CREATIVE KNITTING

CREATIVE KNITTING

NEWNES BOOKS

Consultant Editor: Sandy Carr
Editor: Janie Ryan
Designer: Liz Rose
Production: Dennis Hovell

Published by Newnes Book, a division
of The Hamlyn Publishing Group Limited,
84-88, The Centre, Feltham, Middlesex, England
and distributed for them by
Hamlyn Distribution Services Limited,
Sanders Lodge Estate, Rushden, Northants, England

Contents

Introduction

In recent years knitting has shed much of its rather dowdy old-fashioned image. Shops selling hundreds of wonderful new yarns in fashion colours have sprung up on every high street and there are lots more interesting patterns to choose from than there used to be. As a result there are many people now who would like to learn to knit but are, perhaps, discouraged because it seems hopelessly difficult. Expert knitters seem to knit so quickly that it's impossible to see what they are doing and how. In fact, basic knitting skills are easy and the Know-how section of this book will teach you everything you need to know to produce some highly impressive results.

Armed with this knowledge (and you don't need to know it all before you begin) you can try one of the forty-six patterns in the following pages — all right up-to-date and the work of some of our top knitting designers. There are garments for men, women and children, for summer and winter, and, as well as main items like sweaters, dresses and coats, there are accessories — shawls, gloves, socks, scarves and hats — something, in fact, for everyone.

Know-how

Knitting is one of the easiest and quickest crafts to learn. You don't have to be an expert to produce acceptable results and there is very little specialist equipment that you have to buy before you can begin — just needles and some yarn. The very basic skills you need are casting on and off, knitting and purling (see pages 14-18). Increasing and decreasing (pages 19-21) is also important for shaping garments. The other more advanced techniques like bobbles and cables you can leave until later.

Equipment and Materials

Knitting equipment is extremely simple and has remained virtually unchanged for hundreds of years. Yarns, on the other hand, are continually changing. Apart from the traditional plain yarns, there are many wonderful new fibres and finishes to choose from every year.

The basics

Pattern It is best to use a given pattern when beginning to knit. With experience you may prefer to design your own patterns.

Yarn Make sure that the yarn you buy can be knitted to the stated pattern tension. Buy one ball first and experiment, then buy or reserve sufficient yarn to complete the garment to avoid any slight change in the dye. When buying note the dye lot number in case you do need more. You are especially likely to need extra yarn when replacing four ply or double knitting with crêpe yarn.

Pair of needles For flat knitting along the rows. The knobs prevent the stitches from dropping off the ends. Use good needles: bent, uneven or easily breakable ones spoil your knitting. Most are coated metal, plastic or wooden for large sizes. They are sold in metric (mm) but you may have some marked in old British sizes. The chart will tell you whether you already have the needles you need. The size relates to the tension. For a tighter tension use smaller needles and *vice versa*. Needles come in different lengths as well as different sizes. Choose a suitable length for the number of stitches you are going to carry. Remember to take into account any increasing you may have to do.

Additional equipment

Gauge For checking needle sizes, both British and metric.

Row counter For counting increased and decreased stitches; also rows.

Stitch holder For holding a number of stitches on any part of the work until they are needed later on.

Safety pins For holding a few stitches, say for a front band on a cardigan.

Cable needle For holding stitches at the back or front of the work while twisting a cable. The cable needle size should be similar to the main needles.

Double-pointed needles For seamless, circular knitting—either tubular or flat. Four or five needles can be used, each with points at both ends. Useful for socks, collars, armholes and neckbands.

Circular needles For flat or seamless circular knitting with a large number of stitches. Choose a suitable length for your stitch number and tension.

Scissors For cutting yarn. Medium size and clean cutting.

Tape measure Choose one marked in both inches and centimetres.

Pins For checking tension. Choose ones with big coloured heads for thick yarn.

Pressing cloth For making up. Use a fine cotton.

Sewing needles For sewing pieces together. Use one with a blunt end to prevent the yarn splitting and a large eye to take the thickness of the yarn.

Needle sizes			
Metric	**British**	**Metric**	**British**
2mm	14	5mm	6
2¼mm	13	5½mm	5
2½mm	—	6mm	4
2¾mm	12	6½mm	3
3mm	11	7mm	2
3¼mm	10	7½mm	1
3½mm	—	8mm	0
3¾mm	9	9mm	00
4mm	8	10mm	000
4½mm	7		

Types of yarn

Yarns are generally sold by weight in balls, hanks or cones. They can be made from natural fibres like wool, cotton or silk; man-made fibres like nylon, acrylic, or viscose; or a mixture of the two. The ball band or label will usually give guidance as to the most suitable method of cleaning and pressing and, in some cases, a needle or hook size and tension measurement are given.

Plain yarns

Two-, three- and four-ply The ply of a yarn is usually an indication of its thickness. A ply is a single thread of spun yarn. Generally the more plies the thicker the yarn.

Double knitting A commonly used yarn; fairly thick and hardwearing.

Double-double knitting, chunky and Aran Even thicker than double knitting and very quick to knit up.

Baby yarn A soft light yarn available in several thicknesses.

Crêpe Highly twisted double knitting or four-ply; a tough durable yarn.

Tweed A multi-coloured yarn producing a speckled tweedy fabric.

Textured yarns

Bouclé A loopy yarn available in various thicknesses. It produces an attractive bobbly texture.

Slub An unevenly spun yarn which knits up to a soft irregular fabric. Like many highly textured yarns it is most suitable for hand knitting.

Chenille A velvety tufted yarn producing a smooth rich fabric.

Natural yarns

Cotton Available in many thicknesses from very fine to double knitting.

Silk A luxury yarn produced in a range of thicknesses and textures.

Mohair Fluffy goat-hair yarn often combined with other fibres.

Angora A delicate soft yarn made from rabbit fur.

Alpaca A slightly hairy yarn obtained from llamas, usually sold undyed.

All-synthetic yarns

Many of these imitate the qualities of natural yarns, but are often preferable as they are relatively cheap and can often be machined-washed.

Fancy yarns

Glitter Metallized man-made threads in gold, silver, copper and other metallic finishes.

Other unusual yarns Practically any thread-like material can be used in knitting and crochet. String, raffia, plastic or cloth strips, ribbon and braid can all be knitted, alone or with other yarns.

Understanding Knitting Patterns

The shorthand format used in knitting and crochet patterns is designed to avoid repetition. To follow a pattern successfully a thorough understanding of the abbreviations is essential.

If you intend to use a pattern always buy it before buying your yarn and read it through. If you are going to use an alternative yarn to the one recommended in the pattern pay particular attention to the size, tension and materials sections.

Abbreviations can vary considerably from pattern to pattern, so read and note them before beginning work. The abbreviations used in this book are shown below.

Size The *'to fit'* measurement is not intended as a precise measurement of the garment. The actual measurement is sometimes given after the 'to fit' measurement or in a measurement diagram. Continually refer to this diagram to check all your actual measurements. The 'to fit' size is what it says. If it is a tight-fitting garment then the measurement is that intended to fit tightly and *vice versa.*

The figures in the *square brackets* are the larger sizes given in the pattern. Choose your size and encircle or underline all the instructions for that size throughout the pattern before beginning work. This way you will follow through the instructions consistently for your size.

The *length measurement* refers most usually to the length from shoulder seam down to the bottom of the garment.

The *sleeve seam measurement* is from the end of the shoulder seam to the end of the sleeve.

Tension This is very important, especially where you have chosen to substitute the recommended yarn, so always work a tension sample. Some patterns only give the number of stitches, while others also give the number of rows. For more information about tension, see page 11.

Materials If you decide to substitute the recommended yarn make sure you buy enough — weight is not necessarily an indication of length i.e. a 50g ball of an alternative yarn may not go as far as a 50g ball of the recommended yarn.

Main pattern To keep your place through the pattern it may help to cross off the rows with a pencil as you work them. Where a section of the pattern is to be repeated several times it is as well to use a row counter.

Never deviate from the *order of the pattern*. If you do, you may find that you are unable to make up as instructed because the necessary stages have not been completed beforehand.

Where instructions are grouped together in *round brackets* read just beyond them and you will see that they tell you how often to repeat the instructions in brackets e.g. (K1, P1) to end, (rib 4, M1) 4 times. Sometimes, instructions are grouped together in brackets to indicate they should all be worked into the one stitch e.g. (K1, yfwd, K1, yfwd, K1) all into next st. Always note *asterisks*. A single asterisk is usually used to indicate a repetition of the stitch pattern within the row. Double, treble and even quadruple asterisks usually indicate the repetition of larger areas of instruction.

Abbreviations

alt = alternate (ly)	P-wise = purlwise
approx = approximately	rem = remain (ing)
beg = begin (ning)	rep = repeat
cm = centimetre (s)	RH = right hand
cont = continu (e) (ing)	RS = right side
dc = double crochet	sl = slip
dec = decreas (e) (ing)	sl st = slip stitch (knitting)
foll = follow (s) (ing)	ss = slip stitch (crochet)
g = gram (s)	st (s) = stitch (es)
g st = garter stitch	st st = stocking stitch
inc = increas (e) (ing)	tbl = through back of loop (s)
K = knit	tog = together
K up = pick up and knit	tr = treble
K-wise = knitwise	WS = wrong side
LH = left hand	ybk = yarn back
P = purl	yfwd = yarn forward
patt = pattern	yon = yarn over needle
psso = pass slipped stitch over	yrh = yarn round hook
P up = pick up and purl	yrn = yarn round needle

Tension

Tension, or gauge, is the most important single factor in the success of any piece of knitting. However imaginative the design, or beautiful the yarn, the final result will inevitably be disappointing if the tension has not been carefully checked at the start.

What is tension?

At its simplest, the tension of knitting is a measurement of its tightness or looseness. It describes the number of stitches and rows it takes to achieve a given width and length. Tension is affected by four factors: type of yarn, needle size, stitch pattern and the individual knitter.

Yarn

Yarns come in a wide range of thicknesses and finishes. The ball bands of many yarns nowadays recommend a tension measurement. This is the tension which, in the manufacturer's opinion, will produce the most suitable finish for that particular yarn, and is especially useful when designing your own garments or when substituting a new yarn for the one specified in the pattern. Often pattern designers use the 'wrong' tension deliberately, to achieve special effects — a floppier or more rigid fabric, for example — so whatever the ball band says always match your tension to the one given in the pattern. In general, however, thicker, chunkier yarns must be knitted on larger needles than fine yarns, and produce a tension of fewer rows and stitches to the square centimetre. Even yarns apparently of the same weight and thickness can display variations in tension. All double knitting yarns, for example, do not knit up to the same tension.

Needle size

This has an obvious effect on knitting tension. The larger the needles, the looser the fabric and the fewer the rows and stitches to the square centimetre. This is clearly demonstrated by casting on a given number of stitches and knitting in stocking stitch for, say, 20cm, using the same yarn

throughout but changing to smaller needles every few rows. Work a purl row on the right side between each needle size. The width of the knitting and the distance between the rows will gradually decrease.

Stitch pattern

Different stitch patterns are designed to produce fabrics with widely varying surface textures and properties. Some, like moss stitch, are tight firm fabrics which hold their shape well. Lacy patterns are, by definition, loose and open, Ribs are stretchy, tending to pull inwards widthways. All these properties affect tension measurement. The same yarn and needle size will result in widely differing tension over different stitch patterns. For this reason you cannot substitute a new stitch pattern for the one specified and assume that the resulting garment will be the correct measurements. The tension of the new stitch pattern must be carefully checked against the original one. Often it is not possible to match both row and stitch tension simultaneously. In such cases you should use a needle size which will achieve the correct stitch tension and follow the measurement diagram for length.

The knitter

Tension is almost as personal a thing as handwriting or fingerprints. It is rarely possible to find two people who knit to the same tension. It is therefore never advisable to allow anyone else to finish a piece of knitting which you have started. It is also the reason why you must adjust your personal tension to that of any pattern before beginning work on it. The tension of the pattern is that of the designer of the pattern and the chances are that his or her tension will be different from yours. You can not adjust your tension successfully by trying to knit more loosely or more tightly than you usually do. This will simply interrupt the natural rhythm of your knitting. It will be uncomfortable to work and, as you relax into your normal style it will almost certainly produce an unevenness of tension over the whole garment. If your tension needs adjusting it must be done by changing the needle size.

Checking tension

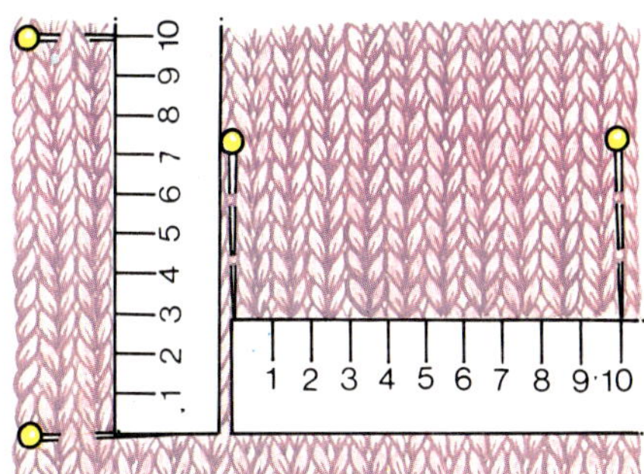

1 *Knit up a tension sample using the same yarn, needle size and stitch pattern specified in the tension measurement (in this case 10 stitches and 14 rows to 10cm), casting on a few more stitches and working more rows than given. Place a ruler along the width of the sample and mark off the measurement with pins at right angles to the ruler. Place the ruler vertically on the sample and mark off the measurement with pins. Count the stitches and rows between pins.*

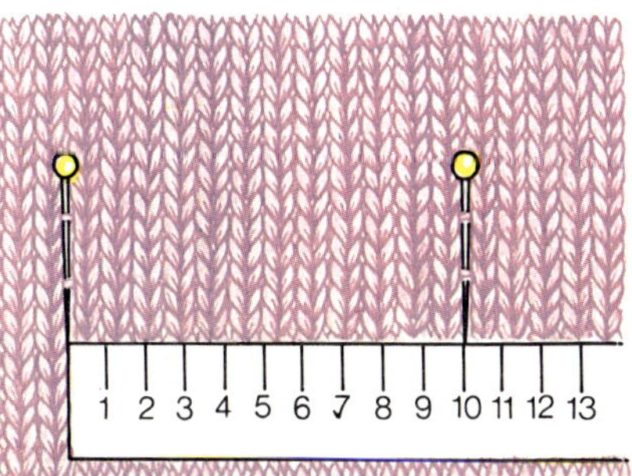

2 *If there are too many stitches or rows your tension is tighter than that of the designer. Knit up another sample using larger needles and check it again.*

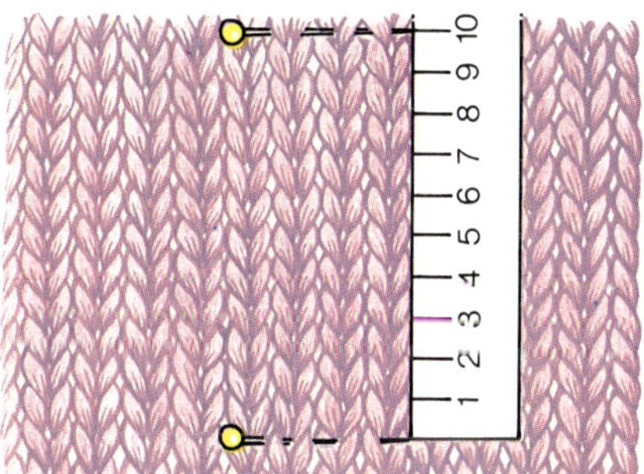

3 *If there are too few stitches and rows between the pins your tension is looser than that of the designer. Knit up another sample on smaller needles and check it again.*

Making Up

Bad making up can ruin the most skilful knitting, so take plenty of time and extra care over blocking, pressing and piecing the garment together for a really professional finish.

Making up is the final stage in making a crocheted or knitted garment. Perhaps because of this there is a tendency even among otherwise careful knitters - to rush it, but poorly made-up garments with lumpy seams look dreadful however good the actual knitting. There are five basic stages in making up: blocking, pressing, seaming, knitting on (edgings, for example) and finishing (sewing on buttons, zips and so on). Some but not all of these stages are described in detail in the making-up section of patterns.

Blocking

First check whether or not the yarn used for the garment should be pressed. Sometimes the pattern gives pressing instructions. If not, they should be printed on the ball band. If the yarn cannot be pressed go straight to the seaming stage.. If it can be pressed each piece of the garment must be blocked to the correct shape and measurements before pressing. Use a thick ironing pad (a folded towel or blanket is ideal). Lay the knitting right-side downwards on this and begin pinning it out all round. Push the pins into the pad right up to the head and just over a centimetre apart, keeping the edge of the knitting straight and flat. Check the measurement diagram for the *actual* measurements of each part of the pieces and first pin out the widest point (usually the chest measurement). One of the advantages of blocking is that the knitting can be eased into or slightly stretched to the correct measurement if necessary. After the chest pin out the rest of the basic shape — length, armhole depth, shoulder width and so on — then fill in between these points with pins. Pin around the whole piece, except for the ribbing

which is never blocked or pressed. Place the pins along the top edge of the rib where it meets the main part of the back, front or sleeves of the garment.

Pressing

The pressing instructions on the ball band of the yarn should tell you not only whether it can be pressed but also how — dry or damp, and hot, warm or cool. Always use a cloth; the iron should never come into direct contact with the knitted fabric. Press very lightly using up and down movements. Avoid ribbed sections and any knitted in garter stitch or heavily textured stitch patterns. Some fabrics, like mohair and angora are lightly steamed rather than pressed. Block them right side up and hold a wet cloth just above the surface. Press the cloth with a hot iron so that the steam is forced down into the fabric. The same method can be used to 'raise' stitches which have been flattened by heavy pressing.

Blocking and pressing

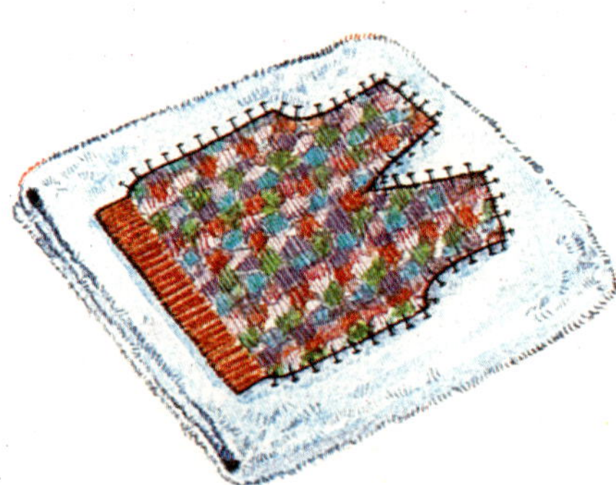

1 *Place the knitted pieces right side down on a thick pad—a folded towel or blanket, for example—and block them out to correct measurements.*

2 *Cover the knitting with a clean cloth—dry or damp according to the instructions on the ball band.*

3 *Using a warm iron, press the knitting with vertical rather than horizontal movements, lifting the iron off the knitting between each press. Keep the pressure even over the whole garment. Do not press the ribbing.*

Seaming

The knitted pieces are usually joined together by seaming. In some cases they can be grafted together (see page 143) making a join which is totally invisible. There are several seams suitable for joining knitting.
Back-stitch seam Use this on shoulder seams to set in sleeves and for the main garment seams.

Flat seam Use this to join ribbed edges, button and buttonhole bands and on heavily textured fabrics.

Invisible seam Use this on straight-sided pieces worked in stocking stitch, for ver-vertical joins only.

Always use a blunt-ended wool needle for seaming. Use the garment yarn if possible. If it is unsuitable for some reason (it may be too thick or textured) use a matching finer yarn with the same fibre content. The order in which seams should be joined is usually given in the making up instructions in the pattern. Generally the shoulder seams are

Back-stitch seam

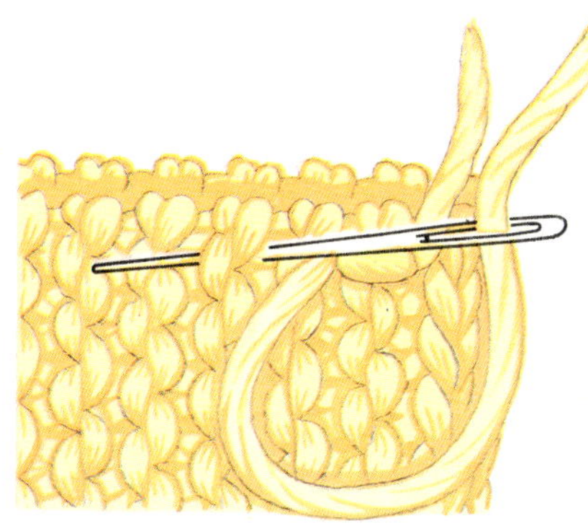

1 Thread a blunt-ended wool needle with matching yarn and begin at the right-hand end of the seam securing the end of the yarn with a double stitch. Make a stitch by pushing the needle through both layers and bringing it back again to the front of the seam.

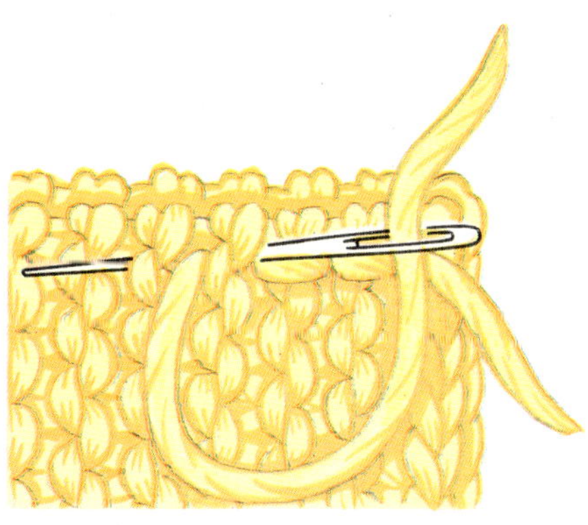

2 Insert the needle back into the fabric as shown and bring it to the front again. Continue in this way to the end of the seam.

joined first. There are several methods of setting in sleeves. They can be joined before or after the side seams.

When joining sections of the garment which fold over on to the right side (for example, a polo neck) remember to reverse the seam at the appropriate point. Press completed seams lightly on the right side if the yarn is suitable for pressing. Darn in loose yarn ends.

Flat seam

1 Use a flat seam when seaming heavily textured fabrics. Place the two edges together RS facing, and secure the end of the yarn with a double stitch.

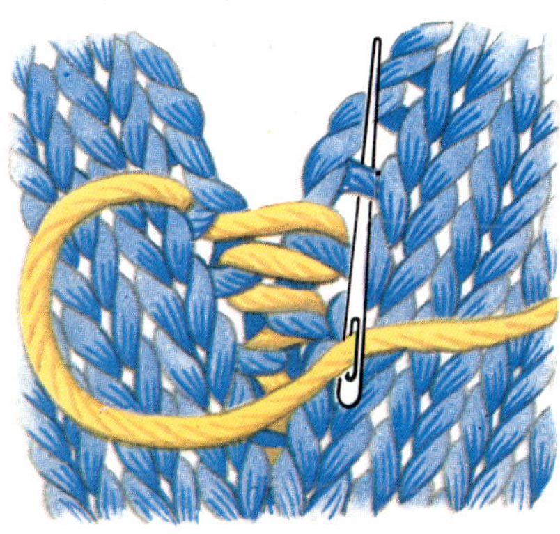

2 Continue along the seam as shown, taking care to match rows or stitches on the two pieces of knitting.

Knitting on

Some edgings can be worked only after certain seams have been joined so the instructions for these are usually included in the making up section of the pattern. This applies to neckbands, armbands, collars and sometimes to button and buttonhole bands. Since these parts of the garment are usually worked in rib it is not necessary to block or press them at this stage.

Invisible seam

1 Place the two edges side by side right sides uppermost, matching stitches and rows exactly. Secure yarn at bottom right-hand edge. Pick up stitch just opposite on left-hand edge. Pull yarn through and tighten. Pick up stitch in row above on right-hand edge. Pull yarn through and tighten.

2 Carry on in this way moving from edge to edge, pulling yarn through and tightening after each stitch until the seam is completed. Fasten off. This seam produces a flat join. It is particularly suitable for straight-sided pieces knitted in stocking stitch.

Finishing

Depending on the type of garment it may be necessary to insert a zip, case a waistband, sew up a hem, make button loops, sew on buttons and so on. Buttons which are likely to receive a great deal of wear can be reinforced by sewing a smaller button behind the button on the wrong side. Stitch through the holes in both buttons at the same time. Finally add the decorative touches — pompons, tassels, beads, cords and any embroidery.

Basic Skills

Holding the yarn and the needles

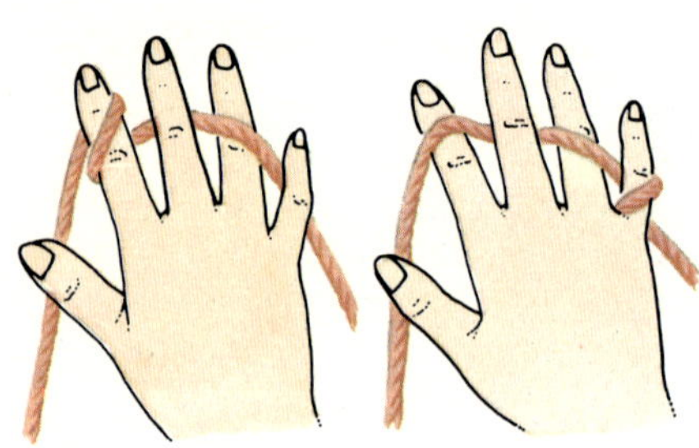

1 *The working yarn can be held in either the left or right hand. Threading the yarn between the fingers helps control both the speed and evenness of the knitting. The two methods shown are right-hand methods— usually easier for beginners where the yarn is looped either round the index finger or round the little finger.*

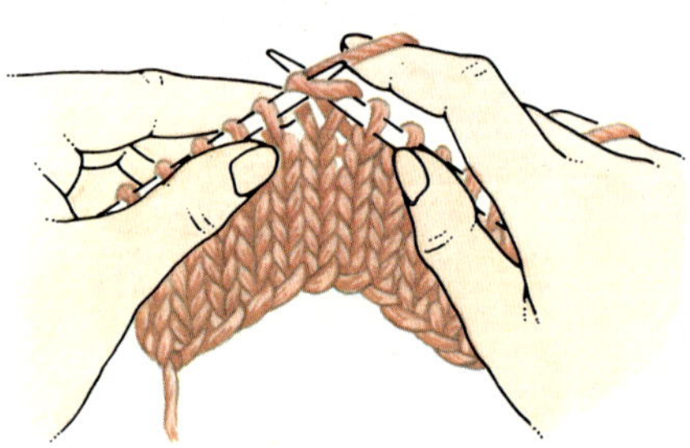

2 *There are several ways of holding the needles. Most people experiment until they find a method which suits them and is both comfortable and efficient. The method shown is popular since it provides a firm, but not rigid, hold in which the needles can be easily used. The needle in the left hand is referred to as the left-hand needle, the needle held in the right hand as the right-hand needle.*

Casting on

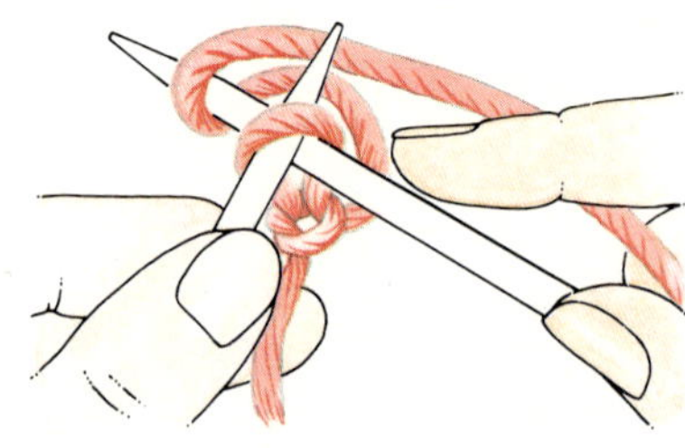

1 *The English cable method produces a firm, elastic edge suitable for most purposes. Make a slip loop and place it on the left-hand needle. Insert the right-hand needle through the front of the loop as shown. Take the yarn under and over the point of the right-hand needle.*

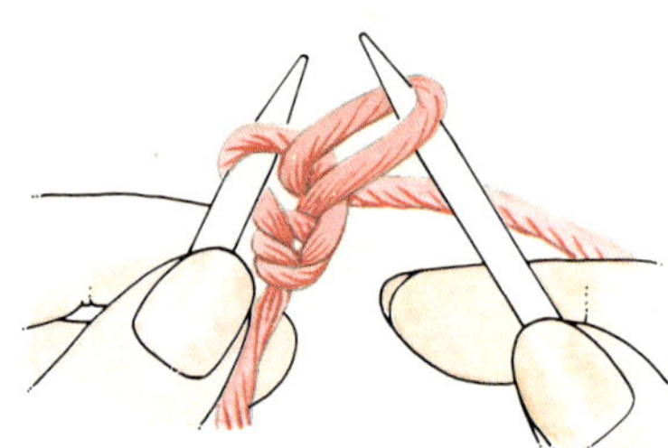

2 *Draw the yarn through the loop on the left-hand needle, thus making a new loop on the right-hand needle. Transfer the loop on the right hand needle to the left-hand needle.*

3 *Insert the right-hand needle between the loops on the left-hand needle. Take the yarn under and over the point of the right-hand needle.*

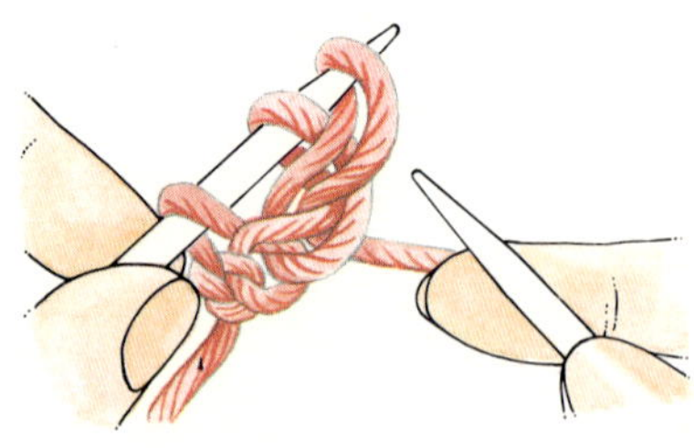

4 *Draw the yarn between the loops on the left-hand needle. Place the new loop on the left-hand needle. Repeat stages 3 and 4 until the required number of stitches have been cast on.*

Casting on (French method)

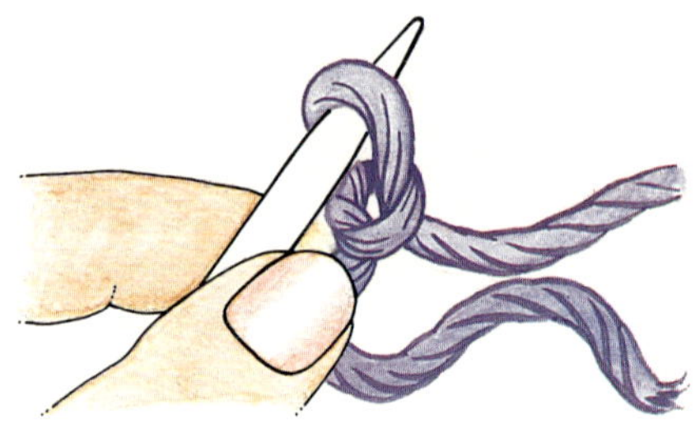

1 *This produces a looser more elastic edge than the English cable method. Make a slip loop and place it on the left-hand needle.*

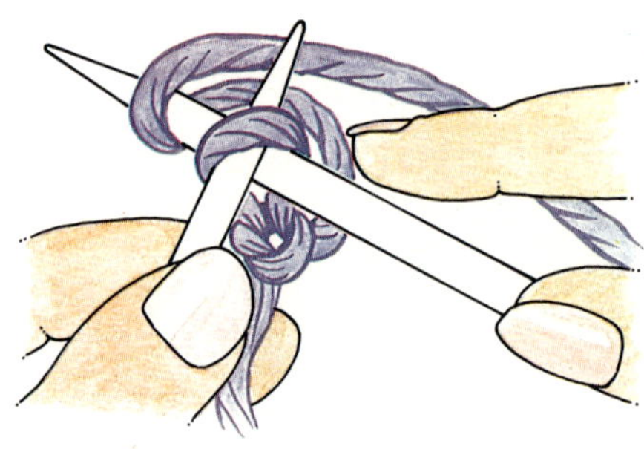

2 *Insert the right-hand needle through the loop from front to back. Take the yarn under and over the point of the right hand needle.*

Single casting on

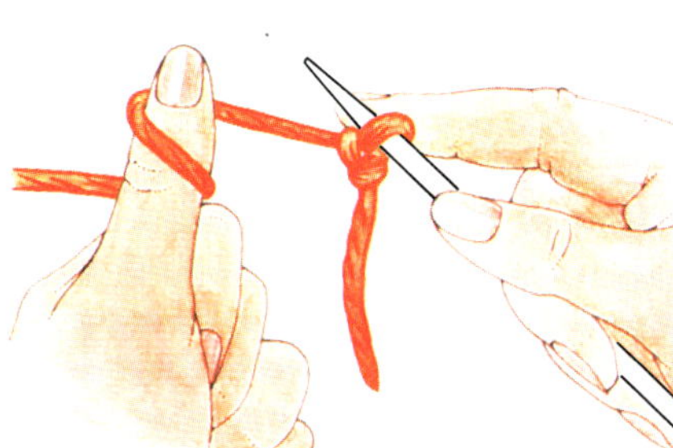

3 *Draw a loop through and place it on the left-hand needle. Tighten the loop.*

1 *This is a light-weight edge ideal for children's and baby clothes and for casting on when making buttonholes. Place a slip loop on the right-hand needle and wind the yarn from the ball round the left thumb as shown above.*

4 *In a variation of this technique (known as the Continental method) the stitches are cast on to two needles held together and the yarn wound round the thumb and third finger as shown. This edge is looser and more elastic.*

5 *A further variation produces a decorative knotted edge. Cast on two stitches singly. Lift the second stitch over the first. Cast on two more stitches. Slip second stitch over the first. Continue until required number of stitches has been cast on.*

4 *Insert the right-hand needle through the new loop on the left-hand needle. Take the yarn under and over the point of the right hand needle and draw the loop through. Place the new loop on the left-hand needle. Carry on in this way until all the stitches have been cast on.*

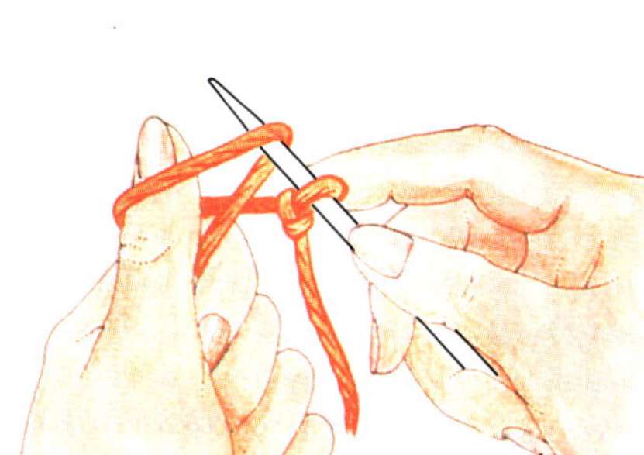

2 *Take the needle up through the loop on the thumb and take it on to the needle.*

Invisible casting on

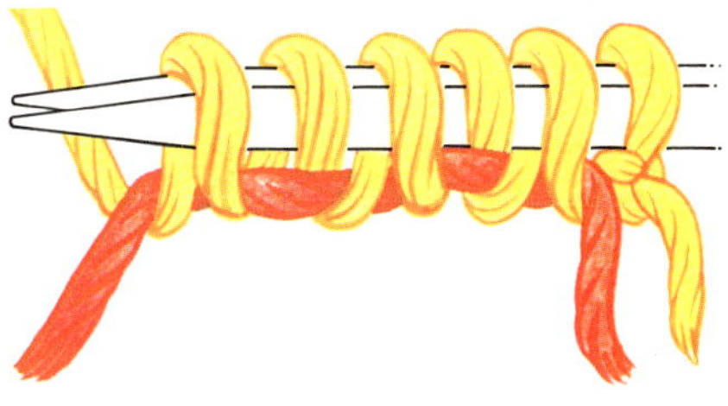

This method produces an edge which can be picked up and knitted in the opposite direction. Place a slip loop on two wheels held together. Hold a length of contrast yarn under the needles. With the yarn from the ball make loops on the needles taking them in front of the contrast yarn and behind it alternately as shown. When the required stitches have been cast on, remove one needle. Knit first row through the front of the loops. Remove the contrast yarn and pick loops to knit in the opposite direction.

5 *The edge can be made slightly firmer by knitting the first row through the back of the loops.*

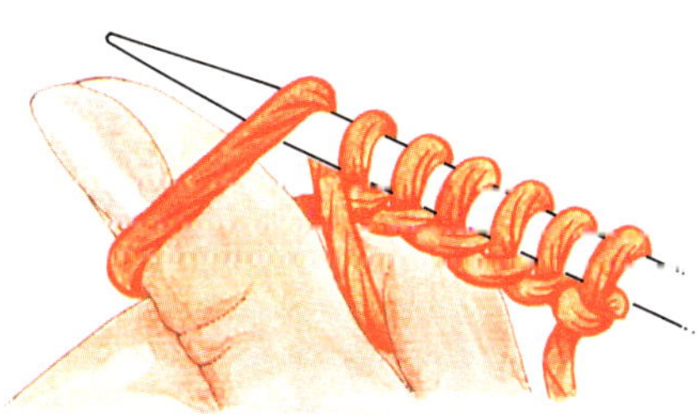

3 *Continue making loops on the right-hand needle until the required stitches have been cast on.*

The knit stitch (K)

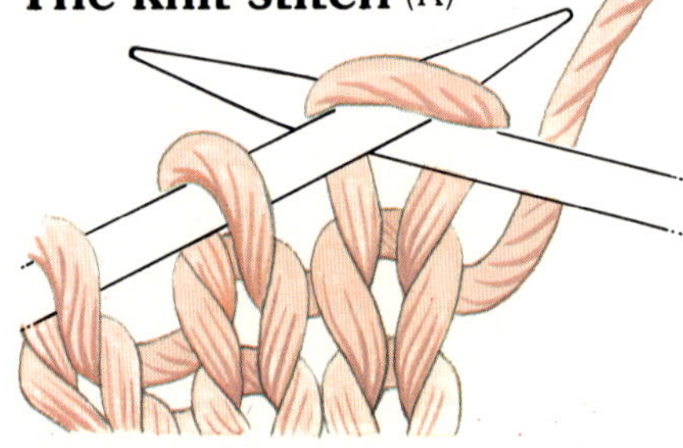

1 Take the needle holding the stitches in your left hand. With the yarn at the back of the work insert the right-hand needle through the front of the first stitch.

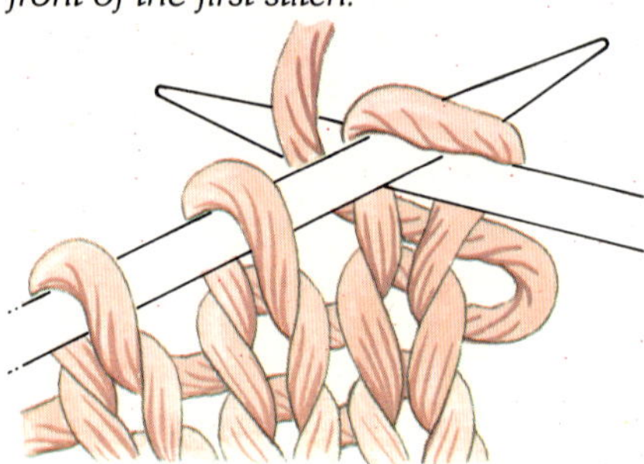

2 Take the yarn under and over the point of the right-hand needle.

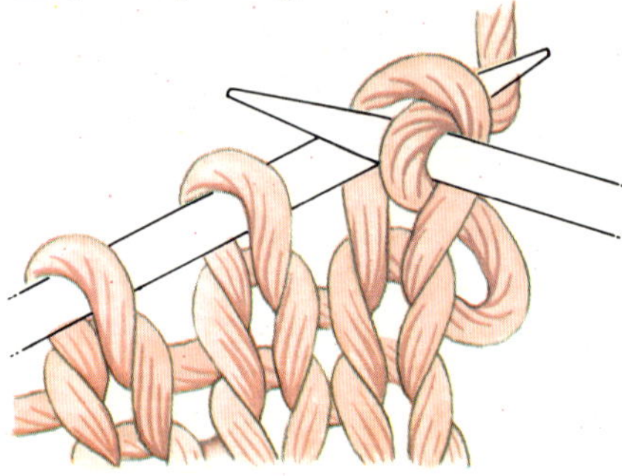

3 Draw the yarn on the right-hand needle through the stitch on the left-hand needle.

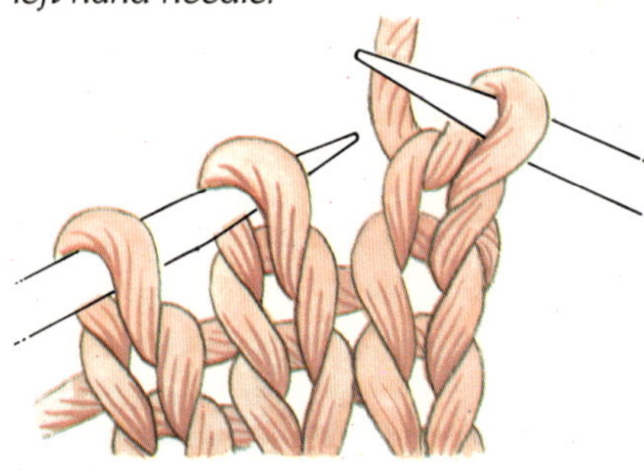

4 Slip the left-hand stitch off the needle, so completing the knit stitch. Knitting every row forms a garter stitch (g st) fabric.

The purl stitch (P)

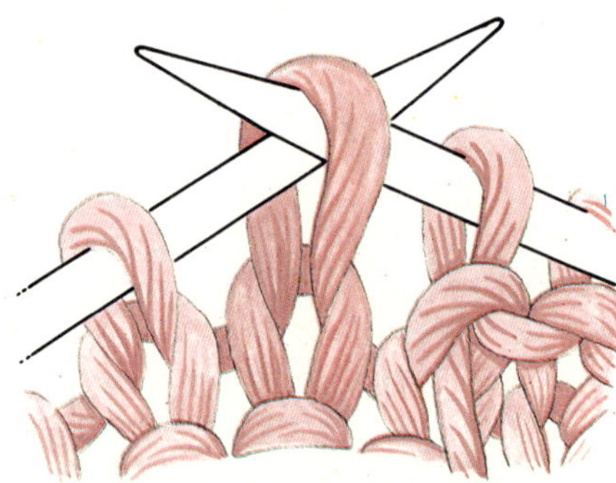

1 Hold the needle with the cast-on stitches in your left hand. With the yarn at the front of the work insert the right-hand needle through the front of the first stitch from right to left.

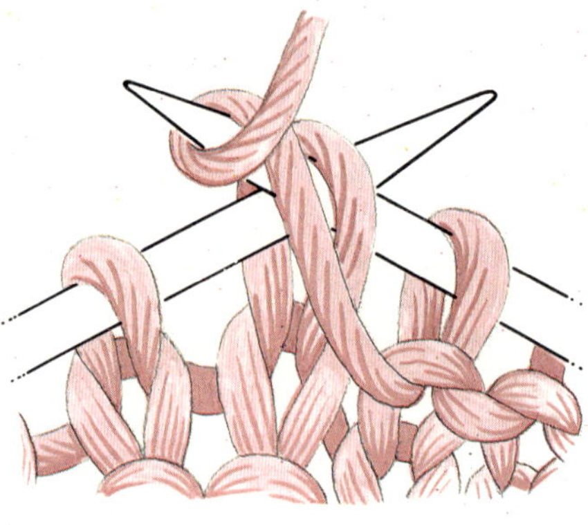

2 Take the yarn over and under the point of the right-hand needle.

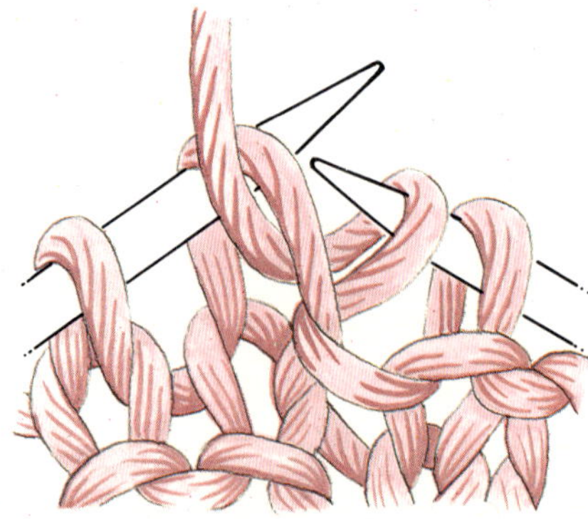

3 Draw the yarn on the right-hand needle through the stitch on the left-hand needle. Slip the left-hand stitch off the needle, so completing the purl stitch.

Joining in new yarn

Ideally new yarn should be joined in at the beginning of a row. It takes a length of yarn roughly four times the width of the knitting to complete a row. If the yarn is too short, let it hang at the edge of the work. Take a new ball and start the new row. Knot and darn both ends in at the wrong side when making up.

Splicing yarn

Occasionally new yarn must be joined in the middle of a row: for example, to avoid excessive wastage of expensive yarn or when knitting a scarf where yarn joins at the edge would show. In such cases the best method is to splice the ends of the old and new balls. Unravel both ends for about 8cm. Twist the ends together to make a single thread. Work the next stitches very carefully.

Casting off knitwise

1 With the yarn at the back of the work, knit the first two stitches on the left-hand needle as usual.

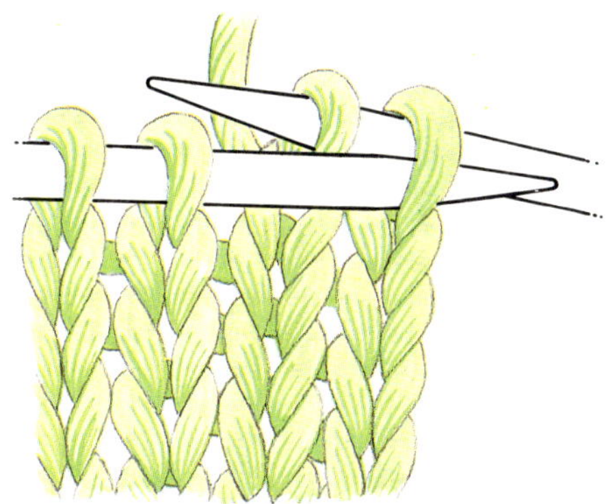

2 *With the tip of the left-hand needle lift the first stitch knitted over the second stitch knitted and off the needle. One stitch has been cast off.*

Casting off purlwise

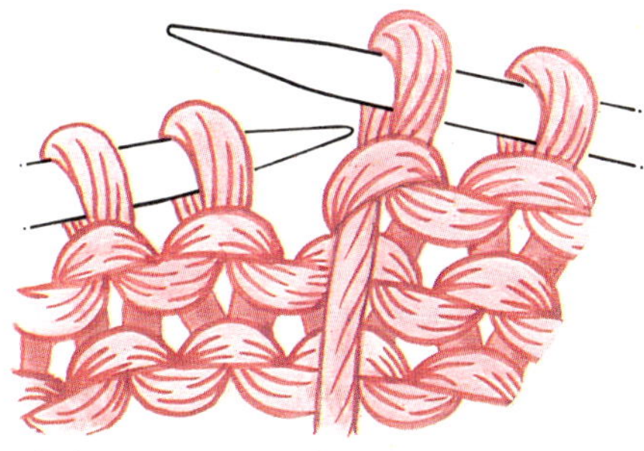

1 *Occasionally it is necessary to cast off on purl rows. Purl the first two stitches on the left-hand needle.*

Casting off in rib

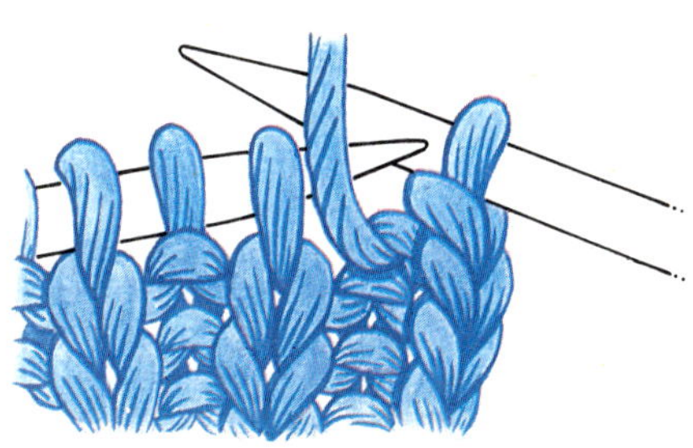

1 *Ribbed edgings are usually cast off in rib, producing a more elastic edge. On a single rib, knit the first stitch on the left-hand needle and purl the second stitch. Lift the knit stitch over the purl stitch and off the needle.*

3 *Work the next stitch on the left-hand needle as usual. Lift the second stitch knitted over it and off the needle. Two stitches have been cast off.*

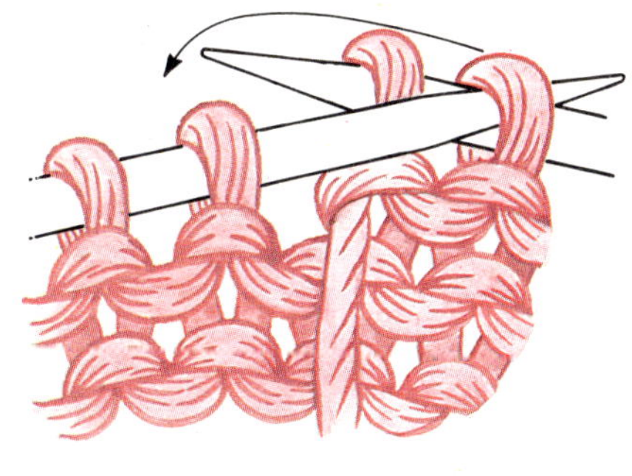

2 *Lift the first stitch on the right-hand needle over the second stitch on the right-hand needle and off the needle.*

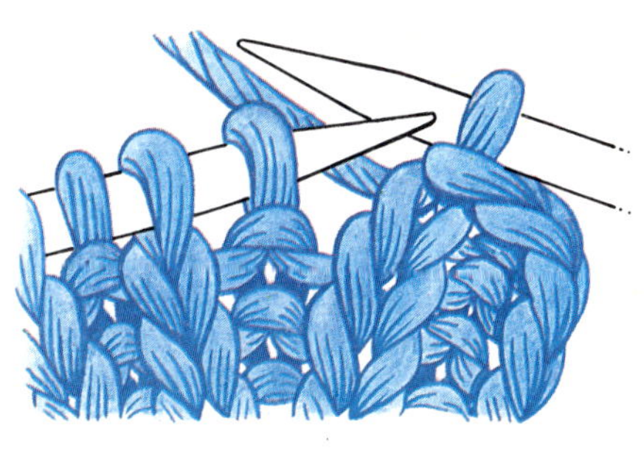

2 *Knit the next stitch on the left-hand needle. Lift the purl stitch over the knit stitch and off the needle.*

4 *Repeat step 3 across the row. Break off the yarn, thread it through the last stitch and tighten.*

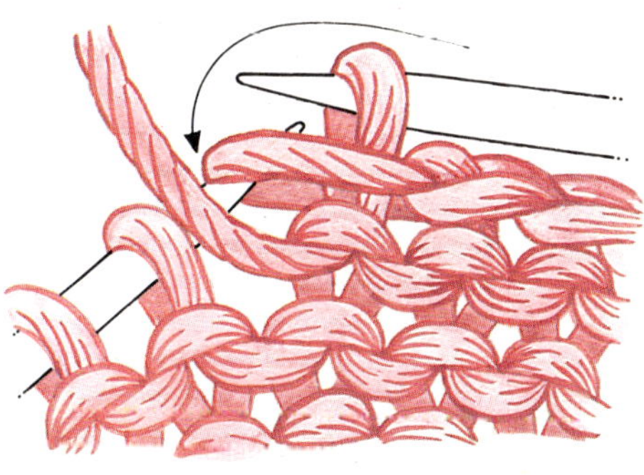

3 *Purl the next stitch on the left-hand needle. Lift the first stitch on the right-hand needle over the second stitch on the right-hand needle and off the needle. Carry on in this way until all the stitches have been cast off.*

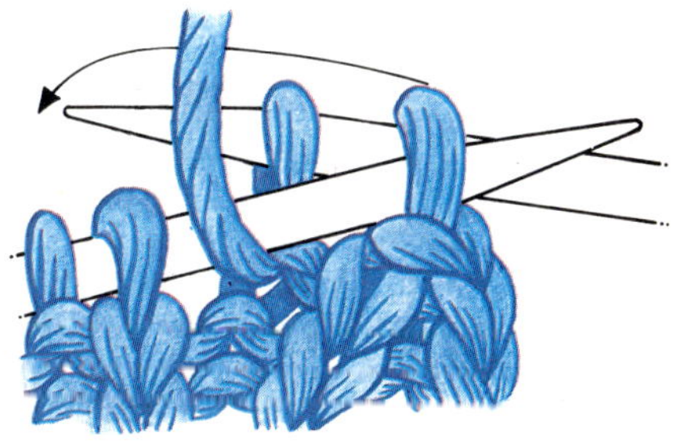

3 *Purl the next stitch on the left-hand needle. Lift the knit stitch over the purl stitch and off the needle. Carry on in this way until all the stitches have been cast off.*

Holding stitches

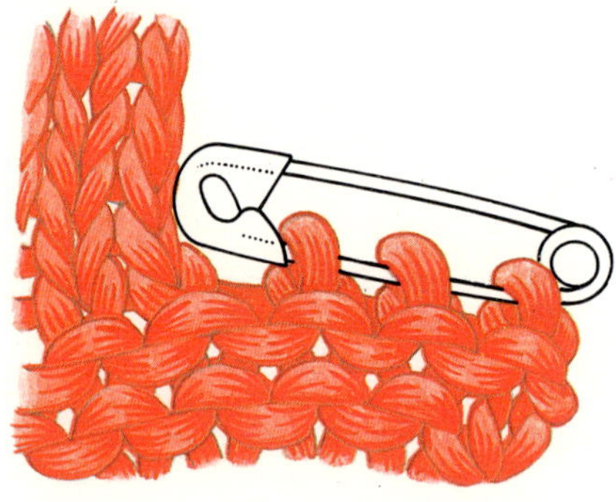

1 *Inserting pockets or working neckbands and neck edges usually requires that a number of stitches be held without being cast off until later in the pattern. If the number of stitches is very small they can be held on a safety pin.*

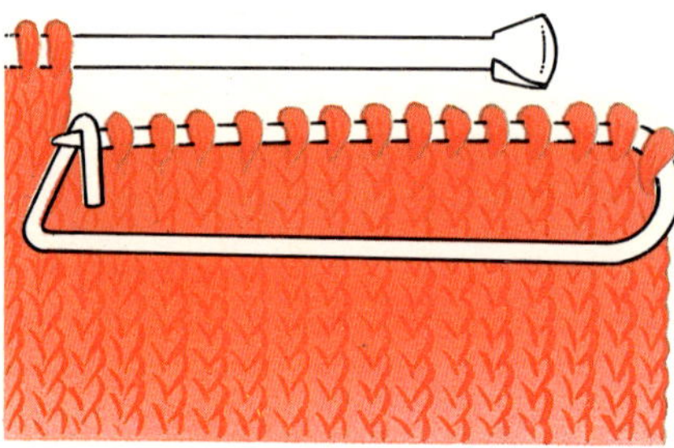

2 *More than ten stitches should be held on a special stitch holder with the end closed to secure them.*

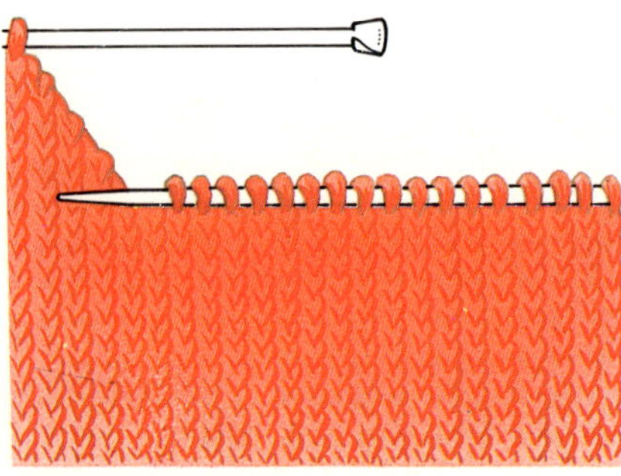

3 *Large numbers of stitches, for example, on the front of a V-necked sweater, can be held on a spare needle.*

4 *In intricate patterns where a spare needle or stitch holder would be awkward to handle (for example, on gloves) the stitches can be held on a piece of spare yarn.*

Picking up stitches

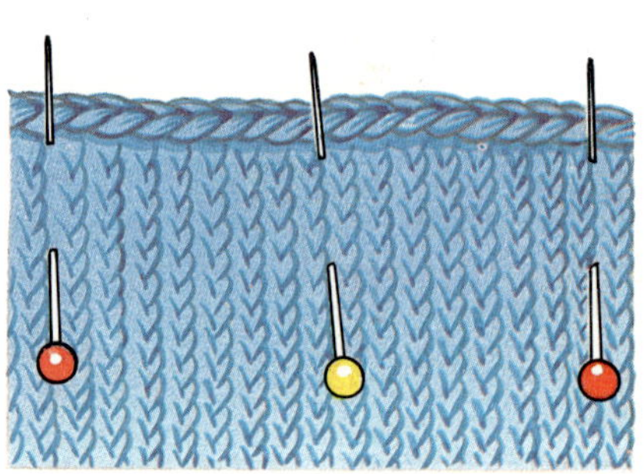

1 *Stitches often need to be picked up round neck edges and armholes so that a neckband and armhole band can be knitted. To ensure they are picked up evenly, divide the edge into equal sections and mark them with pins.*

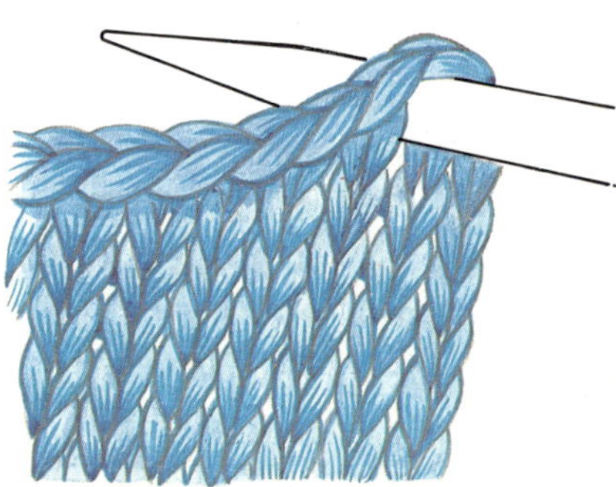

2 *Divide the number of sections into the number of stitches specified in the pattern and start picking up an equal number of stitches per section. Insert the tip of the needle into a row end on vertical edges or a stitch on horizontal edges.*

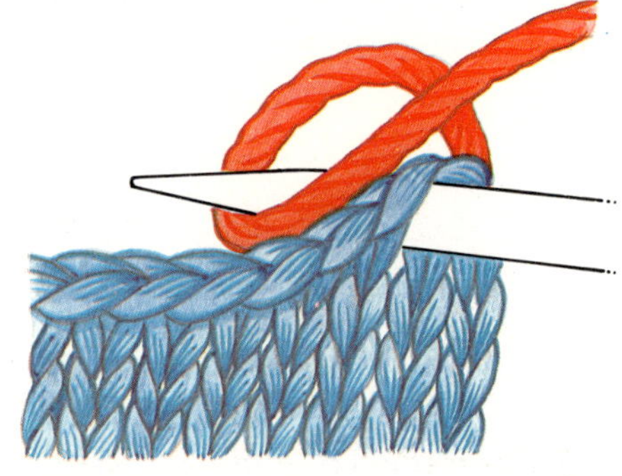

3 *With the yarn at the back of the work, take it under and over the point of the needle, and draw a loop through.*

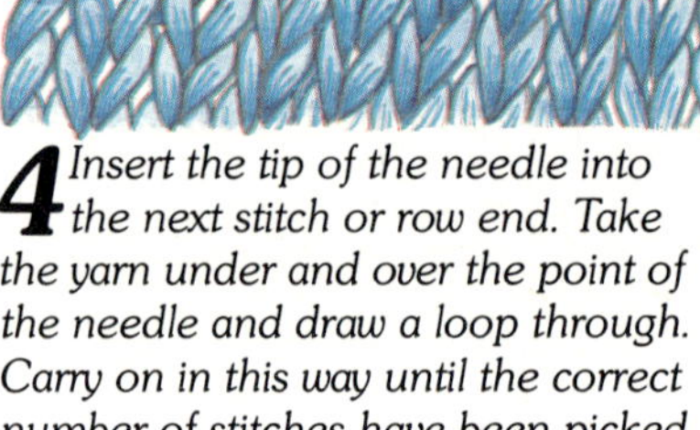

4 *Insert the tip of the needle into the next stitch or row end. Take the yarn under and over the point of the needle and draw a loop through. Carry on in this way until the correct number of stitches have been picked up.*

Picking up a dropped stitch ladder

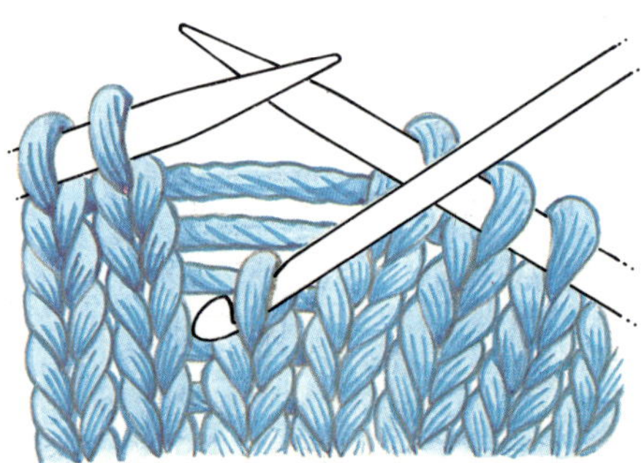

Dropping stitches, even several rows down, is not necessarily a disaster. If the stitch is a simple one like stocking stitch the stitch can be picked up easily with a crochet hook. With the right side of work facing, insert the hook from the front into the dropped stitch, then under the horizontal thread just above it. Pull the thread through the dropped stitch. Continue upwards until all the threads of the ladder have been picked up.

Increasing and Decreasing

Simple increasing
Increase one stitch (inc 1)

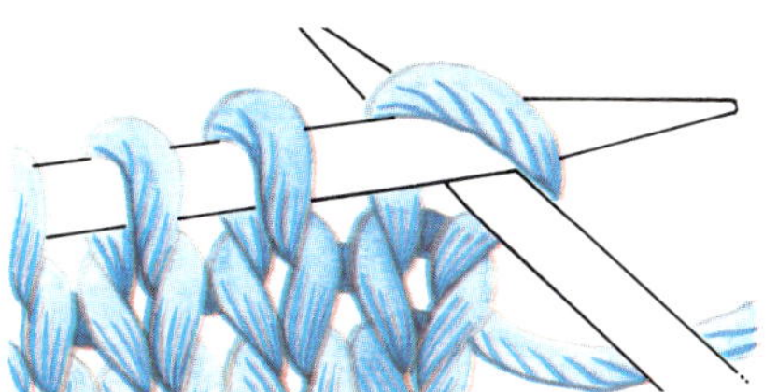

1 This method is used most often to make increases at the beginnings and ends of rows. Insert the right-hand needle knitwise into the front of the stitch on the left-hand needle.

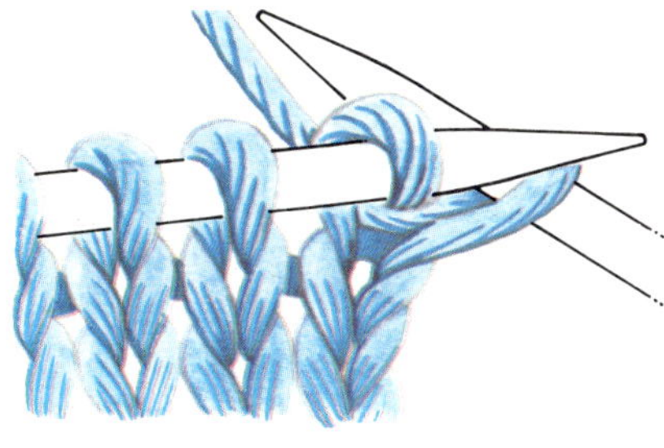

2 Knit the stitch on the left-hand needle as usual but without slipping it off the needle.

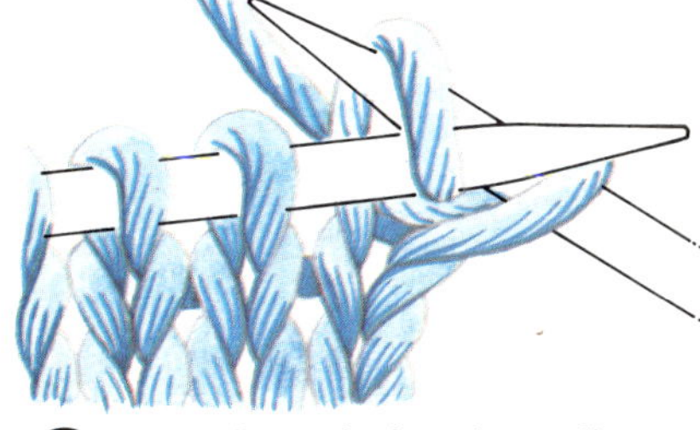

3 Insert the right-hand needle into the back of the same stitch knitwise. Take the wool under and over the point of the right-hand needle.

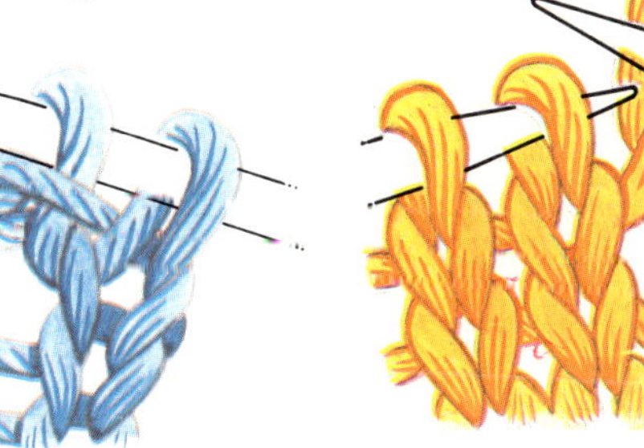

4 Draw the loop through, discarding the stitch on the left-hand needle, thus making two stitches out of one. This method is also called 'knitting into the front and back of the same stitch'.

Make one knitwise

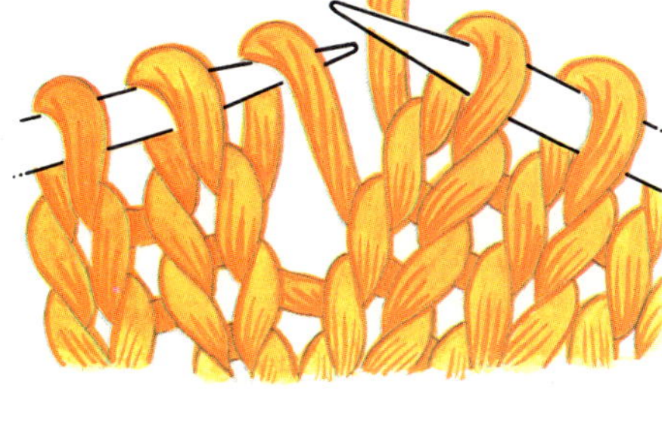

1 With the left-hand needle pick up the loop between the stitch just worked and the next stitch on the left-hand needle from front to back.

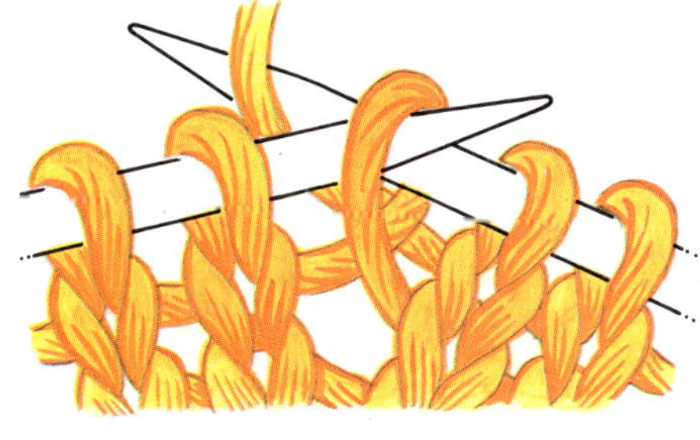

2 Knit as usual into the back of the raised loop on the left-hand needle. This makes an almost invisible increase.

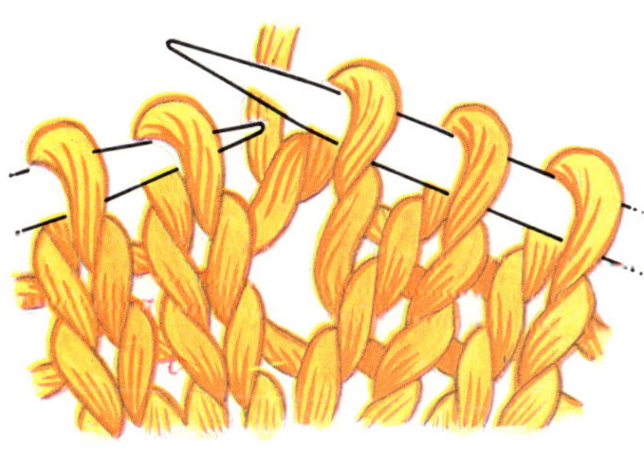

3 A visible hole which can be used for decorative purposes is formed by knitting the raised loop through the front rather than the back.

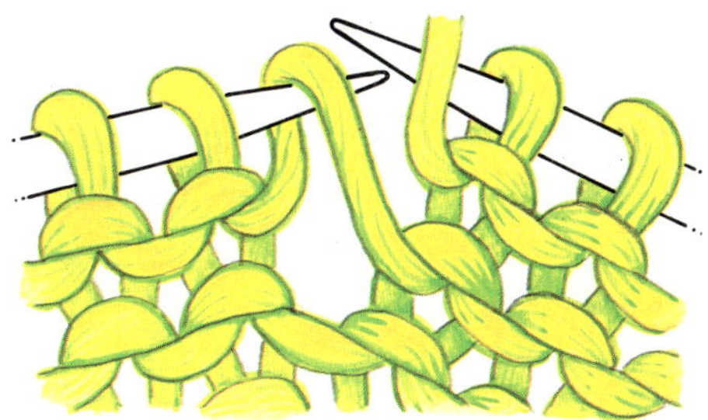

1 On purl rows, with the left-hand needle pick up the loop between the stitch just worked and the next stitch on the left-hand needle from front to back.

2 Purl into the back of the raised loop on the left-hand needle. This makes an almost invisible increase.

Make one purlwise

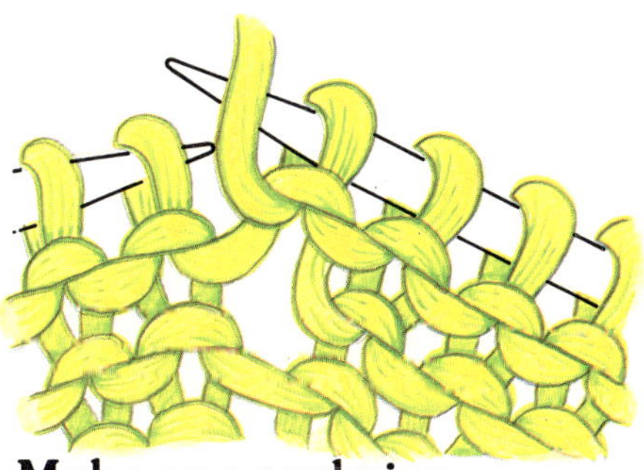

3 This method can also be varied to make a visible hole in the fabric by purling the raised loop through the front rather than the back.

Lifted increase (knitwise)

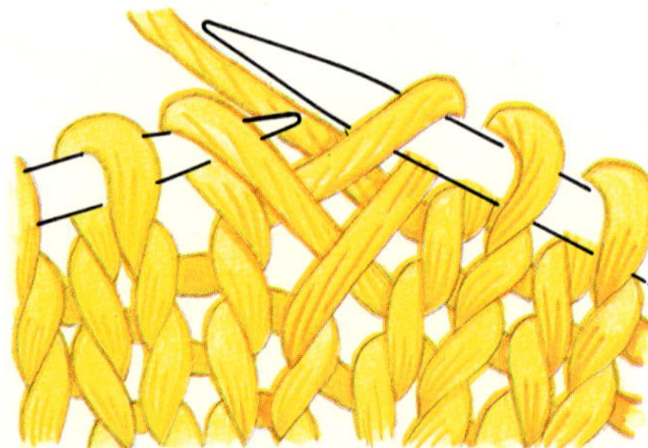

1 *This is one of the least visible forms of increasing. Insert the right-hand needle into the stitch below the next stitch on the left-hand needle from front to back.*

2 *Lift the stitch and knit it in the usual way by taking the yarn under and over the point of the right-hand needle and drawing it through the stitch.*

3 *Knit the stitch above the lifted stitch as usual. This method is often referred to as 'knit one below'.*

Lifted increase (purlwise)

1 *On purl rows, insert the right-hand needle into the stitch below the*

20

next stitch on the left-hand needle from back to front. Lift and purl it.

2 *Insert the needle into the stitch above the lifted stitch and purl it as usual. This method is often referred to as 'purl one below'.*

Double increasing

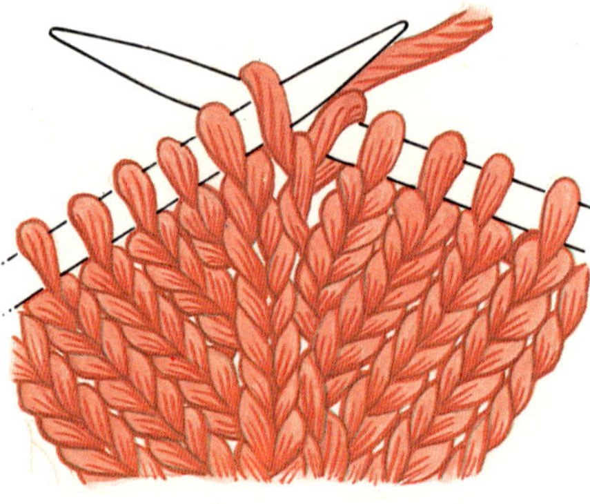

1 *Double increases are made by adding one stitch either side of a centre stitch. Work to the centre stitch. Pick up the loop between the last stitch knitted and the next stitch and knit into the back of it.*

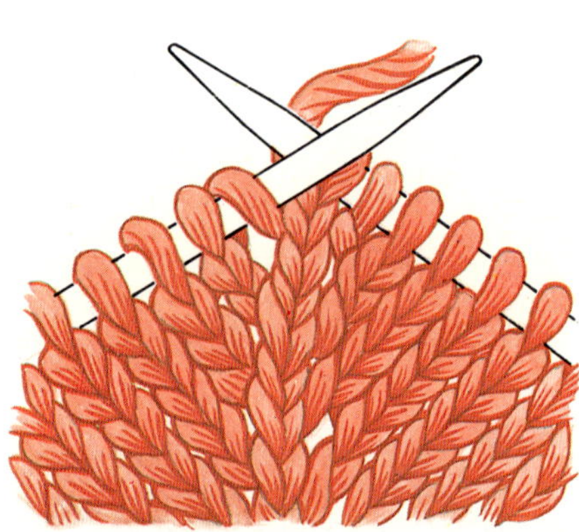

2 *Knit the next stitch as usual. Pick up the loop between the last stitch knitted and and the next stitch and knit into the back of it. Repeat this procedure on all subsequent right-side (knit) rows. All the alternate rows are purled.*

Decorative increasing
Yarn forward (yfwd)

This method is used to make a stitch between two knit stitches. After the first knit stitch the yarn is at the back of the work. Bring the yarn forward between the needles. Knit the next stitch as usual.

Yarn round needle (yrn)

1 *This method is used to make a stitch between two purl stitches. After the first purl stitch the yarn is at the front of the work. Take the yarn over then under the right-hand needle. Purl the next stitch as usual.*

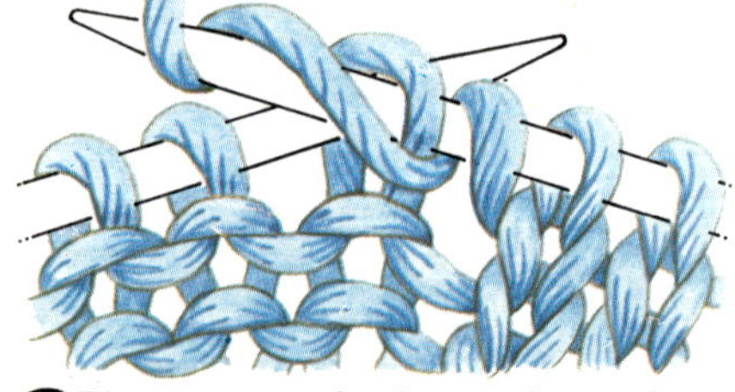

2 *The same method is used to make a stitch between a knit and a purl stitch. After the knit stitch take the yarn under, over, then under the right-hand needle. Purl the next stitch as usual.*

Yarn over needle (yon)

This method is used to make a stitch between a purl and a knit stitch. After the purl stitch the yarn is at the front of the work. Take yarn over the right-hand needle. Knit the next stitch as usual.

Decreasing

Knit two stitches together

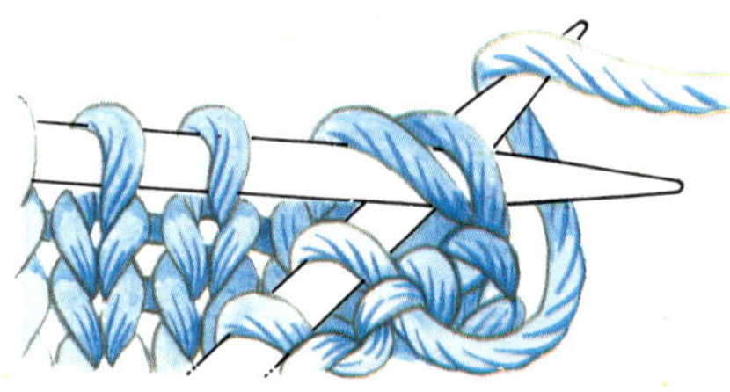

1 Insert the right-hand needle knitwise into the second then the first stitch on the left-hand needle. Take the yarn under and over the point of the right hand needle.

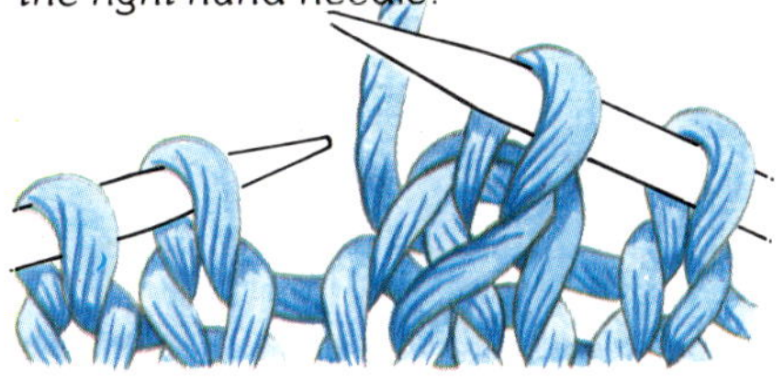

2 Draw the yarn through the first and second stitches on the left-hand needle, discarding both stitches at the same time, thus making one stitch.

Purl two stitches together (P2 tog)

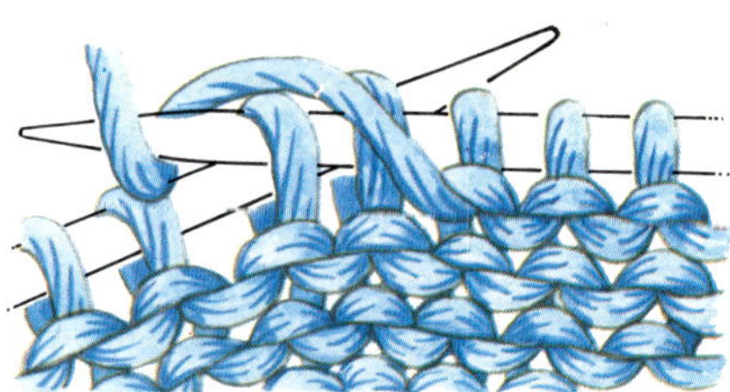

1 Insert the right-hand needle purlwise into the first then the second stitch on the left-hand needle. Take the yarn over and under the point of the right-hand needle.

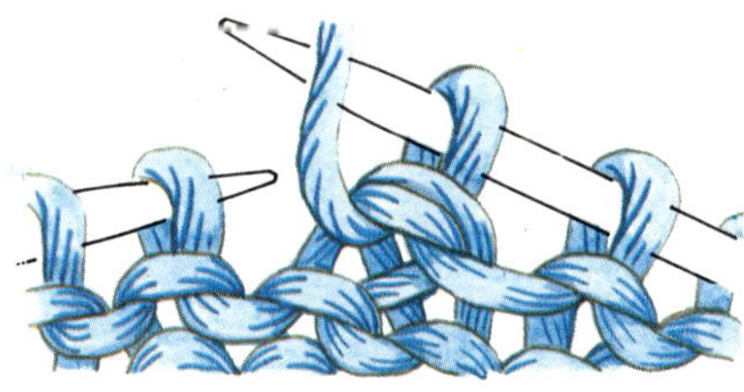

2 Draw the yarn through the first and second stitches on left-hand needle, thus making one stitch out of two.

Slip one, knit one, pass slipped stitch over
(sl1, K1, psso)

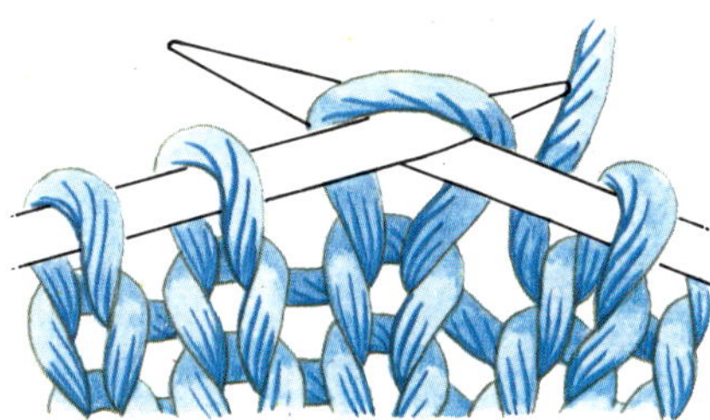

1 Insert the right-hand needle into the next stitch on the left-hand needle as if to knit it. Slip the stitch off the needle on to the right-hand needle.

2 Knit the next stitch on the left-hand needle as usual. With the point of the left-hand needle, lift up the slipped stitch and pass it over the stitch just knitted and off the needle.

Double decreasing

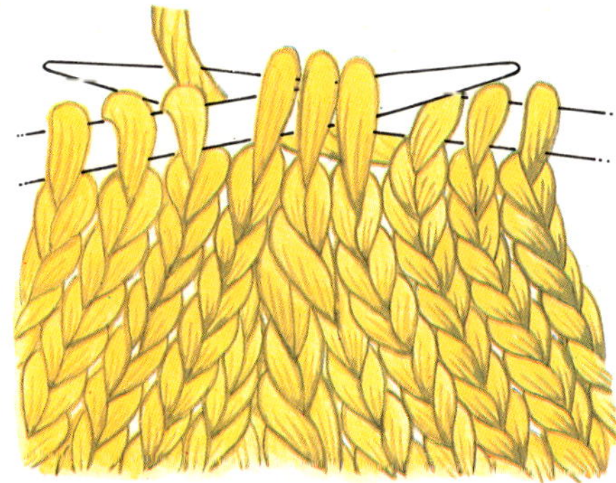

1 Double decreases are made by losing one stitch either side of a centre stitch. Work to within one stitch of the centre stitch. Knit the next three stitches together through the back of the loops. Repeat this on all right-side (knit) rows. All the alternate rows are purled. The decrease overlaps to the left.

2 To overlap the stitches to the right work as given for step one but knit the three stitches through the front of the loops.

Mitred double decrease

1 Work to within one stitch of the centre stitch. slip the next stitch on to the right-hand needle without knitting it. Knit the next two stitches together.

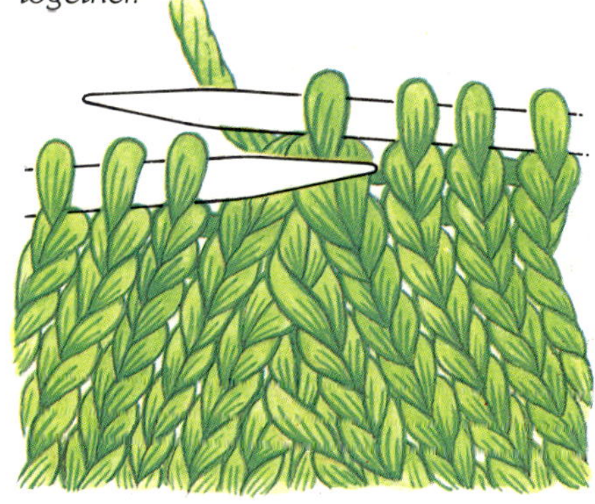

2 Pass the slipped stitch over the first stitch on the right-hand needle completing the decrease. Repeat this procedure on all subsequent right-side (knit) rows. All the alternate rows are purled.

Working into the Back of the Loop

Stitches are usually knitted or purled through the front of the loops. For some stitch patterns, however, they must be worked through the back of the loops thus twisting or crossing them. This technique is characteristic of early Arabic knitting and is similar to the cross-knit looping of early Peruvian textiles. Sometimes the entire fabric is composed of twisted knit and purl stitches. They can also be used singly to emphasize the lines of a textured pattern, as twisted stitches are more prominent than ordinary stitches.

Twisting purlwise

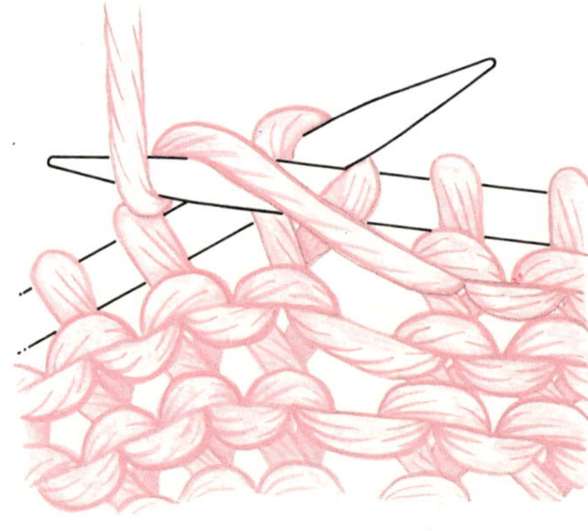

1 *Insert the right-hand needle through the back of the next stitch on the left-hand needle as shown. Take the yarn over and under the point of the right-hand needle.*

2 *Draw a loop through both stitches and drop them off the left-hand needle at the same time to complete the decrease.*

Twisted decreasing (purlwise)

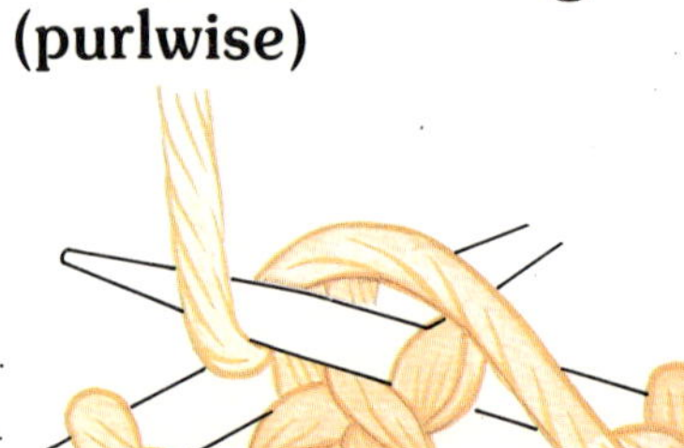

1 *Insert the right-hand needle through the backs of the next two stitches on the left-hand needle as shown. Take the yarn over and under the point of the right-hand needle.*

Twisting knitwise

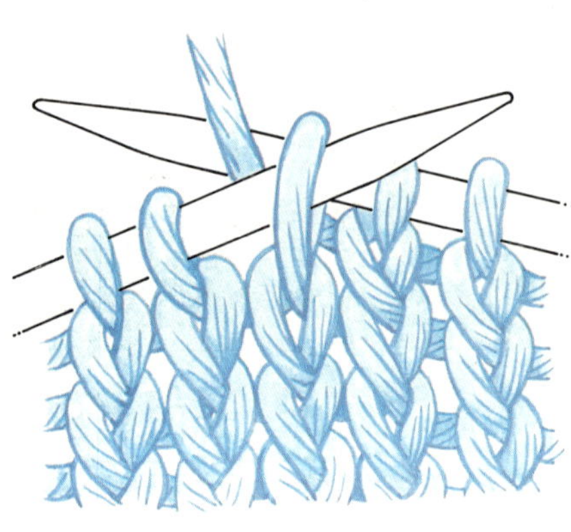

1 *Insert the right-hand needle through the back of the next stitch on the left-hand needle as shown. Take the yarn under and over the point of the right-hand needle.*

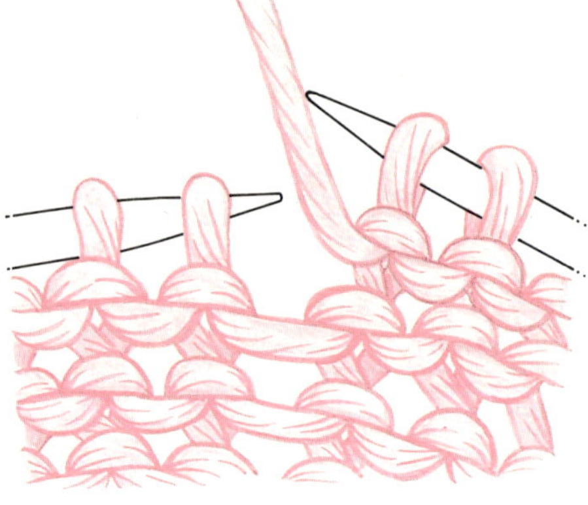

2 *Draw a loop through the stitch and drop the stitch off the left-hand needle to complete it.*

Twisted decreasing (knitwise)

2 *Draw a loop through the stitch and drop the stitch off the left-hand needle to complete it.*

1 *Insert the right-hand needle through the backs of the next two stitches on the left-hand needle as shown. Take the yarn under and over the point of the right-hand needle.*

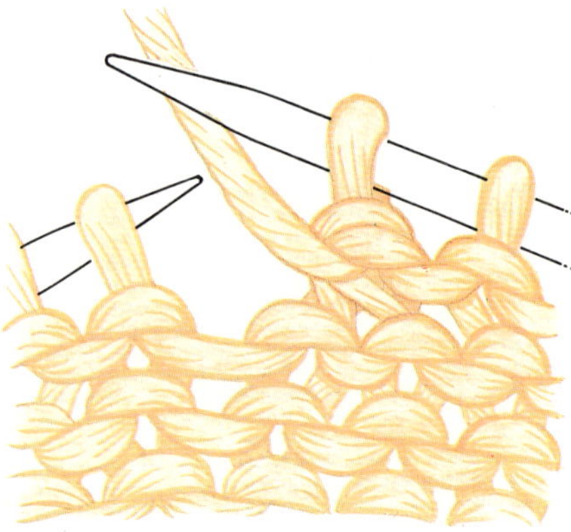

2 *Draw a loop through both stitches and drop them off the left-hand needle, so completing the decrease.*

Slipping Stitches

Stitches are 'slipped', that is, passed from one needle to another without being worked, for a variety of reasons. They can be slipped knitwise or purlwise and with the yarn at the front or back. Stitches may be slipped singly or several stitches may be slipped at a time.

Slipping knitwise

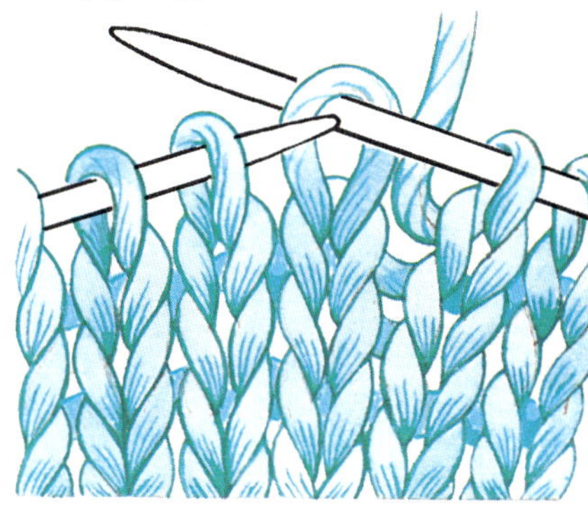

1 *Stitches are always slipped knitwise when they form part of a slipstitch decrease on a knit row. Insert the right-hand needle into the front of the next stitch on the left-hand needle as if to knit it but transfer the stitch on to the right-hand needle without knitting it. Work the next stitch as usual.*

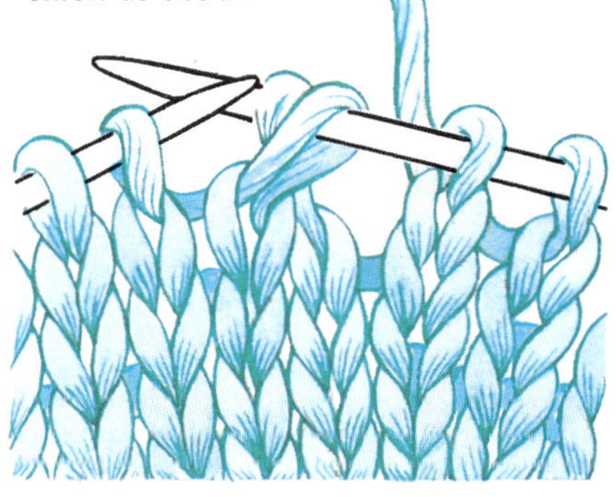

2 *On some double decreases two stitches must be slipped at once. In such cases insert the right-hand needle into the fronts of the next two stitches on the left-hand needle as if to knit them together and transfer them to the left-hand needle without knitting them.*

Slipping purlwise

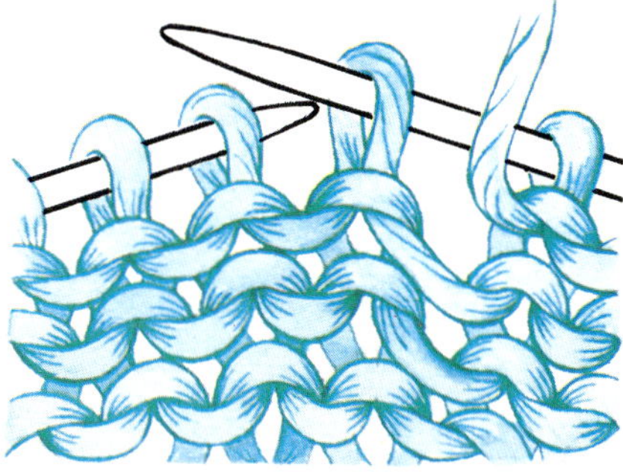

1 *Stitches are slipped purlwise when they form part of a decrease on a purl row or of any fancy pattern which requires the same stitch to be worked on the next or subsequent rows, for example, mosaic stitches and slipstitch textured patterns. Insert the right-hand needle into the next stitch on the left-hand needle as if to purl it but pass it to the right-hand needle without purling it.*

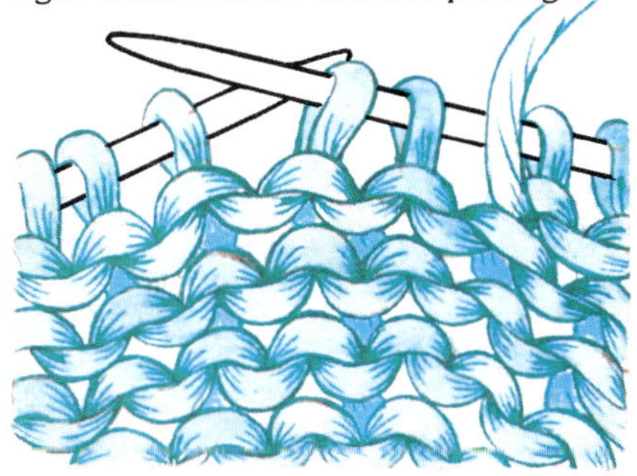

2 *To slip more than one stitch purlwise simply insert the right-hand needle into the required number of stitches as if to purl them and transfer them straight on to the right-hand needle without purling them.*

Yarn front

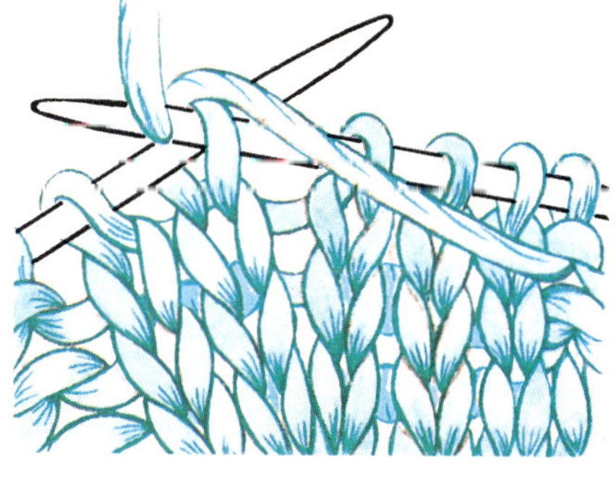

1 *The front of the work refers to the side facing the knitter regardless*

of whether it is the right or wrong side of the fabric. When slipping after purl stitches the yarn is already in front. Slip the required number of stitches and knit or purl the next stitch as instructed.

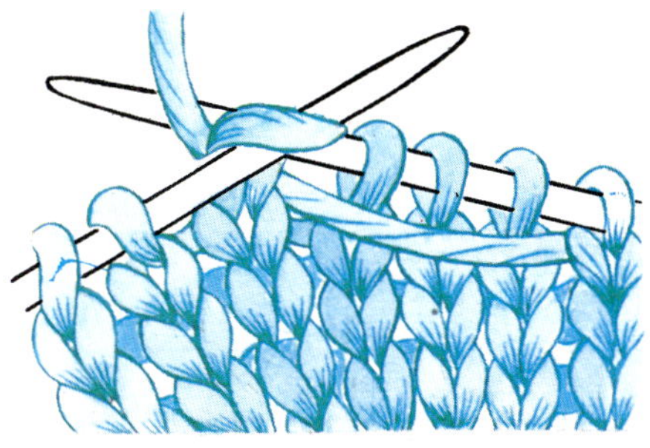

2 *After knit stitches bring the yarn to the front between the needles, slip the required number of stitches and purl or knit the next stitch as instructed in the pattern.*

Yarn back

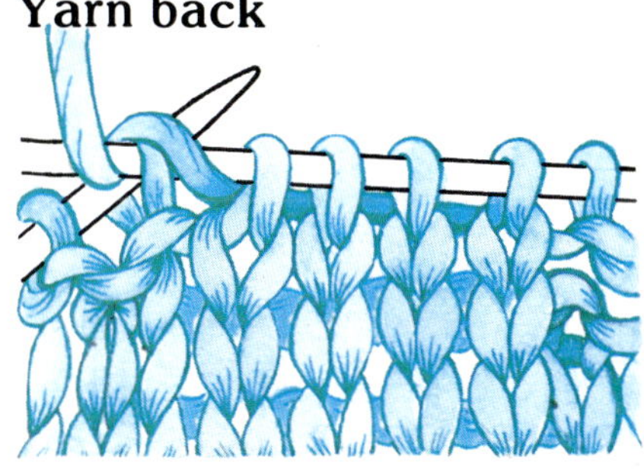

1 *The back of the work refers to the side facing away from the knitter regardless of whether it is the right or wrong side of the fabric. When slipping after knit stitches the yarn is already at the back. Slip the required number of stitches and knit or purl the next stitch as instructed.*

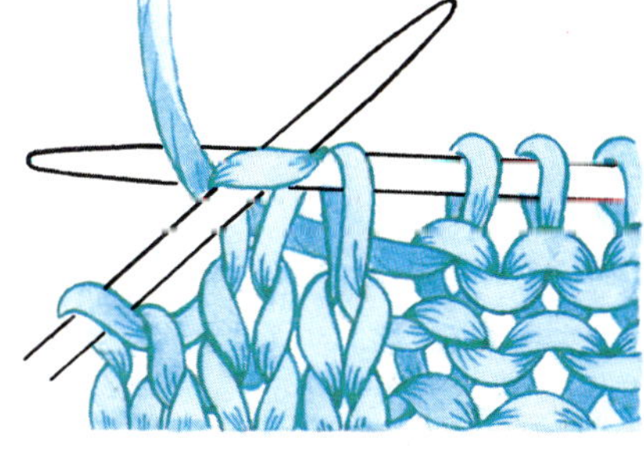

2 *After purl stitches take the yarn back between the needles, slip the required number of stitches and knit or purl the next stitch.*

Working with Colour

Knitting with several different coloured yarns is not easy but the results are so spectacular that it's worth making the effort to learn the technique.

Using a bobbin

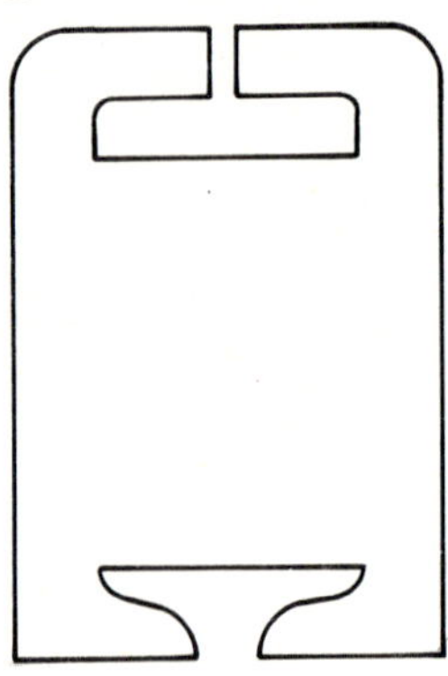

1 *When working single motifs in plain knitting, wind contrast colours on a notched card, called a bobbin. Trace the shape shown on stiff card. Cut one for each contrast colour.*

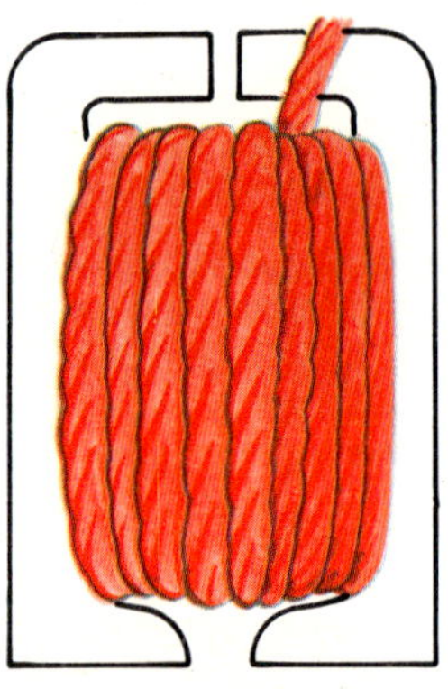

2 *Wind the yarn round the card until it is full, passing the working end through the thinner notch.*

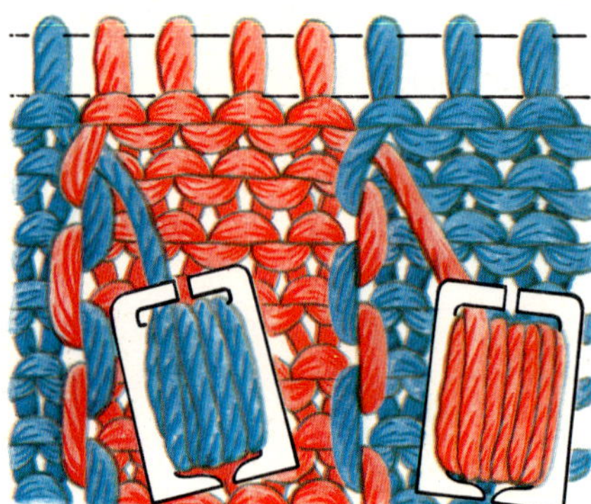

3 *When in use the bobbins hang down at the back of the work keeping the colours separate, and preventing the different yarns from tangling.*

Weaving yarns

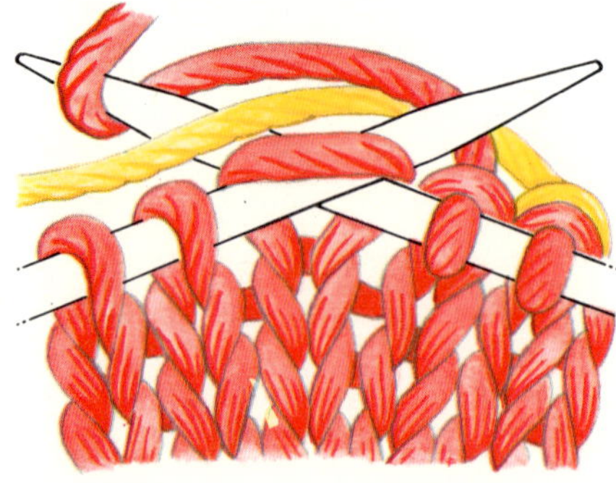

1 *Hold the yarn in use in your right hand and the yarn not in use in your left hand. Knit the first stitch as usual. On the next and every alternate stitch insert the right-hand needle knitwise. Take the yarn in the left hand over the right-hand needle, then knit with the yarn in the right hand as usual.*

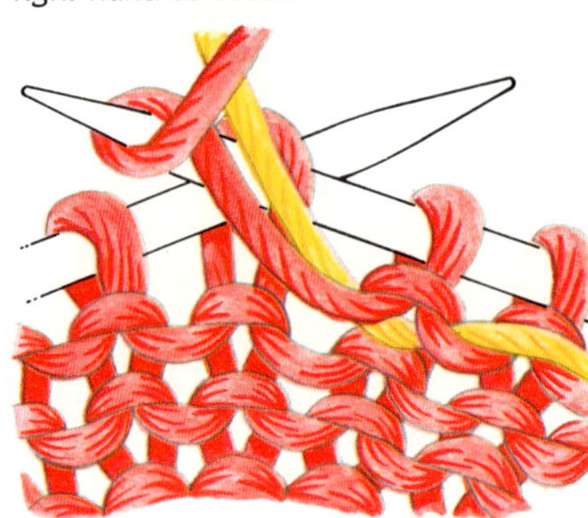

2 *On purl rows, work in exactly the same way. Bring the yarn not in use over the top of the right-hand needle on every alternate stitch, but the weaving takes place at the front of the work and the stitches are purled. This method is used where the yarn is carried over more than five stitches.*

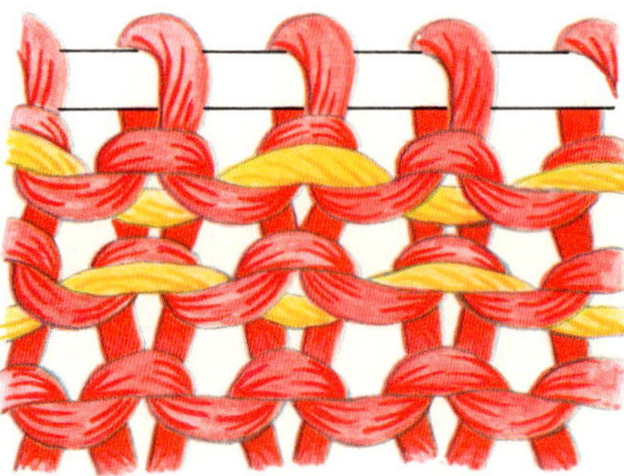

3 *Weaving yarns avoids untidy long strands at the back of the work.*

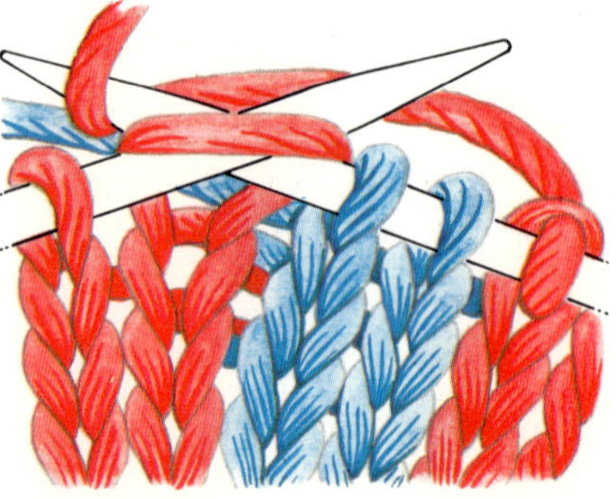

1 *On right-side rows, knit the required number of stitches with the first colour. Drop the yarn. Pick up the second colour and knit the required number of stitches with that. Pick up the first colour again and carry it loosely across the back of the work before knitting the next stitches.*

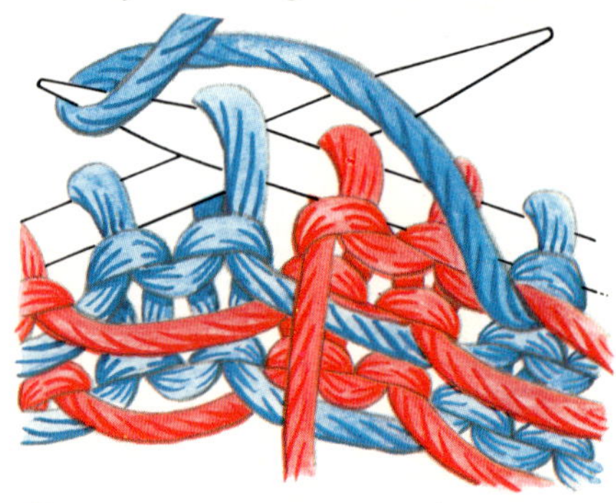

2 *On wrong-side rows, work in exactly the same way as for right-side rows but purl the stitches and carry the yarn loosely across the front of the work. This method is used where the yarn is carried over no more than three or four stitches.*

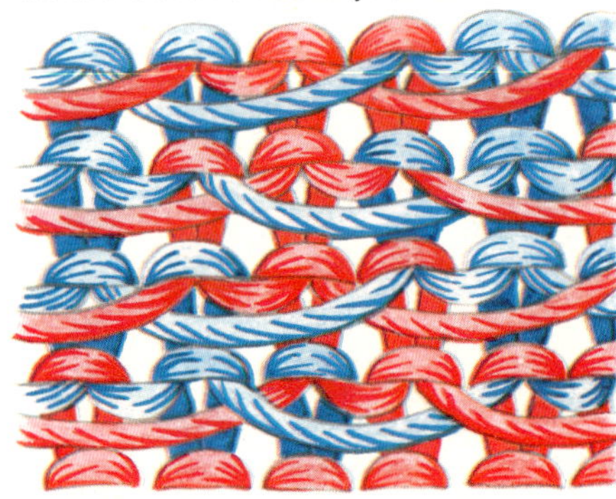

3 *The back of the work will be neat provided the yarns are carried evenly and at the same tension as the knitting. If the yarns are carried too tightly the right side of the work will pucker.*

Using a Cable Needle

The use of a cable needle is the basis of many knitting techniques including cable stitch patterns, Aran and travelling stitches.
Cable needles are short double-pointed needles. They are used to move stitches from one position to another in the same row and so change the order in which they are worked. On knit rows, cabling to the front twists the stitches to the left on the right side of the work; cabling to the back twists them to the right on the right side. On purl rows cabling front twists the stitches to the right and cabling back to the left.

Cable four front

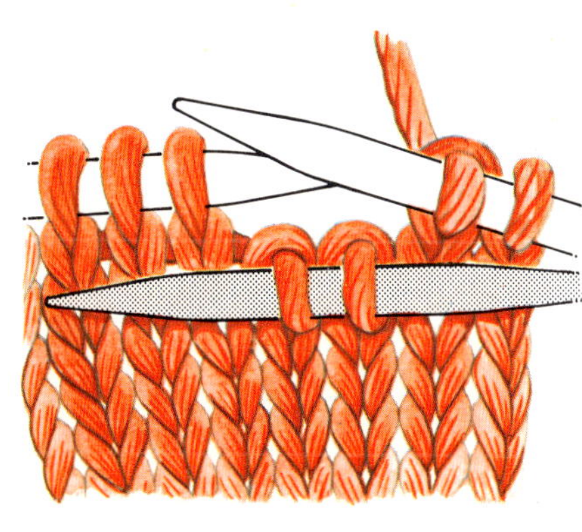

1 *Slip the next 2 stitches on to the cable needle and leave it at the front of the work.*

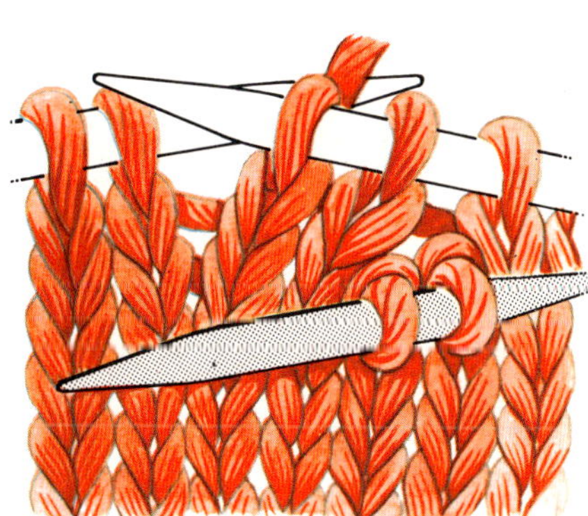

2 *Knit the next 2 stitches on the left-hand needle in the usual way.*

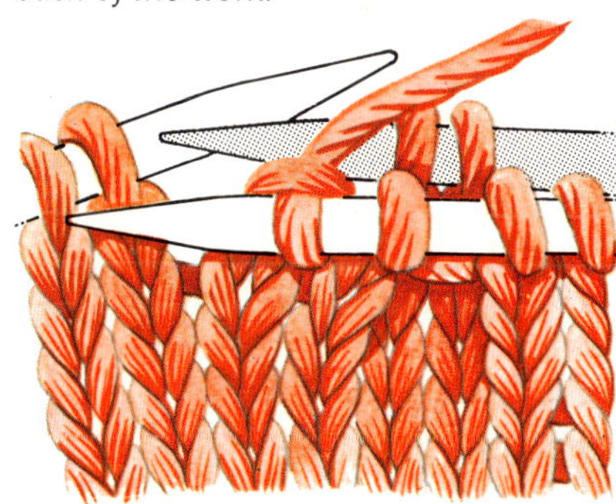

3 *Holding the cable needle in your left hand, knit off the two stitches on the cable needle.*

Cable four back

1 *Slip the next 2 stitches on to the cable needle and leave it at the back of the work.*

2 *Knit the next two stitches on the left-hand needle in the usual way.*

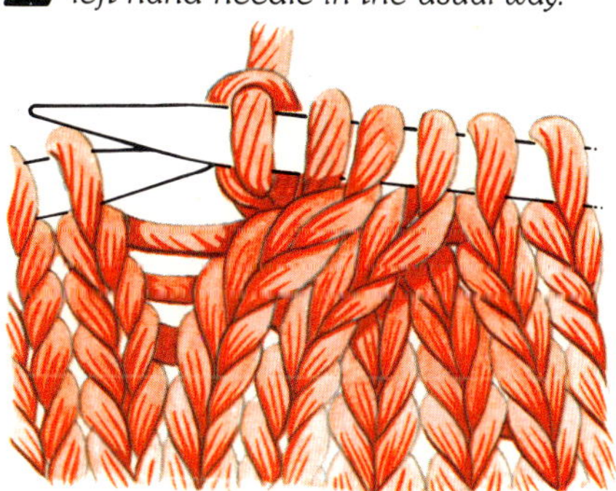

3 *Holding the cable needle in your left hand, knit off the two stitches on the cable needle.*

Cable 4 front purlwise

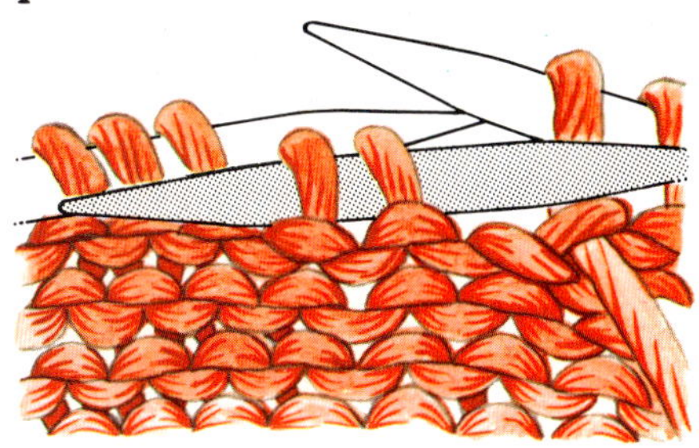

1 *Slip the next two stitches on to the cable needle and leave it at the front of the work.*

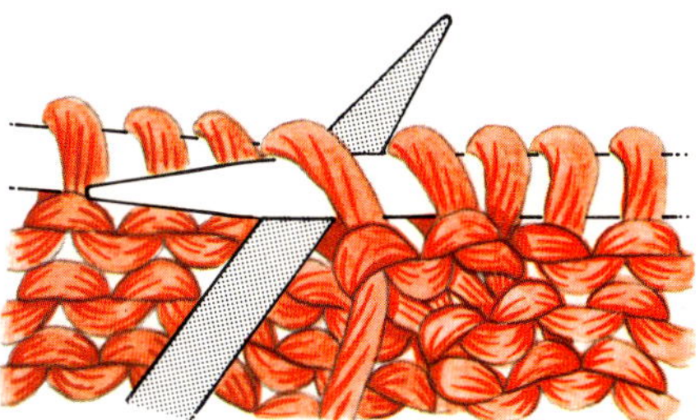

2 *Purl the next two stitches on the left-hand needle in the usual way, then purl the two stitches on the cable needle.*

Cable 4 back purlwise

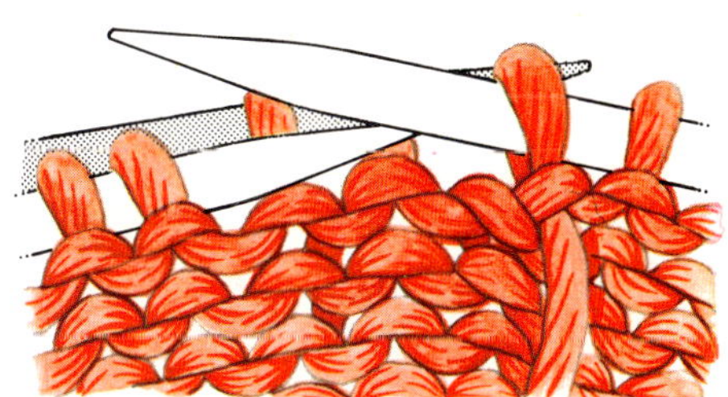

1 *Slip the next two stitches on to the cable needle and leave it at the back of the work.*

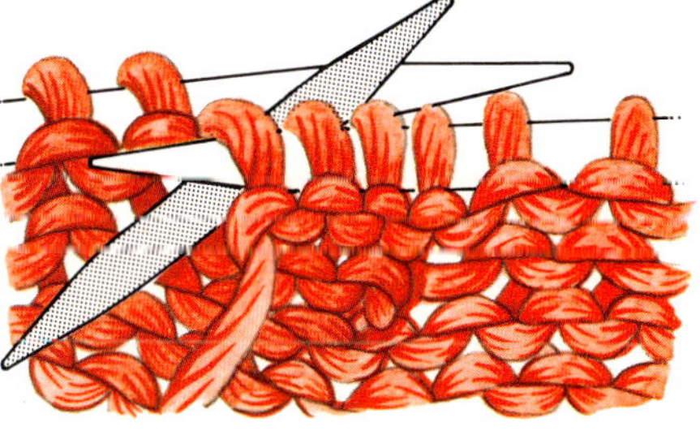

2 *Purl the next two stitches on the left-hand needle in the usual way, then purl the two stitches on the cable needle.*

Making Eyelets

Eyelets are small holes arranged decoratively on a knitted background. They are formed in many different ways but the basic principle is the same: each eyelet is composed of a decorative increase and a compensating decrease.

2 Purl the next row including the yarn taken over the needle.

Double eyelet

Picot eyelet

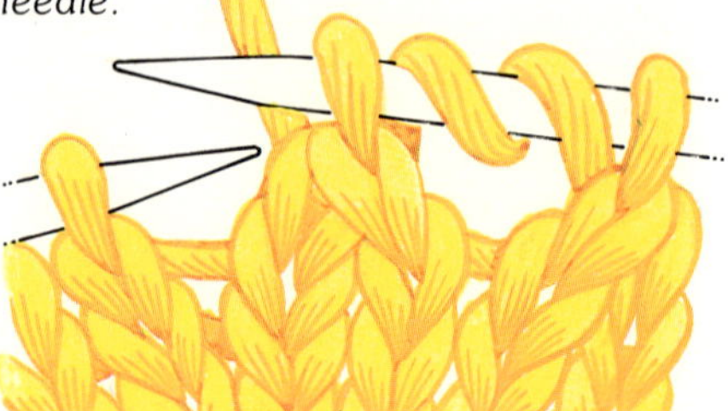

1 Work to the eyelet position. Knit the next two stitches together. Take the yarn twice round the needle.

Chain eyelet

1 This is the most popular single eyelet method. Work to the position of the eyelet. Bring the yarn forward between the needles and take it over the needle to knit the next two stitches together.

2 Purl the next row including the yarn taken over the needle.

Open eyelet

1 This makes a large round eyelet. Work to the eyelet position. Knit the next two stitches together. Bring the yarn forward.

2 Slip the next stitch knitwise. Take the yarn over the needle to knit the following stitch. Pass the slipped stitch over the knit stitch.

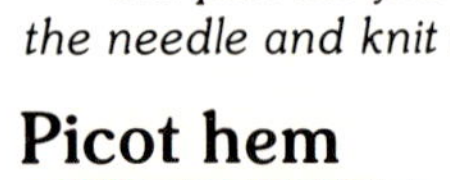

2 Slip the next stitch knitwise. Knit the following stitch. Pass the slipped stitch over the knit stitch.

3 On the next row, purl every stitch but purl the first loop taken over the needle and knit the second.

Picot hem

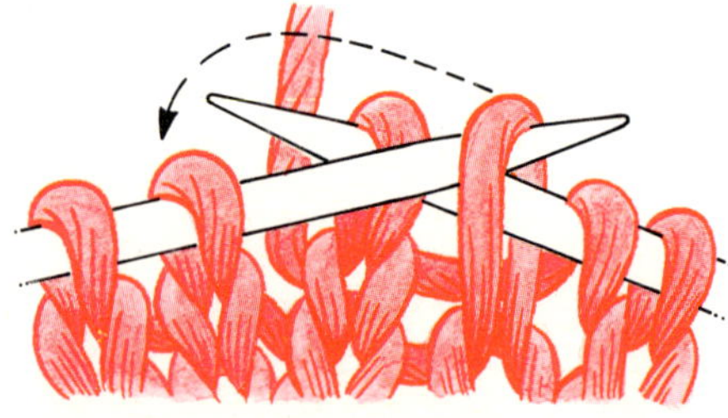

1 This is rounder and more clearly defined than the chain eyelet. Work to the eyelet position. Bring the yarn forward between the needles. Slip the next stitch knitwise. Take the yarn over the needle to knit the following stitch. Pass the slipped stitch over the knit stitch.

3 On the next row, purl every stitch but purl and knit into the yarn taken over the needle.

Eyelets are used to make picot hems. Work a row of chain eyelets along the fold line of the hem as close together as possible. When the garment is completed, fold the hem along the picot row and slipstitch the edge in place.

Making Bobbles

Bobbles are made in various ways depending on whether they are large or small, and knit or purl, but the basic principle remains the same: several increases are made into one stitch; these stitches are worked on in various ways to form a small piece of knitting attached to the main work by one stitch, then decreased until only one stitch is left. The bobble 'sits' on top of the background fabric.

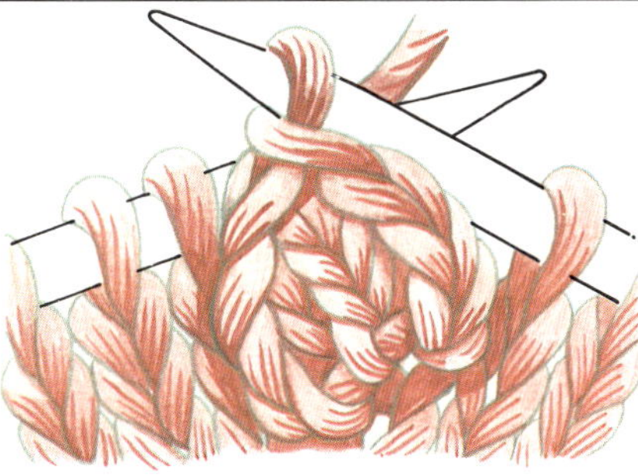

4 Turn the work. Slip one stitch, knit two stitches together. Pass the slipped stitch over the decrease to complete the bobble.

Small knit bobble

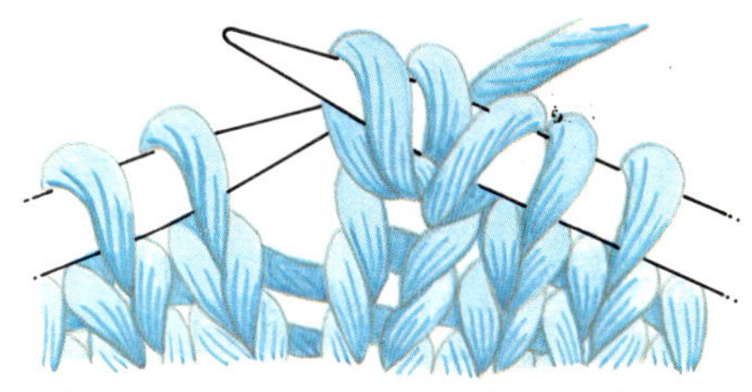

1 To make a knit bobble, work to the bobble position. Knit into the next stitch without slipping it off the needle, bring the yarn forward, knit again into the same stitch and slip if off the needle.

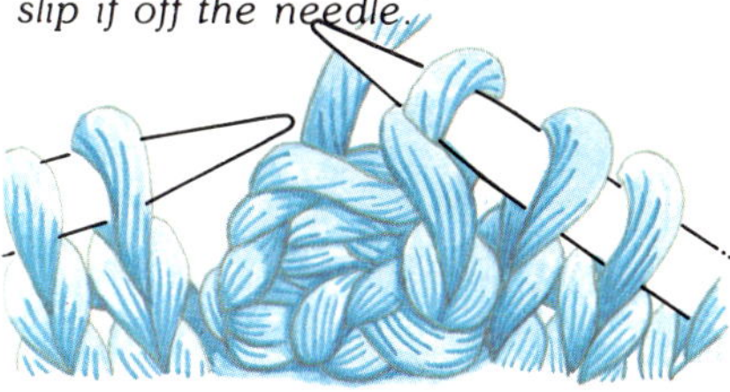

2 Turn the work. Purl the three 'made' stitches. Turn the work and knit the three made stitches. Turn the work, purl two stitches together, purl one stitch. Turn the work slip one stitch, knit one stitch, pass the slipped stitch over the knit stitch to complete the bobble.

Large knit bobble

1 Work to the bobble position. Knit into the next stitch without slipping it off the needle, bring the yarn forward, knit again into the same stitch, bring the yarn forward, knit again into the same stitch and slip it off the left-hand needle.

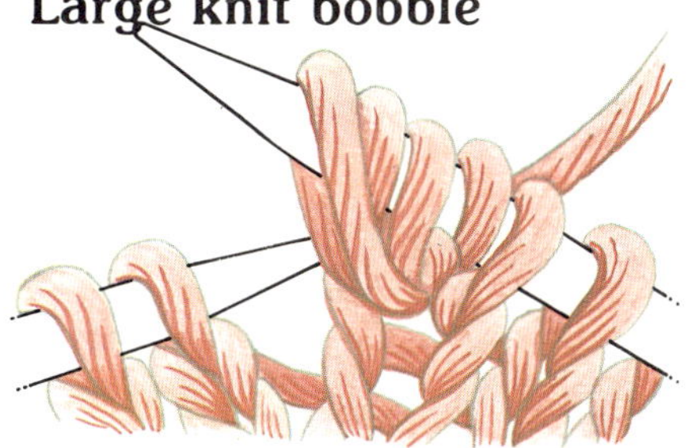

2 Turn the work. Purl across the five 'made' stitches. Turn the work and knit across the five stitches.

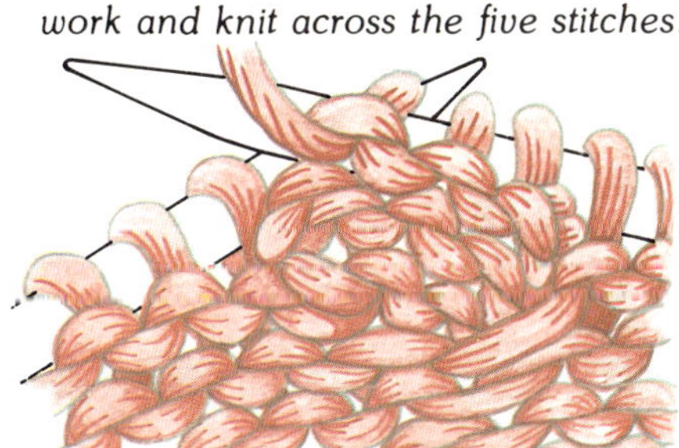

3 Turn the work and purl two stitches together, purl one stitch, purl two stitches together across the five stitches.

Large purl bobble

1 Work as for step one of the large knit bobble. Turn the work and knit across the five made stitches. Turn the work and purl across the five made stitches.

2 Turn the work and knit two stitches together, knit one stitch, knit two stitches together across the five stitches.

3 Turn the work. Slip one stitch, purl two stitches together. Pass the slipped stitch over the decrease to complete the bobble.

Small purl bobble

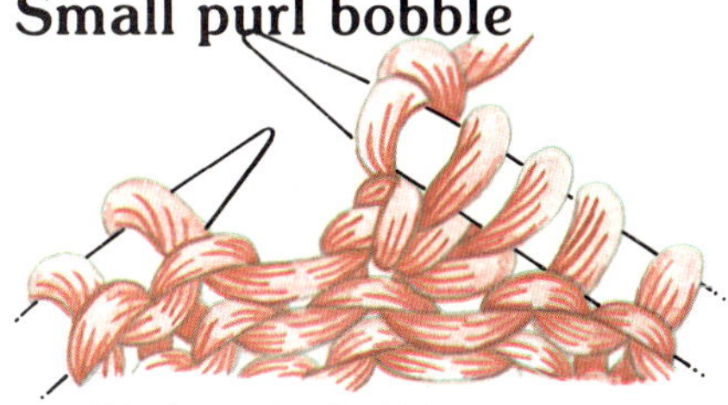

1 Work to the bobble position. Knit into the next stitch without slipping it off the needle, bring the yarn forward, knit again into the same stitch and slip it off the needle. Turn the work. Knit the three 'made' stitches.

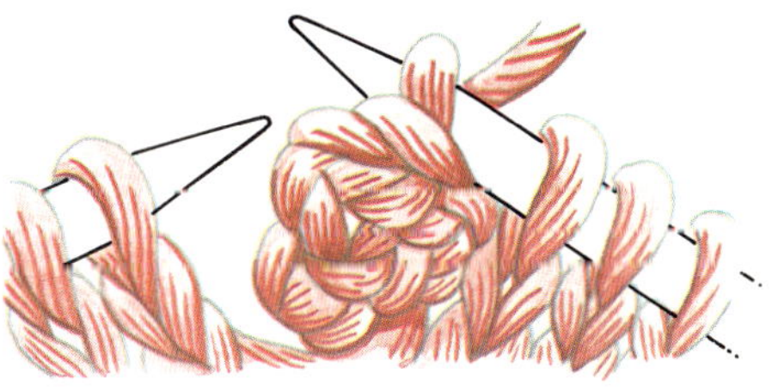

2 Turn the work. Purl the three made stitches. Turn the work, knit two stitches together, knit one stitch. Turn the work, slip one stitch, purl one stitch, pass the slipped stitch over the purl stitch and off the needle.

Swiss Darning

Swiss darning is one of the most popular and versatile ways of decorating knitted garments. As its name suggests, it was originally a means of reinforcing worn areas of a garment and was worked in the same yarn and colour as the original knitting. Now it is usually worked in contrast colours to add motifs to plain stocking stitch fabrics. The object is to cover the stitches entirely with the new yarn which must be the same as the background.

Horizontal lines

1 Thread a blunt-ended wool needle with the chosen yarn and begin at the lower right-hand corner of the motif to be worked. Bring the yarn through from back to front of the base of the first stitch to be covered. Insert the needle from right to left behind the base of the stitch above.

2 Pull the yarn through. Insert the needle through the base of the stitch from front to back, then through the base of the stitch to the left.

3 Pull the yarn through, thus covering the first stitch. Continue

28

in this way across the row, covering each stitch in turn and working from right to left.

4 Work the next row of stitches above the first working from left to right, as shown.

Vertical lines

1 Beginning at the bottom of the line bring the yarn through from back to front at the base of the first stitch. Insert the needle from right to left behind the base of the next stitch above. Pull the yarn through, then insert the needle vertically behind the head of the stitch below as shown.

2 Pull the yarn through thus covering the first stitch. Continue in this way working from the bottom of the line to the top.

Working from charts

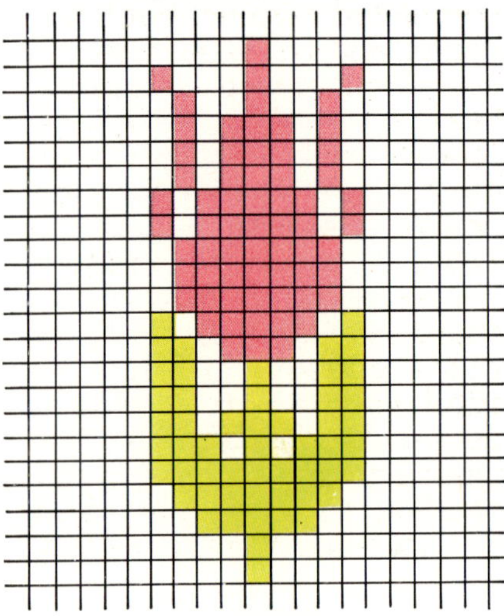

1 Swiss darning is usually worked from charts similar to those used for Fair Isle and jacquard patterns. Each square on the chart represents one stitch on the knitted fabric. Since knitted stitches are rectangular rather than square the motif on the knitted fabric will appear rather more flattened than it does on the chart.

2 Use each colour separately, working as far as possible from right to left, then from left to right, to keep the back of the work neat and smooth. Keep an even tension on the yarn, taking particular care not to pull it too tightly. Finish off the ends at the back of the work by threading them through two or three stitches before cutting off the surplus.

Beading

Beads can be sewn on to a completed garment but it is neater and, in the long run, easier and quicker to knit them in as you go along. In order to prevent the beads slipping to the back of the work they must be placed securely in position. There are various methods depending on the size and shape of bead, and on whether they are used to highlight the stitch pattern or to provide a densely beaded fabric (called purse beading). Except in purse beading, beads are placed on the right-side (knit) rows only.

Threading beads

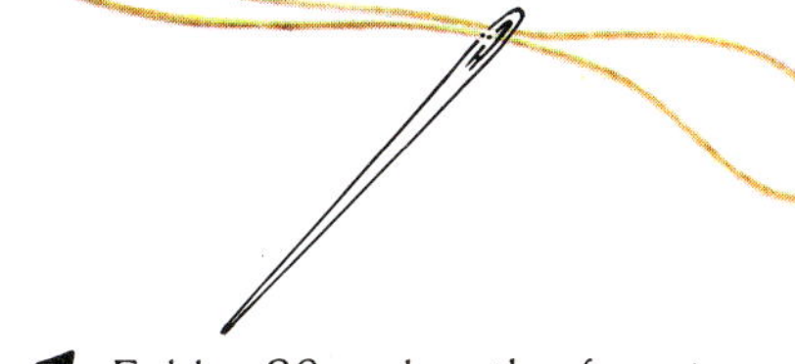

1 Fold a 30cm length of sewing thread in half. Thread both ends together through the eye of a sharp-pointed sewing needle.

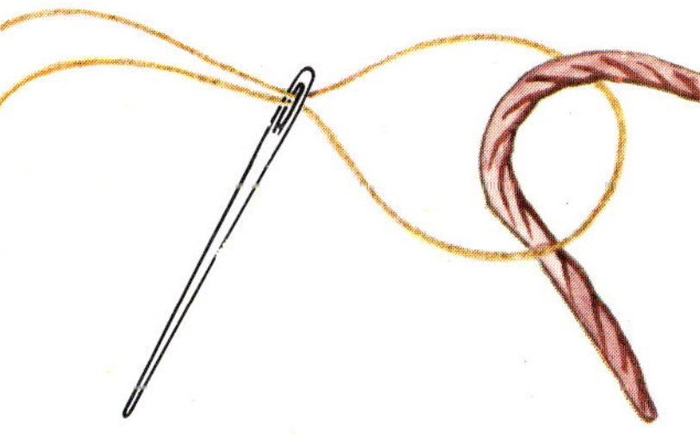

2 Thread the end of the knitting yarn through the loop in the thread.

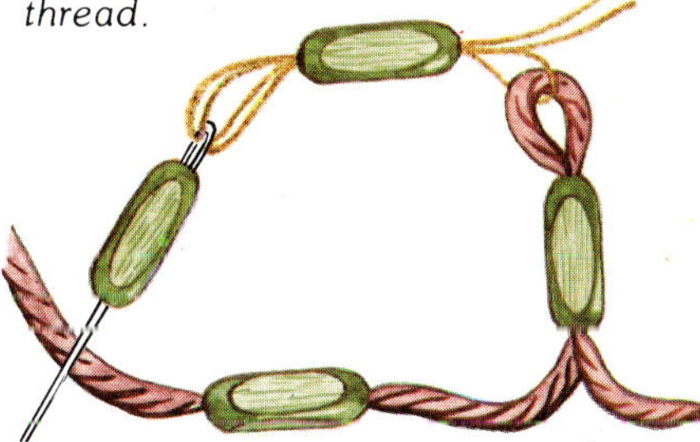

3 Insert the point of the needle into the bead and pass it down over the needle and thread and on to the yarn. Thread the beads in reverse order to the way they are worked before beginning to knit.

Placing small beads

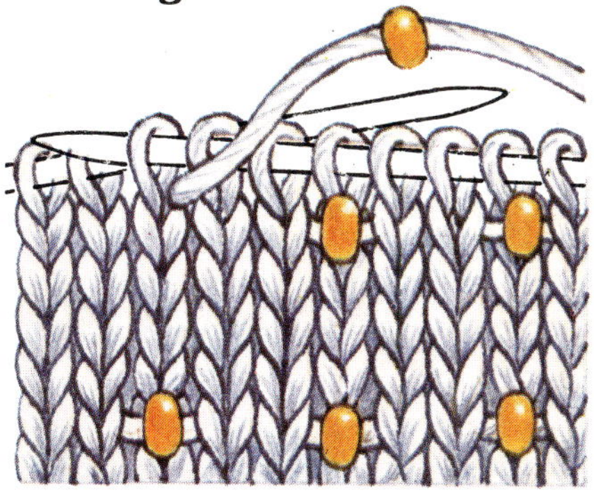

1 This method places the bead in front of the stitch on the right side of the work. Knit to the bead position. Pass the yarn forward to the right side of the work. Slip the next stitch.

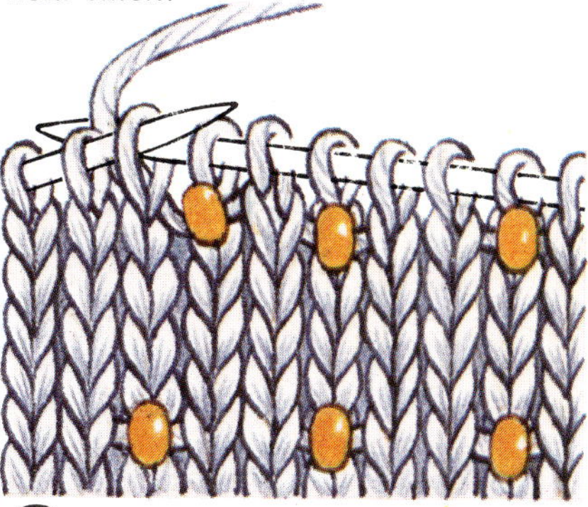

2 Push the bead down the yarn as close as possible to the last stitch knitted. Take the yarn back. Knit the next stitch on the left-hand needle. This method is also suitable for placing horizontal beads. More than one stitch can be slipped if necessary.

Placing large beads

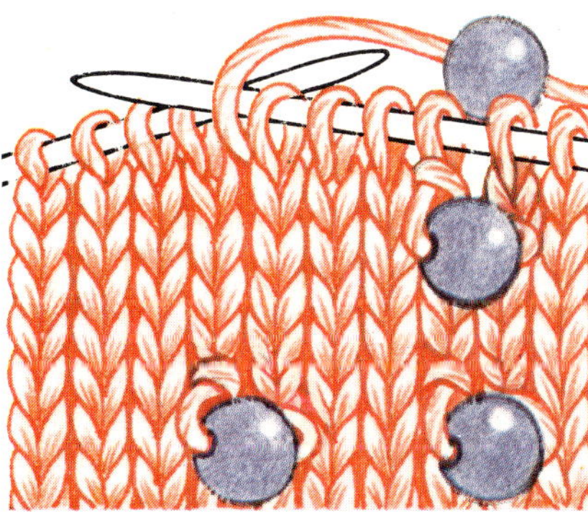

1 This method places the beads between the stitches on the right side of the work. Knit as usual to the bead position. Pass the yarn forward to the right side of the work.

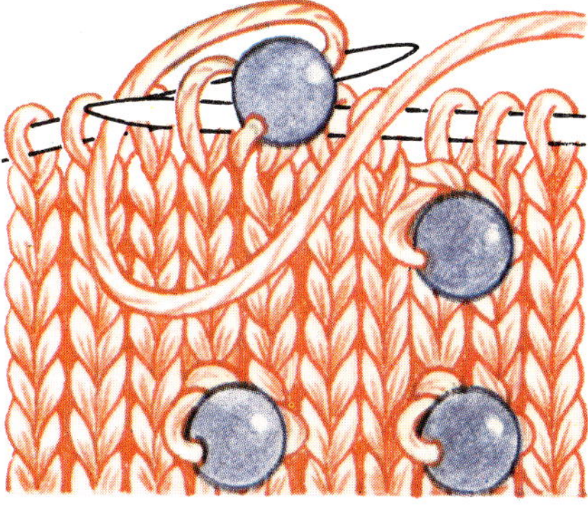

2 Slip the bead as close as possible to the last stitch knitted. Purl the next stitch, then knit as usual.

Purse beading

2 In purse beading the beads sit on top of the knitted stitches completely covering them. On knit rows, knit the first stitch through the back of the loop. Knit the next stitch through the back of the loop, pushing the bead through the stitch to the front of the work as the yarn is pulled through. Beads are placed on every stitch except the first and last.

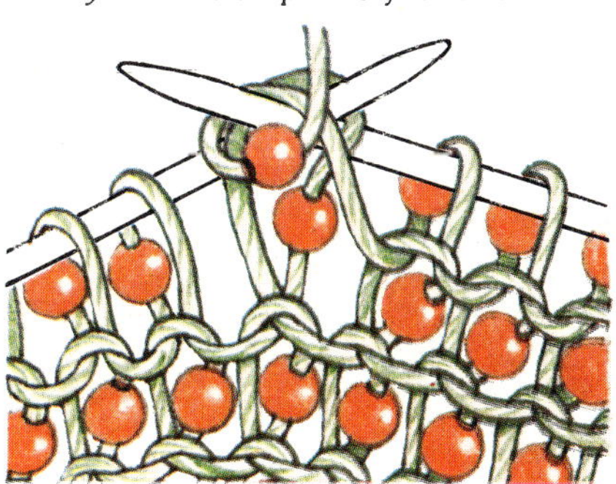

2 On purl rows, purl the first stitch through the back of the loop. Purl the next stitch through the back of the loop pushing the bead through the stitch to the back of the work as the yarn is pulled through. Beads are placed on every stitch in the row except the first and the last one. All the knit rows and all the purl rows are beaded.

Left-handed Skills

Many left-handed people learn to knit in a 'right-handed' way. This has advantages since the instructions in most publications (including this one) are written for right-handed people. However, there are ways of handling the needles and making the stitches that are much more natural for a left-handed person, so here is a guide to both basic and more complicated techniques for those knitters.

Equipment

The basic tools of knitting — the needles — are the same whether you are left- or right-handed, but there are left-handed versions of items like scissors and tape measures. The crucial difference for left-handed knitters is that the needle which holds the stitches is held in the right rather than left hand, and the working needle is held in the left rather than right hand.

Casting on and off

1 *Make a slip loop as usual and place it on one of the needles. Hold this needle in your right hand.*

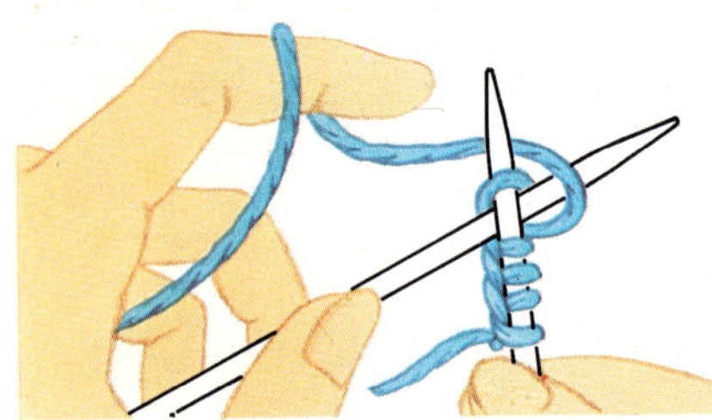

2 *Hold the other needle in your left hand and insert it into the slip loop. Take the yarn under and over the left-hand needle. Draw a loop through and place it on the right-hand*

needle. Now insert the left-hand needle between the two loops and take the yarn under and over it.

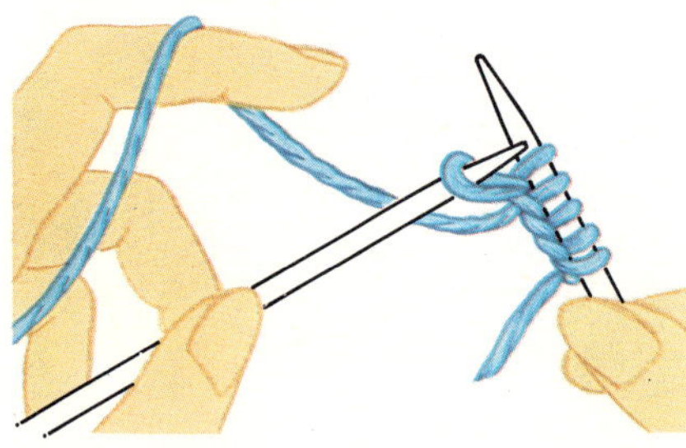

3 *Draw a loop through between the stitches and place it on the right-hand needle. Continue in this way until the required number of stitches has been cast on.*

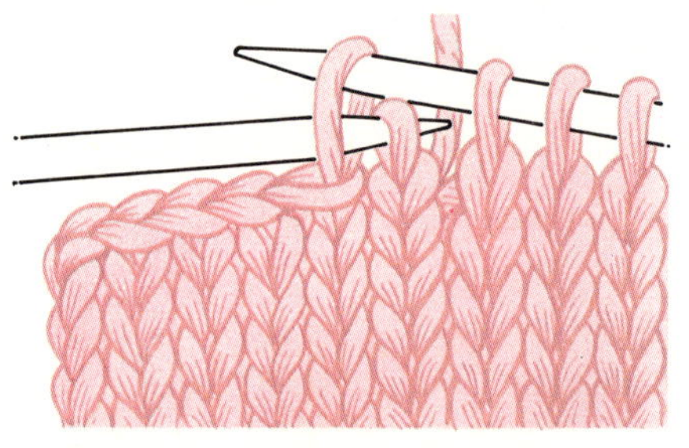

4 *Casting off is worked as the right-handed method (pages 16-17) except that the stitches are cast off from left to right rather than from right to left.*

Knit

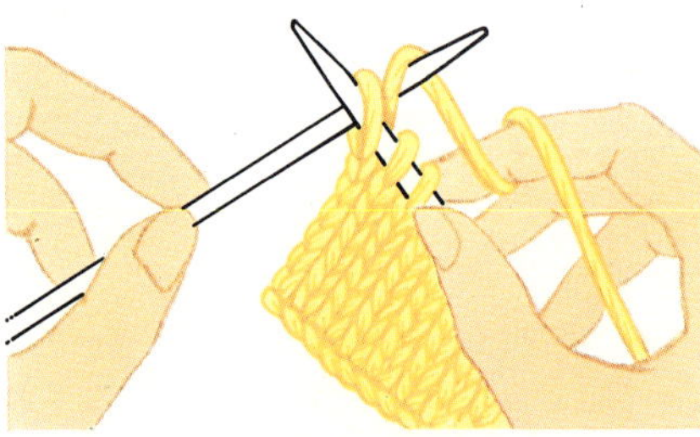

1 *The 'continental method' of knitting is generally the most comfortable for left-handed knitters. The yarn is held by the same hand that holds the needle with the stitches (in this case the right hand). Insert the left-hand needle through the next stitch on the right-hand needle. Loop it under the yarn held in the right hand.*

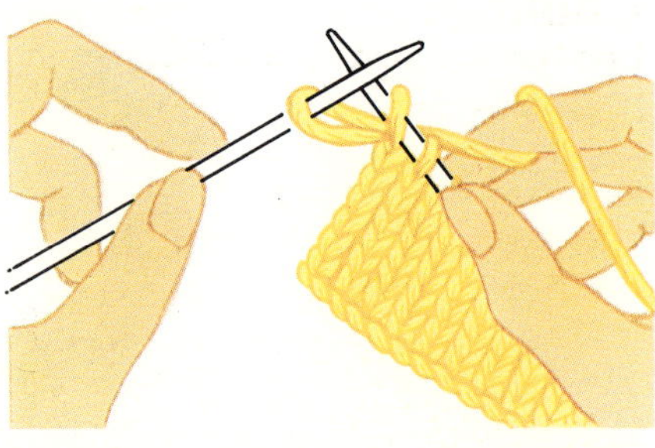

2 *Draw a loop through the stitch. Drop the original stitch off the right-hand needle thus completing a new stitch. Carry on in this way across the row. For left-handers, rows are thus worked from left to right instead of from right to left.*

Purl

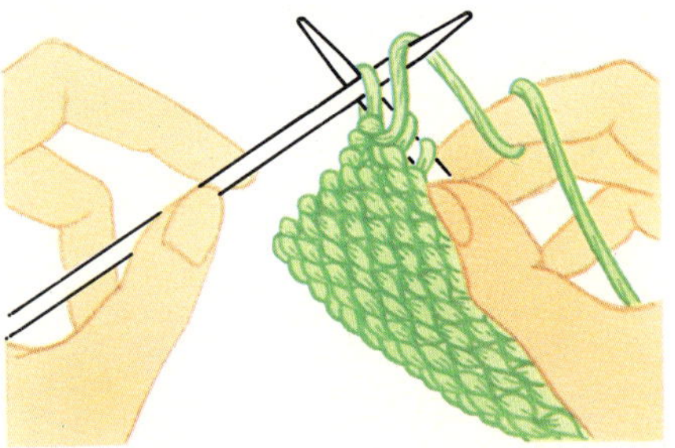

1 *Hold the needle with the stitches in your right hand looping the yarn round the right forefinger. Insert the left-hand needle through the next stitch on the right-hand needle and hook it under the yarn.*

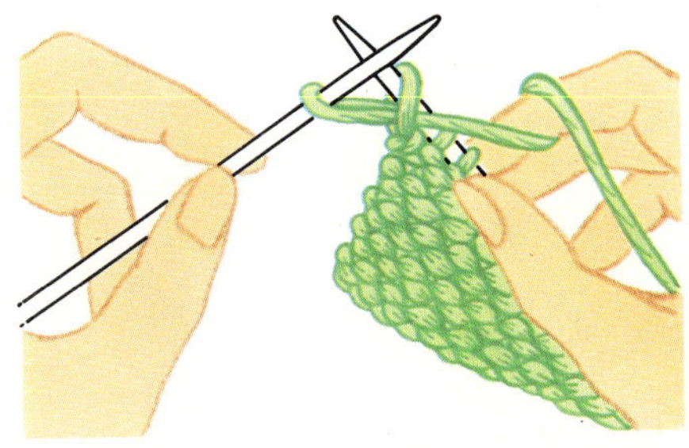

2 *Draw a loop through the stitch. Drop the original stitch off the right-hand needle thus completing a new stitch. Carry on in this way across the row, thus working from left to right instead of right to left.*

Cabling

Left-handed knitters work rows from left to right rather than right to left. This has the effect of reversing the twist on cable patterns.

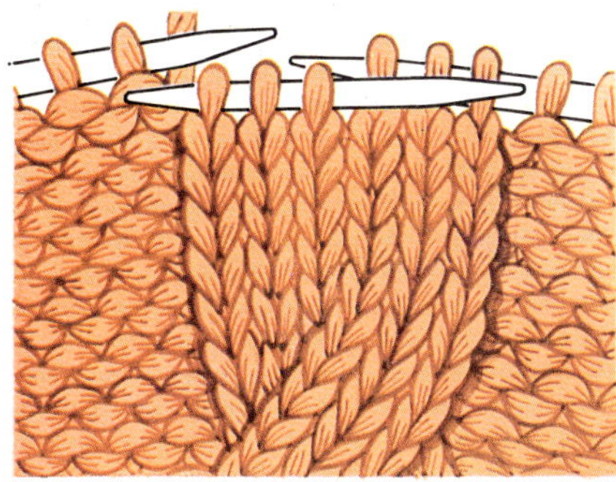

1 For right-handers, cabling forwards (holding the cable needle with the stitches at the front of the work) produces a twist to the left. For left-handers, it produces a twist to the right.

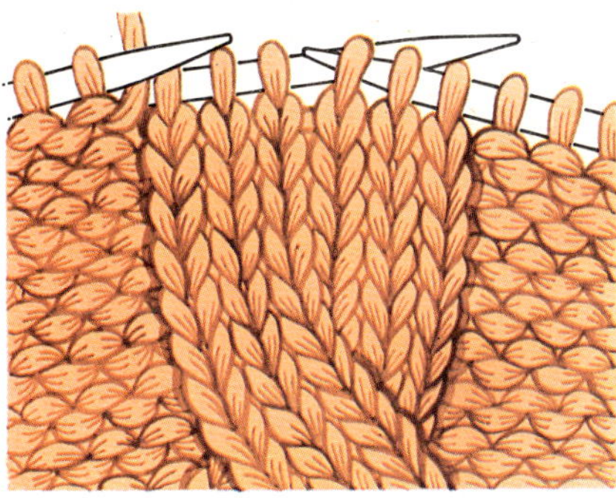

2 Cabling back (holding the needle at the back of the work) produces a twist to the left for left-handed knitters. When following a right-handed pattern left-handers should cable back when the pattern says cable forward, and forward when it says cable back.

Decreasing

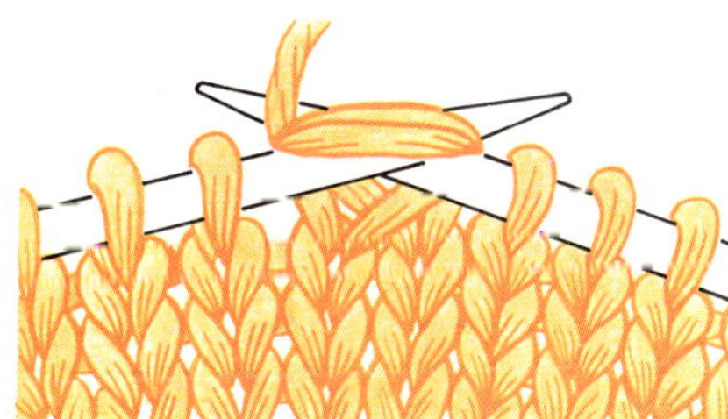

1 The direction of decreases is reversed for left-handed knitters. For example, knitting two stitches together through the front of the loops produces a decrease which slants to the left rather than the right.

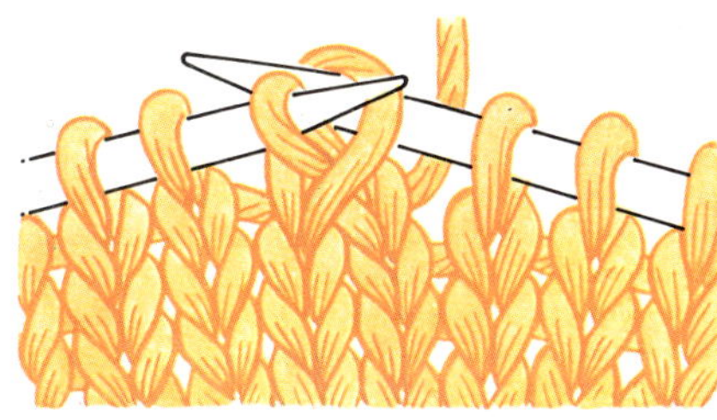

2 The slipstitch decrease (slip one, knit one, pass slipped stitch over) produces a decrease which slants to the right rather than the left. When reading a right-handed pattern where decreases are paired (for instance in raglan shaping), read 'K2 tog' for 'sl 1, K1, psso' and vice versa.

Decorative increasing

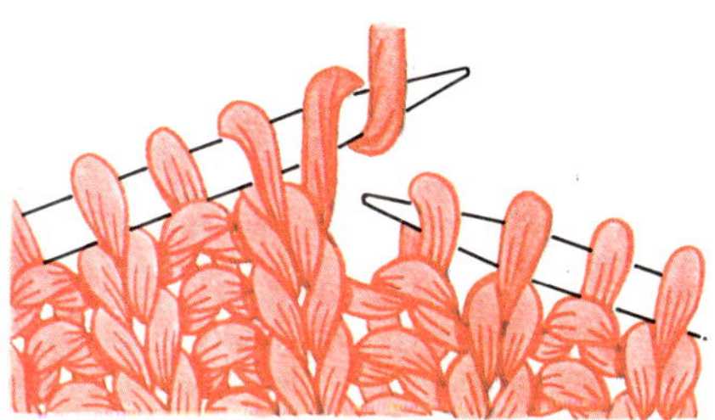

1 Eyelets and lace stitches are worked similarly for left-handers as for right-handers. 'Yarn overs' create new stitches between existing stitches. Between a knit and a purl stitch hook the needle round the yarn as shown before purling.

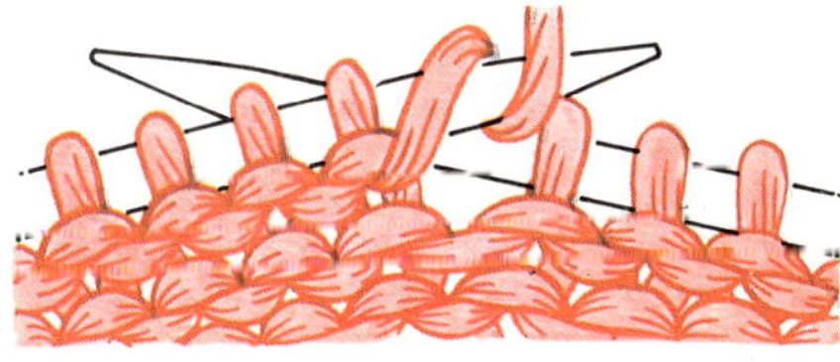

2 Between two purl stitches hook left-hand needle round yarn as shown. The techniques in steps 1 and 2 are abbreviated as 'yrn'.

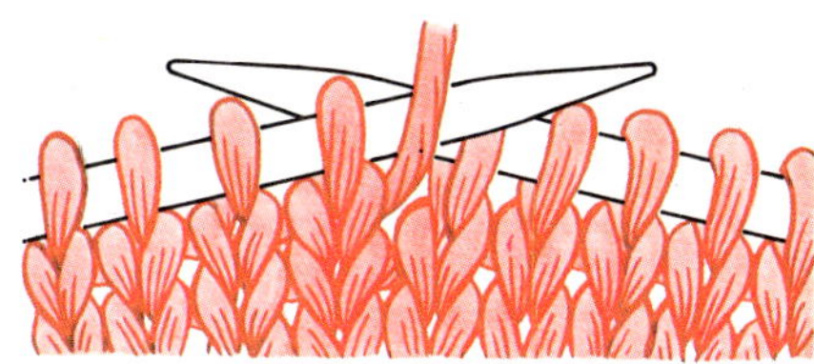

3 Between two knit stitches bring the yarn forward between the needles before inserting the left-hand needle to knit the next stitch. This is abbreviated as 'yfwd'.

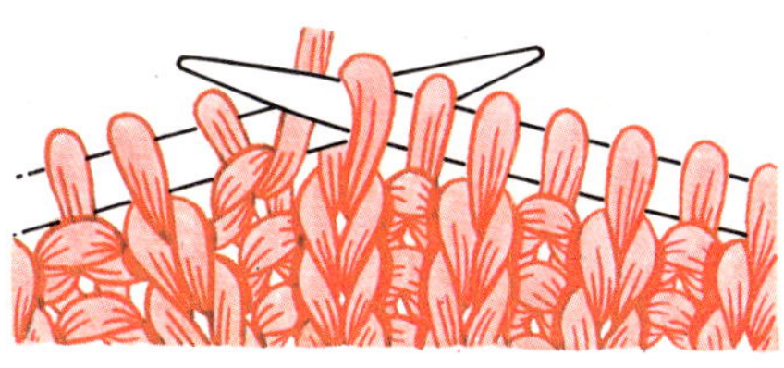

4 Between purl and knit stitches simply take the yarn over the needle from its position at the front of the work to knit the next stitch. This is abbreviated as 'yon'.

Following patterns

Most patterns are written for right-handed knitters. However, these can be used by left-handed knitters providing that they follow a few basic guidelines. All references to left-hand and right-hand needle should be reversed. When reading charts knit rows should be read from left to right and purl rows from right to left. Be especially careful when reading shaping instructions. In right-handed knitting the shaping of right-hand edges is carried out at the beginnings of right-side rows and/or the ends of wrong-side rows, while the shaping of left-hand edges is carried out at the ends of right-side rows and/or the beginnings of wrong-side rows. The situation is reversed for left-handed knitters.

Circular Knitting

Circular knitting is carried out using a set of four or more double-pointed needles or a circular needle. It produces a tubular seamless fabric, ideal for items such as socks and gloves. Many traditional types of sweater such as Aran, Fair Isle and especially Guernsey were also worked in the round. Since circular knitting is worked with the right side facing on every round, the construction of stitch patterns is different from that which obtains in flat knitting. Stocking stitch, for example, is worked by knitting every round, and garter stitch by alternately knitting and purling rounds. Circular needles can also be used for flat knitting when the number of stitches is too great for ordinary needles.

Casting on to four needles

1 *Using any of the usual methods, cast on the required number of stitches on to one of the needles.*

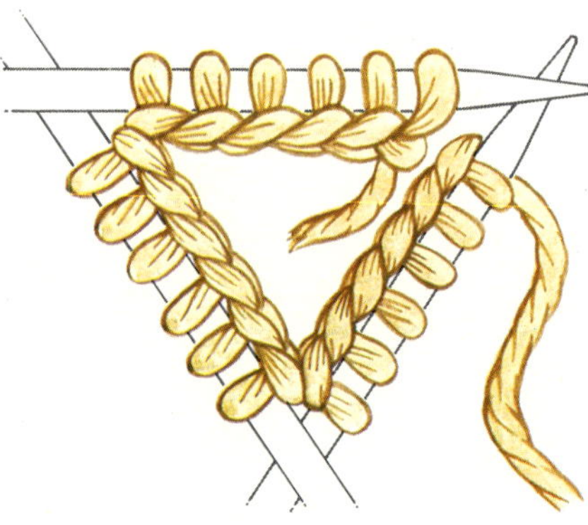

2 *Distribute these stitches among three of the set of four needles. Form the needles into a triangle making sure that the stitches are not twisted as you do so.*

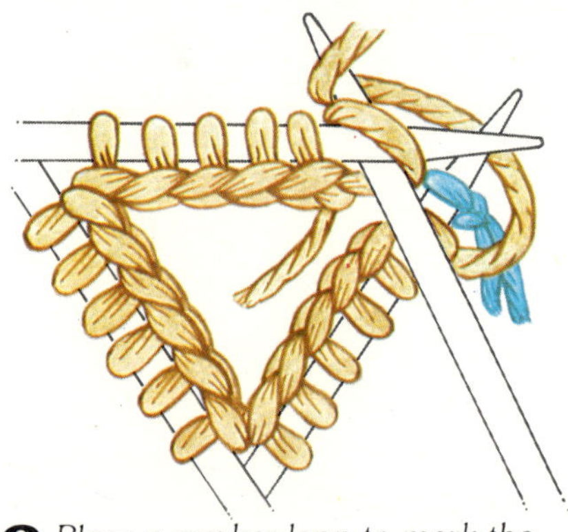

3 *Place a marker loop to mark the beginning of rounds. Join the stitches into a round by using the fourth needle and the working yarn from the last stitch on the third needle to knit first stitch on first needle.*

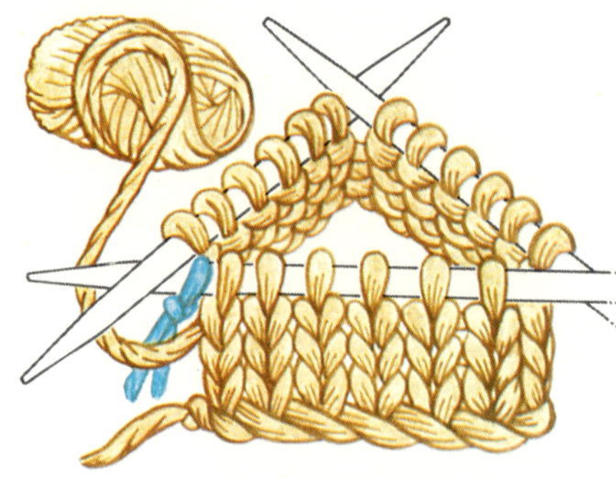

4 *Continue knitting off the stitches on the first needle. then use the first needle to knit off the stitches on the second needle and so on until the round is completed. Slip the marker loop at the beginning of each round. Alternatively the end of yarn left after casting on can be used as a marker.*

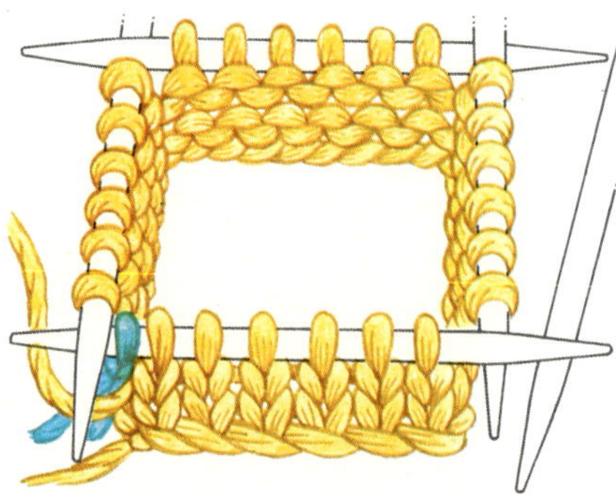

5 *When using a set of five needles. cast on the stitches on to four needles and use the fifth needle to work off the stitches. The same principle holds for working with larger sets of needles — cast on to one less than the total number of needles and use the spare needle as the actual working needle.*

Using a circular needle

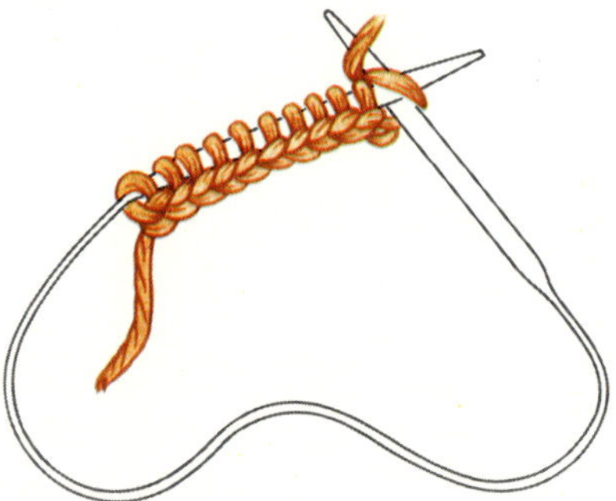

1 *Circular needles come in lengths varying from 40 to 100cm. They can only be used where the number of cast-on stitches is sufficient to reach from one point to the other. Use one point to cast on stitches on to the other point in the usual way.*

2 *When the stitches have been cast on. join them into a round by transferring the left-hand point to the right hand and vice versa. then knit first cast-on stitch using the working yarn from the right-hand point.*

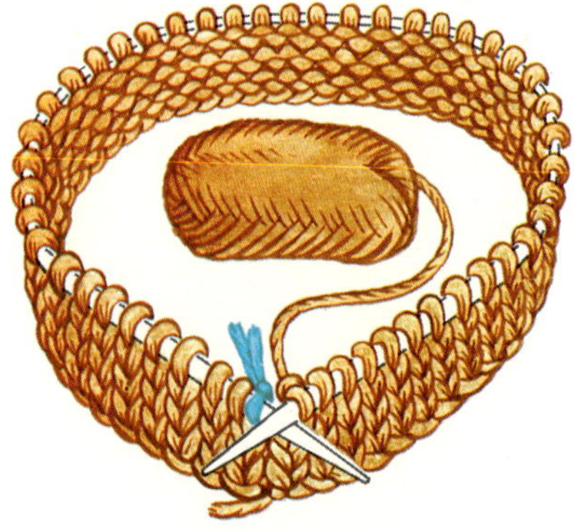

3 *Continue using the right-hand point to knit off the stitches until the round is completed. Mark the beginning of rounds using a marker loop or the cast-on end of yarn.*

Textured Patterns

Knitting is one of the few textile crafts in which it is possible to produce an extraordinarily wide range of textured fabrics. With even the simplest, most basic stitches, straightforward knit and purl, you can make different textures including the smoothness of stocking stitch, vertical ribbed stitches, basketweave (page 56) and horizontal ridges (page 37). Then there is a whole range of embossed stitches like that used in the loganberry sweater on page 34 and in the leaf-stitch sweater on page 46, where the embossing is used to create a raised leaf motif on plain background.

With twisted stitches (page 40) and cabling techniques the possibilities for spectacularly textured effects become almost limitless with fabrics taking on a beautiful, three-dimensional effect. The dress on page 49 and the tweedy coat on page 58 are exceptionally fine examples.

Loganberry Sweater

This tight-fitting 30's style sweater is knitted in a pretty openwork embossed stitch. The shaped side seams and V-shaped ribbing on the yoke add to the period flavour.

Sizes
To fit 81-87 [92-97] cm bust
Length 57 [60] cm
Sleeve seam 49cm

Note Instructions for the larger size are in square brackets []; where there is one set of figures it applies to both sizes.

Tension
30 sts and 29 rows to 10cm over patt on 4mm needles.

Materials
450[600] g double knitting yarn
1 pair each 3¼mm and 4mm knitting needles

Back
** Using 3¼mm needles, cast on 100 [112] sts. Work in K1, P1 rib for 8cm, ending with a RS row.
Next row Rib 9 [7], *work twice into next st, rib 9 [11], rep from * ending last rep rib 10 [8]. 109 [121] sts.
Change to 4mm needles and commence loganberry patt.
1st row (RS) P3, *K1, P5, rep from * to last 4 sts, K1, P3.

2nd row K3 tog, *yfwd, (K1, yfwd, K1) all into next st, yfwd, K2 tog tbl, K3 tog, sl the 2nd st on RH needle over the last st, rep from * to last 4 sts, yfwd, (K1, yfwd, K1) all into next st, yfwd, K3 tog tbl.
3rd row K1, *P5, K1, rep from * to end.
4th row P1, *K5, P1, rep from * to end.
5th row As 3rd row.
6th row Work twice into first st, *yfwd, K2 tog tbl, K3 tog, sl the 2nd st on RH needle over the last st, yfwd, (K1, yfwd, K1) all into next st, rep from * to last 6 sts, yfwd, K2 tog tbl, K3 tog, sl the 2nd st on RH needle over the last st, yfwd, inc into last st.
7th row As 1st row.
8th row K3, *P1, K5, rep from * to last 4 sts, P1, K3.
These 8 rows form the patt. Rep these 8 rows 2 [3] times more.
Cont in patt, inc 1 st at each end of the 4th and 8th patt rows until there are 133 [145] sts, ending with an 8th patt row. Cont without shaping. Work 1st-8th patt rows twice more, then 1st-6th rows once.

Commence yoke
Next row P3, (K1, P5) 10 [11] times, (K1, P1) 3 times, (K1, P5) 10 [11] times, K1, P3.
Next row K3, (P1, K5) 10 [11] times, (P1, K1) 3 times, (P1, K5) 10 [11] times, P1, K3.
These 2 rows establish the yoke, keeping loganberry patt correct, cont as foll.
Next row Patt 63 [69], (K1, P1) 3 times, K1, patt 63 [69].
Next row Patt 63 [69], (P1, K1) 3 times, P1, patt 63 [69].
Next row Patt 60 [66], (K1, P1) 6 times, K1, patt 60 [66].
Next row Patt 60 [66], (P1, K1) 6 times, P1, patt 60 [66].
Rep the last 2 rows once.
Next row Patt 57 [63], (K1, P1) 9 times, K1, patt 57 [63].
Next row Patt 57 [63], (P1, K1) 9 times, P1, patt 57 [63].
Rep the last 2 rows once.
Next row Patt 54 [60], (K1, P1) 12 times, K1, patt 54 [60].
Next row Patt 54 [60], (P1, K1) 12 times, P1, patt 54 [60].
Rep the last 2 rows once. **
Cont in this way, working 3 sts less in

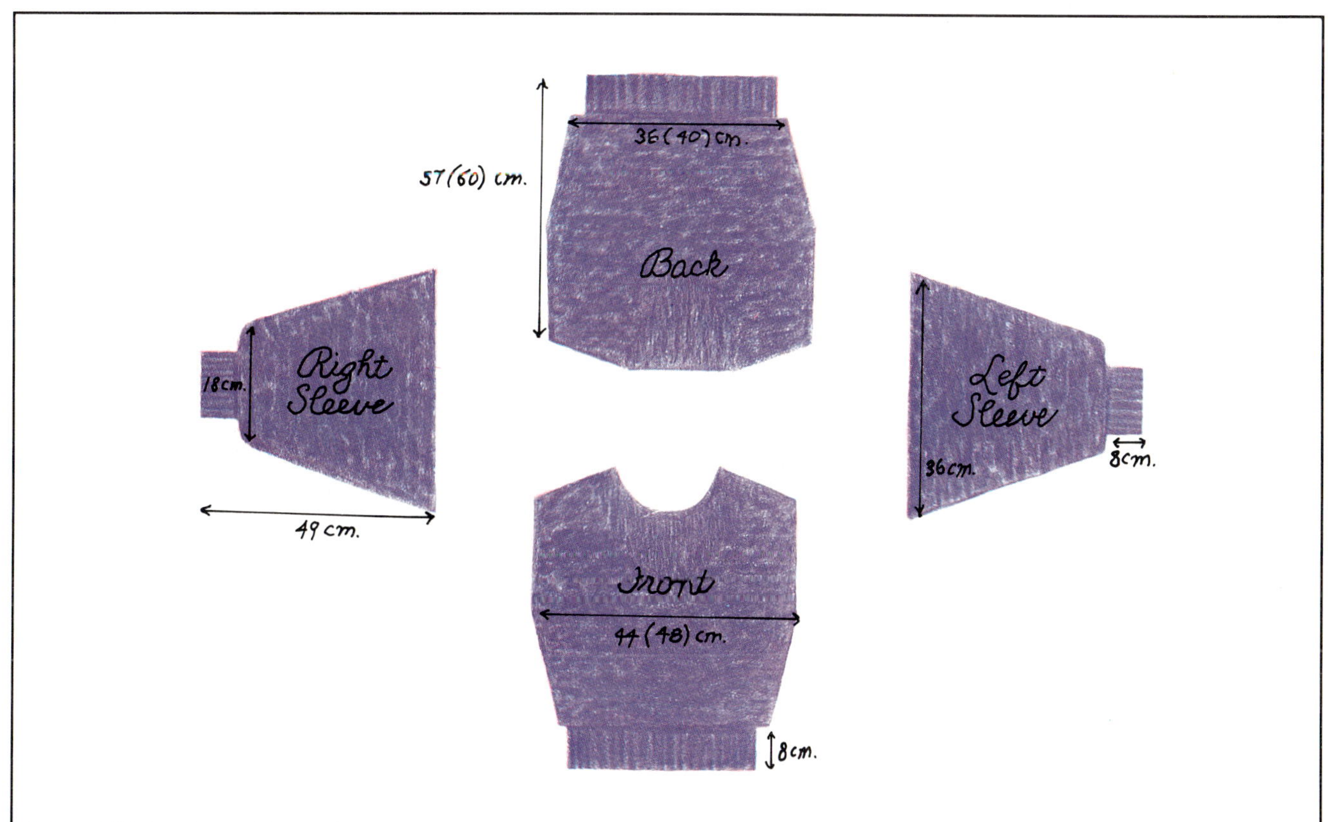

patt at each side of rib on the next and every foll 4th row until the row Patt 30 [36], (K1, P1) 36 times, K1, patt 30 [36] has been worked.
Work 3 rows.

Shape shoulders
Still inc rib sts as before, cast off 9 sts at beg of next 2 rows, 6 sts at beg of foll 2 rows, 9 sts at beg of next 2 rows and 9 [10] sts at beg of foll 2 rows.
Now cast off 8 [9] sts at beg of next 2 rows and 8 [10] sts at beg of foll 2 rows.
Leave the rem 35 [39] sts on a spare needle.

Front
Work as given for back from ** to **
Cont in this way, working 3 sts less in patt at each side of rib on the next and every foll 4th row until the row Patt 36 [42], (K1, P1) 30 times, K1, patt 36 [42] has been worked.

Divide for neck
Next row Patt 36 [42], (P1, K1) 12 times, P1, cast off 11, (P1, K1) 12 times, P1, patt 36 [42].
Still inc rib sts as before, complete left side of neck first.

*** **Next row** Work to last 2 sts, work 2 tog.
Next row Cast off 2 [3] sts, work to end.
Repeat last 2 rows once.
Dec 1 st at neck edge on next foll 5 rows, ending at armhole edge.

Shape shoulder
Cast off 9 sts at beg of next row and 6 sts at beg of foll alt row.
Cast off 9 sts at beg of next row and 9 [10] sts at beg of foll row.
Cast off 8 [9] sts at beg of next row.
Work 1 row.
Cast off rem 8 [10] sts.
With RS of work facing, rejoin yarn to sts for right side of neck.
Work 1 row.
Then work as given for first side from *** to end.

Sleeves
Using 3¼mm needles cast on 42 sts.
Work in K1, P1 rib for 8cm, ending with a RS row.
Next row Rib 3, *work twice into next st, rib 2, rep from * to end. 55 sts.
Change to size 4mm needles and cont in loganberry patt as given for back,

inc 1 st at each end of every 4th and 8th patt row until there are 109 sts.
Cont in patt without shaping until the patt has been worked 15 times.
Cast off.

To make-up
Join left shoulder.
Neck border

With RS of work facing, using 3¼mm needles, work in K1, P1 rib across sts on back neck, K up 49 sts from front neck. 84 [88] sts.
Work in K1, P1 rib for 6cm.
Cast off loosely in rib.
Join right shoulder and neck border. Set in sleeves. Join side and underarm seams. Press with a cool iron over a dry cloth.

Special technique — casting off in mid-row

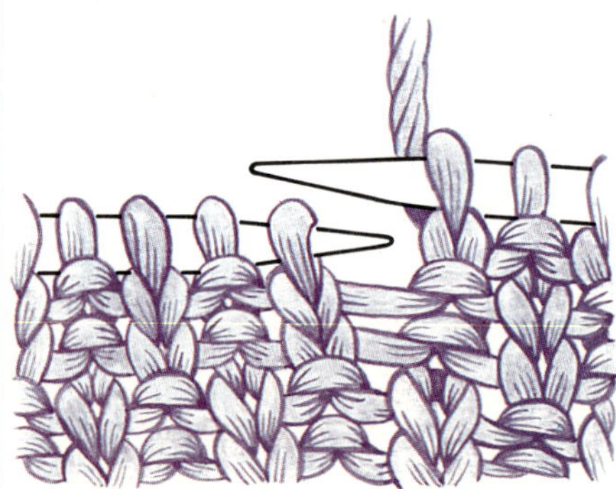

1 *The neck shaping on the basic sweater involves casting off stitches in the middle of a row. Work the pattern as instructed to the cast-off position.*

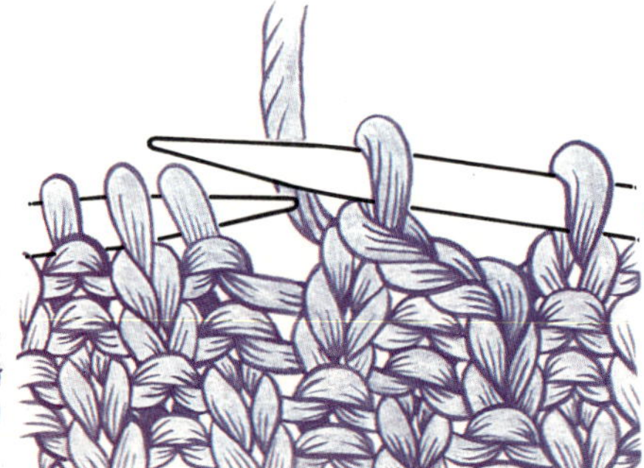

2 *Then cast off the next stitch as follows. Knit the next two stitches. Lift the 2nd stitch on the right-hand needle over the 1st stitch and off the needle. Knit the next stitch. Lift the 2nd stitch on the right-hand needle over the 1st stitch and off the needle.*

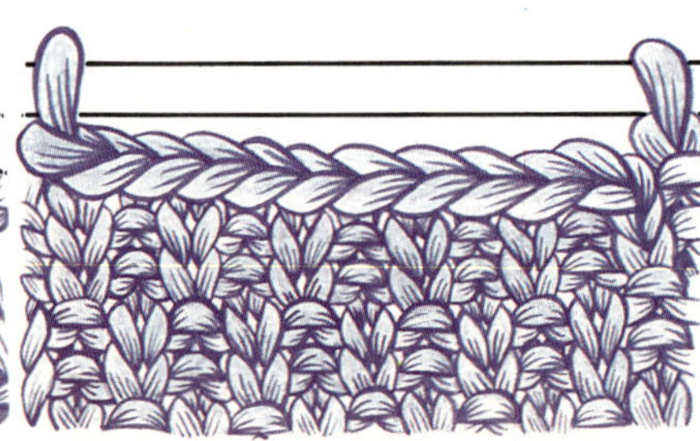

3 *Carry on in this way until the required number of stitches (in this case 11) has been cast off. Then work in pattern to the end of the row. The stitch used in casting off is counted as the first pattern stitch on the left-hand side on the neck.*

T-shape Dress and Sweater

This simple sporty dress and
sweater are both so easy to knit.
Made from basic rectangular shapes in stocking stitch
with garter stitch ridges and borders,
they are ideal garments for beginners.

Sizes
To fit 81 [86:91:97]cm bust
Sweater length 71 [71:76:76]cm
Dress length 91 [91:97:97]cm
Sleeve seam 36cm.
Note Instructions for larger sizes are in square brackets [ ]; where there is only one set of figures it applies to all sizes.

Tension
22 sts and 30 rows to 10cm over st st on 4mm needles.

Materials
Sweater
600 [600:700:700] g double knitting yarn.
Dress
700 [800:900:900] g double knitting yarn.
1 pair each 3¼mm and 4mm knitting needles.

Sweater
Back
Using 3¼mm needles, cast on 108 [114:120:126] sts.
Next row (WS) K.

Next row K.
Cont in garter st (every row K). Work 45 [45:39:39] rows.
Change to 4mm needles.
*Beg with a K row work 15 rows in st st.
Next row (WS) K.
Next row K.
Next row K. *
Rep from * to * 7 [7:8:8] times more.
Work 15 rows st st, ending with a K row.
Change to 3¼mm needles.
Work 35 rows garter st.
Cast off.

Front
Work as given for back.

Sleeves
Using 3¼mm needles, cast on 82 [88:94:100] sts.
Work 23 rows in garter st.
Change to 4mm needles.
Work as given for back from * to * 3 times.
Work 15 rows st st, ending with a K row.
Change to 3¼mm needles.

Work 35 rows garter st.
Cast off.

To make up
Press lightly, omitting garter st borders. Using a back-stitch seam,

---

Special technique–setting sleeves in flat

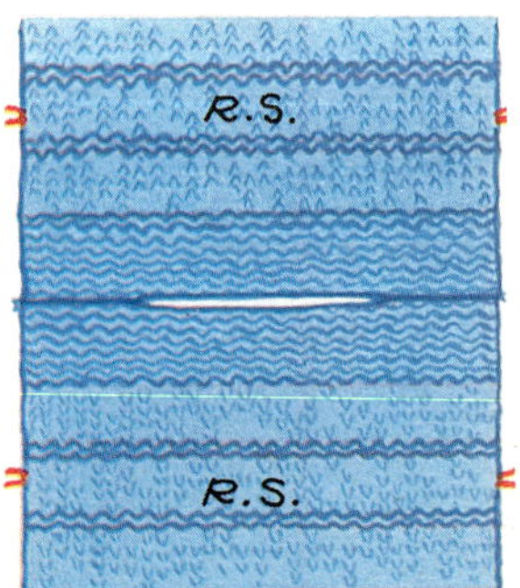

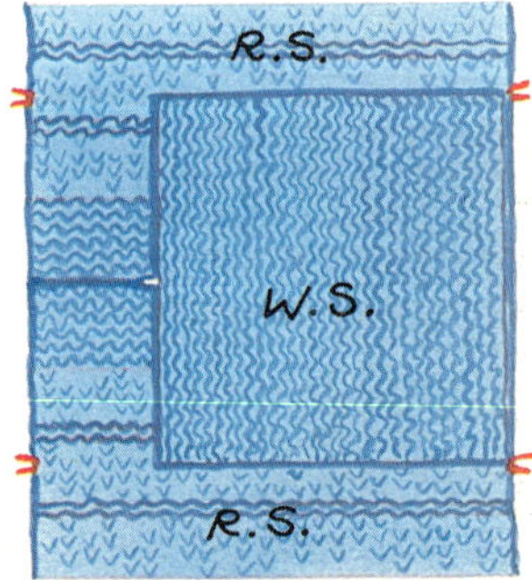

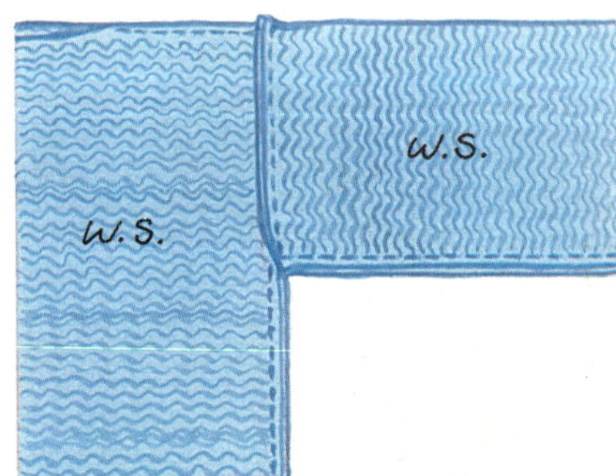

1 *Join the shoulder seam. Place a marker on the front and back of the garment at the distance from the shoulder seam given in the pattern.*

2 *With right sides together, place the centre of the cast-off edge of the sleeve to the shoulder seam.*

3 *Join the seam between the markers. Join the side and sleeve seams.*

join shoulder seams leaving the centre 25cm free for neck opening. Mark down 19 [20:22:23]cm from shoulder on back and front. Placing the centre of cast-off edge of sleeve to shoulder seam, set in sleeves between markers. Join sleeve and side seams leaving garter st border at hem free to form slits.

Dress
Back
Using 3¼mm needles, cast on 108 [114:120:126] sts.
Next row (WS) K.
Next row K.
Cont in garter st (every row K). Work 51 [51:49:49] rows.
Change to 4mm needles.
Work as given for back of sweater from * to * 11 [11:12:12] times.
Work 15 rows in st st, ending with a K row.
Change to 3¼mm needles.
Work 35 rows in garter st.
Cast off.

Front
Work as given for back.

Sleeves
Work as given for sweater.

To make up
Complete as given for sweater, but join garter stitch border to hem omitting slits.

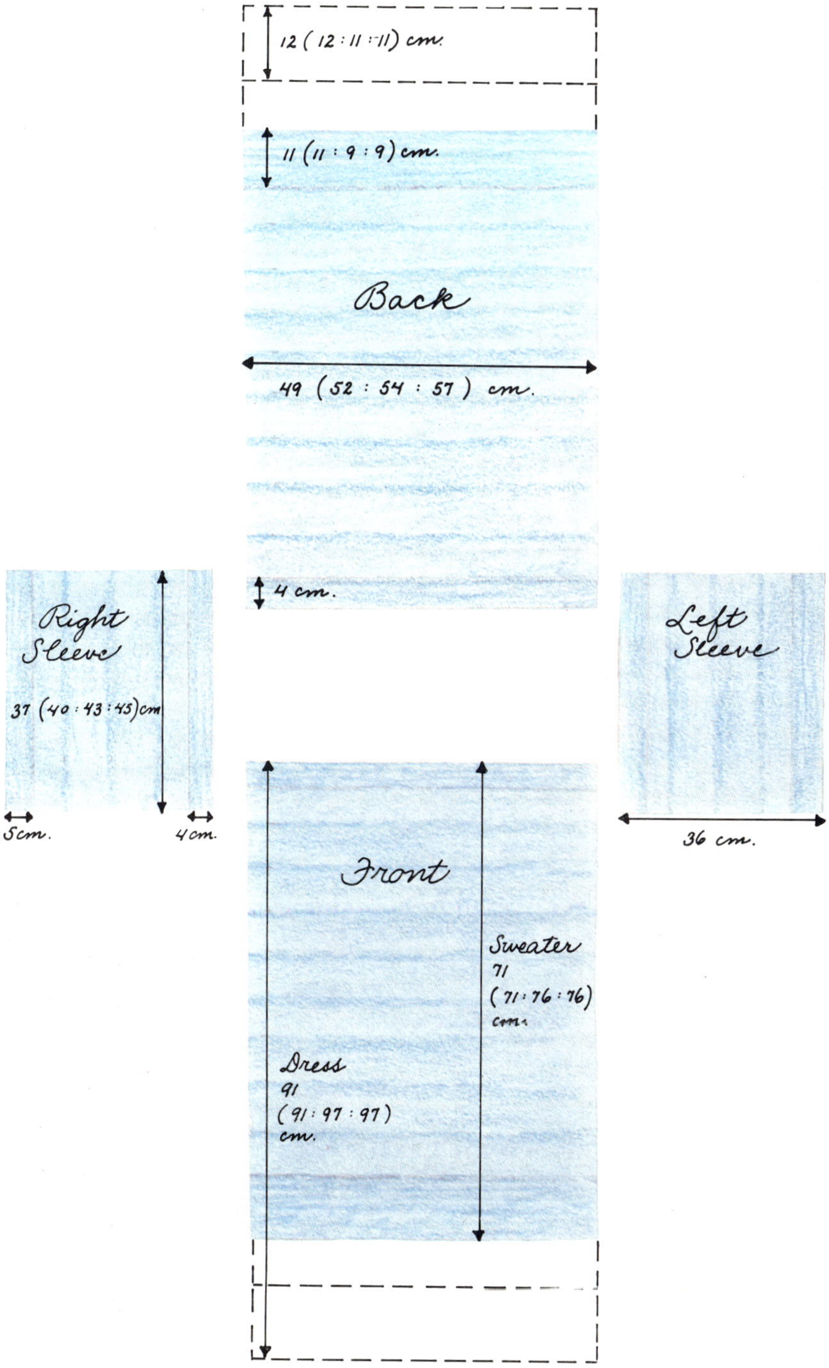

Country Casuals

A crunchy textured twisted fern stitch is worked all over this
loose easy-to-wear jerkin and echoed in panels on a
matching polo jumper and legwarmers.

Sizes
To fit 97[102:107]cm chest
Sweater length 67[69:71]cm
Sweater sleeve seam 57[59:61]cm
Jerkin length 79[81:83]cm
Legwarmers length 61cm
Note Instructions for the larger sizes are in square brackets []; where there is only one set of figures it applies to all three sizes.

Tension
20 sts and 24 rows to 10cm over reverse st st on 4½mm needles
24 sts and 28 rows to 10cm over twisted-stitch patt on 4½mm needles

Materials
Sweater
1100 [1150:1200] g Aran-weight yarn
Jerkin
1150 [1200:1250] g Aran-weight yarn
Legwarmers
450g Aran-weight yarn
1 pair each 3¾mm and 4½mm knitting needles

Sweater
Back
****Using 3¾mm needles, cast on 100[106:112] sts. Work in twisted rib as foll:
1st row *K1 tbl, P1, rep from * to end.
This row forms twisted rib. Cont in rib for 8cm.**
Change to 4½mm needles.
Next row (WS) K.
Next row P.
These 2 rows form reverse st st.
Rep these 2 rows until work measures 41[42:43]cm from cast-on edge, ending with a K row.
Shape armholes
Cast off 3 sts at beg of next 2 rows. 94[100:106] sts.
Cont without shaping until work measures 23[24:25]cm from beg of armholes, ending with a K row.
Change to twisted rib.
Work a further 3cm.
Shape shoulders
Cast off 28[30:32] sts in rib at beg of next 2 rows. Cast off in rib rem 38[40:42] sts.

Front
Work as given for back from ** to **,
inc 6 sts evenly across last row. 106[112:118] sts.
Change to 4½mm needles and commence working in reverse st st with twisted stitch panels as foll:
1st, 3rd, 5th, 7th and 9th rows (WS) K9[11:13], *P1, (K2, P5, K2, P1) twice*, K46[48:50], rep from * to * again, K to end.
2nd, 4th, 6th, 8th and 10th rows P9[11:13], *K1 tbl, (P2, K2 tog but do not sl sts off LH needle, K 1st st again, then sl both sts from needle, — called RT —, K1, K tbl 2nd st on LH needle but do not sl sts off needle, K2 tog tbl 1st and 2nd sts and sl both sts from needle — called LT —, P2, K1 tbl) twice*, P46[48:50], rep from * to * again, P to end.
11th, 13th, 15th, 17th and 19th rows K9[11:13], *P3, (K2, P1, K2, P5) twice ending last rep P3*, K46[48:50], rep from * to * again, K to end.
12th, 14th, 16th, 18th and 20th rows P9[11:13], *K1, (LT, P2, K1 tbl, P2, RT, K1) twice,* P46[48:50], rep from * to * again, P to end.
These 20 rows form the patt.
Cont in patt until work measures 41[42:43]cm from cast-on edge, ending with a WS row.
Shape armholes
Cast off 3 sts at beg of next 2 rows. 100[106:112] sts.
Cont without shaping until work measures 16[17:18]cm from beg of armholes, ending with a WS row.
Shape neck
Next row Patt 39[41:43] sts and turn, leave rem sts on a spare needle.
Dec 1 st at neck edge of next and every foll alt row until 31[33:35] sts rem. Cont without shaping until work measures 23[24:25]cm from beg of armholes, ending with a WS row.
Change to twisted rib.
Next row K1 tbl, *P1, K1 tbl, rep from * to end.
Next row P1, *K1 tbl, P1, rep from * to end.
Rep last 2 rows for 3cm, ending at armhole edge.
Shape shoulder
Cast off rem sts in rib. With RS of work facing, return to sts on spare needle, cast off centre 22[24:26] sts, patt to end.
Complete to match first side of neck, reversing shapings.

Sleeves
Using 3¾mm needles, cast on 50[52:54] sts. Work 8cm twisted rib as given for back.
Change to 4½mm needles. Beg with a P row cont in reverse st st, inc 1 st at each end of every foll 4th row until there are 104[108:112] sts.
Cont without shaping until work measures 56[58:60]cm from cast-on edge, ending with a K row. Change to twisted rib as given for back. Work a further 3cm. Cast off in rib.

To make up
Join right shoulder seam.
Polo neckband
With RS of work facing, using 4½mm needles, K up 18 sts down left side of neck, K up 22[24:26] sts from centre front, K up 18 sts up right side of neck and 38[40:42] sts across back neck. 96[100:104] sts. Work in twisted rib as given for back for 20cm. Cast off in rib. Join left shoulder and neckband, reversing seam to roll on to RS. Set in sleeves flat joining cast-off sts at underarms to final rows on sleeve. Join side and sleeve seams.

Jerkin
Back
Using 4½mm needles, cast on 131[141:151] sts. Work twisted rib as foll:
1st row (RS) K1 tbl, * P1, K1 tbl, rep from * to end.
2nd row P1, * K1 tbl, P1, rep from * to end.
Rep last 2 rows for 5cm ending with a RS row.
Commence twisted-stitch patt.
1st, 3rd, 5th, 7th and 9th rows (WS) P1, (K2, P5, K2, P1) to end.
2nd, 4th, 6th, 8th and 10th rows K1 tbl, (P2, RT, K1, LT, P2, K1 tbl) to end.
11th, 13th, 15th, 17th and 19th rows P3, (K2, P1, K2, P5) to last 8 sts, K2, P1, K2, P3.
12th, 14th, 16th, 18th and 20th rows K1, (LT, P2, K1 tbl, P2, RT, K1) to end.
These 20 rows form the patt.
Cont in patt until work measures 51[52:53]cm from cast-on edge, ending with a WS row.
Shape armholes
Cast off 5 sts at beg of next 2 rows. 121[131:141] sts.

Cont without shaping until work measures 25[[26:27]cm from beg of armholes, ending with a WS row. Change to twisted rib as for back. Work 3cm, ending with a WS row.

Shape shoulders

Cast off in rib 40 [44:48] sts at beg of next 2 rows. Cast off in rib rem sts.

Pocket linings (make 2)

Using 4½mm needles, cast on 26 sts. Work 15cm st st, ending with a P row. Leave sts on a holder.

Right front

Using 4½mm needles, cast on 75[79:85] sts. Work 5cm twisted rib as given for back. Inc 1 st at end of last row on 2nd size only. 75[80:85] sts.

Commence twisted-stitch patt with rib border as foll:

1st, 3rd, 5th, 7th and 9th rows (WS) P1, (K2, P5, K2, P1) to last 14[19:14] sts, K0[5:0], rib to end.

2nd, 4th, 6th, 8th and 10th rows Rib 14, P0[5:0], K1 tbl, (P2, RT, K1, LT, P2, K1 tbl) to end.

11th, 13th, 15th, 17th and 19th rows P3, (K2, P1, K2, P5) to last 22 [27:22] sts, K2, P1, K2, P3, K0[5:0], rib to end.

12th, 14th, 16th, 18th and 20th rows Rib 14, P0[5:0], K1, (LT, P2, K1 tbl, P2, RT, K1) to end.

These 20 rows form twisted-stitch patt. *** Cont in patt, taking 1 more st into rib at inner border edge on the 8th and every foll 10th row, *at the same time,* place pocket when work measures 20cm from cast-on edge, ending at side edge, as foll:

Next row Patt 15, cast off 26 sts, patt across sts of pocket lining, patt to end. Cont as set, taking sts into rib as before until work measures 51[52:53]cm ending at side edge.

Shape armhole

Cast off 5 sts at beg of next row. 70[75:80] sts.

Cont without further shaping until there are 30[31:32] sts in rib and 40[44:48] sts in patt.

Cont as set until work measures 25[26:27]cm from beg of armhole shaping, ending with a WS row. Cont in twisted rib only. Work 3cm, ending at armhole edge. ***

Shape shoulder

Cast off these sts in rib.

Left front

Using 4½mm needles, cast on 75[79:85] sts. Work 5cm twisted rib as given for back. Inc 1 st at beg of last row on 2nd size only. Commence twisted-stitch patt with rib border as foll:

1st, 3rd, 5th, 7th and 9th rows (WS) Rib 14, K0[5:0], P1, (K2, P5, K2, P1) to end.

2nd, 4th, 6th, 8th and 10th rows K1 tbl, (P2, RT, K1, LT, P2, K1 tbl) to last 14[19:14] sts, P0[5:0], rib to end.

11th, 13th, 15th, 17th and 19th rows Rib 14, K0[5:0], P3, (K2, P1, K2, P5) to last 8 sts, K2, P1, K2, P3.

12th, 14th, 16th, 18th and 20th rows, K1, (LT, P2, K1 tbl, P2, RT, K1) to last 14[19:14] sts, P0[5:0], rib to end.

These 20 rows form the patt. Complete to match right front working from *** to ***.

Shape shoulder

Cast off in rib 40[44:48] sts, rib to end. Cont in rib on rem sts for a further 18[19:20]cm. Cast off in rib.

To make up

Join shoulder seams and sew collar to back of neck. Join collar edges.

Armbands

With RS of work facing, using 4½mm needles, K up 157[167:173] sts around armhole edge. Work 5cm twisted rib as for back. Cast off. Fold rib in half on to WS and catch down.

Pocket edgings

With RS facing, using 4½mm needles, K up 26 sts along pocket edge. Work 3cm twisted rib. Cast off in rib. Sew down pocket linings and edges.

Legwarmers

Using 3¾mm needles, cast on 71 sts. Work 10cm in twisted rib as for jerkin back. Change to 4½mm needles.

1st row K25, work from * to * as for 1st row of sweater front, K25.

2nd row P25, work from * to * as for 2nd row of sweater front, P25.

Cont working patt panel as for sweater front, until work measures 51cm, ending with WS row. Change to 3¾mm needles, work 10cm in twisted rib as for jerkin back. Cast off in rib. Join side seam.

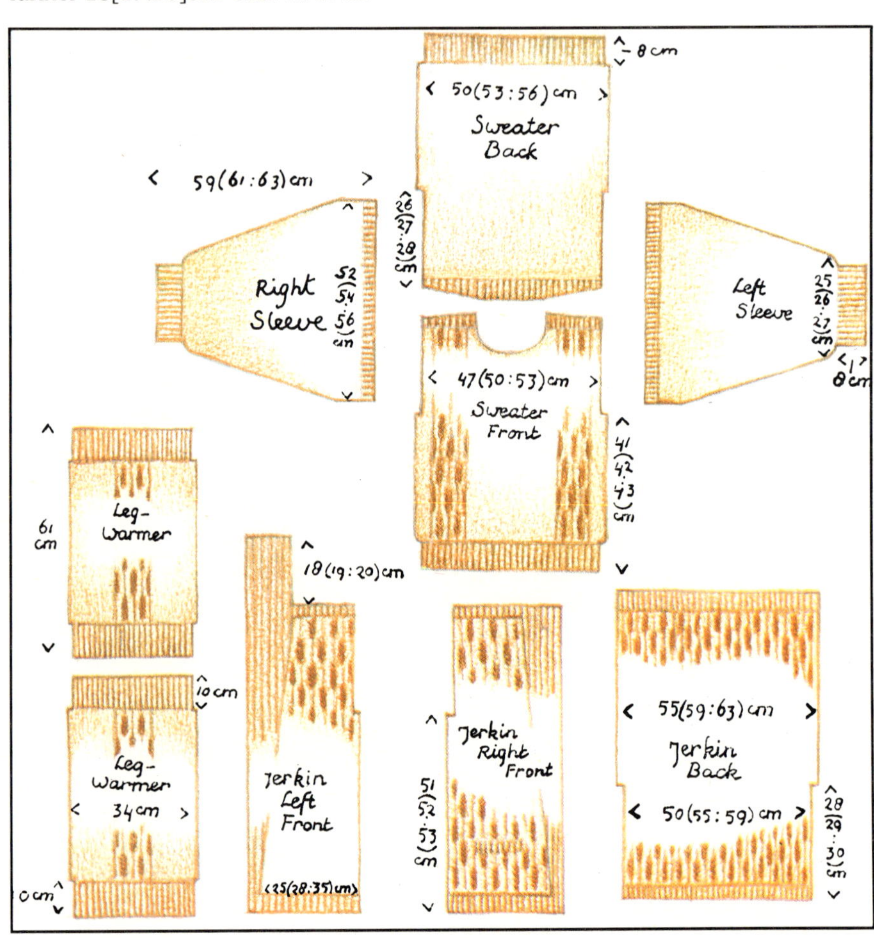

Two-tone Suit

Two different slipstitch patterns are used for the top of this elegant two-piece suit — one for the main fabric and a two-colour slipstitch rib for the welts. The gently flared skirt is knitted in simple stocking stitch.

Sizes
Sweater
To fit 86 [91:97] cm bust
Length 59 [61:62] cm
Sleeve seam 43cm
Skirt
To fit 91 [97:102] cm hips
Length 61 [62:63] cm (adjustable)

Note Instructions for larger sizes are in square brackets []; where there is only one set of figures it applies to all three sizes.

Tension
Sweater
27½ sts and 42 rows to 10cm over patt on 4½mm needles
Skirt
23 sts and 30 rows to 10cm over st st on 3¾mm needles

Materials
Sweater
500 [500:550] g double knitting yarn in main colour (A)
75 [125:125] g in contrast colour (B)
3¼mm circular needle
1 pair each 3¼mm and 4½mm needles
3 buttons
Skirt
400 [450:500] g double knitting yarn in contrast colour (B)
3¼mm circular needle (length 40cm)
3¾mm circular needle (length 50cm)
Length of elastic for waistband

Sweater
Back
**Using 3¼mm circular needle and B, cast on 128 [136:144] sts.
Work in rows in 2-colour rib patt as folls:
1st row (RS) With B, *ybk, sl 2 P-wise, yfwd, P2, rep from * to end, do not turn.
Join in A to beg of 1st row.
2nd row (RS) With A, *K2, sl 2 P-wise, rep from * to end, turn.
3rd row (WS) With B, *K2, yfwd, sl 2 P-wise, ybk, rep from * to end, do not turn.
4th row (WS) With A, *sl 2 P-wise, P2, rep from * to end, turn work.
These 4 rows form the 2-colour rib patt.
Rep these 4 rows for 8cm, ending with a 2nd row.
Cont in A only.

Next row (WS) P to end, inc 1 st at each end of row. 130 [138:146] sts. Change to 4½mm needles and commence patt. Work backwards and forwards in rows.
1st row (RS) *K2, yfwd, sl 2 P-wise, ybk, rep from * to last 2 sts, K2.
2nd row P1, *ybk, sl 2 P-wise, yfwd, P2, rep from * to last st, P1.
3rd row *Yfwd, sl 2 P-wise, ybk, K2, rep from * to last 2 sts, yfwd, sl 2 P-wise.
4th row P3, *ybk, sl 2 P-wise, yfwd, P2, rep from * to last 3 sts, ybk, sl 2 P-wise, yfwd, P1.
5th-12th rows Rep 1st-4th rows twice more.
13th row *Yfwd, sl 2 P-wise, ybk, K2, rep from * to last 2 sts, yfwd, sl 2 P-wise.
14th row P1, *ybk, sl 2 P-wise, yfwd, P2, rep from * to last st, P1.
15th row *K2, yfwd, sl 2 P-wise, ybk, rep from * to last 2 sts, K2.
16th row P3, ybk, sl 2 P-wise, yfwd, P2, rep from * to last 3 sts, ybk, sl 2 P-wise, yfwd, P1.
17th-24th rows Rep 13th-16th rows twice more.
These 24 rows form the patt. Cont in patt until work measures approx 38cm from cast-on edge, ending with a 24th patt row.
Shape armholes
Keeping patt correct, cast off 6 [6:7] sts at beg of next 2 rows. Dec 1 st at each end of the next 7 rows. Work 1 row. Dec 1 st at each end of the next and every foll alt row until 98 [106:110] sts rem.**
Cont without shaping until work measures 21 [23:24] cm from beg of armholes, ending with a WS row.
Shape shoulders
Cast off 7 [8:8] sts at beg of next 6 rows and 6 [6:7] sts at beg of foll 2 rows. Cast off rem 44 [46:48] sts.

Front
Work as given for back from ** to **. Cont without shaping until work measures 5 [7:8] cm from beg of armholes, ending with a RS row.
Divide for front opening
Next row Patt 51 [55:57] and leave these sts on a spare needle, patt to end.
Complete left side of neck first.
Next row Patt 47 [51:53], cast on 4 sts for buttonband. 51 [55:57] sts.

Cont in patt until 23 rows less than back to shoulder shaping have been worked, ending with a RS row.
Shape neck
Keeping patt correct, cast off 12 [13:14] sts at beg of next row.
Dec 1 st at neck edge on next 5 rows. Work 1 row.
Dec 1 st at neck edge on next and foll 5 alt rows.
Work 3 rows.
Dec 1 st at neck edge on next row. 27 [30:31] sts.
Work 1 row.
Shape shoulder
Cast off 7 [8:8] sts at beg of next and foll 2 alt rows. Work 1 row. Cast off rem 6 [6:7] sts.
Mark the position of 3 buttons on buttonband, the first to come 2cm above base of opening with the other 2 at 4cm intervals.
With RS of work facing, join in yarn to sts on spare needle, patt to end. Complete to match first side of neck, reversing shapings and making buttonholes opposite markers as foll:
1st buttonhole row (RS) Patt 2. cast off 2 sts, patt to end.
2nd buttonhole row Patt to end. casting on 2 sts over those cast off in previous row.

Sleeves
Using 3¼mm circular needle and B, cast on 52 [56:60] sts.
Work in 2-colour rib patt as given for back for 6cm, ending with a 2nd row. Cont in A.
Next row (WS) P5 [3:4], make 1 by picking up the loop between last st worked and next st on LH needle and working into the back of it — called M1, (P2 [3:2], M1, P3, M1) 8 [8:10] times, P3, M1, P4 [2:3]. 70 [74:82] sts.
Change to 4½mm needles and beg with a 13th row commence patt as given for back. Inc and work into patt 1 st at each end of the 7th and every foll 8th row until there are 106 [110:116] sts.
Cont without shaping until work measures approx 43cm from cast-on edge, ending with a 24th patt row.
Shape top
Keeping patt correct, cast off 6 [6:7] sts at beg of next 2 rows. Dec 1 st at each end of the next and every foll 4th row until 84 [88:92] sts rem.

Dec 1 st at each end of every foll alt row until 44 sts rem, ending with a WS row.
Cast off 2 sts at beg of next 2 rows and 3 sts at beg of foll 2 rows. Cast off 4 sts at beg of next 2 rows and 5 sts at beg of foll 2 rows.
Cast off rem 16 sts.

Collar
Using 3¼mm circular needle and B, cast on 110 [114:122] sts.
Work in rows in 2-colour rib as foll:
1st row (RS) With B, P2, *ybk, sl 2 P-wise, yfwd, P2, rep from * to end, do not turn.
Join in A to beg of 1st row.
2nd row (RS) With A, sl 2 P-wise, *K2, sl 2 P-wise, rep from * to end, turn.
3rd row (WS) With B, K2, *yfwd, sl 2 P-wise, ybk, K2, rep from * to end, do not turn.
4th row (WS) With A, sl 2 P-wise, *P2, sl 2 P-wise, rep from * to end, turn.
These 4 rows form the 2-colour rib patt.
Rep these 4 rows until work measures approx 6cm from cast-on edge, ending with a 4th patt row.

With A only, cast off K-wise.

Front borders (alike)
With RS of work facing, using pair 3¾mm needles and A, K up 27 sts along front opening edge.
Cast off very loosely.

Skirt
Using 3¼mm circular needle and B, cast on 160 [172:184] sts. Mark beg of round. Work in rounds of K2, P2 rib for 3cm for waistband.
Change to 3¾mm circular needle.
Work 7 rounds st st (every round K).
Commence shaping
Next round K9 [10:11], (M1, K1, M1, K19 [20:22], M1, K1, M1, K19 [21:22]) 3 times, M1, K1, M1, K19 [20:22], M1, K1, M1, K10 [11:11]. 176[188:200] sts.
Work 8 rounds st st.
Next round K10 [11:12], (M1, K1, K21 [22:24], M1, K1, M1, K21 [23:24]) 3 times, M1, K1, M1, K21 [22:24], M1, K1, M1, K11 [12:12]. 192[204:216] sts.
Work 8 rounds st st.
Next round K11 [12:13], (M1, K1, M1, K23 [24:26], M1, K1, M1, K23 [25:26]) 3 times, M1, K1, M1, K23 [24:26], M1, K1, M1, K12 [13:13].
Work 10 rounds st st. 208[220:232] sts.
Cont in this way, inc on next and 2 foll 11th rounds. 256 [268:280] sts.
Work 14 rounds st st.
Now cont to inc as before on the next and every foll 15th round until there are 320[332:344] sts. Cont without shaping until work measures 61[62:63]cm from waistband, (length may be adjusted here).
Next row (to form hem-line) P.
Work 6 rounds st st.
Cast off.

To make up
Do not press.
Sweater
Join shoulders. Place collar 1cm from front border edges and sew to neck. Join side and sleeve seams. Set in sleeves. Stitch base of buttonband under buttonhole band. Sew on buttons.
Skirt
Cut elastic to fit waist. Join in a ring and sew to rib waistband using herringbone stitch.
Fold lower edge on to WS at hem line and slipstitch down.

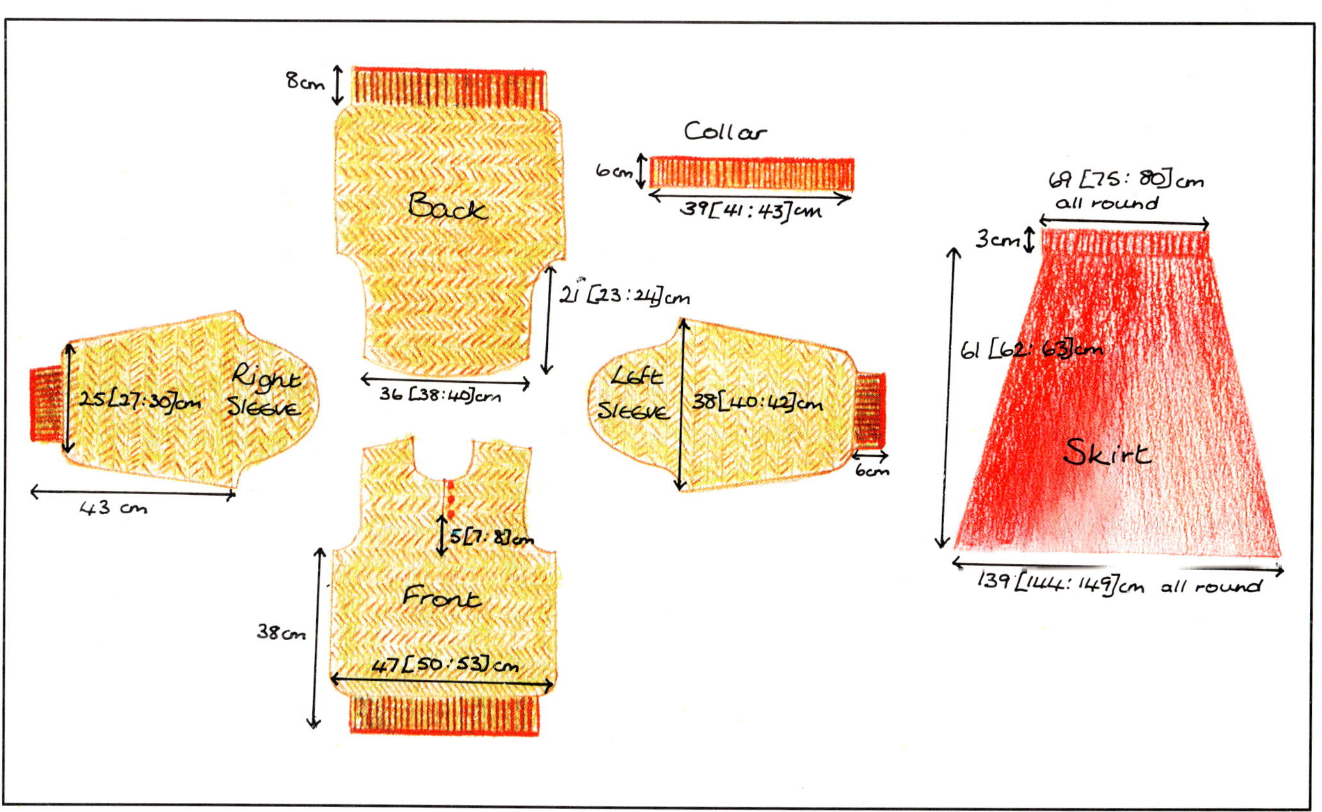

Leaf-stitch Sweater

The leaves are falling all over this beautiful cowl-necked sweater — just right for long country walks on misty autumnal mornings

Sizes
To fit 86 [91:97]cm bust
Length 67cm
Sleeve seam 44cm

Note Instructions for larger sizes are in square brackets []; where there is only one set of figures it applies to all sizes.

Tension
22 sts and 30 rows to 10cm over st st on 4mm needles

Materials
600 [650:650] g double knitting yarn
1 pair each 3¼mm and 4mm knitting needles

Back
**Using 3¼mm needles, cast on 94 [100:106] sts. Work in K1, P1 rib for 10cm, ending with a RS row.
Next row Rib 7 [10:5], pick up the loop lying between st just worked and next st on LH needle and work into the back of it — called M1 —, (rib 5 [5:6], M1) 16 times, rib to end. 111 [117:123] sts.
Change to 4mm needles and commence patt.
1st row (RS) P11 [8:11], *P2, K1 tbl, P9, rep from * to last 4 [1:4] sts, P to end.
2nd row K4 [1:4], *K9, P1 tbl, K2, rep from * to last 11 [8:11] sts, K to end.
3rd-6th rows Rep 1st and 2nd rows twice.
7th row P11 [8:11], *P2, (K1, yfwd, K1, yfwd, K1) all into next st, P9, rep from * to last 4 [1:4] sts, P to end.
8th row K4 [1:4], *K9, P5, K2, rep from * to last 11 [8:11] sts, K to end.
9th row P11 [8:11], *P2, K into front and back of next st — called inc 1 F —, K3, K into back and front of next st — called inc 1 B —, P9, rep from * to last 4 [1:4] sts, P to end.
10th row K4 [1:4], *K9, P7, K2, rep from * to last 11 [8:11] sts, K to end.
11th row P11 [8:11], *P2, inc 1 F, K5, inc 1 B, P9, rep from * to last 4 [1:4] sts, P to end.
12th row K4 [1:4], *K9, P9, K2, rep from * to last 11 [8:11] sts, K to end.
13th row P7 [4:7], K1 tbl, P3, * P2, sl 1, K1, psso, K5, K2 tog, P5, K1 tbl, P3, rep from * to last 4 [1:4]

sts, P to end.
14th row K4 [1:4], *K3, P1 tbl, K5, P2 tog, P3, P2 tog tbl, K2, rep from * to last 11 [8:11] sts, K3, P1 tbl, K to end.
15th row P7 [4:7], K1 tbl, P3, *P2, sl 1, K1, psso, K1, K2 tog, P5, K1 tbl, P3, rep from * to last 4 [1:4] sts, P to end.
16th row K4 [1:4], *K3, P1 tbl, K5, P3 tog, K2, rep from * to last 11 [8:11] sts, K3, P1 tbl, K to end.
17th row P7 [4:7], K1 tbl, P3, *P8, K1 tbl, P3, rep from * to last 4 [1:4] sts, P to end.
18th row K4 [1:4], *K3, P1 tbl, K8, rep from * to last 11 [8:11] sts, K3, P1 tbl, K to end.
19th-22nd rows Rep 17th-18th rows twice.
23rd row P7 [4:7], (K1, yfwd, K1, yfwd, K1) all into next st, P3, *P8, (K1, yfwd, K1, yfwd, K1) all into next st, P3, rep from * to last 4 [1:4] sts, P to end.
24th row K4 [1:4], *K3, P5, K8, rep

from * to last 15 [12:15] sts, K3, P5, K7 [4:7].
25th row P7 [4:7], inc 1 F, K3, inc 1 B, P3, *P8, inc 1 F, K3, inc 1 B, P3, rep from * to last 4 [1:4] sts, P to end.
26th row K4 [1:4], *K3, P7, K8, rep from * to last 17 [14:17] sts, K3, P7, K to end.
27th row P7 [4:7], inc 1 F, K5, inc 1 B, P3, *P8, inc 1 F, K5, inc 1 B, P3, rep from * to last 4 [1:4] sts, P to end.
28th row K4 [1:4], *K3, P9, K8, rep from * to last 19 [16:19] sts, K3, P9, K to end.
29th row P7 [4:7], sl 1, K1, psso, K5, K2 tog, P3, *P2, K1 tbl, P5, sl 1, K1, psso, K5, K2 tog, P3, rep from * to last 4 [1:4] sts, P to end.
30th row K4 [1:4], *K3, P2 tog, P3, P2 tog tbl, K5, P1 tbl, K2, rep from * to last 17 [14:17] sts, K3, P2 tog, P3, P2 tog tbl, K to end.
31st row P7 [4:7], sl 1, K1, psso, K1, K2 tog, P3, *P2, K1 tbl, P5, sl 1,

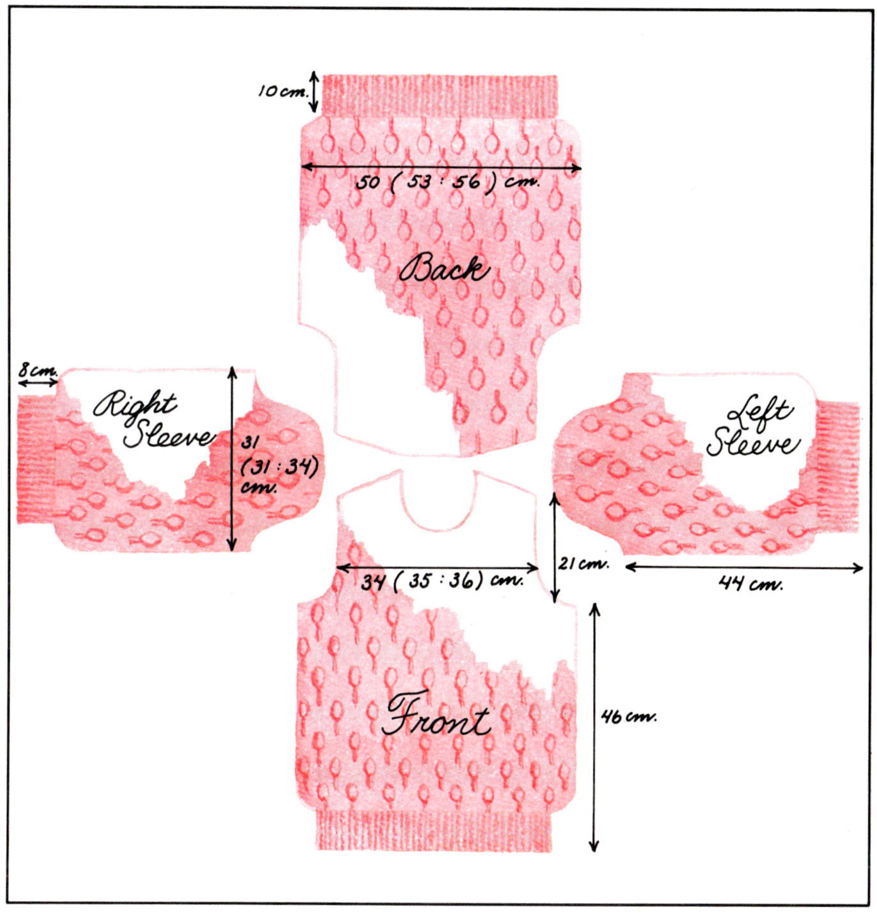

K1, psso, K1, K2 tog, P3, rep from *
to last 4 [1:4] sts, P to end.
32nd row K4 [1:4], *K3, P3 tog, K5,
P1 tbl, K2, rep from * to last 13
[10:13] sts, K3, P3 tog, K to end.
These 32 rows form the patt.
Cont in patt until work measures
46cm approx from cast-on edge,
ending with a 12th patt row.
Shape armholes
Keeping patt correct, cast off 4 sts at
beg of next 2 rows. Dec 1 st at each
end of the next 7 [7:11] rows, then
dec 1 st at each end of the next and
every foll alt row until 75 [77:79] sts
rem. ** Cont without shaping until
work measures approx 66[67:68] cm
from cast-on edge, ending with a 12th
patt row.
Shape shoulders
Keeping patt correct, cast off 6 sts at
beg of next 4 rows, and 6 [6:5] sts at
beg of next 2 rows. Leave rem 45
[51:55] sts on a spare needle.

Front
Work as given for back from ** to
**. Cont without shaping until work
measures 58cm from cast-on edge,
ending with a 16th patt row.
Shape neck
Next row Patt 26 [27:26], P2 tog,
turn leaving rem sts on spare needle.
Complete left side of neck first.
Dec 1 st at neck edge on every foll alt
row until 18 [18:17] sts rem.
Cont without shaping until work
matches back to shoulder shaping,
ending with a WS row.
Shape shoulder
Cast off 6 sts at beg of next and foll
alt row. Work 1 row. Cast off rem
6 [6:5] sts. With RS facing, return to
sts on spare needle, sl centre 19
[19:23] sts on to a stitch holder, join
in yarn to rem sts, P2 tog, patt to
end. Complete to match first side,
reversing shapings.

Sleeves
Using 3¼mm needles, cast on 40
[44:46] sts. Work in K1, P1 rib for
8cm, ending with a RS row.
Next row Rib 6 [10:9], M1, (rib 1,
M1) 28 [24:28] times, rib to end. 69
[69:75] sts.

Change to 4mm needles and cont in
patt as given for 2nd [2nd:1st] size
on back until work measures approx
44cm from cast-on edge, ending with
a 12th patt row.
Shape top
Cast off 4 sts at beg of next 2 rows.
Dec 1 st at each end of next and
every foll 4th row until 57 [57:63]
sts rem. Work 1 row. Dec 1 st at each
end of next and every foll alt row until
35 sts rem. Work 1 row. Cast off.

To make up
Join right shoulder seam.
Collar
With RS of work facing, using 4mm
needles, K up 24 sts down left side of
neck, K19 [19:23] sts from centre
front, K up 24 sts up right side of
neck and K across 45 [51:55] sts
across back neck. 112 [118:126] sts.
Beg with a P row, cont in reverse st st
until border measures 18cm from beg
ending with a K row. Cast off.
Join left shoulder and neck border.
Join side and sleeve seams.
Set in sleeves.

Special technique — working a cluster

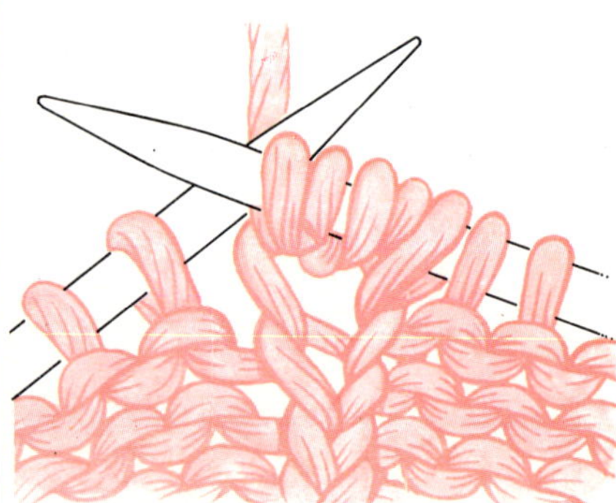

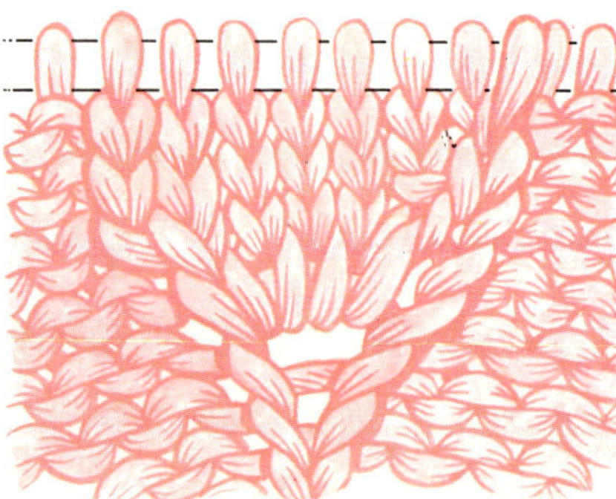

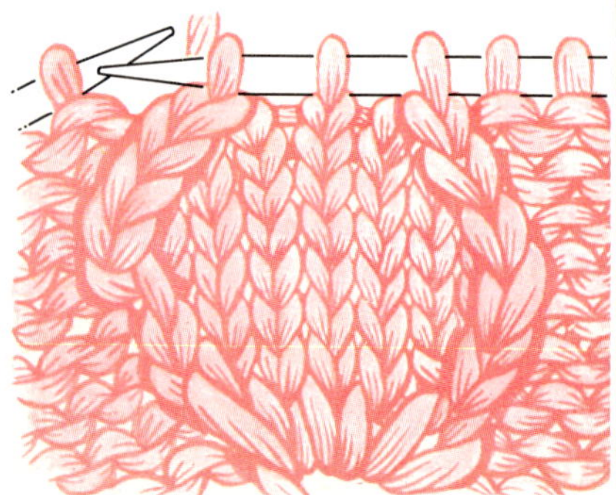

1 *The leaf motif on the basic sweater is formed from a cluster worked on the 7th-16th rows. On the 7th row work to the cluster position and make five stitches from one. Purl these stitches on wrong-side rows.*

2 *Increase one stitch on either side of the cluster on the 9th and 11th rows. Continue to purl the cluster stitches on wrong-side rows.*

3 *Now decrease one stitch on either side of the cluster stitches on every row until three cluster stitches remain. Purl these three stitches together completing the cluster. Clusters are worked the same way on the 23rd-32nd rows.*

Multi-textured Dress

Interlaced cables woven through with contrast-coloured threads add an original touch to an attractive Aran-knit sweater dress that's both warm and stylish.

Sizes
To fit 81[87:91]cm bust
Length 90[91:92]cm
Sleeve seam 45[46:47]cm

Note Instructions for larger sizes are in square brackets []; where there is only one set of figures it applies to all sizes.

Tension
20 sts and 24 rows to 10cm over moss st on 4½mm needles
28 sts and 24 rows to 10cm over central cable panel on 4½mm needles

Materials
1500 [1600:1700] g double knitting yarn in main colour (A)
75g in each of two contrast colours (B) and (C)
1 pair each 4mm and 4½mm knitting needles

1 4mm circular needle 40cm long
Cable needle

Special note When weaving contrast yarns on patchwork panels, use separate balls of yarn for each panel, carrying yarn up WS of work when not in use. See also Special Technique.

Patchwork cable panel patt
(worked over 19 sts)
1st row (RS) P2, K2, (K1 weaving B on RS thus, bring contrast yarn B to RS, K1A, take B to WS — called K1wB —, P1) 3 times, K1wB, K4, P4.
2nd row K4, P4, (K1, P1 weaving B on RS thus, take contrast yarn B to RS, P1A, bring B to WS — called P1wB —), 3 times, K1, P2, K2.
3rd row P2, sl next 2 sts on to cable needle and hold at front of work, P1,

then K2 from cable needle — called Tw3F —,(P1, K1wB) 3 times, sl next 2 sts on to cable needle and hold at front of work, K2, then K2 from cable needle — called C4F —, P4.
4th row K4, P4, (K1, P1wB), 3 times, P2, K3.
5th row P3, Tw3F, K1wB, P1, K1wB, sl next 2 sts on to cable needle and hold at back of work, K2, then P2 from cable needle — called Tw4B —, sl next 2 sts on to cable needle and hold at front of work, K1, then K2 from cable needle — called C3F —, P3.
6th row K3, P2, P1 tbl weaving C on RS thus, take contrast yarn C to RS, P1A tbl, bring C to WS — called P1 tblwC —, K1, P1 tblwC, P2, K1, P1wB, K1, P2, K4.
7th row P4, Tw3F, Tw4B, K1 tbl weaving C on RS thus, bring contrast yarn C to RS, K1 tbl, take C to WS

Special technique— knitting in weaving threads

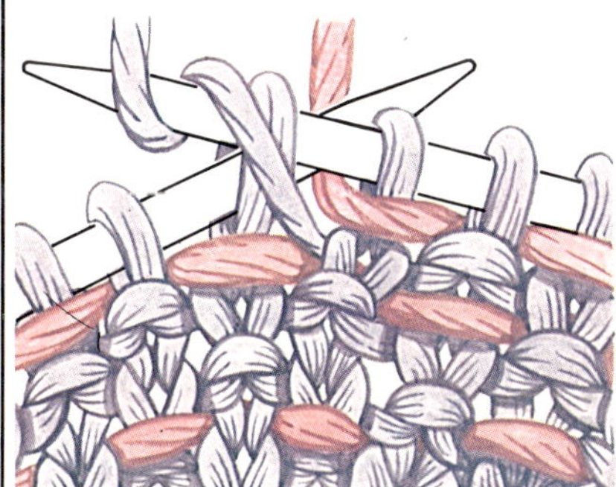

1 The woven-look effect on the patchwork cable is achieved by weaving in contrast yarns as you knit. On right-side rows secure the end of the weaving thread at the back of the work, bring it to the front then work the next stitch in the main colour. Take the weaving thread to the back.

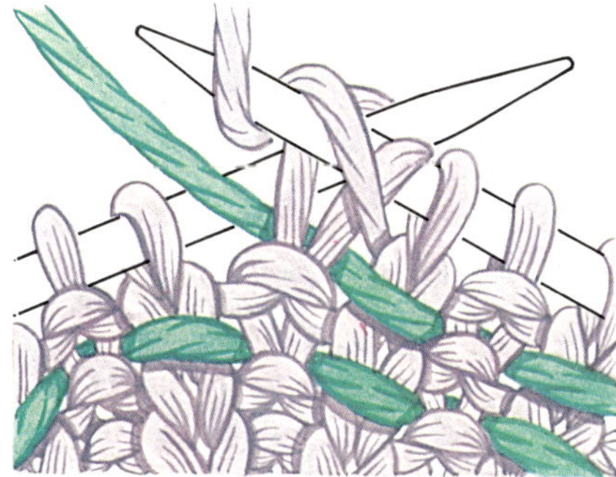

2 On wrong-side rows the weaving thread begins at the front of the work. Take it through to the back (the right side of the work), work the next stitch in the main colour, then bring the weaving thread back to the front. The contrast yarns are thus woven from back to front of the work but never actually knitted.

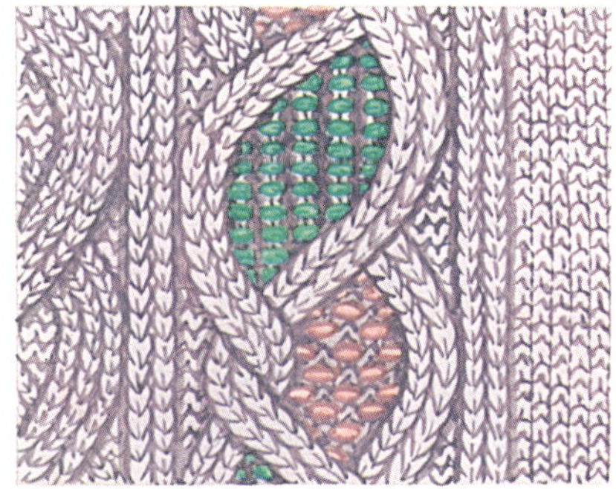

3 The weaving threads are arranged in two different ways in the basic pattern. On one section of the cable the threads on the right side are staggered above each other. On the other section they lie directly above each other.

— called K1 tblwC—, P1, K1 tblwC) Tw3F, P2.
8th row K2, P2, (K1, P1 tblwC) 3 times, P4, K5.
9th row P5, Tw4B, (K1 tblwC, P1) 3 times, K2, P2.
10th row K2, P2, (K1, P1 tblwC) 4 times, P2, K5.
11th row P3, Tw4B, (K1 tblwC, P1) 3 times, K1 tblwC, sl next st on to cable needle and hold at back of work, K2, then P1 from cable needle — called Tw3B —, P2.
12th row K3, P2, (P1 tblwC, K1) 4 times, P1 tblwC, P2, K3.
13th row P2, Tw3B, (K1 tblwC, P1) 3 times, K1 tblwC, Tw4B, P3.
14th row K5, P2, (P1 tblwC, K1) 4 times, P2, K2.
15th row P2, K2, (P1, K1 tblwC) 3 times, sl next 2 sts on to cable needle and hold at back of work, K2, then K2 from cable needle — called C4B—, P5.
16th row K5, P4, (P1 tblwC, K1) 3 times,P2, K2.
17th row P2, Tw3F, K1 tblwC, P1, K1 tblwC, Tw4B, C3F, P4.
18th row K4, P2, K1, P1wB, K1, P2, P1 tblwC, K1, P1 tblwC, P2, K3.
19th row P3, Tw3F, Tw4B, K1wB, P1, K1wB, Tw3F, P3.
20th row K3, P2, (P1wB, K1) 3 times, P4, K4.
21st row P4, C4F, (K1wB, P1) 3 times, C3F, P2.
22nd row K2, P2, (K1, P1wB) 3 times, K1, P4, K4.
23rd row P4, K4, (K1wB, P1) 3 times, K1wB, K2, P2.
24th row K2, P2, (K1, P1wB) 3 times, K1, P4, K4.
25th row P4, C4F, (K1wB, P1) 3 times, Tw3B, P2.
26th row K3, P2, (P1wB, K1) 3 times, P4, K4.
27th row P3, sl next st on to cable needle and hold at back of work, K2, then K1 from cable needle — called Cr3B, —, sl next 2 sts on to cable needle and hold at front or work, P2, then K2 from cable needle — called Tw4F—, K1wB, P1, K1wB, Tw3B, P3.
28th row K4, P2, K1, P1wB, K1, P2, P1 tblwC, K1, P1 tblwC, P2, K3.
29th row P2, Tw3B, K1 tblwC, P1, K1 tblwC, Tw4F, Tw3B, P4.
30th row K5, P4, (P1 tblwC, K1) 3 times, P2, K2.

31st row P2, K2, (P1, K1 tblwC) 3 times, Tw4F, P5.
32nd row K5, P2, (P1 tblwC, K1) 4 times, P2, K2.
33rd row P2, Tw3F, (K1 tblwC, P1) 3 times, K1 tblwC, Tw4F, P3.
34th row K3, P2, (P1 tblwC, K1) 4 times, P1 tblwC, P2, K3.
35th row P3, Tw4F, (K1 tblwC, P1) 3 times, K1 tblwC, Tw3F, P2.
36th row K2, P2, (K1, P1 tblwC) 4 times, P2, K5.
37th row P5, C4F, (K1 tblwC, P1) 3 times, K2, P2.
38th row K2, P2, (K1, P1 tblwC) 3 times, P4, K5.
39th row P4, Cr3B, Tw4F, K1 tblwC, P1, K1 tblwC, Tw3B, P2.
40th row K3, P2, P1 tblwC, K1, P1 tblwC, P2, K1, P1wB, K1, P2, K4.
41st row P3, Tw3B, K1wB, P1, K1wB, Tw4F, Tw3B, P3.
42nd row K4, P4, (K1, P1wB) 3 times, P2, K3.
43rd row P2, Cr3B, (P1, K1wB) 3 times, C4F, P4.
44th row K4, P4, (K1, P1wB) 3 times, K1, P2, K2.
These 44 rows form patchwork cable panel patt, referred to throughout as 'cable 19'.

Central cable panel patt (worked over 31 sts)
1st row (RS) K2, P1, K3, (P4, K6) twice, P3, K2.
2nd and foll alt rows K the P sts and P the K sts of previous row.
3rd row K2, P1, K3, (P4, sl next 3 sts on to cable needle and hold at front of work, K3, then K3 from cable needle) twice, P3, K2.
5th row K2, P1, (sl next 3 sts on to cable needle and hold at front of work, P2, then K3 from cable needle — called C5F — , sl next 2 sts on to cable needle and hold at back of work, K3, then P2 from cable needle — called C5B —,) twice, C5F, P1, K2.
7th row K2, P3, (sl next 3 sts on to cable needle and hold at back of work, K3, then K3 from cable needle, P4) twice, K3, P1, K2.
9th row K2, P1, (C5B, C5F) twice, C5B, P1, K2.
10th row As 2nd row.
These 10 rows form the central cable panel patt, referred to throughout as 'cable 31'.

Back
**** Using 4mm needles and A, cast on 114[118:122] sts. Work in twisted K1, P1 rib as foll:
1st row (RS) *K1 tbl, P1, rep from * .
2nd row *K1, P1 tbl, rep from * .
Rep the last 2 rows until work measures 3cm from cast-on edge, ending with a WS row.
Next row Rib 29[30:31], (work twice into next st — called inc 1 —, rib 27[28:29]) twice, inc 1, rib to end. 117[121:125] sts.
Next row K.
Change to 4½mm needles and commence patt.
1st row (RS) (K1, P1) 11[12:13] times, K2, work 1st row of cable 19, 1st row of cable 31, 1st row of cable 19, K2, (P1, K1) 11[12:13] times.
2nd row (K1, P1) 11[12:13] times, P2, work 2nd row of cable 19, 2nd row of cable 31, 2nd row of cable 19, P2, (P1, K1) 11[12:13] times.
These 2 rows establish the patt of cable panels between st st borders and moss st edge sts.
Keeping patt correct, inc and work into moss st 1 st at each end of 18th and every foll 20th row until there are 125[131:137] sts. Cont in patt until work measures 65[66:67]cm ending with a WS row.
Shape armholes
Next row Patt 26[29:32] sts and sl on to a st holder, patt 73, turn, sl last 26[29:32] sts on to a st holder.**
Cont in patt until work measures 90[91:92]cm from cast-on edge, ending with a RS row.
Next row P3, K to last 3 sts, P3.
Leave these sts on a spare needle.

Front
Work as given for back from ** to **.
Cont in patt until work measures 5 rows less than back.
Shape neck
Next row (WS) P2, K2 tog, turn.
Next row P1, K2, turn.
Next row P1, P2 tog, turn.
Next row K2, turn.
Next row P2 tog, K 65 sts at centre, K2 tog, P2, turn.
Next row K2, P1, turn.
Next row P2 tog, P1, turn.
Next row K2, turn.
Next row P2 tog.
Break off yarn, leave rem 67 sts on a spare needle.

Left sleeve

***Using 4mm needles and A, cast on 50[52:54] sts. Work 3cm twisted K1, P1 rib as given for back, ending with a WS row.

Next row Rib 3[2:14], *inc 1, rib 1[1:0], rep from * to last 3[2:14] sts, inc 1, rib to end. 73[77:81] sts.

Next row K.

Change to 4½mm needles and commence patt.

1st size only

1st row K2, cable 19, cable 31, cable 19, K2.

2nd row P2, cable 19, cable 31, cable 19, P2.

These 2 rows establish the patt.

2nd and 3rd sizes only

1st row (K1, P1) [1:2] times, K2, cable 19, cable 31, cable 19, K2 (P1, K1) [1:2] times.

2nd row (K1, P1) [1:2] times, P2, cable 19, cable 31, cable 19, P2, (P1, K1) [1:2] times.

These 2 rows establish the patt.

All sizes

Keeping patt correct, inc and work into moss st, 1 st at each end of the 2nd[4th:4th] and every foll 4th row until there are 121 sts.***

Cont without shaping until work measures 45[46:47]cm from cast-on edge, ending with a RS row.

Shape pocket lining

Next row Cast on 20 sts, P20, patt to end.

Next row Patt to last 20 sts, K20.

Rep the last 2 rows until work measures 13[14:16]cm from beg of pocket lining, ending with a RS row.

Next row K.

Cast off loosely.

Right sleeve

Work as given for left sleeve from *** to ***. Cont without shaping until work measures 45[46:47]cm from cast-on edge, ending with a WS row.

Shape pocket lining

Next row Cast on 20 sts, K20, patt to end.

Next row Patt to last 20 sts, P20.

Complete to match left sleeve.

To make up

Join side seams.

Left pocket border

Using 4mm needles and A, with WS of work facing, K across the 26[29:32] sts left on stitch holder at left front armhole, then K across the 26[29:32] sts on stitch holder at left back armhole. 52 [58:64] sts. Work 8 rows twisted K1, P1 rib as given for back, beg with a 2nd row. Cast off in rib.

Right pocket border

Work as given for left pocket border but K across stitches on holder at right back armhole, then across sts on holder at right front armhole. 52 [58:64] sts. Complete as for left pocket border.

Join underarm seams to pocket lining. Fold pocket borders on to RS and catch down sides.

Set in sleeves. Catch down pocket linings to WS.

Collar

Using 4mm circular needle, with RS of work facing, K up 4 sts from left side of neck, K across 67 sts at centre front, K up 4 sts up right side of neck, K across 73 sts on back neck. 148 sts. Work in rounds.

1st round *P1 tbl, K1, rep from * to end.

Rep this round until work measures 28cm from beg.

Cast off in rib.

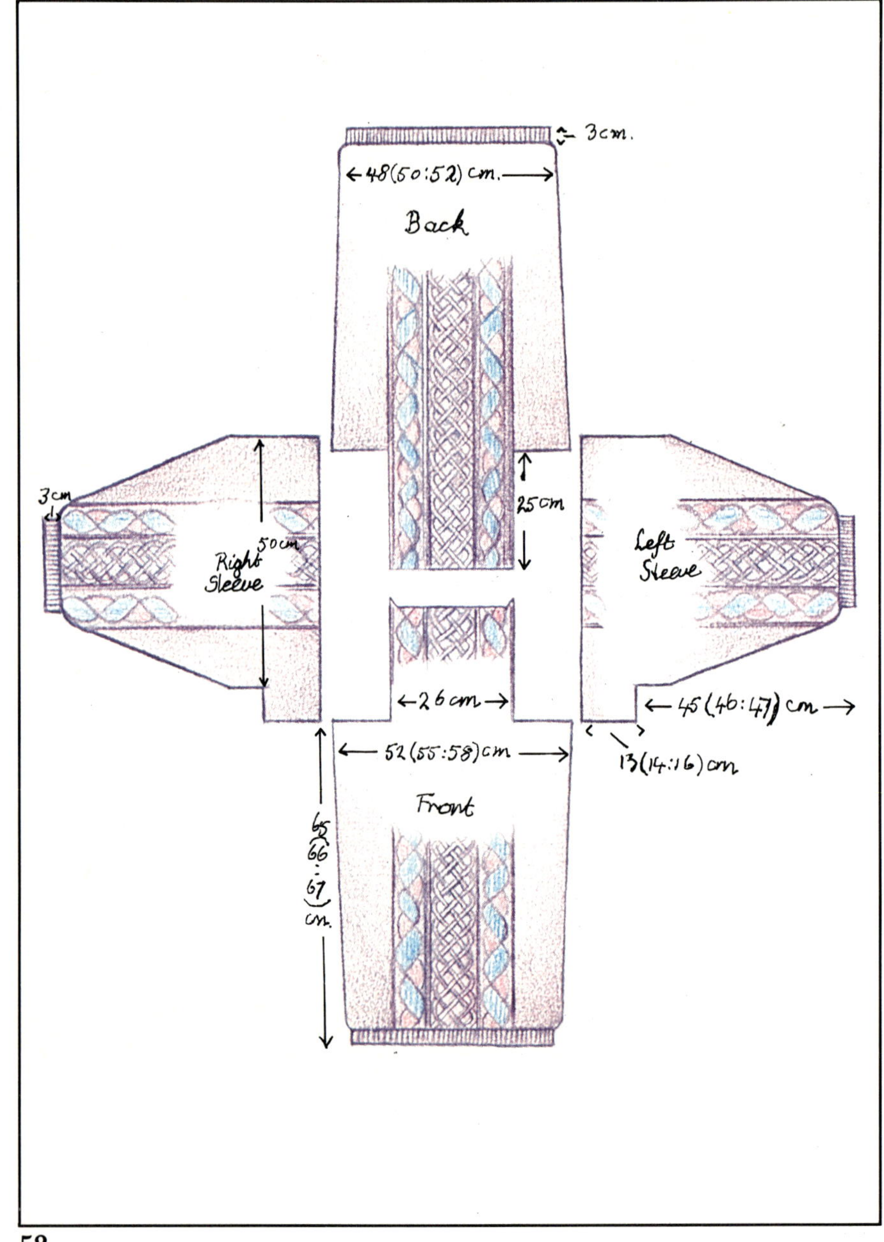

Woven-look Sweater

This military-style sweater in an interesting woven-look stitch
pattern has practical shoulder buttoning and would
look good on any active youngster.

Sizes
To fit 61-69 [71-79] chest
Length 49 [54] cm
Sleeve seam 33 [39] cm

Note Instructions for larger size are in square brackets [ ]; where there is only one set of figures it applies to both sizes.

Tension
28 sts and 36 rows to 10cm over st st on 3¼mm needles

Materials
300 [350] g four-ply yarn in main colour (A)
125g in contrast colour (B)
1 pair each 2¾mm and 3¼mm knitting needles
6 buttons

Back
Using 3¼mm needles and A, cast on 64[72] sts loosely. Form base triangles by working turning rows.
1st row (WS) P2, turn.
2nd row K2.
3rd row P3, turn.
4th row K3.
5th row P4, turn.
6th row K4.
7th row P5, turn.
8th row K5.
9th row P6, turn.
10th row K6.
11th row P7, turn.
12th row K7.
13th row P8, do not turn.
First triangle completed. Leave these 8 sts on right-hand needle and rep last 13 rows 7[8] times more, so forming 8[9] triangles.
Cut off A.
*Join in B and work across first 8 sts for selvedge triangle.
1st row K2, turn.
2nd row P2.
3rd row Inc in first st by working into front and back of st, sl 1, K1, psso, turn.
4th row P3.
5th row Inc in first st, K1, sl 1, K1, psso, turn.
6th row P4.
7th row Inc in first st, K2, sl 1, K1, psso, turn.
8th row P5.
9th row Inc in first st, K3, sl 1, K1,

psso, turn.
10th row P6.
11th row Inc in first st, K4, sl 1, K1, psso, turn.
12th row P7.
13th row Inc in first st, K5, sl 1, K1, psso, do not turn.
Selvedge triangle completed. Leave these 8 sts on right-hand needle and work first rectangle.
****1st row** K up 8 sts along side of base triangle, turn.
2nd row P8.
3rd row K7, sl 1, K1, psso, turn — two sections joined.
Rep 2nd and 3rd rows until all 8 sts from base triangle have been dec, ending with a 3rd row.******
Rep from ****** to ****** 6[7] times more. Work selvedge triangle.
1st row K up 8 sts along side of last triangle worked, turn.
2nd row P2 tog, P6, turn.
3rd and every foll alt row K.
4th row P2 tog, P5, turn.
6th row P2 tog, P4, turn.
8th row P2 tog, P3, turn.
10th row P2 tog, P2, turn.
12th row P2 tog, P1, turn.
14th row P2 tog.
Cut off B.
Join in A and work rectangles.
1st row P up 7 sts along side of triangle just worked. 8 sts.
2nd row K8.
3rd row P7, P2 tog, turn.
Rep 2nd and 3rd rows until all 8 sts from next rectangle have been dec, ending with a 3rd row.
Do not turn after last row.
Leave these 8 sts on right-hand needle.
******* P up 8 sts along side of next rectangle.
Rep 2nd and 3rd rows until all 8 sts from next rectangle have been dec, ending with a 3rd row.
Do not turn after last row. *******
Rep from ******* to ******* 6[7] times more.
Cut off A.*
Rep from * to * until work measures approx 29[33]cm from beg, ending with a row of rectangles and two selvedge triangles worked in B.
Cut off B.
Join in A and work a row of triangles to complete patt.
1st row P up 8 sts along side of last triangle worked, turn. 9sts.

2nd row K9.
3rd row P2 tog, P6, P2 tog, turn.
4th row K8.
5th row P2 tog, P5, P2 tog, turn.
6th row K7.
7th row P2 tog, P4, P2 tog, turn.
8th row K6.
9th row P2 tog, P3, P2 tog, turn.
10th row K5.
11th row P2 tog, P2, P2 tog, turn.
12th row K4.
13th row P2 tog, P1, P2 tog, turn.
14th row K3.
15th row (P2 tog) twice, turn.
16th row K2.
17th row P3 tog, do not turn.
Rep 1st to 17th rows until 8[9] triangles have been worked and 1 st remains. Do not cut off yarn, turn.
Commence yoke
With RS facing using 3¼mm needles and A, K up 98[110] sts across top of triangles just worked. 99[111] sts.
Beg with a P row, work 10[11]cm st st, ending with a K row.
Shape shoulders
1st row P to last 8[9] sts, turn.
2nd row Sl 1, K to last 8[9] sts, turn.
3rd row Sl 1, P to last 16[18] sts, turn.
4th row Sl 1, K to last 16[18] sts, turn.
5th row Sl 1, P to last 24[26] sts, turn.
6th row Sl 1, K to last 24[26] sts, turn.
7th row Sl 1, P to last 31[34] sts, turn.
8th row Sl 1, K to last 31[34] sts, turn.
9th row P across all 99 [111] sts.
Cut off A.

Back neck border
Sl 31[34] sts from each side on to a holder.
With RS facing, using 2¾mm needles and A, K across centre 37[43] sts inc 2 sts evenly across the row: 39[45] sts.
Next row P1, *K1, P1, rep from * to end.
Next row K1, *P1, K1, rep from * to end.
Rep the last 2 rows 3 times more.
Cast off in rib.

Front
Work as for back until 11[13] rows less have been worked to beg of shoulder shaping, ending with a P row.
Divide for neck
Next row K37[42], K2 tog, turn and leave rem sts on a spare needle.
Complete left side of neck first.
Dec 1 st at neck edge on next 6[8] rows.

Work 1 row.
Dec 1 st at neck edge on next row.
31[34] sts.
Work 2 rows.

Shape shoulder
1st row (WS) P23[25], turn.
2nd and every foll alt row Sl 1, K to end.
3rd row P15[16], turn.
5th row P7[8], turn.
6th row K.
Leave all 31[34] sts on a holder.
With RS facing place centre 21[23]sts from spare needle on to a holder, join A to next st, K2 tog, K to end. 38[43] sts.
Work to match first side, reversing shaping.

Sleeves
Using 2¾mm needles and A, cast on 46[50] sts.
Work 6cm in K1, P1 rib.
Next row (WS) Rib 1[5], pick up and K the loop between last st worked and next st on left-hand needle — called M1—, (rib 4[3], M1) 11[13] times, rib 1[6]: 58[64] sts.
Change to 3¼mm needles and beg with a K row, work in st st inc 1 st each end of every foll 5th row until there are 90[102] sts.
Cont without shaping until work measures 33[39]cm from cast-on edge ending with a P row.
Cast off.

To make up
Press sleeves and yoke only on WS following instructions on ball band.
Front neck border
With RS facing, using 2¾mm needles and A, K up 14[16] sts down left side of neck, K the sts from holder, then K up 14[16] sts up right side of neck. 49[55] sts.
Work 8 rows in K1, P1 rib, as given for back neck border.
Cast off in rib.
Shoulder borders
Right back
With RS facing, using 2¾mm needles and A, K31[34] sts from shoulder inc 2 sts evenly across, then K up 6 sts evenly from side of the back neck border. 39[42] sts.
Work 8 rows in K1, P1 rib as for back neck border.
Cast off in rib.

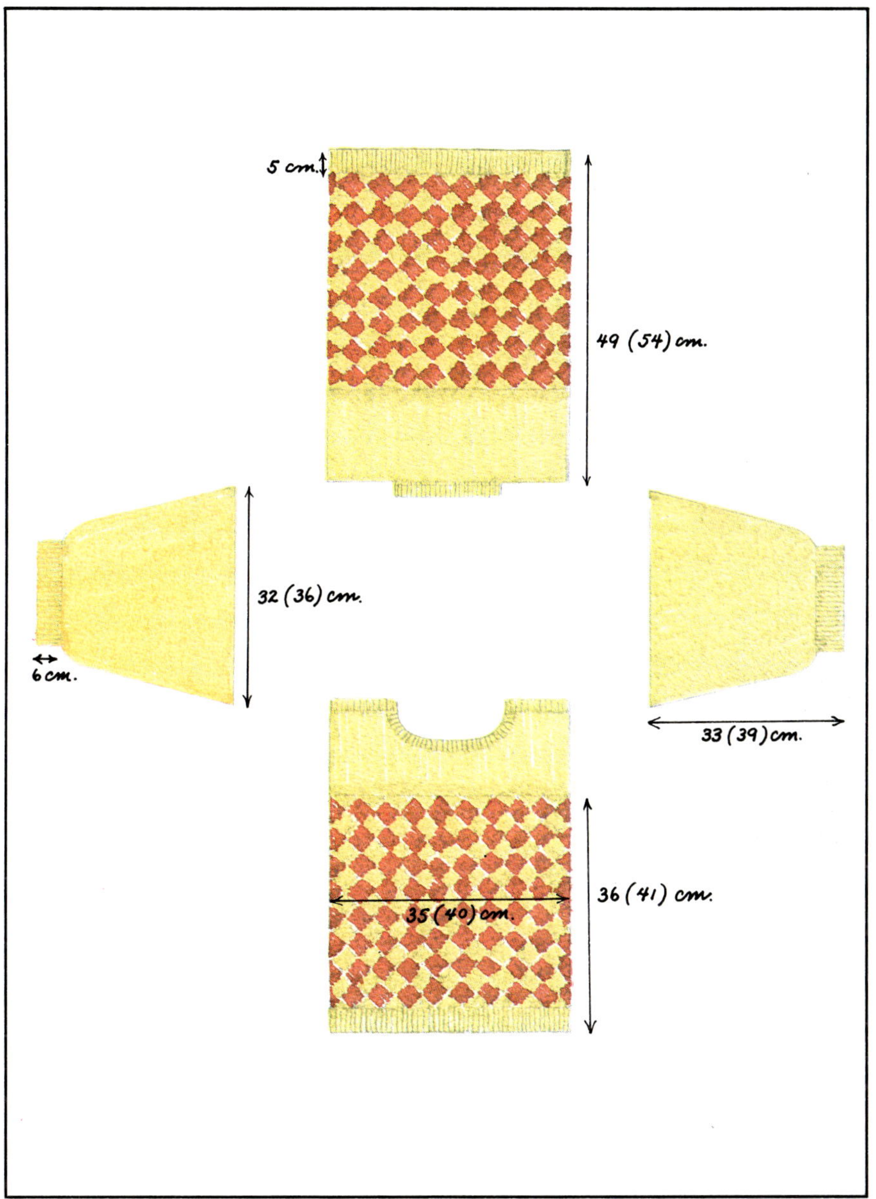

Left back
Start at top of back neck border and work as for right back border.
Left front
With RS facing, using 2¾mm needles and A, K31[34] sts from shoulder inc 2[3] sts evenly, then K up 6 sts up side of front neck border. 39[43] sts.
Work 3 rows K1, P1 rib as for back neck border.
1st buttonhole row (Rib 10[11], cast off 2) 3 times, rib 3[4].
2nd buttonhole row Rib to end, casting on 2 sts over those cast off in previous row.
Work 3 rows in rib.
Cast off in rib.

Right front
Work as for left front, starting at top neck border and working 1st buttonhole row as foll:
Buttonhole row Rib 3[4], (cast off 2, rib 10[11] sts) 3 times.
Welts (back and front alike)
With RS facing, using 2¾mm needles and A, K up 96[102] sts evenly along lower edge.
Work 5cm K1, P1 rib. Cast off in rib.
Lap front over back to depth of rib.
Place markers 16[18] cm down from shoulders on back and front.
Sew in sleeves between markers, then join side and sleeve seams.
Sew on buttons.

Basketweave Sweater

Casual and sporty, but elegant enough for town wear, a
classic V-necked sweater is given textural interest with a
basketweave pattern

Sizes
To fit 97[102:107]cm chest
Length 64[64:68]cm
Sleeve seam 52.5cm

Note Instructions for larger sizes are in square brackets []; where only one set of figures it applies to all sizes.

Tension
12 sts and 20 rows to 10cm over patt using 6mm needles.

Materials
950 [1050:1150] g chunky yarn
1 pair each 5mm and 6mm needles

Back
Using 5mm needles, cast on 62[65:68] sts.
Work in K2, P2 rib as follows:
Next row K2[1:0], *P2, K2, rep from * to end of row.
Next row *P2, K2, rep from * to last 2[1:0] sts, P2 [1:0].
Rep last 2 rows until work measures 8cm.
Change to 6mm needles and work in patt as follows:
****1st, 3rd, 5th and 7th rows** K1, *K3, P3, rep from * to last 1 [4:1] sts, K1 [4:1].
2nd and every alt row K1, P to last st, K1.
9th, 11th, 13th and 15th rows K1, *P3, K3, rep from * to last 1 [4:1] sts, K1 [(P3, K1):K1].
16th row As 2nd row.**
These 16 rows form patt.
Rep from ** to ** 6 times. Work first 0 [0:8]rows of patt once more.
Shape shoulders
Keeping patt correct, cast off 11 [11:12] sts at beg of next 4 rows.
Leave rem 18 [21:20] sts on stitch holder for neckband.

Front
Work 46cm from beg, ending with WS row.
Divide for neck
Work in patt for 31 [32:34] sts, turn leaving rem sts on a spare needle.
Next row P2 tog, P to last st, K1.
Keeping patt correct, dec 1 st at neck edge on every foll 4th row until 22 [22:24] sts rem.

Work in patt without shaping until front matches back to beg of shoulder shaping, ending with a WS row.
Shape shoulders
Cast off 11 [11:12] sts at beg of next row. Work 1 row. Cast off.
Rejoin yarn to centre front.
Next row Dec 0 [1:0] sts, work in patt to end of row.
Next row K1, P to last 2 sts, P2 tog.
Complete to match first side, reversing all shaping.

Sleeves (alike)
Using 5mm needles, cast on 32 sts and work in K2, P2 rib until work measures 8cm.
Change to 6mm needles and work in patt as given for first size of back.
Keeping patt correct, inc 1 st at each end of every foll 6th row until there are 56 sts, ending with a WS row.
Work in patt for 17 rows without shaping.

Cast off loosely P-wise.

To make up
Join right shoulder seam.

Neckband
With RS facing, using 5mm needles K up 52 [53:58] sts along right front edge, K the 18 [21:20] sts on stitch holder for back. 70 [74:78] sts.
Next row P2, *K2, P2, rep from *.
Next row K2, *P2, K2, rep from *.
Rep these 2 rows for 5cm.
Cast off loosely in rib.
With RS facing, using 5mm needles K up 52 [52:56] sts along left front neck edge. Work in K2, P2 rib for 5cm.
Cast off loosely in rib.
Join left shoulder seam and neckband seam. Slipstitch neckband into position at centre front, overlapping left neckband over right. Sew in sleeves. Join sleeve and side seams.

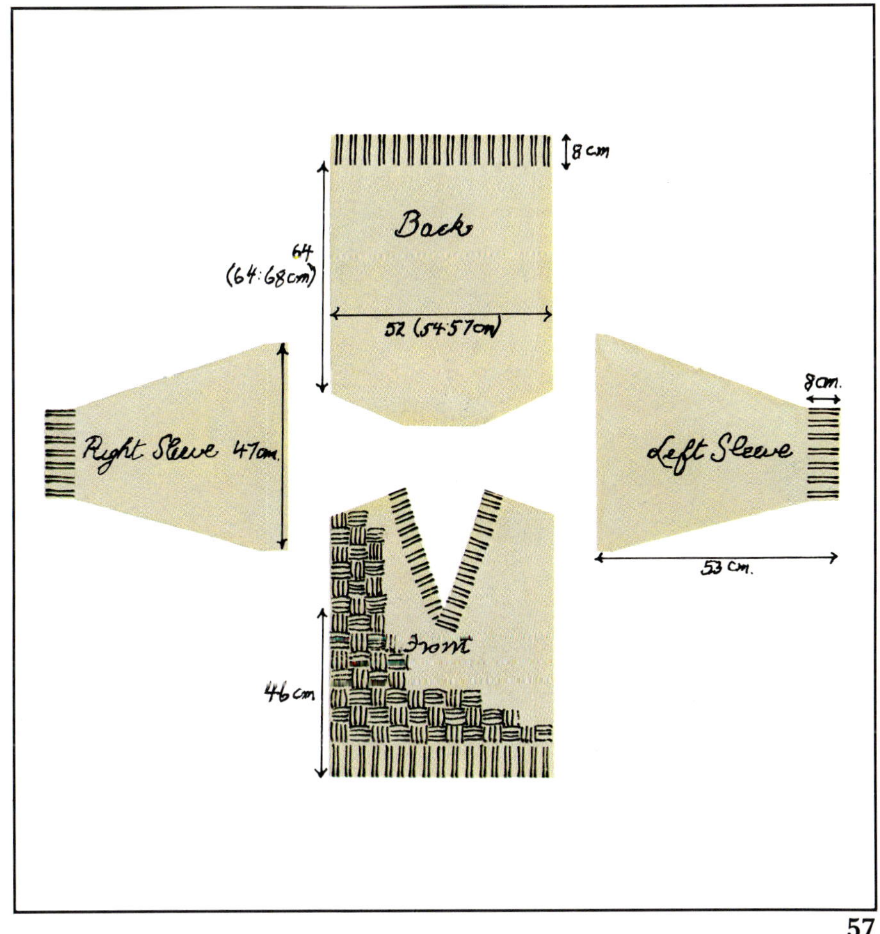

Tweedy Coat and Hat

Treat yourself to a warm winter in a beautiful tweedy coat
encrusted with richly textured stitch patterns. Complete the
picture with a snug ribbed hat to match.

Sizes
To fit 81[87:91] cm bust
Length 98[99:100] cm
Sleeve seam 44cm

Note Instructions for larger sizes are in square brackets []; where there is only one set of figures it applies to all sizes.

Tension
15 sts and 20 rows to 10cm over st st on 6mm needles.

Materials
Coat
1650 [1700:1750] g chunky yarn
Hat
175g chunky yarn
1 pair each 5mm and 6mm needles
5mm circular needle
Cable needle
11 buttons

Back
Using 5mm needles, cast on 66[70:74] sts.
Work in K2, P2 rib as foll:
1st row K2, *P2, K2, rep from * to end.
2nd row P2, *K2, P2, rep from * to end.
Rep the last 2 rows for 8cm, ending with a 1st row.
Next row Rib 8[10:10] pick up loop between last st worked and next st on LH needle and work into the back of it — called M1 —, (rib 2, M1) 25[25:27] times, rib to end.
92[96:102] sts.
Change to 6mm needles and commence patt.
1st row (RS) P4[6:2], K1 tbl, *P4, sl next 2 sts on to cable needle and leave at front of work, K2, then K2 from cable needle — called C4F —, P4, sl next st on to cable needle and hold at front of work K1 tbl, then K1 tbl from cable needle — called C2Ftbl —, rep from * to last 17[19:15] sts, P4, C4F, P4, K1 tbl, P4[6:2].
2nd and every foll alt row K the P sts and P the K sts of previous row.
3rd row P4[6:2], *sl next st on to cable needle and hold at front of work, P1, then K1 tbl from cable needle — called Tw2F —, P2, sl next st on to cable needle and hold at back of work, K2, then P1 from cable needle — called Tw3B—, sl next 2

sts on to a cable needle and hold at front of work, P1, then K2 from cable needle, — called Tw3F —, P2, sl next st on to cable needle and hold at back of work, K1 tbl then P1 from cable needle, — called Tw2B —, rep from * to last 4[6:2] sts, P to end.
5th row P4[6:2], *P1, Tw2F, Tw3B, P2, Tw3F, Tw2B, P1, rep from * to last 4[6:2] sts, P to end.
7th row P4[6:2], *P2, sl next st on to cable needle and hold at back of work, K2, then K1 tbl from cable needle — called Cr3B —, P4, sl next 2 sts on to cable needle and hold at front of work, K1 tbl, then K2 from cable needle — called Cr3F —,P2, rep from * to last 4[6:2] sts, P to end.
9th row P4[6:2], *P1, Tw3B, Tw2F, P2, Tw2B, Tw3F, P1, rep from * to last 4[6:2] sts, P to end.
11th row P4[6:2], *Tw3B, P2, Tw2F, Tw2B, P2, Tw3F, rep from * to last 4[6:2] sts, P to end.
13th row P4[6:2], K2, *P4, sl next st on to cable needle and hold at back of work, K1 tbl, then K1 tbl from cable needle — called C2Btbl —,P4, sl next 2 sts on to cable needle and hold at back of work, K2, then K2 from cable needle — called C4B —, rep from * to last 16[18:14] sts, P4, C2Btbl, P4, K2, P to end.
15th row P4[6:2], *Tw3F, P2, Tw2B, Tw2F, P2, Tw3B, rep from * to last 4[6:2] sts, P to end.
17th row P4[6:2], P1, Tw3F, Tw2B, P2, Tw2F, Tw3B, P1, rep from * to last 4[6:2] sts, P to end.
19th row P4[6:2], *P2, Cr3F, P4, Cr2B, P2, rep from * to last 4[6:2] sts, P to end.
21st row P4[6:2], *P1, Tw2B, Tw3F, P2, Tw3B, Tw2F, P1, rep from * to last 4[6:2] sts, P to end.
23rd row P4[6:2], *Tw2B, P2, Tw3F, Tw3B, P2, Tw2F, rep from * to last 4[6:2] sts, P to end.
24th row As 2nd row.
These 24 rows form the patt. Rep these 24 rows 4 times more.
Now cont in bobble patt as foll:
1st row (RS) P4[6:2], K1 tbl, *P5, K2, rep from * to last 10[12:8] sts, P5, K1 tbl, P4[6:2].
2nd and every foll alt row K4[6:2], P1, *K5, P2, rep from * to last 10[12:8] sts, K5, P1, K4[6:2].
3rd row P4[6:2], K1 tbl, *P5, (K1,

P1) twice into next st, P4, turn, K4, turn, P2 tog, P2 tog tbl, turn, sl 1, K1, psso, — called make bobble (MB) —, K1, P5, K2, rep from * to last 17[19:15] sts, P5, MB, K1, P5, K1 tbl, P4[6:2].

5th row P4[6:2], K1 tbl, *P4, MB, K1, MB, P5, K2, rep from * to last 17[19:15] sts, P4, MB, K1, MB, P5, K1 tbl, P4[6:2].
7th row P4[6:2], K1 tbl, *P3, MB, P1, MB, K1, MB, P4, K2, rep from * to last 17[19:15] sts, P3, MB, P1, MB, K1, MB, P4, K1 tbl, P4[6:2].
9th row As 1st row.
11th row P4[6:2], K1 tbl, *P5, K2, P5, MB, K1, rep from * to last 17[19:15] sts, P5, K2, P5, K1 tbl, P4[6:2].
13th row P4[6:2], K1 tbl, *P5, K2, P4, MB, K1, MB, rep from * to last 17[19:15] sts, P5, K2, P5, K1 tbl, P4[6:2].
15th row P4[6:2], K1 tbl, P1, *P4, K2, P3, MB, P1, MB, K1, MB, rep from * to last 16[18:14] sts, P4, K2, P5, K1 tbl, P4[6:2].
16th row As 2nd row.
These 16 rows form bobble patt.
Shape armholes
Keeping patt correct, cast off 3 sts at beg of next 2 rows.
Dec 1 st at each end of next 7[7:5] rows and then on every foll alt row until 62[62:76] sts rem.
Cont without shaping until work measures 98[99:100]cm from cast-on edge, ending with a WS row.

Shape shoulders
Keeping patt correct, cast off 8[8:11] sts at beg of next 2 rows and 8[7:10] sts at beg of foll 2 rows. Cast off rem 30[32:34] sts.

Left front
** Using 5mm needles cast on 34[34:38] sts. Work 8cm K2, P2 rib as given for back, ending with a 1st row.
Next row Rib 5[3:1], ,M1, (rib 2[2:3], M1), 12[14:12] times, rib to end. 47[49:51] sts.**
Change to 6mm needles and commence patt.
1st row (RS) P4[6:2], K1 tbl, *P4, C4F, P4, C2Ftbl, rep from * to last 14[14:20] sts, P4, C4F, P4, K1 tbl, P1[1:7].

2nd and every foll alt row K the P sts and P the K sts of previous row.
3rd row P4[6:2], *Tw2F, P2, Tw3B, Tw3F, P2, Tw2B, rep from * to last 1[1:7] sts, P1[1:7].
5th row P4[6:2], *P1, Tw2F, Tw3B, P2, Tw3F, Tw2B, P1, rep from * to last 1[1:7] sts, P1[1:7].
7th row P4[6:2], *P2, Cr3B, P4, Cr3F, P2, rep from * to last 1[1:7] sts, P1[1:7].
9th row P4[6:2], *P1, Tw3B, Tw2F, P2, Tw2B, Tw3F, P1, rep from * to last 1[1:7] sts, P1[1:7].
11th row P4[6:2], *Tw3B, P2, Tw2F, Tw2B, P2, Tw3F, rep from * to last 1[1:7] sts, P1[1:7].
13th row P4[6:2], K2, *P4, C2Btbl, P4, C4B, rep from * to last 13[13:19] sts, P4, C2Btbl, P4, K2, P to end.

15th row P4[6:2], *Tw3F, P2, Tw2B, Tw2F, P2, Tw3B, rep from * to last 1[1:7] sts, P1[1:7].
17th row P4[6:2], *P1, Tw3F, Tw2B, P2, Tw2F, Tw3B, P1, rep from * to last 1[1:7] sts, P1[1:7].
19th row P4[6:2], *P2, Cr3F, P4, Cr3B, P2, rep from * to last 1[1:7] sts, P1[1:7].
21st row P4[6:2], *P1, Tw2B, Tw3F, P2, Tw3B, Tw2F, P1, rep from * to last 1[1:7] sts, P1[1:7].
23rd row P4[6:2], *Tw2B, P2, Tw3F, Tw3B, P2, Tw2F, rep from * to last 1[1:7] sts, P1[1:7].
24th row As 2nd row.
These 24 rows form the patt. Rep these 24 rows 4 times more.
Now cont in bobble patt as foll:
1st row (RS) P4[6:2], K1 tbl, *P5, K2, rep from * to last 7[7:13] sts, P5, K1 tbl, P1[1:7].

2nd and every foll alt row K1[1:7], P1, K5, *P2, K5, rep from * to last 5[7:3] sts, P1, K4[6:2].
3rd row P4[6:2], K1 tbl, *P5, MB, K1, P5, K2, rep from * to last 14[14:20] sts, P5, MB, K1, P5, K1 tbl, P1[1:7].
5th row P4[6:2], K1 tbl, *P4, MB, K1, MB, P5, K2, rep from * to last 14[14:20] sts, P4, MB, K1, MB, P5, K1 tbl, P1[1:7].
7th row P4[6:2], K1 tbl, *P3, MB, P1, MB, K1, MB, P4, K2, rep from * to last 14[14:20] sts, P3, MB, P1, MB, K1, MB, P4, K1 tbl, P1[1:7].
9th row As 1st row.
11th row P4[6:2], K1 tbl, *P5, K2, P5, MB, K1, rep from * to last 14[14:20] sts, P5, K2, P5, K1 tbl, P1[1:7].
13th row P4[6:2], K1 tbl, *P5, K2, P4, MB, K1, MB, rep from * to last 14[14:20] sts, P5, K2, P5, K1 tbl, P1[1:7].
15th row P4[6:2], K1 tbl, P1, *P4, K2, P3, MB, P1, MB, K1, MB, rep from * to last 13[13:19] sts, P4, K2, P5, K1 tbl, P1[1:7].
16th row As 2nd row.
These 16 rows form bobble patt.
Shape armhole and neck
Next row Cast off 3 sts, patt to last 2 sts, P2 tog.
Patt 1 row.
Dec 1 st at neck edge on next and every foll alt row, *at the same time*, dec 1 st at armhole edge on next

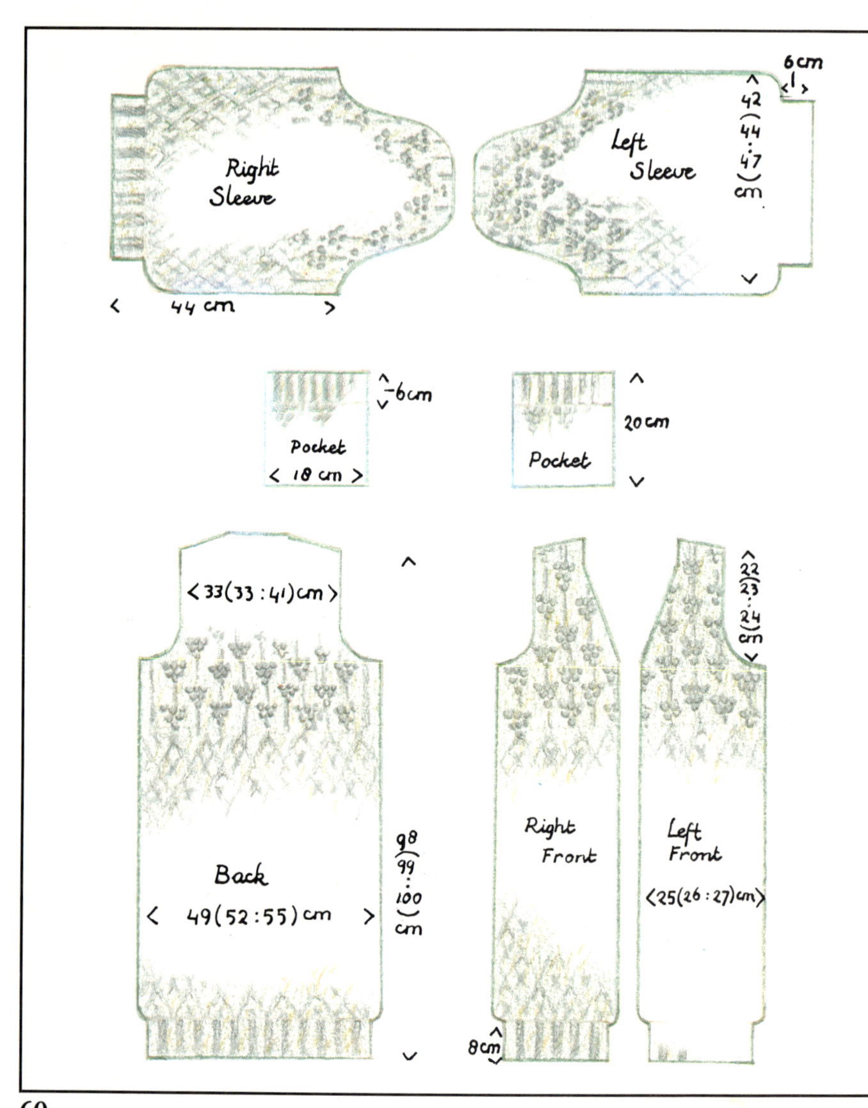

7[7:5] rows, then on every foll alt row until 22[20:29] sts rem.
Keeping armhole edge straight cont to dec at neck edge as before until 16 [15:21] sts rem. Cont without shaping until work matches back to shoulder shaping, ending at armhole edge.
Shape shoulder
Cast off 8[8:11] sts at beg of next row.
Work 1 row.
Cast off rem 8[7:10] sts.

Right front
Work as given for left front from ** to **. Change to 6mm needles and commence patt.
1st row (RS) P1[1:7], K1 tbl, *P4, C4F, P4, C2Ftbl, rep from * to last 17[19:15] sts, P4, C4F, P4, K1 tbl, P4[6:2].
2nd and every foll alt row K the P sts and P the K sts of previous row.
3rd row P1[1:7], *Tw2F, P2, Tw3B, Tw3F, P2, Tw2B, rep from * to last 4[6:2] sts, P4[6:2].
5th row P1[1:7], *P1, Tw2F, Tw3B, P2, Tw3F, Tw2B, P1, rep from * to last 4[6:2] sts, P4[6:2].
7th row P1[1:7], *P2, Cr3B, P4, Cr3F, P2, rep from * to last 4[6:2] sts, P4[6:2].
9th row P1[1:7], *P1, Tw3B, Tw2F, P2, Tw2B, Tw3F, P1, rep from * to

last 4[6:2] sts, P4[6:2].
11th row P1[1:7], *Tw3B, P2, Tw2F, Tw2B, P2, Tw3F, rep from * to last 4[6:2] sts, P4[6:2].
13th row P1[1:7], K2, *P4, C2Btbl, P4, C4B, rep from * to last 16[18:14] sts, P4, C2Btbl, P4, K2, P to end.
15th row P1[1:7], *Tw3F, P2, Tw2B, Tw2F, P2, Tw3B, rep from * to last 4[6:2] sts, P4[6:2].
17th row P1[1:7], * P1, Tw3F, Tw2B, P2, Tw2F, Tw3B, P1, rep from * to last 4[6:2] sts, P4[6:2].
19th row P1[1:7], *P2, Cr3F, P4, Cr3B, P2, rep from * to last 4[6:2] sts, P4[6:2].
21st row P1[1:7], *P1, Tw2B, Tw3F, P2, Tw3B, Tw2F, P1, rep from * to last 4[6:2] sts, P4[6:2].
23rd row P1[1:7], *Tw2B, P2, Tw3F, Tw3B, P2, Tw2F, rep from * to last 4[6:2] sts, P4[6:2].
24th row As 2nd row.
These 24 rows form the patt. Rep these 24 rows 4 times more.
Now cont in bobble patt as foll:
1st row (RS) P1[1:7], K1 tbl, *P5, K2, rep from * to last 10[12:8] sts, P5, K1 tbl, P4[6:2].
2nd and every foll alt row K4[6:2], P1, K5, *P2, K5, rep from * to last 2[2:8] sts, P1, K1[1:7].
3rd row P1[1:7], K1 tbl, *P5, MB,

K1, P5, K2, rep from * to last 17[19:15] sts, P5, MB, K1, P5, K1 tbl, P4[6:2].
5th row P1[1:7], K1 tbl, *P4, MB, K1, MB, P5, K2, rep from * to last 17[19:15] sts, P4, MB, K1, MB, P5, K1 tbl, P4[6:2].
7th row P1[1:7], K1 tbl, *P3, MB, P1, MB, K1, MB, P4, K2, rep from * to last 17[19:15] sts, P3, MB, P1, MB, K1, MB, P4, K1 tbl, P4[6:2].
9th row As 1st row.
11th row P1[1:7], K1 tbl, *P5, K2, P5, MB, K1, rep from * to last 17[19:15] sts, P5, K2, P5, K1 tbl, P4[6:2].
13th row P1[1:7], K1 tbl, *P5, K2, P4, MB, K1, MB, rep from * to last 17[19:15] sts, P5, K2, P5, K1 tbl, P4[6:2].
15th row P1[1:7], K1 tbl, P1, *P4, K2, P3, MB, P1, MB, K1, MB, rep from * to last 16[18:14] sts, P4, K2, P5, K1 tbl, P4[6:2].
16th row As 2nd row.
These 16 rows form the bobble patt. Complete to match left front, reversing all shapings.

Sleeves
Using 5mm needles, cast on 30[34:34] sts. Work 6cm K2, P2 rib as given for back, ending with a 1st row.

Special technique–sewing on a patch pocket

1 Patch pockets can be sewn on with decorative embroidery stitches such as cross stitch or blanket stitch, or as on the basic coat, almost invisibly. First position the pocket on the coat matching the pattern on the pocket to that on the coat, then pin it in place.

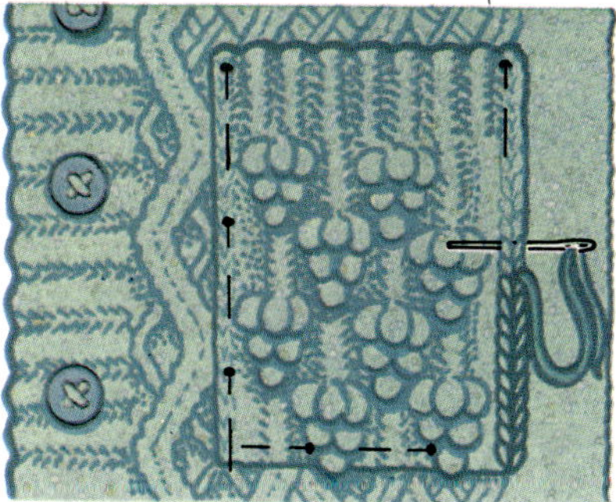

2 Thread a wool needle with matching yarn and, working through both layers, work a vertical line of Swiss darning (see page 28) through the edge stitches of the pocket on both sides.

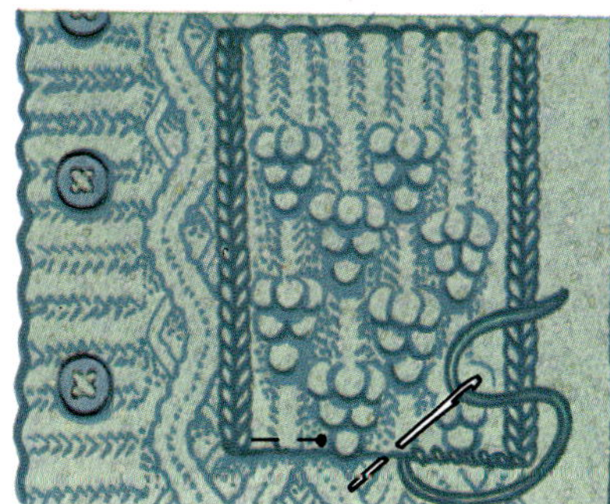

3 Join the bottom edge of the pocket to the coat with neat over-stitching. (On plain stocking stitch pockets this join can also be made with Swiss darning.)

Next row Rib 1, *M1, rib 1, rep from * to end. 59[67:67] sts.
Next row K3[6:4], M1, *K3[4:3], M1, rep from * to last 2[5:3] sts, K to end. 78[82:88] sts.
Change to 6mm needles and commence patt as give for back beg with a 13th patt row. Work 13th-24th rows once, then work 1st-24th rows again.
Now work 1st-16th rows of bobble patt as given for back.
Shape top
Keeping continuity of patt, cast off 3 sts at beg of next 2 rows. Dec 1 st at each end of next and every foll alt row until 30[36:44] sts rem. Work 1 row.
2nd and 3rd sizes only
Dec 1 st at each end of every row until 30 sts rem. Work 1 row.
All sizes
Cast off.

Pockets (make 2)
Using 6mm needles, cast on 37 sts and work in patt as foll:
1st row (RS) K2, *P5, K2, rep from * to end.
2nd and every foll alt row P2, *K5, P2, rep from * to end.
3rd row K2, (P5, MB, K1, P5, K2) twice, P5, K2.

5th row K2, (P4, MB, K1, MB, P5, K2) twice, P5, K2.
7th row K2, (P3, MB, P1, MB, K1, MB, P4, K2) twice, P5, K2.
9th row As 1st row.
11th row K2, (P5, K2, P5, MB, K1) twice, P5, K2.
13th row K2, (P5, K2, P4, MB, K1, MB) twice, P5, K2.
15th row K2, P1, (P4, K2, P3, MB, P1, MB, K1, MB) twice, P4, K2.
16th row As 2nd row.
Rep these 16 rows once more, dec 3 sts evenly across last row.
Change to 5mm needles and work 6cm K2, P2 rib as given for back.
Cast off in rib.

To make up
Join shoulders.
Button band
With RS of work facing, using 5mm circular needle, K up 9[11:12] sts from centre back neck to shoulder seam, 35[37:40] sts from shoulder seam to beg of neck shaping, then 114 sts from beg of neck shaping to cast-on edge. 158[162:166] sts. Work in rows. Beg with a 2nd row work 15 rows K2, P2 rib as given for back. Cast off in rib.
Buttonhole band
With RS of work facing, using 5mm

needles, K up 114 sts from cast-on edge to beg of neck shaping, 35[37:40] sts from beg of neck shaping to shoulder, and 9[11:12] sts from shoulder to centre back neck. 158[162:166] sts.
Beg with a 2nd row work 7 rows K2, P2 rib as given for back.
1st buttonhole row Rib 6, cast off 2 sts, *rib 8, (including st used in casting off), cast off 2, rep from * 9 times more, rib to end.
2nd buttonhole row Rib to end, casting on 2 sts over those cast off in previous row.
Rib a further 6 rows. Cast off in rib. Join centre back neck seam of bands. Join side and sleeve seams. Set in sleeves, easing fullness at top. Sew on pockets. (See Special Technique.) Sew on buttons.

Hat
Using 5mm needles, cast on 74 sts.
1st row K2, *P2, K2, rep from *.
2nd row P2, *K2, P2, rep from *.
Rep last 2 rows for 20cm, ending with a 1st row.
Next row Rib 19, (M1, rib 18) twice, M1, rib 19. 77 sts.
Change to 6mm needles and commence patt.
1st row (RS) K1, *P3, K1, rep from * to end.
2nd row P1, *K3, P1, rep from *.
Rep these 2 rows until work measures 35cm from cast-on edge, ending with a WS row.
Shape crown
1st row K1, *P2 tog, P1, K1, rep from * to end. 58 sts.
2nd row P1, *K2, P1, rep from *.
3rd row K1, *P2, K1, rep from *.
4th row As 2nd row.
5th row K1, *P2 tog, K1, rep from * to end. 39 sts.
6th row P1, *K1, P1, rep from *.
7th row K1, *P1, K1, rep from *.
8th row As 6th row.
9th row K1, *K2 tog, rep from * to end. 20 sts.
10th row (P2 tog) 10 times. 10 sts.
Break yarn, thread through rem sts, draw up and fasten off.

To make up
Join seam, reversing K2, P2 rib section to roll back. Roll brim on to RS and catchstitch in position.

Lacy Patterns

Knitting is such a versatile craft: it can produce the thick crunchy textures of cable patterns but also the fine delicacy of lace. Lace knitting is often thought to be impossibly difficult and it is true that there are some stitch patterns which demand a high degree of skill. However, there are many others which are well within the capabilities of most average knitters. Lace knitting is based largely on a technique known as 'decorative increasing' (see page 20) and on basic eyelet formations (page 26). It's worth persevering with these skills as the results are so impressive.

The patterns in the following pages include several lacy garments that are quite easy and would make sensible starting points for newcomers to this type of knitting. The openwork sweater on page 70 and the striped lace top on page 77 come into this category. The exquisite lace collar on page 80, on the other hand, should be attempted only by experienced knitters.

Frilly Bedjacket

This extravagantly pretty bedjacket is knitted in a lacy chevron pattern and bordered with a deep lace edging. The toning ribbon ties are further decorated with tiny beads and sequins.

Sizes
To fit 86-91 [96-101] cm bust
Length 65cm including edging
Sleeve seam 47cm including edging

Note Instructions for the larger size are in square brackets []; where there is only one set of figures it applies to both sizes.

Tension
24 sts and 34 rows to 10cm over st st on 3mm needles

Materials
450 [500] g four-ply yarn
1 pair 3mm knitting needles
4m narrow satin ribbon
Beads or sequins to trim ribbon ties

Back
Using 3mm needles, cast on 137 [154] sts.
**Commence patt.
1st row (WS) P.
2nd row K1, *(yfwd, sl 1, K1, psso, K4, K2 tog) twice, yfwd, K1, rep from * to end.
3rd row P8, *K1, P15, rep from * to last 9 sts, K1, P8.
4th row K1, *yfwd, sl 1, K1, psso, K3, K2 tog, yrn, P1, yon, sl 1, K1, psso, K3, K2 tog, yfwd, K1, rep from * to end.
5th row P7, *K3, P13, rep from * to last 10 sts, K3, P7.
6th row K1, *yfwd, sl 1, K1, psso, K2, K2 tog, yrn, P3, yon, sl 1, K1, psso, K2, K2 tog, yfwd, K1, rep from * to end.
7th row P6, *K5, P11, rep from * to last 11 sts, K5, P6.
8th row K1, *yfwd, sl 1, K1, psso, K1, K2 tog, yfwd, K1, yrn, P3 tog, yon, K1, yfwd, sl 1, K1, psso, K1, K2 tog, yfwd, K1, rep from * to end.
9th row P8, *K into front and back of next st, P15, rep from * to last 9 sts, K into front and back of next st, P8.
10th row K1, *yfwd, sl 1, K1, psso, K2 tog, yfwd, K8, yfwd, sl 1, K1, psso, K2 tog, yfwd, K1, rep from * to end.
11th row P.
12th row K1, *yfwd, sl 1, K2 tog, psso, yfwd, K10, yfwd, K3 tog, yfwd, K1, rep from * to end.
These 12 rows form the patt. Rep them 15 times more.
Cast off**.

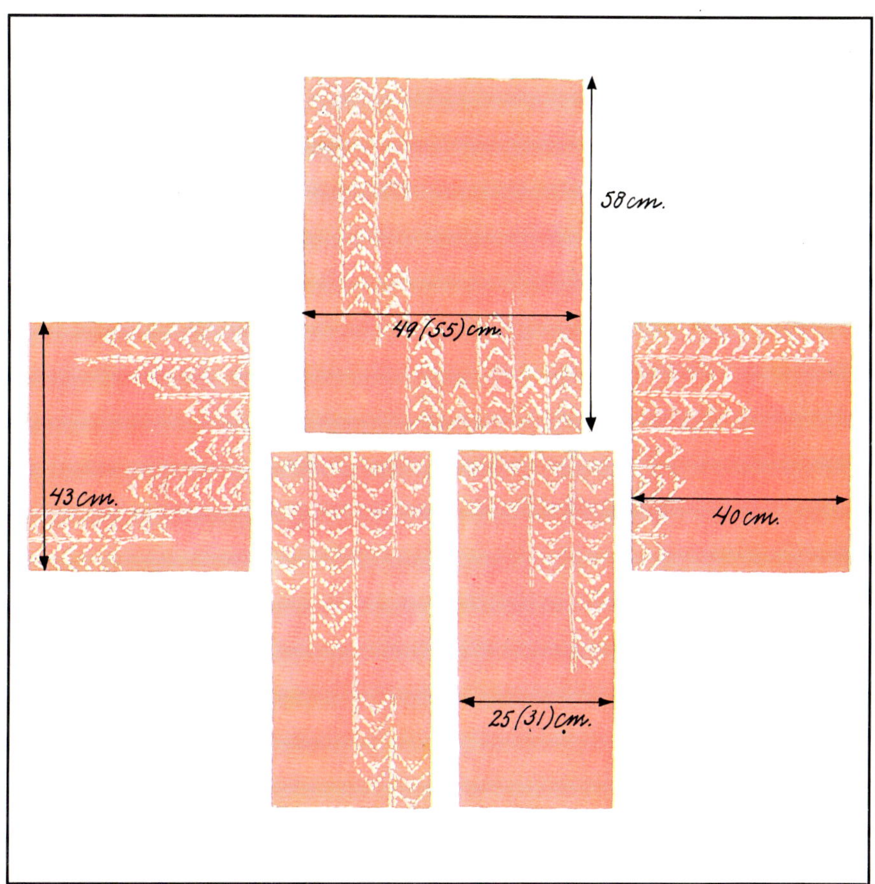

Left and right front (alike)
Using 3mm needles, cast on 69 [86] sts. Work as given for back from ** to **.

Sleeves
Using 3mm needles, cast on 120 sts. Cont in patt as given for back. Rep the 12 patt rows 11 times.
Cast off loosely.

Sleeve edging (make 2)
***Using 3mm needles, cast on 11 sts. K one row. Commence patt.
1st row K3, yfwd, K2 tog, K1, sl 1, K1, psso, cast on 4 sts, K2 tog, K1. 13 sts.
2nd row K10, yfwd, K2 tog, K1.
3rd row K3, yfwd, K2 tog, sl 1, K1, psso, (yfwd, K1) 4 times, yfwd, K2 tog. 16 sts.
4th row K13, yfwd, K2 tog, K1.
5th row K3, yfwd, K2 tog, sl 1, K1, psso, (yfwd, K1) twice, yfwd, sl 1, K2 tog, psso, (yfwd, K1) twice, yfwd, K2 tog. 18 sts.
6th row K15, yfwd, K2 tog, K1.
7th row K3, yfwd, K2 tog, K11, K2 tog. 17 sts.

8th row Cast off 6 sts, K7, yfwd, K2 tog, K1. 11 sts.
These 8 rows form the patt. ***Rep the last 8 rows until edging fits edge of sleeve. Cast off.

Front and hem edging (one piece)
Work as given for sleeve edging from *** to ***.
Rep the last 8 rows until work measures 262cm from cast-on edge. Cast off.

To make up
Press. Join shoulder seams, matching patt and making a 8cm tuck, 1 patt rep wide, on front shoulder.
Mark 23cm down from shoulders on back and front. Set in sleeves between markers. Join side and sleeve seams. Sew on sleeve edging. Beg at centre back hem edge, sew on front and hem edging, gathering slightly at corners and across back neck. Thread ribbon through lace patt at wrists and waist-line. Decorate ribbon ends with beads or sequins.

Party Dress and Pinafore

This gorgeous party dress, straight from the pages of a fairy tale, will delight any little girl. The dress is trimmed with two layers of bell-like frills. The matching over-pinafore is knitted in a delicate eyelet pattern with lacy edging round the hem and yoke.

Sizes
Dress
To fit 59[61:63]cm chest
Length 46[49:51]cm
Sleeve seam 6cm
Pinafore
To fit 59-63cm chest
Length 45cm

Note Instructions for larger sizes are in square brackets []; where there is only one set of figures it applies to all sizes.

Tension
Dress
28 sts and 32 rows to 10cm over st st on 3mm needles.
Pinafore
32 sts and 40 rows to 10cm over st st on 2½mm needles.

Materials
Dress
350 [350:400] g four-ply yarn (or No 5 cotton)
1 pair each 2¼mm and 3mm knitting needles
3 buttons
Ribbon (optional)
Pinafore
350g four-ply yarn (or No 5 cotton)
1 pair 2½mm knitting needles
2 buttons
Ribbon (optional)

Dress
Back
Using 3mm needles cast on 160 [168:176] sts.
Next row *K1 tbl, P1, rep from * to end.
Rep the last row until work measures 1 cm from the beg.
Commence patt.
1st row P4, * cast on 10 sts on to RH needle, P8, rep from * ending last rep P4.
2nd row K4, *P10, K8, rep from * ending last rep K4.
3rd row P4, *K10, P8, rep from * ending last rep P4.
4th row As 2nd row.
5th row As 3rd row.
6th row As 2nd row.
7th row P4, *sl 1, K1, psso, K6, K2 tog, P8, rep from * ending last rep P4.

8th row K4, *P8, K8, rep from * ending last rep K4.
9th row P4, *sl 1, K1, psso, K4, K2 tog, P8, rep from * ending last rep P4.
10th row K4, *P6, K8, rep from * ending last rep K4.
11th row P4, *sl 1, K1, psso, K2, K2 tog, P8, rep from * ending last rep P4.
12th row K4, *P4, K8, rep from * ending last rep K4.
13th row P4, *sl 1, K1, psso, K2 tog, P8, rep from * ending last rep P4.
14th row K4, *P2, K8, rep from * ending last rep K4.
15th row P4, *K2 tog, P8, rep from * ending last rep P4.
16th row K4, *P1, K8, rep from * ending last rep K4.
17th row P3, *K2 tog, P7, rep from * ending last rep P4.
18th row K to end.
These 18 rows form the patt. Work a further 18 rows.
Change to st st. Beg with a K row work a further 4[5:6]cm, ending with a P row.
This point marks 'hipline' — skirt length may be adjusted here.
Next row K2[0:1], *K1, K2 tog, rep from * to last 2[0:1] sts, K2[0:1]. 108 [112:118] sts.
Next row P.
Next row K10[1:4], *K2[3:3], K2 tog, rep from * to last 10[1:4] sts, K10[1:4]. 86[90:96] sts.
Beg with a P row cont in st st until work measures 36[39:41]cm from the beg, ending with a P row. Length to armhole may be adjusted here.
Shape armholes
Cast off 6[8:11] sts at beg of next 2 rows and 2 sts at beg of foll 4 rows. 66 sts.**
Cont in st st until work measures 46 [49:51]cm from the beg, ending with a P row.
Shape shoulders
Cast off 4 sts at beg of next 4 rows and 10 sts at beg of foll 2 rows.
Cast off the rem sts.

Front
Work as given for back to **. Cont in st st until work measures 41[44:46]cm from the beg, ending with a P row.
Shape neck
Next row K22, cast off 22 sts, K to end.

Work right side of neck first.
Next row P to last 2 sts, P2 tog.
Next row K2 tog, K to end.
Rep the last 2 rows once more. 18 sts.
Beg with a P row cont in st st until work matches back to shoulder shaping ending at armhole edge.
Shape shoulder
Cast off 4 sts at beg of the next and foll alt row. Work 1 row. Cast off rem sts.
Return to sts on left side of neck. With WS facing, rejoin yarn to next st.
Next row P2 tog, P to end.
Next row K to last 2 sts, K2 tog.
Rep the last 2 rows once more.
Complete to match first side of neck, reversing shaping.

Sleeves
Using 2¼mm needles cast on 60 sts.
Next row *K1 tbl, P1, rep from *.
Rep the last row until work measures 3cm from the beg.
Change to 3mm needles.
Next row *K twice into next st, rep from * to end. 120 sts.
Beg with a P row, cont in st st until work measures 6cm from beg, ending with a P row. Sleeve length may be adjusted here.
Shape sleeve top
Cast off 8 sts at beg of next 2 rows and 2 sts at beg of foll 4 rows. 96 sts.
Dec 1 st at each end of every row until 48 sts rem. Cast off 6 sts at beg of next 4 rows. Cast off the rem 24 sts.

Detachable collar
Using 3mm needles cast on 18 sts.
Next row (WS) K6, P7, K5.
Commence patt.
1st row Sl 1, K2, yfwd, K2 tog, K2, K2 tog, yfwd, K5, yfwd, K2 tog, (yfwd, K1) twice.
2nd row K6, yfwd, K2 tog, P7, K2, yfwd, K2 tog, K1.
3rd row Sl 1, K2, yfwd, K2 tog, K1, (K2 tog, yfwd) twice, K4, yfwd, K2 tog, (yfwd, K1) twice, K2.
4th row K8, yfwd, K2 tog, P7, K2, yfwd, K2 tog, K1.
5th row Sl 1, K2, yfwd, K2 tog, (K2 tog, yfwd) 3 times, K3, yfwd, K2 tog, (yfwd, K1) twice, K4.
6th row K10, yfwd, K2 tog, P7, K2, yfwd, K2 tog, K1.
7th row Sl 1, K2, yfwd, K2 tog, K1,

(K2 tog, yfwd) twice, K4, yfwd, K2 tog, (yfwd, K1) twice, K6.
8th row Cast off 8 sts, K4 including st used in casting off, yfwd, K2 tog, P7, K2, yfwd, K2 tog, K1.
These 8 rows form the patt.
Rep these 8 rows 14 times more.
* * * Cont in garter st (every row K).
Cast off 4 sts at beg of next 2 rows.
Dec 1 st at each end of the next and every foll alt row until 2 sts rem.
Next row K2 tog and fasten off.
With RS of work facing, K up 10 sts from cast on edge.
Work from * * * to end.

To make up
Join right shoulder seam.

Neckband
With RS of work facing, using 2¼mm needles K up 84 sts evenly around neck edge.
Work in rib as given for back for 1cm, ending with a WS row. Cast off in rib.
Press lightly as instructed on ball band, taking care not to flatten patt. Join side seams, matching patt. Sew together 1cm at armhole edge of left shoulder seam. Join sleeve seams, set in sleeves gathering sleeve head to fit. Sew buttons to front shoulder and make button loops to correspond.
Pin collar to a curve to fit neck edge and press firmly. Either thread ribbon through eyelet holes on collar or make a plaited cord.

Pinafore
Back
Using 2½mm needles cast on 336 sts. Beg with a K row work 5 rows in st st.
Next row * P2 tog, rep from * to end. 168 sts.
Commence patt.
1st row K.
2nd and every alt row P.
3rd row *K6, yfwd, K2 tog, rep from * to end.
5th row K.
7th row K2, *yfwd, K2 tog, K6, rep from * ending last rep K4.
8th row P.
These 8 rows form the patt. Cont in patt until work measures 23cm from the beg, ending with an 8th patt row.

Pinafore length may be adjusted here.
Next row (RS) *K2 tog, rep from * to end. 84 sts.
Next row P. * *
Next row *K1 tbl, P1, rep from * to end.
Rep the last row 5 times more.
Cast off in rib.

Front
Work as given for back to * *.
1st row (K1 tbl, P1) 10 times, K7, (yfwd, K2 tog, K6) 4 times, yfwd, K2 tog, K3 (P1, K1 tbl) 10 times.
2nd row (P1, K1 tbl) 10 times, P44, (K1 tbl, P1) 10 times.
3rd row (K1 tbl, P1) 10 times, K44, (P1, K1 tbl) 10 times.
4th row As 2nd row.
5th row (K1 tbl, P1) 10 times, K3, (yfwd, K2 tog, K6) 5 times, K1 (P1, K1 tbl) 10 times.
6th row As 2nd row.
7th row Cast off 20 sts in rib, K to last 20 sts, (P1, K1 tbl) 10 times.
8th row Cast off 20 sts in rib, P to end. 44 sts.

Cont in patt.

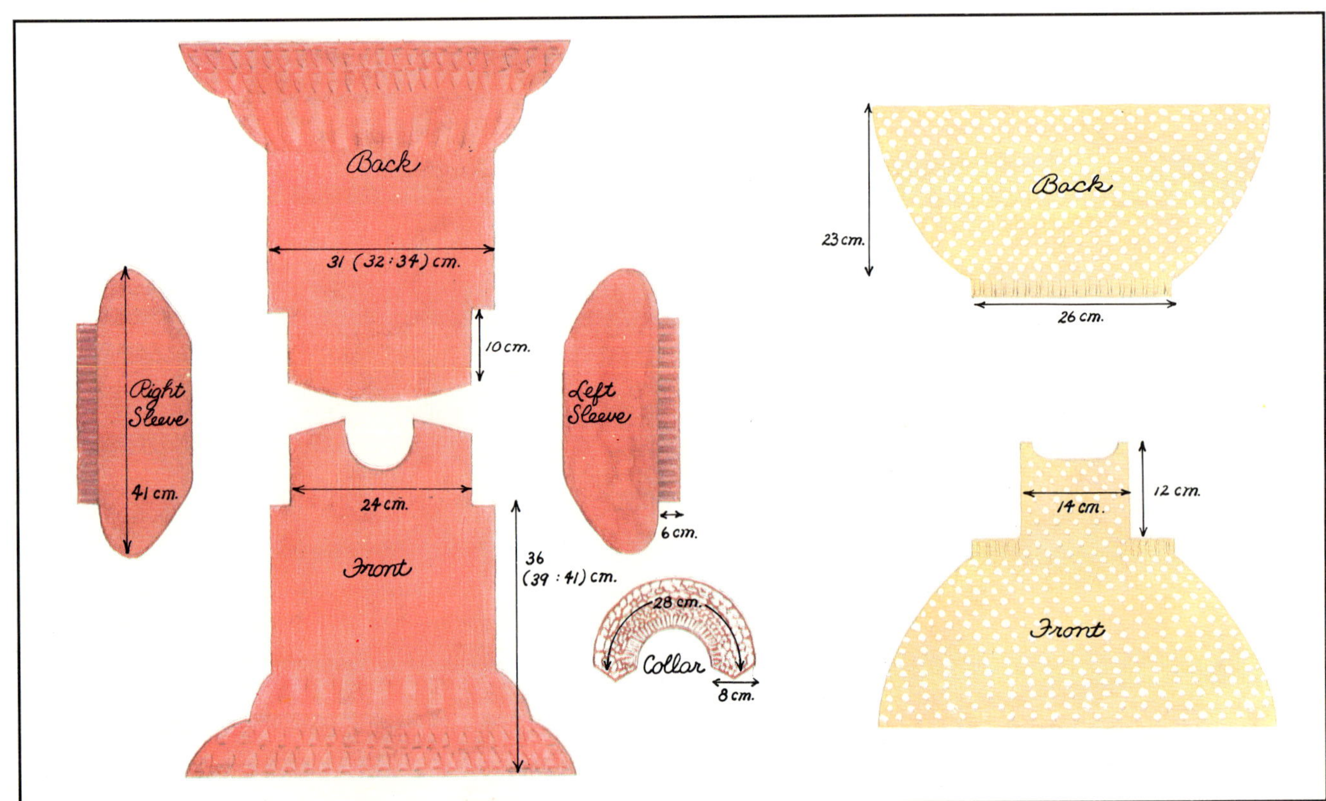

1st row (RS) K1, *K6, yfwd, K2 tog, rep from * to last 3 sts, K3.
2nd and every alt row P.
3rd row K.
5th row K3, yfwd, K2 tog, *K6, yfwd, K2 tog, rep from * to last 7 sts, K7.
7th row K.
8th row P.
These 8 rows form the patt. Rep these 8 rows 4 times more, ending with an 8th patt row. Length of pinafore may be adjusted here.
Shape neck
Next row K8, cast off 28 sts, K to end.
Complete right side of neck first.
Next row P to last 2 sts, P2 tog.
Next row K2 tog, K to end.
Rep the last 2 rows twice. Cast off rem 2 sts.
Return to sts at left side of neck. With WS of work facing, rejoin yarn to next st.
Next row P2 tog, P to end.
Next row K to last 2 sts, K2 tog.
Rep the last 2 rows twice. Cast off rem 2 sts.

Hem edging (make 2 pieces)
The pieces are worked sideways.
Using 2½mm needles cast on 18 sts.

Next row (WS) K6, P7, K5.
Commence patt.
1st row Sl 1, K2, yfwd, K2 tog, K2, K2 tog, yfwd, K5, yfwd, K2 tog, (yfwd, K1) twice.
2nd row K6, yfwd, K2 tog, P7, K2, yfwd, K2 tog, K1.
3rd row Sl 1, K2, yfwd, K2 tog, K1, K2 tog, yfwd) twice, K4, yfwd, K2 tog, (yfwd, K1) twice, K2.
4th row K8, yfwd, K2 tog, P7, K2, yfwd, K2 tog, K1.
5th row Sl 1, K2, yfwd, K2 tog, (K2 tog, yfwd) 3 times, K3, yfwd, K2 tog, (yfwd, K1) twice, K4.
6th row K10, yfwd, K2 tog, P7, K2, yfwd, K2 tog, K1.
7th row Sl 1, K2, yfwd, K2 tog, K1, (K2 tog, yfwd) twice, K4, yfwd, K2 tog, (yfwd, K1) twice, K6.
8th row Cast off 8 sts, K3, yfwd, K2 tog, P7, K2, yfwd, K2 tog, K1.
These 8 rows form the patt.
Repeat rows 1-8 inclusive 41 times more. Cast off.

Yoke edging (make 2 pieces)
Work as given for hem edging for 40cm ending with an 8th patt row. Cast off.

Neckband and straps
Using 2½mm needles cast on 8 sts.
Next row *K1 tbl, P1, rep from * to end.
Rep the last row until work measures 1cm from the beg.
1st buttonhole row Rib 3, cast off 2, rib to end.
2nd buttonhole row Rib, casting on over those sts cast off in previous row.
Cont in rib until work measures 49cm from the beg, ending with a WS row. Length may be adjusted here.
Now work the 2 buttonhole rows again.
Work a further 1cm in rib.
Cast off in rib.

To make up
Press as instructed on ball band. Join hem edging pieces and sew to hem. Sew neckband on to yoke. Sew edging on to yoke and band, gathering slightly.
Cut ribbon into 4, or make 4 simple plaited cords and sew to pinafore at underarms.
Sew buttons on waistband at centre back.

Special technique — making buttonholes

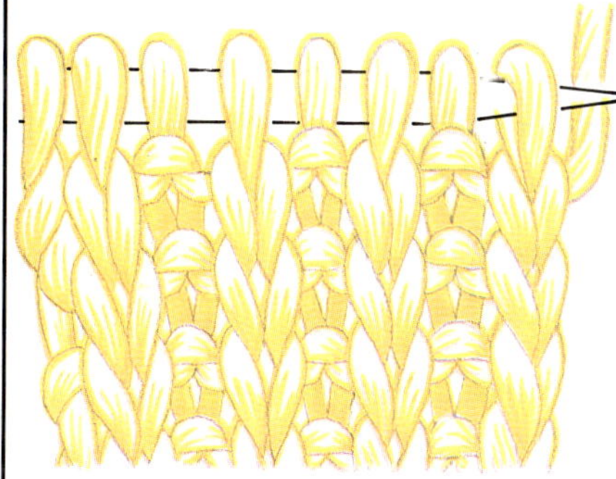

1 The back straps of the pinafore dress are fastened with a small buttonhole on the end of each one, buttoning two buttons on the back waistband. Work in twisted rib to the buttonhole row.

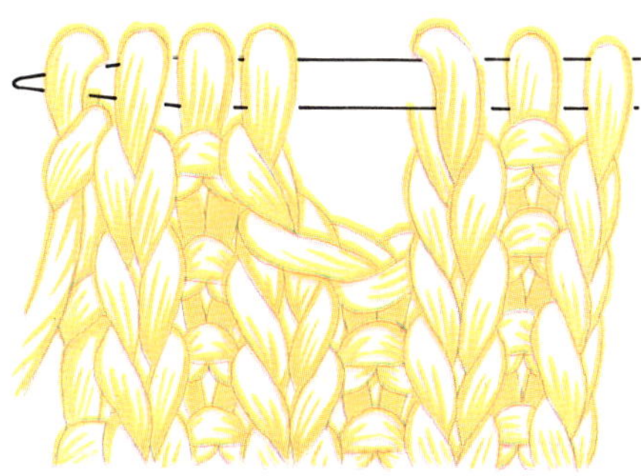

2 On the next row work to the buttonhole position. Cast off 2 stitches (more stitches can be cast off for a larger buttonhole). Work to the next buttonhole position or to end of row.

3 On the next row work to the buttonhole position. Cast on to the right-hand needle the same number of stitches as were cast off on the previous row. Work to the next buttonhole position or to end of row.

Openwork Sweater

This lovely summer sweater is knitted in a cool cotton yarn. Its fresh, crisp look is accentuated by a geometric arrangement of faggot stitch motifs crossed by garter stitch ridges.

Sizes
To fit 82 [86:91:97] cm bust
Length 56 [57:58:60] cm
Sleeve seam 43cm
Note Instructions for larger sizes are in square brackets []; where there is only one set of figures it applies to all sizes.

Tension
22 sts and 30 rows to 10cm over st st on 4mm needles

Materials
725 [775:775:825] g double knitting yarn
1 pair each 3¼mm and 4mm knitting needles

Back
Using 3¼mm needles, cast on 86 [94:98:106] sts. Work in K2, P2, rib as foll.
1st row (RS) *K2, P2, rep from * to last 2 sts, K2.
2nd row *P2, K2, rep from * to last 2 sts, P2.
Rep the last 2 rows for 6cm, ending with a WS row.
Next row Rib 8 [9:13:10], pick up loop between needles and work into the back of it — called M1—, (rib 14 [15:24:17], M1) 5 [5:3:5] times, rib 8 [10:13:11]. 92 [100:102:112] sts.
Change to 4mm needles and commence patt.
1st row (WS) P.
2nd row P.
3rd row K.
4th row K2 [2:3:0], *K1, (yfwd, K2 tog tbl) 3 times, K1, rep from * to last 2 [2:3:0] sts, K2 [2:3:0].
5th, 7th, 9th and 11th rows P.
6th row K2 [2:3:0], *K2, (yfwd, K2 tog tbl) twice, K2, rep from * to last 2 [2:3:0] sts, K2 [2:3:0].
8th row K2 [2:3:0], *K3, yfwd, K2 tog tbl, K3, rep from * to last 2 [2:3:0] sts, K2 [2:3:0].
10th row As 6th row.
12th row As 4th row.

Rep the last 12 rows working K2 tog, yfwd instead of yfwd, K2 tog tbl.
The last 24 rows form the patt. Cont in patt until work measures 37 [37:38:38] cm from beg, ending with a WS row.
Shape armholes
Cast off 11 sts at beg of next 2 rows. 70 [78:80:90] sts.
Cont without shaping until work measures 56 [57:58:60] cm from beg, ending with a WS row.
Shape shoulders
Cast off 7 [7:7:9] sts at beg of next 2 rows and 6 [8:8:9] sts at beg of foll 4 rows. Leave rem 32 [32:34:36] sts on a spare needle.

Front
Work as given for back until work measures 36 [40:42:46] rows less than back to shoulder shaping, ending with a WS row.
Divide for neck
Next row Patt 19 [23:23:27], turn,

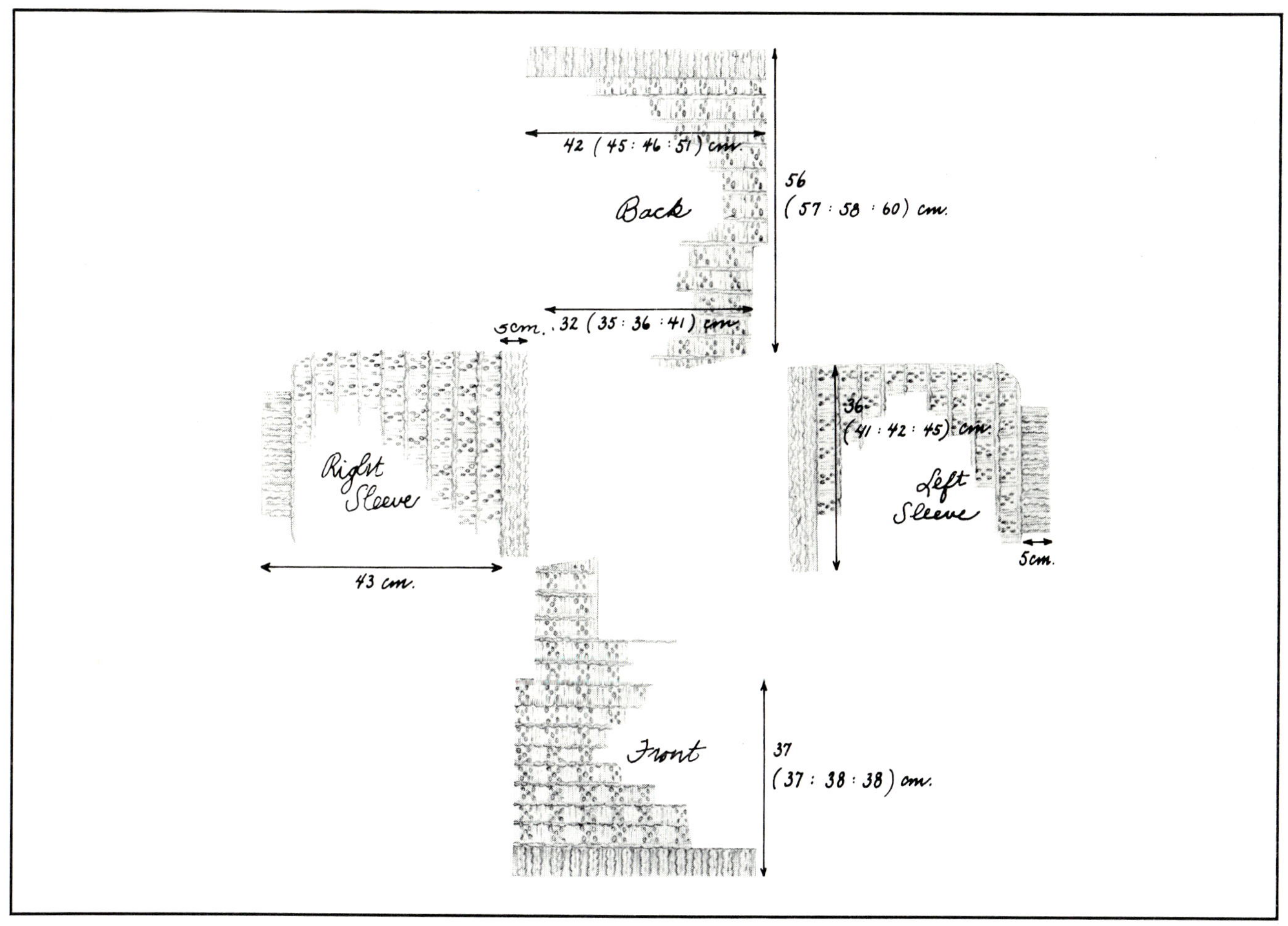

leaving rem sts on a spare needle.
Complete left side of neck first.
Cont without shaping until work
matches back to shoulder shaping,
ending at armhole edge.

Shape shoulder

Cast off 7 [7:7:9] sts at beg of next
row and 6 [8:8:9] sts at beg of foll alt
row.

Patt 1 row. Cast off rem 6 [8:8:9]
sts.

With RS of work facing, return to sts
on spare needle, sl centre 32
[32:34:36] sts on to a stitch holder,
rejoin yarn to next st, patt to end.
Complete to match first side of neck
reversing shaping.

Sleeves

Using 3¼mm needles, cast on 38
[42:42:46] sts and work in K2, P2 rib
as given for back, for 5cm, ending with
a WS row.

Next row (Work 3 times into next st)
2 [3:4:4] times, *work twice into next
st, rep from * to last 2 [3:4:4] sts,
(work 3 times into next st) 2 [3:4:4]
times. 80 [90:92:100] sts.
Change to 4mm needles and
commence patt.

1st row (WS) P.
2nd row P.
3rd row K.
4th row K0 [1:2:2] *K1, (yfwd, K2
tog tbl) 3 times, K1, rep from * to last
0 [1:2:2] sts, K0 [1:2:2].
5th, 7th 9th and 11th rows P.
6th row K0 [1:2:2], *K2, (yfwd, K2
tog tbl) twice, K2, rep from * to last 0
[1:2:2] sts, K0 [1:2:2].
8th row K0 [1:2:2], *K3, yfwd, K2
tog tbl, K3, rep from * to last 0
[1:2:2] sts, K0 [1:2:2].
10th row As 6th row.
12th row As 4th row.
Rep the last 12 rows working K2 tog,
yfwd instead of yfwd, K2 tog tbl.
The last 24 rows form the patt. Cont
in patt until work measures approx
43cm from beg, ending with a 12th
patt row.
Change to 3¼mm needles and cont
in garter st (every row K) for 5cm,
ending with a RS row.
Cast off loosely.

To make up

Darn in yarn ends neatly.
Omitting garter st borders, press
lightly on WS using a warm iron over
a damp cloth.
Using a back-stitch seam join right
shoulder seam.

Neck border

With RS of work facing, using 3¼mm
needles, K up 20 [21:21:22] sts
down left side of neck, K up 1 st from
corner (mark this st with a coloured
thread), K across the 32 [32:34:36]
sts from front neck, K up 1 st from
corner (mark this st with a coloured
thread), K up 20 [21:21:22] sts up
right side of neck, K across 32
[32:34:36] sts from back neck. 106
[108:112:118] sts.
Next row (K to within 2sts of
coloured thread, K2 tog, K1, K2 tog)
twice, K to end.
Next row K.
Rep the last 2 rows until 90
[92:96:102] sts rem, ending with a
RS row.
Cast off loosely, dec on this row as
before.
Join left shoulder and neck border.
Place centre of cast-off edge of sleeve
to shoulder seam and set in sleeve,
joining garter st section of sleeve to
cast-off sts at underarm. Join side and
sleeve seams.

Special technique — garter-stitch mitred corners

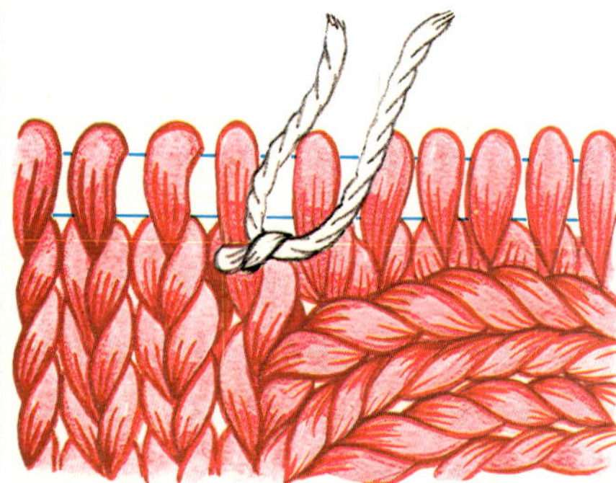

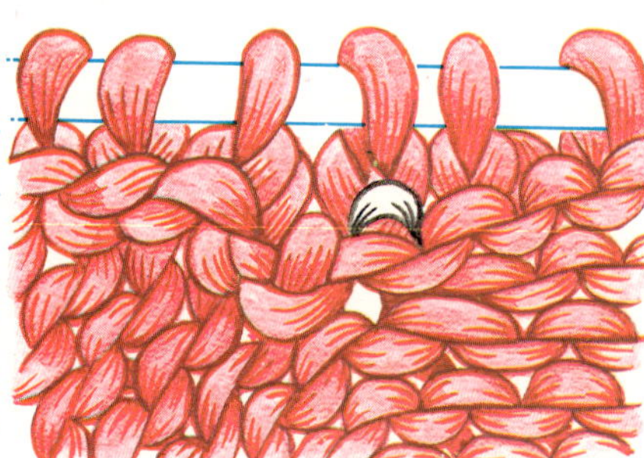

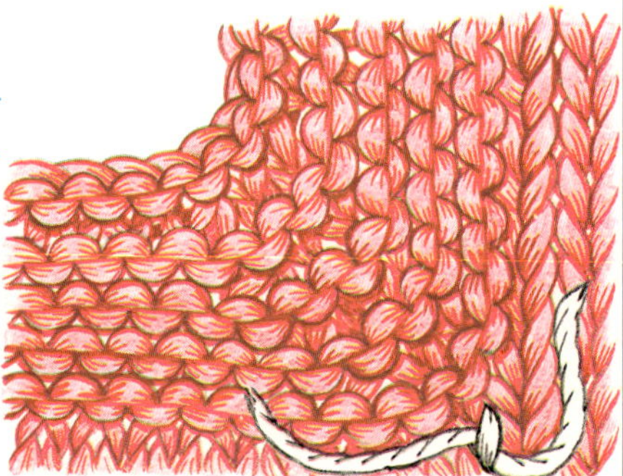

1 *The corners of the square
neckband on the sweater are
mitred. Knit up the stitches around
the neck edge as instructed in the
pattern, marking the corner stitch with
a coloured thread.*

2 *On the next row knit to within
two stitches of the corner stitch,
then knit two together, knit one, knit
two together. Work the next corner
stitch in the same way.*

3 *Knit the next row. Repeat the last
two rows until the neckband is
the required depth. Cast off loosely,
decreasing at the corners as before.*

Mohair Shawl

This long, luxurious shawl will add a sparkle to any party.
Wrap it loosely around your neck and shoulders, leaving the
pompons to hang freely and you will see how naturally the
folds of the shawl will fall.

Shawl
216cm from end to end

Tension
8 sts and 7 rows to 10cm
over mesh patt.

Materials
275g mohair with glitter in main colour
(A)
25g in 3 contrast colours (for
pompons)
1 pair 10mm knitting needles
Artificial flowers (for decoration)

Shawl
Using 10mm needles and A, cast on
3 sts.
Next row K.
Next row K.
Cont in garter st (every row K),
inc 1 st at beg of next and every
alt row until there are 12 sts.
Next row K.
1st row K into front and back of
first st — called inc 1 — , K4, yfwd,
K2 tog, K5.
2nd row K5, P to last 5 sts, K5.
3rd row Inc 1, K4, yfwd, K2 tog, K6.
**4th, 6th, 8th, 10th, 12th and 14th
rows** As 2nd row.
5th row Inc 1, K4, (yfwd, K2 tog)
twice, K5.
7th row Inc 1, K4, (yfwd, K2 tog)
twice, K6.
9th row Inc 1, K4, (yfwd, K2 tog)
3 times, K5.
11th row Inc 1, K4, *yfwd, K2 tog,
rep from * to last 6 sts, K6.
13th row Inc 1, K4 * yfwd, K2 tog,
rep from * to last 5 sts, K5.
Rep 11th-14th rows until 79 sts on
needle.
Next row K2 tog, K4, * yfwd, K2 tog,
rep from * to last 5 sts, K5.
Next row As 2nd row.
Next row K2 tog, K4 * yfwd, K2 tog,
rep from * to last 6 sts, K6.
Next row As 2nd row.
Rep last 4 rows until 13 sts on needle.

Next row K2 tog, K4, yfwd, K2 tog,
K5.
Next row K5, P2, K5.
Cont in g st, dec 1 st at beg of next
and every alt row until 3 sts rem.
K1 row. Cast off.

To make up
Make six pompons in a variety of
colours. Attach them to the corners of
the shawl with plaited cords of varying
lengths. Wind artificial flowers into
the pompons.

Bobble Lace Sweater

An openwork chevron stitch pattern dotted with tiny bobbles
creates a delightfully pretty top in a light cool cotton yarn.
It can be knitted with long or short sleeves.

Sizes
To fit 86[91]cm bust
Length 54[55]cm
Short sleeve seam 15cm
Long sleeve seam 44cm

Tension
28 sts and 32 rows to 10cm over patt on 3¼mm needles

Materials
Short sleeve version
400g four-ply yarn (or No 5 cotton)
Long sleeve version
450g four-ply yarn (or No 5 cotton)
1 pair each 2¾mm and 3¼mm knitting needles
1 2.50mm crochet hook
2 small buttons

Back
Using 2¾mm needles cast on 100[120] sts, working into the back of every st for a firm edge.
Work 33 rows K2, P2 rib.
Next row Rib 10, *work into the front and back of next st, rib 3[4], rep from * to last 10 sts, work into the front and back of next st, rib to end. 121[141]sts.

Change to 3¼mm needles and patt.
1st row K1, *yfwd, sl 1, K1, psso, K15, K2 tog, yfwd, K1, rep from * to end.
2nd row P2, *yrn, P2 tog, P13, P2 tog tbl, yrn, P3, rep from * to last 19 sts, yrn, P2 tog, P13, P2 tog, yrn, P2.
3rd row K3, *yfwd, sl 1, K1, psso, K11, K2 tog, yfwd, K5, rep from * to last 18 sts, yfwd, sl 1, K1, psso, K11, K2 tog, yfwd, K3.
4th row P4, *yrn, P2 tog, P9, P2 tog tbl, yrn, P7, rep from * to last 17 sts, yrn, P2 tog, P9, P2 tog, yrn, P4.
5th row K5, *yfwd, sl 1, K1, psso, K3, (K1, P1, K1, P1, K1) all into next st, turn, K5, turn, cast off 4 — called make bobble (MB), K3, K2 tog, yfwd, K9, rep from * to last 16 sts, yfwd, sl 1, K1, psso, K3, MB, K3, K2 tog, yfwd, K5.
6th row P6, *yrn, P2 tog, P5, P2 tog tbl, yrn, P11, rep from * to last 15 sts, yrn, P2 tog, P5, P2 tog, yrn, P6.
7th row K7, *yfwd, sl 1, K1, psso, K3, K2 tog, yfwd, K6, MB, K6, rep from * to last 14 sts, yfwd, sl 1, K1, psso, K3, K2 tog, yfwd, K7.
8th row P8, *yrn, P2 tog, P1, P2 tog tbl, yrn, P15, rep from * to last 13 sts, yrn, P2 tog, P1, P2 tog, yrn, P8.
9th row K9, *yfwd, sl 1, K2 tog, psso, yfwd, K17, rep from * to last 12 sts, yfwd, sl 1, K2 tog, psso, yfwd, K9.
10th row P to end.
These 10 rows form the patt. Cont in patt until work measures 35cm from the beg, ending with a WS row.
Shape armholes
Keeping patt correct cast off 6[8] sts at beg of the next 2 rows and 5 sts at beg of foll 2[4] rows. 99[105] sts.**
Cont without shaping until work measures 19[20]cm from beg of armhole shaping, ending with a WS row.
Shape shoulders
Cast off 10[11] sts at beg of next 6 rows.
Cast off rem 39 sts.

Front
Work as given for back to **
Cont without shaping until work measures 10[11]cm from beg of armhole shaping, ending with a WS row.

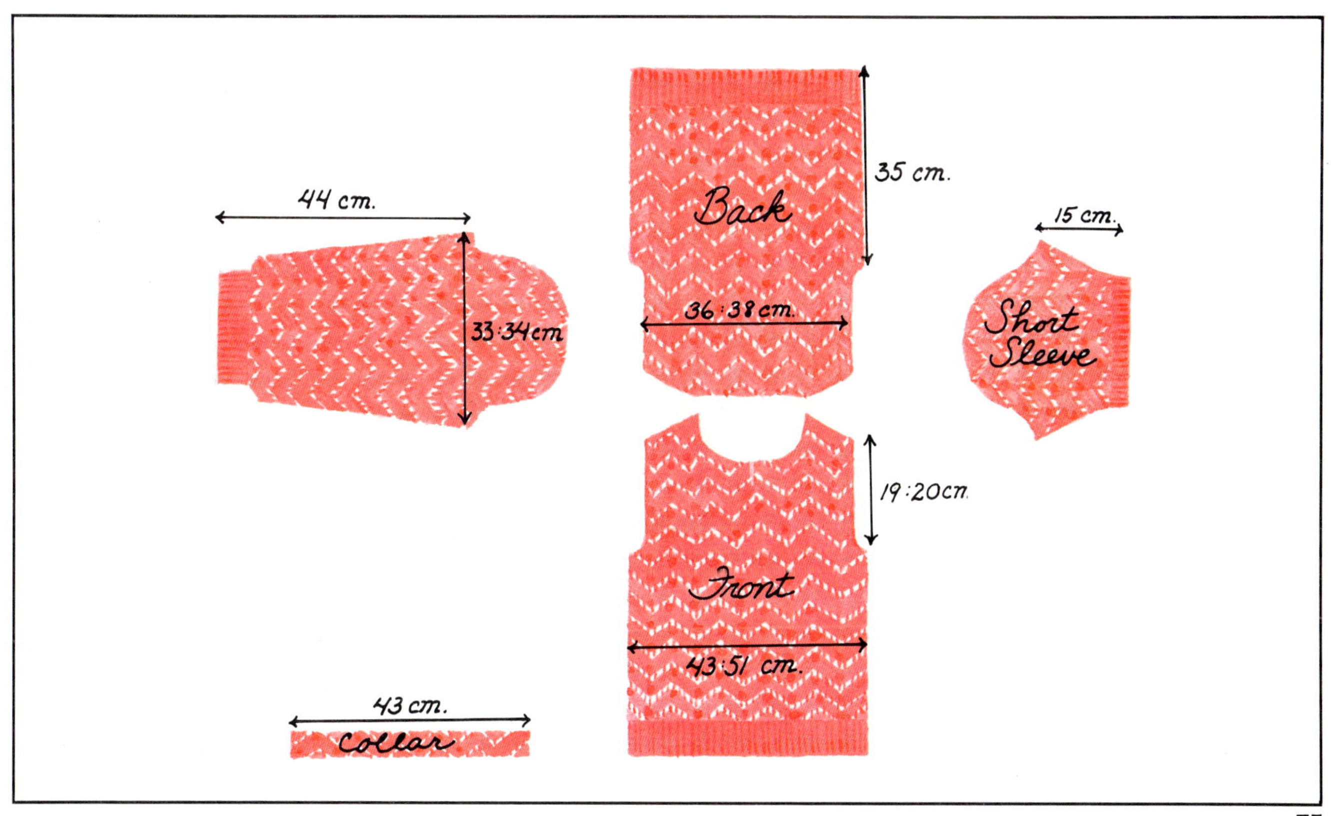

Divide for neck
Next row Patt 49[52], turn and leave rem sts on a spare needle. Complete left side of neck first. Cont without shaping until work measures 14[15]cm from the beg of armhole shaping, ending at neck edge.
Cast off 5 sts at beg of next and foll alt row.
Dec 1 st at neck edge on every row until 30[33] sts rem. Cont without shaping until work matches back exactly to beg of shoulder shaping, ending with a WS row.
Shape shoulder
Cast off 10[11] sts at beg of next and foll alt row.
Work 1 row. Cast off.
Return to sts on spare needle. With RS facing, join yarn to next st, cast off 1 st and patt to end.
Complete to match first side, reversing shaping.

Short sleeves
Using 2¾mm needles cast on 80 sts.

Work 10 rows K2, P2 rib, inc 1 st at end of last row. 81 sts.
Change to 3¼mm needles and patt as given for back, inc and work into st st 1 st at each end of the 3rd and every foll 4th row until there are 91[95] sts. Cont without shaping until work measures 15cm from beg, ending with a WS row.
Shape top
Cast off 2 sts at beg of every row until 21 sts rem.
Cast off.

Long sleeves
Using 2¾mm needles cast on 64 sts. Work 31 rows K2, P2 rib.
Next row Rib 8, *work into front and back of next st, rib 2, rep from * to last 8 sts, work into front and back of next st, rib to end. 81 sts.
Change to 3¼mm needles and patt as given on back, inc and work into st st 1 st at each end of every following 10th row until there are 91[95] sts. Cont without shaping until work measures 44cm from the beg, ending with a WS row.

Shape top
Cast off 2 sts at beg of every row until 21 sts rem. Cast off.

Collar
Using 3¼mm needles cast on 121 sts.
Cont in patt as given for back until work measures 5cm from beg, ending with a WS row. Cast off.

To make up
Do not press. Darn in yarn ends neatly. Join shoulder seams. Set in sleeves. Join side and sleeve seams. Slipstitch the cast-on edge of collar to neck edge.

Collar edging
Join yarn to collar at neck edge. Using a crochet hook, work edging as follows: * 1dc in next st, miss text st, 3tr in next st, miss next st, rep from * around collar, then work 1 row of dc around neck opening. Ss in each dc down first side of opening, then work two 2-ch button loops on other side of opening. Sew buttons in position on front opening.

Special technique — working the bobble

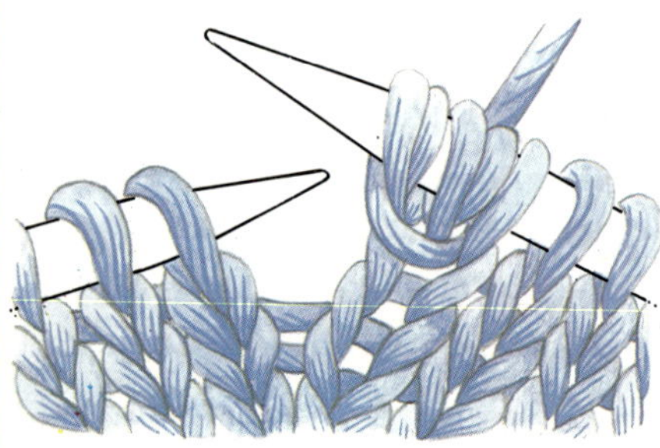

1 All bobbles are made by increasing several times into one stitch. In this case knit, purl, knit, purl, then knit again all into one stitch, making five stitches out of one.

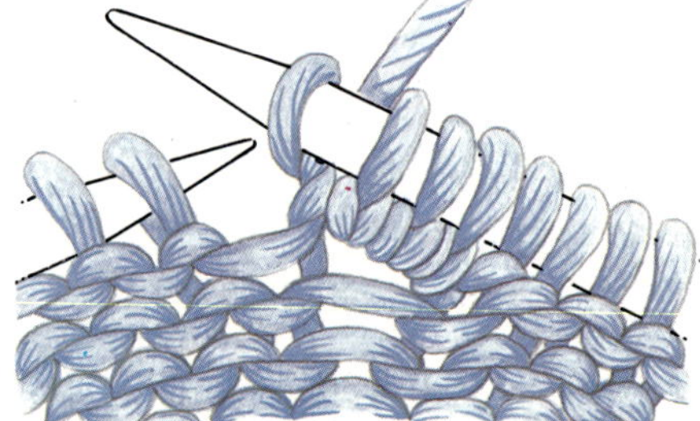

2 Turn the work and hold the RH needle in the left hand and the LH needle in the right hand. Knit the five stitches made from one stitch.

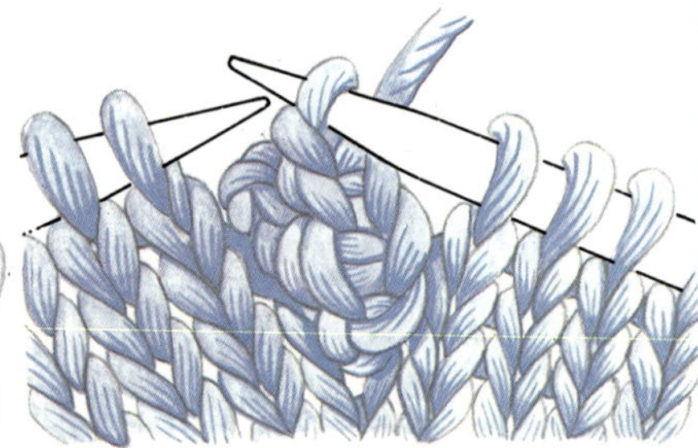

3 Turn the work again. Cast off four of the five stitches. The bobble is now complete. Carry on working in pattern to the next bobble.

Striped Lace Top

This pretty pastel-striped sweater, perfect for summer, can be
worn on or off the shoulder, and it is made in a
marvellously practical thick cotton yarn. The lacy pattern
looks impressive but is very easy to work.

Sizes
To fit 87[91:97]cm bust
Length 55[56:56]cm
Note Instructions for larger sizes are in
square brackets []; where there is only
one set of figures it applies to all three
sizes.

Tension
20 sts and 28 rows to 10cm over st st
on 4mm needles

Materials
350 [450:550] g double knitting
yarn in main colour (A)
125 [225:225] g double knitting
yarn in contrast colour (B)
225 [225:325] in contrast colour
(C)
225 [325:325] in contrast colour
(D)
1 pair each 3¼mm and 4mm knitting
needles
1 each 3¼mm and 4mm circular
needles.

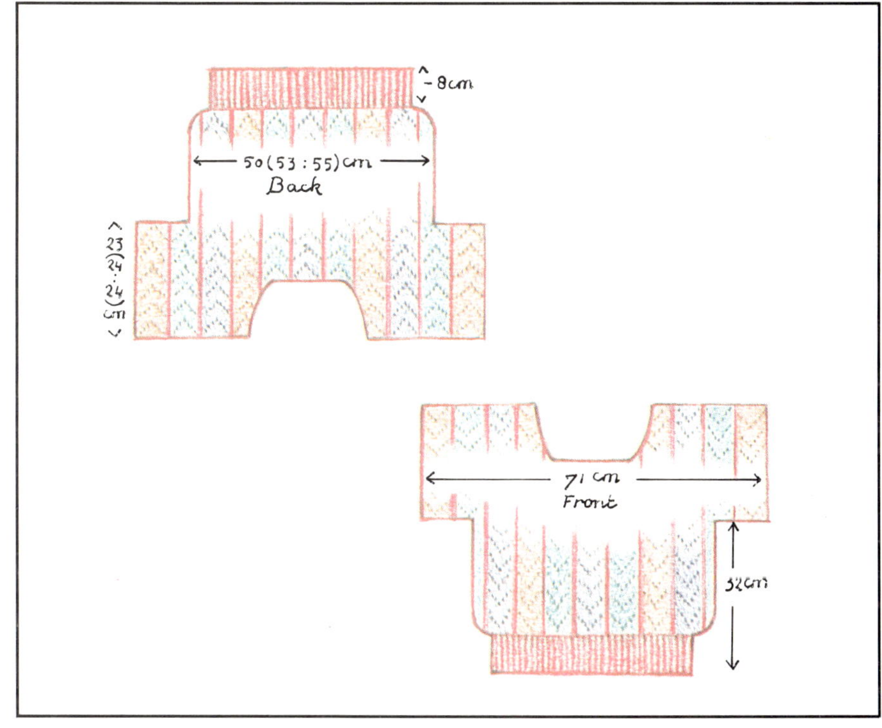

Back and front (alike)
Using 3¼mm needles and A, cast on
96[102:106] sts.
Work 8cm K1, P1 rib.
Next row Rib 9[12:14], *work twice
into next st, rib 18, rep from * ending
last rep rib 10[13:15]. 101[107:111]
sts.
Change to 4mm needles and
commence patt. Use small separate
balls of yarn for each colour section,
twist yarns when changing colour to
avoid a hole.
1st row (RS) K4[7:9]C, K2A, *with
B, K5, yfwd, sl 1, K1, psso, K4,
K2A*, rep from * to * using D
instead of B, rep from * to * using C
instead of B, rep from * to *, rep
from * to * using C instead of B, rep
from * to * using D instead of B, rep
from * to *, K4[7:9]C.
2nd and every foll alt row K1, P to
last st, K1 keeping sections of colour
as set.
3rd row K4[7:9]C, K2A, *with B,
K3, K2 tog, yfwd, K1, yfwd, sl 1, K1,
psso, K3, K2A*, rep from * to *
using D instead of B, rep from * to *
using C instead of B, rep from * to *,
rep from * to * using C instead of B,
rep from * to * using D instead of B,
rep from * to *, K4[7:9]C.
5th row K4[7:9]C, K2A, *with B,
K2, K2 tog, yfwd, K3, yfwd, sl 1, K1,
psso, K2, K2A*, rep from * to *
using D instead of B, rep from * to *
using C instead of B, rep from * to *,
rep from * to * using C instead of B,
rep from * to * using D instead of B,
rep from * to *, K4[7:9]C.
7th row K4[7:9]C, K2A, *with B,
K1, K2 tog, yfwd, K5, yfwd, sl 1, K1,
psso, K1, K2A*, rep from * to *
using D instead of B, rep from * to *
using C instead of B, rep from * to *,
rep from * to * using C instead of B,
rep from * to * using D instead of B,
rep from * to *, K4[7:9]C.
8th row As 2nd row.
These 8 rows form the patt. Cont in
patt until work measures about 32cm

from cast-on edge, ending with a 4th patt row.
Shape sleeves
Next row Cast on 21[18:16] sts, work across these sts as foll:
K1D, using D instead of B, work as given for 5th row from * to *, using C instead of B work as given for 5th row from * to *, patt to end.
Next row Cast on 21[18:16] sts, work across these sts as foll:
K1D, P11D, P2A, P11C, patt to end. 143 sts.
Keeping patt correct, cont without shaping until work measures 12cm from beg of sleeve shaping, ending with a WS row.
Shape neck
Next row Patt 56, turn, leaving rem sts on a spare needle.
Complete left side of neck first.

Keeping patt correct, dec 1 st at neck edge on foll 10 rows. 46 sts.
Cont without shaping until work measures 23[24:24]cm from beg of sleeve shaping, ending with a WS row.
Cast off.
Return to sts on spare needle. Sl centre 31 sts on to a st holder, join in appropriate yarn to next st, patt to end.
Complete to match first side of neck.

To make up
Join shoulder seams.
Collar
With RS of work facing, using 3¼mm circular needle and A, K up 30[32:32] sts down left side of front neck, K31 sts from front neck, K up 30[32:32] sts up right side of front

neck, 30[32:32] sts down right back neck, K31 from centre back neck, and K up 30[32:32] sts up left back neck. 182[190:190] sts. Work in rounds of K1, P1 rib for 8cm.
Change to 4mm circular needle and cont in rounds of rib until work measures 15cm from beg.
Cast off loosely in rib.
Sleeve edgings
Using 3¼mm needles and A, with RS of work facing, K up 128[132:136] sts evenly around sleeve edge.
Next row *K2 tog, P2 tog, rep from * to end. 64[66:68] sts.
Work 6 rows K1, P1 rib.
Cast off loosely in rib.
Join side and underarm seams (see Special Technique).
Roll collar on to RS.

Special technique — edge-to-edge seam selvedge

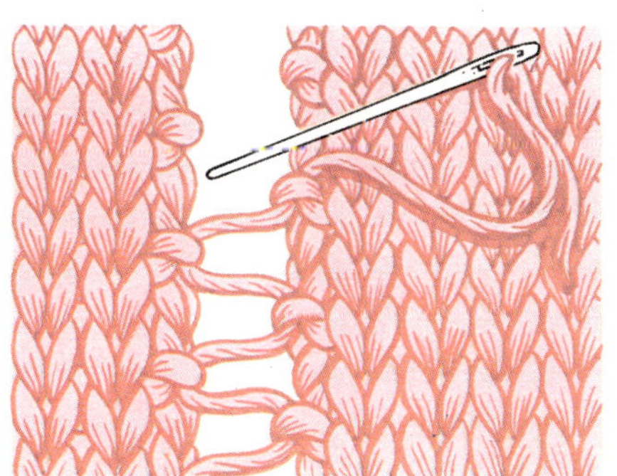

1 *Thick yarns like the double knitting cotton used for the basic sweater can produce bulky seams. These can be avoided by working an edge-to-edge seam. This requires a special selvedge to be knitted in as the work progresses. Knit the first and last stitches on both right-side and wrong-side rows thus producing a line of 'pips' on both edges.*

2 *When the time comes to make up the garment place the edges of the pieces to be joined facing each other matching row to row. Thread a needle with matching yarn and secure it at one side of the bottom of the seam. Insert the needle up through the pip immediately above, then up through the pip opposite. Continue lacing the thread from side to side.*

3 *Pull the thread to tighten and close up the seam as you work. Fasten it off securely when the seam is complete. This seam, which is almost invisible, can be worked with either the right or wrong side of the work facing.*

Fine Lace Collar

Introduce a little old-fashioned elegance into your life with this exquisite lace collar. It transforms the plainest dress into something special.

Size
Collar depth 18cm after stretching

Tension
40 sts and 64 rows to 10cm over garter st on 2¼mm needles

Materials
25g No 60 cotton
1 pair 2¼mm knitting needles
1 small button

To make
Using 2¼mm needles, cast on 39 sts.
Next 2 rows P.
Commence patt.
1st row (RS) P20, K4, (yrn, P2 tog) twice, K4, yfwd, sl 1, K1, psso, (yrn, P2 tog) twice, K1.
2nd row K1, (yrn, P2 tog) 3 times, K4, (yrn, P2 tog) twice, K4, P20.
3rd row P4, (yrn, K2 tog) 8 times, K4, (yrn, P2 tog) twice, K3, K2 tog, yfwd, K1, (yrn, P2 tog) twice, yrn, (P1, K1) into last st.
4th row K1, yfwd, K2, (yrn, P2 tog) twice, K2, yrn, P2 tog, K2, (yrn, P2 tog) twice, K4, P20.
5th row P4, (yon, K2 tog) 8 times, K4, (yrn, P2 tog) twice, K1, K2 tog, yfwd, K3, (yrn, P2 tog) twice, yrn, K3, (P1, K1) into last st, turn, K1, yfwd, K2, yrn, P2 tog, turn, yrn, P2 tog, yon, K3, (P1, K1) into last st.
6th row Cast off 5 sts, yrn, P2 tog, K1, (yrn, P2 tog) twice, K4, (yrn, P2 tog) 3 times, K4, P20.
7th row P4, (yon, K2 tog) 8 times, K4, (yrn, P2 tog) twice, yon, sl 1, K1, psso, K4, (yrn, P2 tog) twice, (P1, K1) into next st, yrn, P2 tog, yrn, (P1, K1) into last st, make picot edge as folls, turn, K3, yrn, P2 tog, turn, yrn, P2 tog, yon, K2, yrn, (P1, K1) into last st, — called make picot.
8th row Cast off 5 sts, yrn, P2 tog, yon, K2, (yrn, P2 tog) twice, K3, P2 tog tbl, yrn, K1, (yrn, P2 tog) twice, K4, P20.
9th row P4, (yon, K2 tog) 8 times, K4, (yrn, P2 tog) twice, K2, yfwd, sl 1, K1, psso, K2, (yrn, P2 tog) twice, K2, (P1, K1) into next st, yrn, P2 tog, yrn, (P1, K1) into last st, make picot.
10th row Cast off 5 sts, yrn, P2 tog, yrn, K4, (yrn, P2 tog) twice, K1, P2 tog tbl, yon, K3, (yrn, P2 tog) twice, K4, P20.
11th row P4, (yon, K2 tog) 8 times, K4, (yrn, P2 tog) twice, K4, yfwd, sl 1, K1, psso, (yrn, P2 tog) twice, K4, (P1, K1) into next st, yrn, P2 tog, yrn, (P1, K1) into last st, make picot.
12th row Cast off 5 sts, yrn, P2 tog, yrn, K6, (yrn, P2 tog) 3 times, K4, (yrn, P2 tog) twice, K4, P20.
13th row P4, (yon, K2 tog) 8 times, K4, (yrn, P2 tog) twice, K3, K2 tog, yfwd, K1, (yrn, P2 tog) twice, K6, (P1, K1) into next st, yrn, P2 tog, yrn, (P1, K1) into last st, make picot.
14th row Cast off 5 sts, yrn, P2 tog, yrn, K8, (yrn, P2 tog) twice, K2, yrn, P2 tog, K2, (yrn, P2 tog) twice, K4, P20.
15th row P4, (yon, K2 tog) 8 times, K4, (yrn, P2 tog) twice, K1, K2 tog, yfwd, K3, (yrn, P2 tog) twice, K8, (P1, K1) into next st, yrn, P2 tog, yrn, (P1, K1) into last st, make picot.
16th row Cast off 5 sts, yrn, P2 tog, yrn, P3 tog, K7, (yrn, P2 tog) twice, K4, (yrn, P2 tog) 3 times, K4, P20.
17th row P4, (yrn, K2 tog) 8 times, K4, (yrn, P2 tog) twice, yon, sl 1, K1, psso, K4, (yrn, P2 tog) twice, K6, K2 tog, K1, yrn, P2 tog, yrn, (P1, K1) into last st, make picot.
18th row Cast off 5 sts, yrn, P2 tog, yrn, P3 tog, K5, (yrn, P2 tog) twice, K3, P2 tog tbl, yrn, K1, (yrn, P2 tog) twice, K4, P20.
19th row P4, (yon, K2 tog) 8 times, K4, (yrn, P2 tog) twice, K2, yfwd, sl 1, K1, psso, K2, (yrn, P2 tog) twice, K4, K2 tog, K1, yrn, P2 tog, yrn, (P1, K1) into last st, make picot.
20th row Cast off 5 sts, yrn, P2 tog, yrn, P3 tog, K3, (yrn, P2 tog) twice, K1, P2 tog tbl, yrn, K3, (yrn, P2 tog) twice, K4, P20.
21st row P4, (yrn, K2 tog) 8 times, K4, (yrn, P2 tog) twice, K4, yfwd, sl 1, K1, psso, (yrn, P2 tog) twice, K2, K2 tog, K1, yrn, P2 tog, yrn, (P1, K1) into last st, make picot.
22nd row Cast off 5, yrn, P2 tog, yrn, P3 tog, K1, (yrn, P2 tog) 3 times, K4, (yrn, P2 tog) twice, K4, P20.
23rd row P4, (yon, K2 tog) 8 times, K4, (yrn, P2 tog) twice, K3, K2 tog, yfwd, K1, (yrn, P2 tog) twice, K2 tog, K1, yrn, P2 tog, yrn, (P1, K1) into last st, make picot.
24th row Cast off 5, yrn, P2 tog twice, (yrn, P2 tog) twice, K2, yrn, P2 tog, K2, (yrn, P2 tog) twice, K4, P20.
25th row P4, (yon, K2 tog) 8 times, K4, (yrn, P2 tog) twice, K1, K2 tog, yfwd, K3, (yrn, P2 tog) twice, sl 1, K2 tog, psso, K1.
26th row K2 tog, (yrn, P2 tog) twice, K4, (yrn, P2 tog) 3 times, K4, P20.
27th row P4, (yon, K2 tog) 8 times, K4, (yrn, P2 tog) twice, yon, sl 1, K1, psso, K4, (yrn, P2 tog) twice, K1.
28th row K1, (yrn, P2 tog) twice, K3, P2 tog tbl, yon, K1, (yrn, P2 tog) twice, K4, P20.
29th row P4, (yon, K2 tog) 8 times, K4, (yrn, P2 tog) twice, K2, yfwd, sl 1, K1, psso, K2, (yrn, P2 tog) twice, K1.
30th row K1, (yrn, P2 tog) twice, K1, P2 tog tbl, yon, K3, (yrn, P2 tog) twice, K4, P20.
31st row P4, (yrn, K2 tog) 8 times, K4, (yrn, P2 tog) twice, K4, yfwd, sl 1, K1, psso, (yrn, P2 tog) twice, K1.
32nd row K1, (yrn, P2 tog) 3 times, K4, (yrn, P2 tog) twice, K4, turn, K4, (yrn, P2 tog) twice, K3, K2 tog, yrn, K1, (yrn, P2 tog) twice, yrn, (P1, K1) into last st.
33rd row K1, yfwd, K2, (yrn, P2 tog) twice, K2, yrn, P2 tog, K2, (yrn, P2 tog) twice, K4, P1, turn, P1, K4, (yrn, P2 tog) twice, K1, K2 tog, yfwd, K3, (yrn, P2 tog) twice, yon, K3, (P1, K1) into last st, turn, K1, yfwd, K2, yrn, P2 tog, turn, yrn, P2 tog, yon, K3, (P1, K1) into last st.
34th row Cast off 5 sts, yrn, P2 tog,

K1, (yrn, P2 tog) twice, K4, (yrn, P2 tog) 3 times, K4, P2, turn, P2, K4, (yrn, P2 tog) twice, yon, sl 1, K1, psso, K4, (yrn, P2 tog) twice, (P1, K1) into next st, yrn, P2 tog, yrn, (P1, K1) into last st, make picot.

35th row Cast off 5 sts, yrn, P2 tog, yon, K2, (yrn, P2 tog) twice, K3, P2 tog tbl, yon, K1, (yrn, P2 tog) twice, K4, P3, turn, P3, K4, (yrn, P2 tog) twice, K2, yfwd, sl 1, K1, psso, K2, (yrn, P2 tog) twice, K2, (P1, K1) into next st, yrn, P2 tog, yrn, (P1, K1) into last st, make picot.

36th row Cast off 5 sts, yrn, P2 tog, yon, K4, (yrn, P2 tog) twice, K1, P2 tog tbl, yon, K3, (yrn, P2 tog) twice, K4, P4, turn, P4, K4, (yrn, P2 tog) twice, K4, yfwd, sl 1, K1, psso, (yrn, P2 tog) twice, K4, (P1, K1) into next st, yrn, P2 tog, yrn, (P1, K1) into last st, make picot.

37th row Cast off 5 sts, yrn, P2 tog, yrn, K6, (yrn, P2 tog) 3 times, K4, (yrn, P2 tog) twice, K4, P5, turn, P5,

K4, (yrn, P2 tog) twice, K3, K2 tog, yfwd, K1, (yrn, P2 tog) twice, K6, (P1, K1) into next st, yrn, P2 tog, yrn, (P1, K1) into last st, make picot.

38th row Cast off 5 sts, yrn, P2 tog, yrn, K8, (yrn, P2 tog) twice, K2, yrn, P2 tog, K2, (yrn, P2 tog) twice, K4, P6, turn, P6, K4, (yrn, P2 tog) twice, K1, K2 tog, yfwd, K3, (yrn, P2 tog) twice, K8, (P1, K1) into next st, yrn, P2 tog, yrn, (P1, K1) into last st, make picot.

39th row Cast off 5 sts, yrn, P2 tog, yrn, P3 tog, K7, (yrn, P2 tog) twice, K4, (yrn, P2 tog) 3 times, K4, P5, turn, P5, K4, (yrn, P2 tog) twice, yon, sl 1, K1, psso, K4, (yrn, P2 tog) twice, K6, K2 tog, K1, yrn, P2 tog, yrn, (P1, K1) into last st, make picot.

40th row Cast off 5 sts, yrn, P2 tog, yrn, P3 tog, K5, (yrn, P2 tog) twice, K3, P2 tog tbl, yon, K1, (yrn, P2 tog) twice, K4, P4, turn, P4, K4, (yrn, P2 tog) twice, K2, yfwd, sl 1, K1, psso, K2, (yrn, P2 tog) twice, K4, K2

tog, K1, yrn, P2 tog, yrn, (P1, K1) into last st, make picot.

41st row Cast off 5 sts, yrn, P2 tog, yrn, P3 tog, K3, (yrn, P2 tog) twice, K1, P2 tog tbl, yrn, K3, (yrn, P2 tog) twice, K4, P3, turn, P3, K4, (yrn, P2 tog) twice, K4, yfwd, sl 1, K1, psso, (yrn, P2 tog) twice, K2, K2 tog, K1, yrn, P2 tog, yrn, (P1, K1) into last st, make picot.

42nd row Cast off 5 sts, yrn, P2 tog, yrn, P3 tog, K1, (yrn, P2 tog) 3 times, K4, (yrn, P2 tog) twice, K4, P2, turn, P2, K4, (yrn, P2 tog) twice, K3, K2 tog, yfwd, K1, (yrn, P2 tog) twice, K2 tog, K1, yrn, P2 tog, yrn, (P1, K1) into last st, make picot.

43rd row Cast off 5 sts, yrn, (P2 tog) twice, (yrn, P2 tog) twice, K2, yrn, P2 tog, K2, (yrn, P2 tog) twice, K4, P1, turn, P1, K4, (yrn, P2 tog) twice, K1, K2 tog, yfwd, K3, (yrn, P2 tog) twice, sl 1, K2 tog, psso, K1.

44th row K2 tog, (yrn, P2 tog) twice, K4, (yrn, P2 tog) 3 times, K4, turn, K4, (yrn, P2 tog) twice, yon, sl 1, K1, psso, K4, (yrn, P2 tog) twice, K1.

45th row K1, (yrn, P2 tog) twice, K3, P2 tog tbl, yon, K1, (yrn, P2 tog) twice, K4, P20.

46th row P20, K4, (yrn, P2 tog) twice, K2, yfwd, sl 1, K1, psso, K2, (yrn, P2 tog) twice, K1.

47th row K1, (yrn, P2 tog) twice, K1, P2 tog tbl, yon, K3, (yrn, P2 tog) twice, K4, P20.

48th-64th rows Rep 31st-47th rows inclusive once more.

The last 64 rows form the patt repeat.

Rep these 64 rows 4 times more.

Rep 1st-30th rows once more.

Next 2 rows P.

Cast off very loosely.

To make up

Make a line of running stitches at neck edge. Gather into required measurement. Curve collar, stretch and pin into shape.

Starch and press.

Make a button loop at neck edge.

Sew on button to fasten.

Puff-sleeved Evening Top

Brighten up your nightlife in this gorgeous
glittering sweater knitted in fine gold yarn. The central panel
with its pretty eyelet bow motif is bordered by textured
panels in cables and blackberry stitch.

Sizes
To fit 81[86:91]cm bust
Length 51cm
Sleeve seam 15cm

Note Instructions for larger sizes are in square brackets []; where there is only one set of figures it applies to all three sizes.

Tension
38 sts and 48 rows to 10cm over st st on 2¾mm needles

Materials
275 [300:300] g three-ply yarn
1 pair each 2¼mm and 2¾mm knitting needles
Cable needle

Back
*** Using 2¼mm needles, cast on 138[142:146] sts. Work in K2, P2 rib as folls:
1st row *K2, P2, rep from * to last 2 sts, K2.
2nd row *P2, K2, rep from * to last 2 sts, P2.
Rep the last 2 rows until work measures 11[12:12]cm from cast-on edge, ending with a 2nd row.
Next row P8[4:0], *P2, P twice into next st, rep from * to last 10[6:2] sts, P to end. 178[186:194] sts. ***
Commence patt.
1st row (WS) P1, *(K1, P1, K1) all into next st, P3 tog, rep from * to last st, P1.
2nd row K1, P to last st, K1.
3rd row P1, *P3 tog, (K1, P1, K1) all into next st, rep from * to last st, P1.
4th row As 2nd row.
These 4 rows form the patt. Cont in patt for a further 118 rows, ending with a 2nd patt row.
Shape armholes
Keeping patt correct, cast off 20 sts at beg of next 2 rows. 138 [146:154] sts.
Work 1st-2nd patt rows again.
Next row Cast off 4 sts, *P3 tog, (K1, P1, K1) all into next st, rep from * to last st, P1.
Next row Cast off 4 sts, P to last st, K1.
Rep the last 4 rows once more. 122 [130:138] sts.
Cont without shaping, work a further 50 rows in patt.
Cast off.

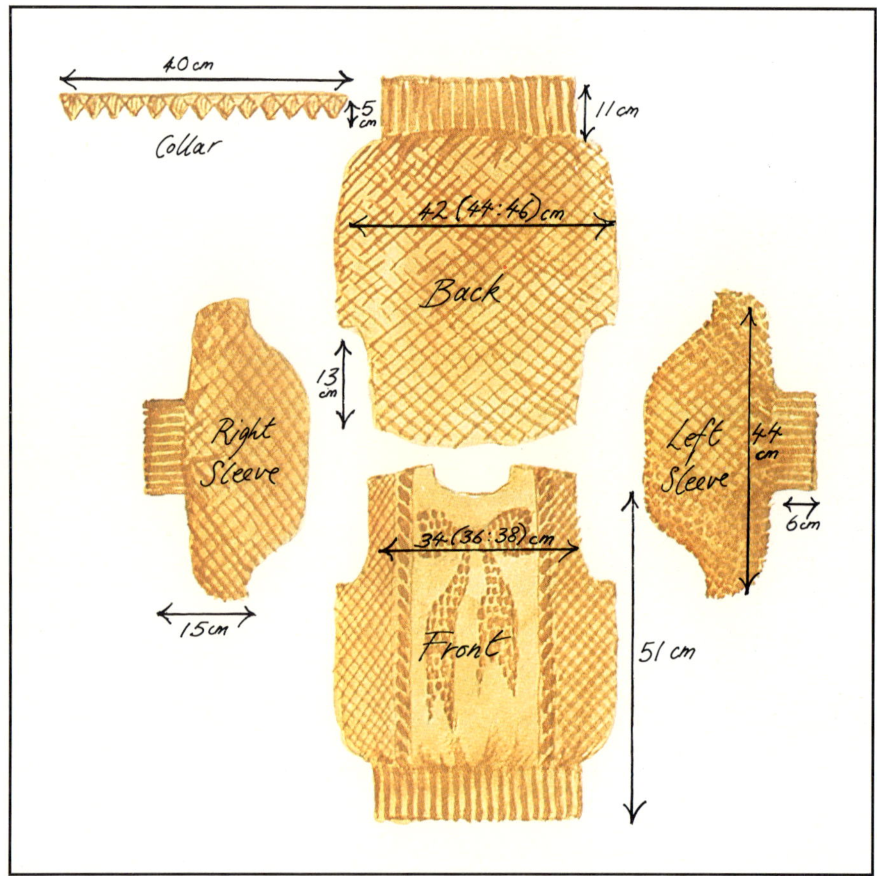

Front
Work as given for back from *** to ***. Commence patt.
1st row (WS) P1, *(K1, P1, K1) all into next st, P3 tog*, rep from * to * 9[10:11] times more, K2, P10, K2, P68, K2, P10, K2, **P3 tog, (K1, P1, K1) all into next st **, rep from ** to **, 9[10:11] times more, P1.
2nd row K1, P42[46:50], K10, P2, K68, P2, K10, P42[46:50], K1.
3rd row P1, *P3 tog, (K1, P1, K1) all into next st *, rep from * to * 9[10:11] times more, K2, P10, K2, P68, K2, P10, K2, **(K1, P1, K1) all into next st, P3 tog **, rep from ** to ** 9[10:11] times more.
4th row K1, P42[46:50], sl next 5 sts on to cable needle and hold at back of work, K5, then K5 sts from cable needle — called C10B, P2, K68, P2, sl next 5 sts on to cable needle and hold at front of work, K5, then K5 sts from cable needle — called C10F, P42[46:50], K1.
5th row As 1st row.
6th row As 2nd row.
7th row As 3rd row.
8th row As 2nd row.
These 8 rows establish the side panel patt with the central panel in st st.
Work the 1st row again.
Now maintaining side panel patt as set, commence working picture eyelets from chart.
1st row Patt 55[59:63], work 1st row from chart as folls: K45, yfwd, K2 tog, K21, patt to end.
2nd row Patt 55[59:63], work 2nd row from chart as folls: P68, patt to end.
3rd row Patt 55[59:63], K68, patt to end.
4th row Patt 55[59:63], P68, patt to end.
5th-8th rows Rep 1st-4th rows again.
9th row Patt 55[59:63], K45, (yfwd, K2 tog) twice, K19, patt to end.
Cont in this way until 113 rows have been worked from chart. (On 107th row refer to Special Technique for how to work a bold eyelet.)
Shape armholes
Keeping patt and chart correct, cast off 20 sts at beg of next 2 rows. 138 [146:174] sts.

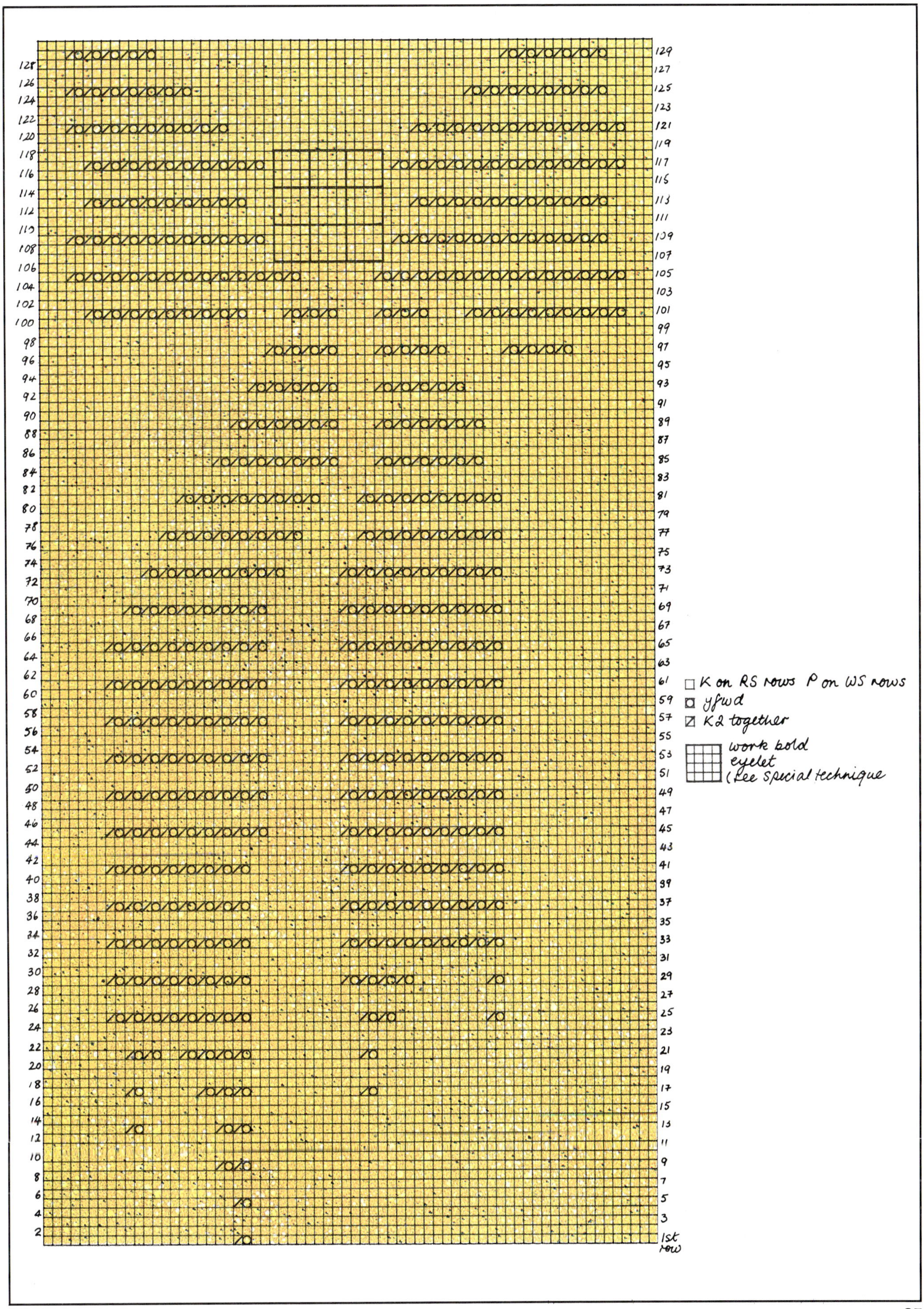

□ K on RS rows P on WS rows
☑ yfwd
☒ K2 together

work bold
eyelet
(See special technique

Work 2 rows.
Cast off 4 sts at beg of next 2 rows.
Rep the last 4 rows once more.
132 [130:138] sts.
Work a further 7 rows until chart is completed.
Now cont with side panel patt as set and central panel in st st.
Work 28 rows.

Shape neck
Next row Patt 57 [61:65] and turn, leaving rem sts on a spare needle.
Complete left side of neck first.
Cast off 4 sts at beg of next row and 2 sts at beg of foll alt row.
Work 1 row.
Dec 1 st at neck edge on next 5 rows and on foll alt row. 35 [39:43] sts.
Cont without shaping until work matches back to shoulder, ending at armhole edge.
Cast off.
With RS of work facing return to sts on spare needle.
Join in yarn, cast off centre 28 sts, patt to end.
Work 1 row.
Complete as given for first side of neck.

Sleeves
Using 2¼mm needles, cast on 94 sts.

Work in K2, P2 rib as given for back for 6cm, ending with a 2nd row.
Change to 2¾mm needles.
Next row P1, *P twice into next st, rep from * to last st, P1. 186 sts.
Cont in patt as given for back until work measures 15cm from cast-on edge, ending with a 2nd or 4th patt row.

Shape top
Keeping patt correct, cast off 20 sts at beg of next 2 rows. Cast off 4 sts at beg of every foll row until 106 sts rem.
Cont without shaping until work measures 24cm from cast-on edge, ending with a 2nd or 4th patt row.
Cast off 4 sts at beg of next 8 rows.
Next row P1, *P3 tog, rep from * to last st, P1.
Cast off.

Collar
Using 2¾mm needles, cast on 12 sts.
Knit 2 rows.
Commence patt.
1st row (RS) K twice into first st — called inc 1, K1, turn.
2nd and every foll alt row K to end.
3rd row Inc 1, K3, turn.
5th row Inc 1, K5, turn.
7th row Inc 1, K7, turn.

9th row Inc 1, K9, turn.
11th row Inc 1, K11, turn.
13th row Inc 1, K13, turn.
15th row Inc 1, K15, turn.
17th row Inc 1, K17, turn.
19th row Inc 1, K19, turn.
21st row K22.
23rd row K2 tog, K19, turn.
25th row K2 tog, K17, turn.
27th row K2 tog, K15, turn.
29th row K2 tog, K13, turn.
31st row K2 tog, K11, turn.
33rd row K2 tog, K9, turn.
35th row K2 tog, K7, turn.
37th row K2 tog, K5, turn.
39th row K2 tog, K3, turn.
41st row K2 tog, K1, turn.
42nd-54th rows K.
These 54 rows form the patt. Rep them 12 times more.
Cast off.

To make up
Join shoulder seams.
Join side and sleeve seams.
Set in sleeves, gathering to form a puff top. Join short ends of collar.
Sew collar to neck edge, placing seam at centre back neck.
Do not press. Remember to wash gently by hand in warm water and dry completely flat on a towel.

Special technique — working a bold eyelet

1 *The knot on the bow motif of the basic sweater is made from a series of bold eyelets worked over four stitches and four rows. On the first row, knit two together, take the yarn round needle twice, then slip one, knit one, then pass the slipped stitch over.*

2 *On the second row, purl together the first stitch and the first yarn round needle, knit together the second yarn round needle and the second stitch.*

3 *On the third row, knit one, yarn round needle twice, knit one. On the fourth row, purl together first stitch, first yarn round needle and the strand below, then knit one and purl one, into second yarn round needle and strand below at the same time, then purl one.*

Elderberry Lace Sweater

A fluffy sweater knitted in an elderberry lace pattern that's delicious enough to make your mouth water. It looks equally good with smart or casual clothes.

Sizes
To fit 81-86[91-97]cm bust.
Length 58[64]cm.
Sleeve seam 43cm.
Note Instructions for larger size are in square brackets []; where there is only one set of figures it applies to all sizes.

Tension
28 sts and 38 rows to 10cm over patt on 3mm needles.

Materials
350 [400]g four-ply yarn
1 pair each 2¼mm and 3mm knitting needles

Back
**Using 2¼mm needles, cast on 120[150] sts.
Next row (RS) (K1, P1) to end.
Next row (K1, P1) to end.
Cont in K1, P1 rib until work measures 8cm from beg, ending with a RS row.
Next row Rib 12[15], pick up loop lying between needles and K tbl — called make 1 or M1 — , (rib 24[30], M1) 4 times, rib to end. 125[155] sts. Change to 3mm needles, start patt.
1st row (RS) K3, *K2 tog, P3, K1, yrn, P8, (K1, yfwd, K1, yfwd, K1) all into next st, turn, P5, turn, K2 tog tbl, K3 tog, pass 1st st over 2nd — called make bobble or MB — , P8, yon, K1, P3, ybk, sl 1 P-wise, K1, psso, K1, rep from * to last 2 sts, K2.
2nd row K2, P2, * K3, P2, K8, P1 tbl, K8, P2, K3, P3, rep from * to last 4 sts, P2, K2 instead of P3.
3rd row K4, *P2 tog, P1, K1, yrn, P5, MB, P3, K1, P3, MB, P5, yon, K1, P1, P2 tog, K3, rep from * to last st, K1.
4th row K2, P2, *K2, P2, K5, P1 tbl, K3, P1, K3, P1 tbl, K5, P2, K2, P3, rep from * to last 4 sts, P2, K2 instead of P3.
5th row K4, *P2 tog, K1, yrn, P2, MB (P3, K1) 3 times, P3, MB, P2, yon, K1 P2 tog, K3, rep from * to last st, K1.
6th row K2, P2, *K1, P2, K2, P1 tbl, (K3, P1) 3 times, K3, P1 tbl, K2, P2, K1, P3, rep from * to last 4 sts, P2, K2 instead of P3.
7th row K4, *K2 tog, yrn, (P3, K1) 5 times, P3, yon, sl 1 P-wise, K1, psso, K3, rep from * to last st, K1.
8th row K2, P4, *(K3, P1) 5 times, K3, P7, rep from * to last 6 sts, P4, K2 instead of P7.

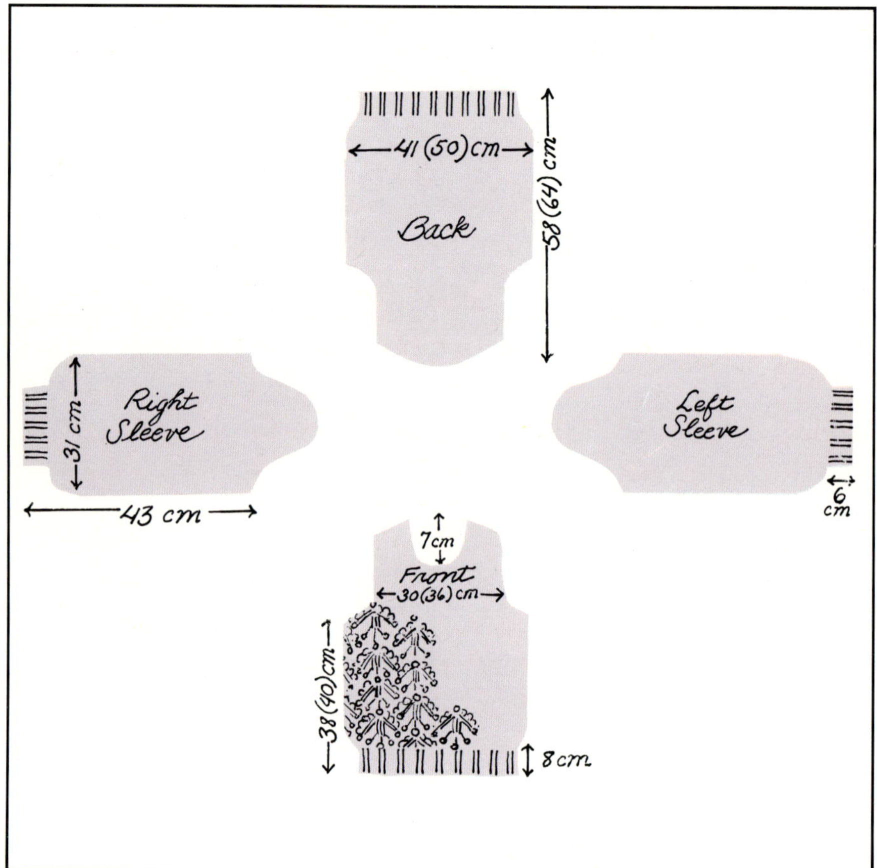

9th row K3, *K2 tog, yrn, P4, yon, K1, P3, K1, P1, P2 tog, K1, P2 tog, P1, K1, P3, K1, yrn, P4, yon, sl 1 P-wise, K1, psso, K1, rep from * to last 2 sts, K2.
10th row K2, P3, *K4, P2, K3, (P1, K2) twice, P1, K3, P2, K4, P5, rep from * to last 5 sts, P3, K2 instead of P5.
11th row K2, K2 tog, *yrn, P6, yon, K1, P3, (K1, P2 tog) twice, K1, P3, K1, yrn, P6, yon, sl 1 P-wise, K2 tog, psso, rep from * to last 4 sts, sl 1 P-wise, K1, psso, K2.
12th row K10, *P2, K3, (P1, K1) twice, P1, K3, P2, K15, rep from * to last 10 sts, K10 instead of K15.
13th row K2, *MB, P8, yon, K1, P3, ybk, sl 1 P-wise, K1, psso, K1, K2 tog, P3, K1, yrn, P8, rep from * to last 3 sts, MB, K2.
14th row K2, *P1 tbl, K8, P2, K3, P3, K3, P2, K8, rep from * to last 3 sts, P1 tbl, K2.
15th row K3, P3, MB, P5, yon, K1, P1, P2 tog, K3, P2 tog, P1, K1, yrn, P5, MB, P3, K1, rep from * to last 2 sts, K2.

16th row K2, *P1, K3, P1 tbl, K5, P2, K2, P3, K2, P2, K5, P1 tbl, K3, rep from * to last 3 sts, P1, K2.
17th row K3, *P3, K1, P3, MB, P2, yon, K1, P2 tog, K3, P2 tog, K1, yrn, P2, MB, (P3, K1) twice, rep from * to last 2 sts, K2.
18th row K2, * (P1, K3) twice, P1 tbl, K2, P2, K1, P3, K1, P2, K2, P1 tbl, K3, P1, K3, rep from * to last 3 sts, P1, K2.
19th row K3, * (P3, K1) twice, P3, yon, sl 1 P-wise, K1, psso, K3, K2 tog, yrn, (P3, K1) 3 times, rep from * to last 2 sts, K2.
20th row K2, * (P1, K3) 3 times, P7, (K3, P1) twice, K3, rep from * to last 3 sts, P1, K2.
21st row K3, * P2 tog, P1, K1, P3, K1, yrn, P4, yon, sl 1 P-wise, K1, psso, K1, K2 tog, yrn, P4, yon, K1, P3, K1, P1, P2 tog, K1, rep from * to last 2 sts, K2.
22nd row K2, * P1, K2, P1, K3, P2, K4, P5, K4, P2, K3, P1, K2, rep from * to last 3 sts, P1, K2.
23rd row K3, * P2 tog, K1, P3, K1, yrn, P6, yon, sl 1 P-wise, K2 tog, psso, yrn, P6, yon, K1, P3, K1, P2 tog, K1, rep from * to last 2 sts, K2.

24th row K2, * P1, K1, P1, K3, P2, K15, P2, K3, P1, K1, rep from * to last 3 sts, P1, K2.

These 24 rows form the elderberry lace patt. Cont in patt until work measures 38 [40]cm from beg, ending with a WS row.

Shape armholes

Keeping patt correct, cast off 6 sts at beg of next 2 rows.

Dec 1 st at each end of next 5[9] rows, then dec 1 st at each end of every foll alt row until 93 [111] sts rem * *.

Cont without further shaping until work measures 58 [64] cm from beg, ending with a WS row.

Shape shoulders

Keeping patt correct, cast off 8[9] sts at beg of next 4 rows, then 9[10] sts at beg of next 2 rows. Leave rem 43[55] sts on a spare needle.

Front

Work as given for back from * * to * *

Cont without further shaping until work measures 51 [57]cm from beg, ending with a WS row.

Shape left front neck

Next row Patt 35 [44] sts, P2 tog, turn, leaving rem sts on a spare needle.

Dec 1 st at neck edge on every foll row until 25[28] sts rem.

Cont without further shaping until front matches back exactly to beg of shoulder shaping, ending with a WS row.

Shape shoulder

Keeping patt correct, cast off 8[9] sts at beg of next and foll alt row. Work 1 row.

Cast off rem 9[10] sts.

Shape right front neck

Return to sts on spare needle and beg at neck edge, slip 19 sts on to a holder. Rejoin yarn to rem sts, P2 tog, patt to end.

Complete to match left side, reversing shapings.

Sleeves (alike)

Using 2¼mm needles, cast on 56[62] sts and work in K1, P1 rib as given for back for 6cm.

Next row Rib 9[15], M1, (rib 1, M1) 38[32] times, rib to end, 95 sts.

Change to 3mm needles and cont in patt as given for back until work measures 43cm from beg, ending with a WS row.

Shape top

Keeping patt correct, cast off 6 sts at beg of next 2 rows.

Dec 1 st at each end of next and every foll 4th row until 79[65] sts rem. Work 1 row.

Dec 1 st at each end of next and every foll alt row until 31 sts rem. Work 1 row. Cast off.

To make up

Do not press.

Join right shoulder seam.

Neck border

Using 2¼mm needles and with RS facing, K up 24 sts down left side of neck, K19 sts from stitch holder, K up 24 sts up right side of neck, then K43[55] from spare needle. 110[122] sts.

Work in K1, P1 rib as given for back for 7cm.

Cast off in rib.

Join left shoulder and neck border seam.

Fold neck border in half to WS and slip stitch loosely in position.

Set in sleeves.

Join side and sleeve seams.

Special technique – working a crew neckband

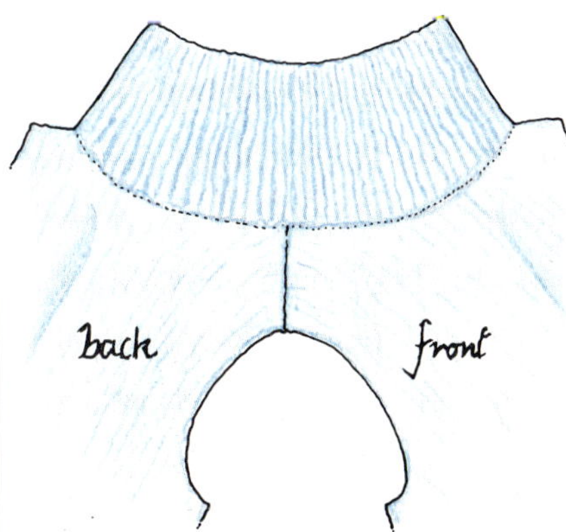

1 Join the right shoulder seam. Pick up the number of stitches specified in the pattern around the neck edge. Work the rib to twice the required depth of neckband. Cast off very loosely in rib.

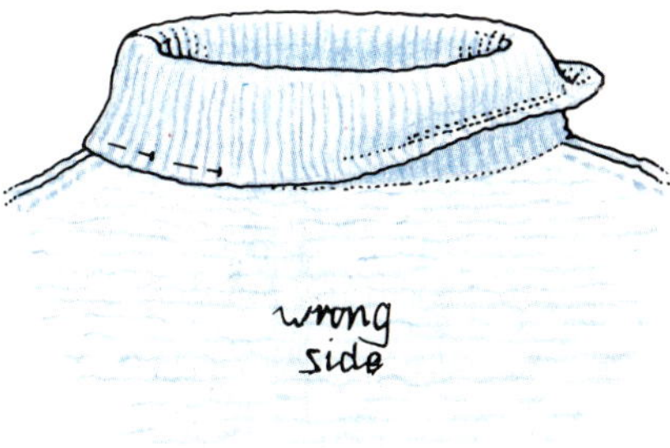

2 Join the left shoulder seam and the neckband seam. Fold the neckband in half to the wrong side of the garment. Pin the cast-off edge to the inner neck edge.

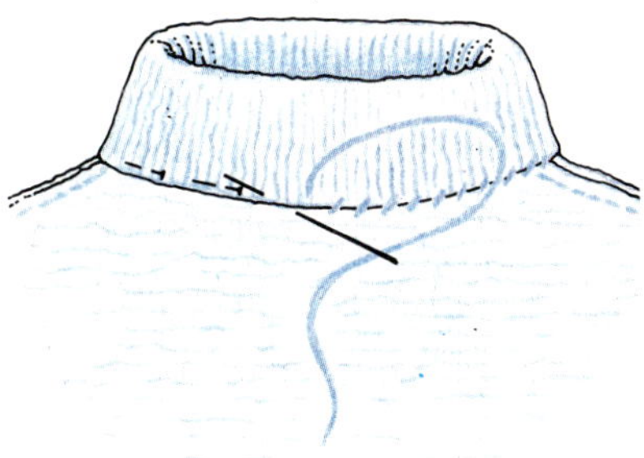

3 Using matching yarn, thread a blunt-ended needle and slipstitch the cast-off edge in position.

Lace Panelled Sweater

**Splurge on ultra-luxurious silk for this superb sweater with
its asymmetrical combination of stitch patterns — strictly
for the experienced knitter and would-be designer!**

Size
To fit 81-86cm bust
Length 55cm
Sleeve seam 52cm

Tension
20 sts and 26 rows to 10cm over st st
on 4mm needles

Materials
1200g Aran-weight yarn
1 pair 3mm knitting needles, 3mm
and 4mm circular needles

Note The sweater is knitted in one
piece, starting at the wrist of one
sleeve, and the work is divided for the
front and back. The following stitch
patterns are used. It is advisable to
knit samples of one or two repeats to
become familiar with the patterns
before the work is started. The
pattern repeats are given between **
and extra stitches have been included
for the first pattern row where
necessary in the instructions to
balance the pattern. Make sure that
these extra stitches are taken into
consideration on the sleeve shaping.

A Bobble stitch pattern
1st-3rd rows K.
4th row (WS) P.
5th row *K5, (K1, yfwd, K1, yfwd,
K1) all into next st, turn, P5, turn,
K5, turn, P2 tog, P1, P2 tog, turn, sl
1, K 2 tog, psso — called MB —, rep
from * to end.
6th row P.
7th-9th rows K.
10th row P. These 10 rows form the
pattern repeat (6 repeat stitches).
B Fan pattern
1st row (RS) K1, *yfwd, sl 1, K1,
psso, K5*, yfwd, K2 tog.
2nd and foll alt rows P.
3rd row K1, *yfwd, K1, sl 1, K1,
psso, K4*, yfwd, K2 tog.
5th row K1, *yfwd, K2, sl 1, K1,
psso, K3*, yfwd, K2 tog.
7th row K1, *yfwd, K3, sl 1 K1,
psso, K2*, ywfd, K2 tog.
9th row K1, *yfwd, K4, sl 1, K1,
psso K1* yfwd, K2 tog.

11th row K1, *yfwd, K5, sl 1 K1,
psso*, yfwd, K2 tog.
12th row P.
These 12 rows form the pattern
repeat. (1 edge stitch, 7 repeat
stitches, 2 edge stitches)

C Triangular leaf pattern
1st row K1, yfwd, sl 1, K1, psso, K1,
*K2, K2 tog, yfwd, K1, yfwd, sl 1,
K1, psso, K1*, K2, K2 tog, yfwd, K1.
2nd and foll alt rows P.
3rd row K1, yfwd, K1, sl 1, K1, psso,
*K1, K2 tog, K1, ywfd, K1, yfwd,
K1, sl 1, K1, psso*, K1, K2 tog, K1,
yfwd, K1.
5th row K1, yfwd, K2, *sl 1, K2 tog,
psso, K2, yfwd, K1, yfwd, K2*, sl 1,
K2 tog, psso, K2, yfwd, K1.
7th row K2, K2 tog, yfwd, *K1,
yfwd, sl 1, K1, psso, K3, K2 tog,
yfwd*, K1, yfwd, sl 1, K1, psso, K2.
9th row K1, K2 tog, K1, yfwd, *K1,
yfwd, K1, sl 1, K1, psso, K1, K2 tog,
K1, yfwd*, K1, yfwd, K1, sl 1, K1,
psso, K1.
11th row K2 tog, K2, yfwd, *K1,
yfwd, K2, sl 1, K2 tog, psso, K2,
yfwd*, K1, yfwd, K2, sl 1, K1, psso.
12th row P.
These 12 rows form the pattern
repeat.
(4 edge stitches, 8 repeat stitches,
5 edge stitches).

D Diamond stitch
1st row (RS) K1*, P1, K1, P1, K1,
P2, K1, P1, K1, P1*, K1.
2nd and foll alt rows P1, *K1, P1,
K1, P1, K2, P1, K1, P1, K1*, P1.
3rd row K1, *P1, yfwd, P3 tog,
yfwd, P2, yfwd, P3 tog, yfwd, P1*,
K1.
5th row As 1st row.
7th row K1, *P2 tog, yfwd, P1,
yfwd, P2 tog, P2 tog, yfwd, P1,
yfwd, P2 tog*, K1.
These 8 rows from the pattern repeat.
(10 repeat stitches)

E Curved leaf pattern
1st row *P2, K5, K2 tog, yfwd, K1,
yfwd, K2*, P2.
2nd row *K2, P5, P2 tog, P4*, K2.

3rd row *P2, K3, K2 tog, K1, yfwd,
K1, yfwd, K3*, P2.
4th row *K2, P7, P2 tog, P2*, K2.
5th row *P2, K1, K2 tog, K2, yfwd,
K1, yfwd, K4*, P2.
6th row *K2, P9, P2 tog*, K2.
These 6 rows form the pattern repeat.
(12 repeat stitches, 2 edge stitches)

Sweater
Sleeve
Using 3mm needles, cast on 36 sts
and work 15 rows in K1, P1 rib.
Change to 4mm circular needle and
work in rows.
Next row P to end, inc 8 sts evenly
across the row. 44 sts.
Cont in bands of patt, *at the same
time*, inc 1 st at each end of every
6th row.
1st-10th rows Work in bobble stitch
pattern A (7 repeats of 6 sts, 2 edge
sts).
11th-34th rows Work in fan pattern
B (2 edge sts, 6 repeats of 7 sts, 2
edge sts in 11th row).
35th-44th rows Work in bobble stitch
pattern A.
45th-80th rows Work in triangular
leaf pattern stitch C (5 edge sts, 6
repeats of 8 sts, 5 edge sts in 45th
row).
81st-90th rows Work in bobble stitch
pattern A (11 repeats of 6 sts, 4 edge
sts in 81st row).
91th-114th rows Work in diamond
stitch pattern D (1 edge st, 6 repeats
of 12 sts, 1 edge st in 91st row).
115th row K.
116th row K, inc 1 st at each end.
84 sts.
117th row K2, *MB, K5*, rep from
* to last 4 sts, MB, K3.
118th row P, inc 1 st at each end.
119th row K.
120th row P, inc 1 st at each end.
88 sts.

Front and back
121st row Cast on 54 sts, K across
these sts, K88 from sleeve, cast on 54
sts. 196 sts.
122nd row P.
123rd-132nd rows Work in bobble

stitch pattern A (2 edge stitches, 32
repeats of 6 sts in bobble row, 2 edge
sts).
133rd row K4, *MB, K5*, rep from
* to end.
134th row P.
135th-137th rows K.
138th row P.
139th row K.
140th row P.

Neck
141st row K92 and leave these sts on
a spare needle, cast off 12 sts K92.
Work front and back separately as foll:
142nd row P.
143rd-160th rows **Work in curved
leaf pattern stitch E (3 edge sts, 7
repeats of 12 sts, 5 edge sts)
161st-170th rows Work in bobble
stitch pattern A (15 repeats of 6 sts, 2
edge sts)
171st-206th rows Work in fan
pattern stitch B (4 edge sts, 12
repeats of 7 sts, 4 edge sts).
207th-216th rows Work in bobble
stitch pattern A (15 repeats of 6 sts, 2
edge sts).**

Cut yarn and leave these sts on a
spare needle.
With WS of work facing return to sts
on spare needle, join in yarn at neck
edge. Work as given from ** to **
again.

Joining back and front
217th row K92, cast on 12 sts and
K92 from spare needle. 196 sts.
218th row P.
219th-230th rows Work in triangular
leaf stitch pattern C (6 edge sts, 23
repeats of 8 sts, 6 edge sts).
221st-237th rows Work 1st-7th rows
of bobble stitch pattern A (32 repeats
of 6 sts, 5 edge sts).

Sleeve
238th row Cast off 54 sts, K142.
239th row Cast off 54 sts, K88.
240th row P, dec 1 st at each end.
86 sts.
241st row K 1, *MB, K5, rep from *
to last st, K 1.
242nd row P, dec 1 st at each end,
84 sts.
243rd row K.

244th row K, dec 1 st at each end.
245th row K.
246th row P, dec 1 st at each end.
80 sts.
Now cont in patt, *at the same time*,
dec 1st at each end of every foll 6th
row.
247th row K1, *MB, K5, rep from *
to last st, K1.
248th row P.
249th-250th rows K.
251st-266th rows Work in diamond
stitch pattern D (4 edge sts, 6 repeats
of 12 sts, 6 edge sts).
267th-276th rows Work in bobble
stitch pattern A (12 repeats of 6 sts, 2
edge sts).
277th-282nd rows Work in curved
leaf pattern E (4 edge sts, 5 repeats of
12 sts, 6 edge sts).
283rd-292nd rows Work in bobble
stitch pattern A (11 repeats of 6 sts, 2
edge sts).
293rd-316th rows Work 2 repeats in
fan pattern B (1 edge st, 9 repeats of
7 sts, 2 edge sts).
317th-326th rows Work in bobble
stitch pattern A (9 repeats of 6 sts, 4
edge sts).
327th-350th rows Work in triangular
leaf pattern C (7 edge sts, 5 repeats
of 8 sts, 7 edge sts).
351st-358th rows Work 1st to 8th
rows of bobble stitch pattern A (7
repeats of 6 sts, 2 edge sts).
Next row K to end, dec 8 sts evenly
across the row. 36 sts.
Change to 3mm needles and work 15
rows in K1, P1 rib. Cast off.

To make up
With RS of work facing, using 3mm
needles K up 39 sts around front neck
edge.
1st row (WS) P1, *K1, P1, rep from
* to end.
2nd row K1, *P1, K1, rep from * to
end.
Rep last 2 rows 3 times more. Cast
off in rib. Work back neck to match.
Using 3mm needles, K up 64 sts
evenly from back lower edge. Work
20 rows in K1, P1 rib. Cast off in rib
and work front lower edge to match.
Sew row ends of neckbands to sts on
shoulders.
Join side and underarm seams.

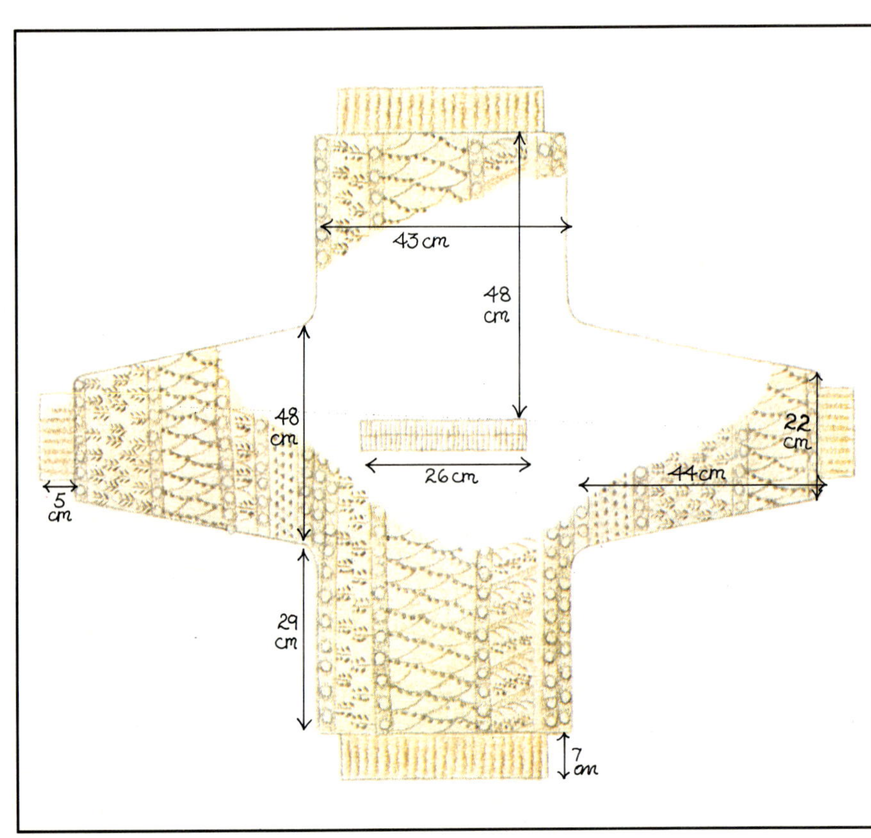

Colour Patterns

Working colour patterns into knitting is surprisingly easy. It involves using several different coloured yarns within the same row — often as few as two but sometimes a great many more. Handling these yarns may seem awkward at first but very quickly improves with practice. One of the most important things is to carry the yarns correctly across the back of the work, either stranding the yarns or weaving them in (see page 24).

Once these techniques have been mastered you will be able to work beautiful all-over patterns like the paisley cardigan on page 98, and the harlequin sweater on page 114, or those with bold pictorial or abstract motifs like the jacket on page 118 and the fireworks sweater (page 111.).

There is also a type of colour-patterned knitting in which amazing geometric patterns can be produced using only one colour to a row. This is 'mosaic' knitting and there is an example of it on page 121. It is one of a large family of patterns which combine different coloured yarns and slip-stitch techniques (see page 23) with some strikingly attractive results.

Jacquard Sweater and Legwarmers

This beautifully patterned sweater set is made in
quick-to-knit chunky wool. To make it even easier the dots
are Swiss-darned afterwards.

Sizes

Sweater
To fit 86-91 [97-102]cm bust
Length 62 [63]cm
Sleeve seam 39cm
Legwarmers
Width round calf 36cm

Note Instructions for the larger size are in square brackets []; where there is only one set of figures it applies to both sizes.

Tension

13½ sts and 15 rows to 10cm over st st on 6mm needles

Materials

250 [350] g chunky yarn in main colour (A)
250 [350] g in 1st contrast colour (B)
150g in each of 5 contrast colours (C), (D), (E), (F) and (G)
1 pair each 5mm and 6mm knitting needles

Back

**Using 5mm needles and A, cast on 62 [68] sts.
1st row K2 [0], *P2, K2, rep from * to end.
2nd row *P2, K2, rep from * to last 2 [0] sts, P2 [0].
Rep the last 2 rows 5 times more. Inc 1 st at end of last row. 63 [69] sts.
Change to 6mm needles and commence patt.
Beg with a K row work 20 rows st st. Now cont in st st, working from chart (page 97) reading K rows from right to left and P rows from left to right.
Work 30 rows, ending with a P row.
Shape armholes
Keeping patt correct, cast off 3 sts at beg of next 2 rows and 2 [3] sts at beg of foll 4 rows. 49 [51] sts.
Cont without shaping until the 52 rows of chart have been completed.**
Cont in F only and st st until work measures 23 [24]cm from beg of armhole shaping, ending with a P row.
Shape shoulders
Cast off 13 sts at beg of next 2 rows. Leave the rem 23 [25] sts on a spare needle.

Front

Work as given for back from ** to **.
Cont in F only and st st until work measures 16 [17]cm from beg of armhole shaping, ending with a P row.
Divide for neck
Next row Patt 18 sts and turn,

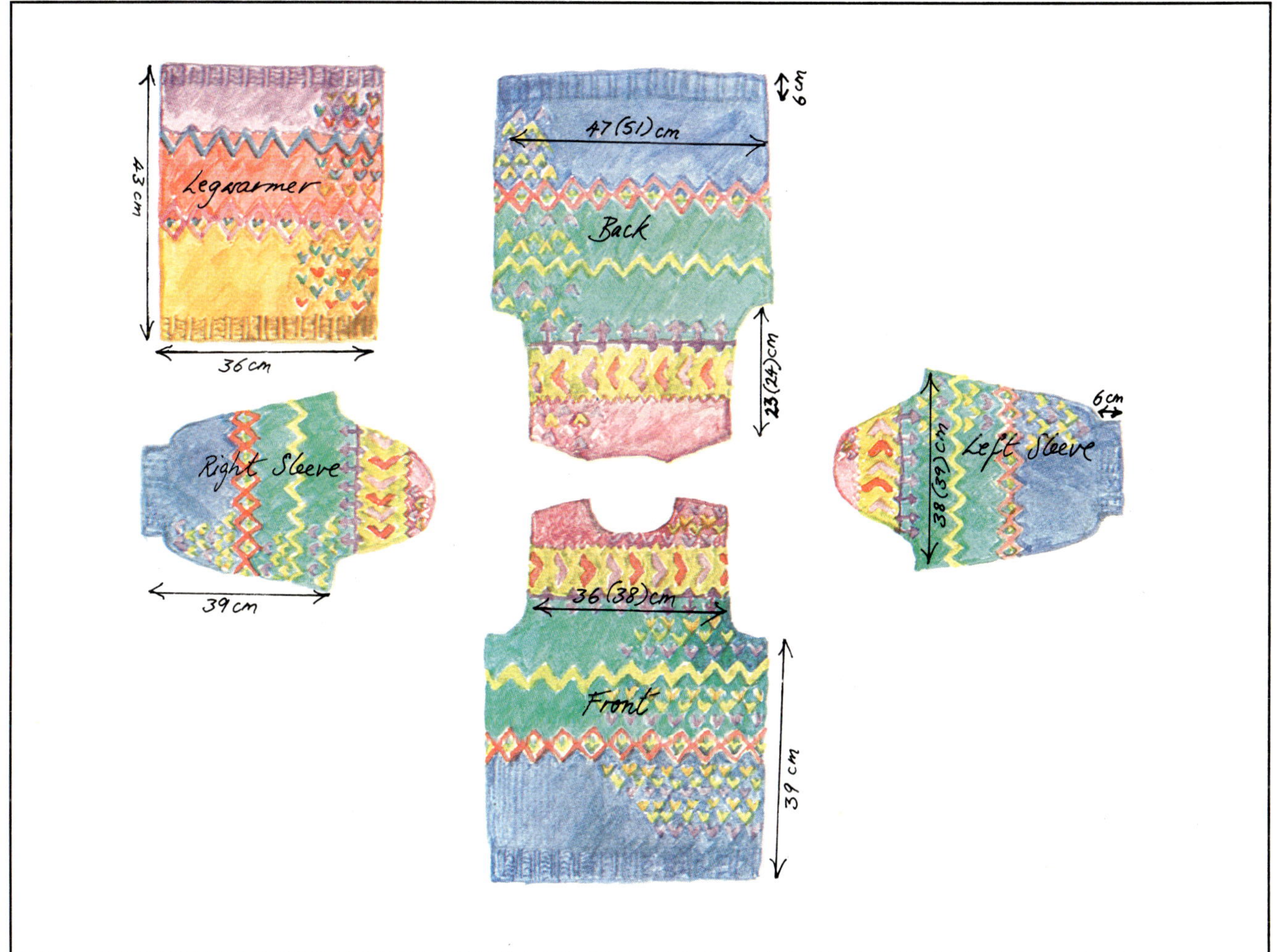

leaving rem sts on a spare needle, patt to end.

Complete left side of neck first.

****Next row Patt to end.

Next row Cast off 3 sts, patt to end.

Next row Patt to end.

Next row Cast off 2 sts, patt to end. Cont without shaping until work matches back to shoulder shaping, ending at armhole edge.

Shape shoulder

Cast off rem 13 sts.****

Return to sts on spare needle. With RS of work facing, sl centre 13 [15] sts on to a stitch holder, join in yarn to next st, patt to end.

Complete to match first side of neck, working from **** to ****.

Sleeves

Using 5mm needles and A, cast on 28 sts.

Work 11 rows K2, P2 rib.

Next row Rib 5, (work into front and back of next st — called M1 —, rib 1) 8 times, M1, rib to end. 37 sts.

Change to 6mm needles and cont in patt as given for back from *** to ***, *at the same time,* inc 1 st at each end of the 7th [5th] row and every foll 6th row until there are 51 [53] sts.

Cont without shaping until 30 rows have been worked from chart, ending with a P row.

Shape sleeve top

Keeping patt correct, cast off 3 sts at beg of next 2 rows and 2 [3] sts at beg of foll 2 rows. Dec 1 st at each end of the next and every foll alt row until 21 [19] sts rem, ending with a P row.

Cast off 2 sts at beg of foll 2 rows and 3 [2] sts at beg of foll 2 rows. Cast off rem 11 sts.

Legwarmers

Using 5mm needles and G, cast on 48 sts.

Work 8 rows in K2, P2 rib. Inc 1 st at end of last row. 49 sts.

Change to 6mm needles and commence patt.

Beg with a K row work 20 rows st st. Now cont in st st, working from chart, reading K rows from right to left and P rows from left to right. Use G instead of A, F instead of B, A instead of C and B instead of D.

Work 21 rows ending with a K row. Beg with a P row cont in E only and work 11 rows in st st. Dec 1 st at end of last row. 48 sts.

Change to 5mm needles and work 8 rows K2, P2 rib. Cast off in rib.

To make up

Join left shoulder seam of sweater. With RS of work facing, using 5mm needles and F, K up 12 sts down left side of neck, K across the 13 [15] sts at centre front, K up 12 sts up right side of neck, K across the 23 [25] sts on back neck. 60 [64] sts.

Work 13 rows in K2, P2, rib. Cast off loosely in rib.

Join right shoulder and neckband seam.

Fold neckband on to WS and slipstitch down. Set in sleeves. Join side and sleeve seams. Swiss darn single stitches for dots on the blank areas of the pattern on every 4th stitch of every 4th row and staggered above each other.

Join side seams of legwarmers. Swiss darn dots as required.

Special technique — Swiss darning dots

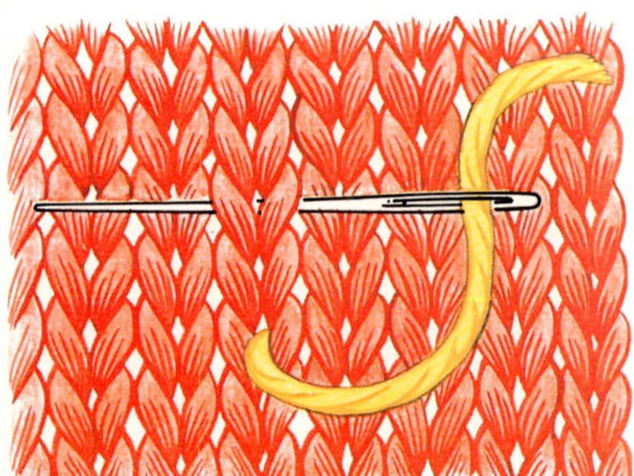

1 *It is usually easier to Swiss darn widely spaced dots than to knit them in. Thread a blunt-ended needle with the chosen yarn. Secure the end of the yarn at the back of the work. Bring the yarn to the front through the base of the stitch. Insert the needle from right to left as shown.*

2 *Pull the yarn through. Push the point of the needle through the base of the stitch and bring it out at the base of the stitch at the next dot position working from right to left.*

3 *Continue in this way working dots in the chosen colours as required. On the basic sweater the dots are worked every 4th row on every 4th stitch in contrast colours and staggered above each other as shown in the photograph.*

pattern repeat 30 sts
1st size Back
sleeve
2nd size Back
legwarmer.
A
B
C
D
E
F

Paisley Cardigan

A string of tiny flowers buttons up this scoop-necked cardigan
worked in a pretty paisley pattern. The sleeves are beautifully
puffed at the top and taper to the wrist.

Sizes
To fit 76[82:86:91]cm bust
Length 50[50:54:54]cm
Sleeve seam 38[40:42:44]cm

Note Instructions for the larger sizes are in square brackets []; where there is only one set of figures it applies to all sizes.

Tension
29 sts and 29 rows to 10cm over patt on 3¼mm needles

Materials
200 [225:250:300] g four-ply yarn in main colour (A)
100 [100:125:125] g in 1st contrast colour (B)
125[125:150:150] g in 2nd contrast colour (C)

1 pair each 2¾mm and 3¼mm knitting needles
13[13:14:14] buttons

Back
Using 3¼mm needles and A, cast on 118[126:136:142] sts.
**Work 6 rows K1, P1 rib.
Beg with a K row cont in st st and patt from chart 1. Read K rows from right to left, P rows from left to right.
Cont until work measures 28[28:30:30] cm from cast-on edge, ending with a P row.**
Shape armholes
Keeping patt correct, cast off 4 sts at beg of next 2 rows, 3 sts at beg of foll 2 rows and 2 sts at beg of next 2 rows.
Dec 1 st at beg of next 2 rows.
98[106:116:122] sts.

Cont without shaping until work measures 50[50:54:54]cm from cast-on edge, ending with a P row.
Shape shoulders
Cast off 24[28:33:36] sts at beg of next 2 rows.
Cast off rem 50 sts.

Right front
Using 3¼mm needles and A, cast on 56[60:64:68] sts.
Work as given for back from ** to **, working patt from chart 2.
Shape armhole
Next row Cast off 4 sts, patt to end.
Next row Patt to end.
Next row Cast off 3 sts, patt to end.
Next row Patt to end.
Next row Cast off 2 sts, patt to end.
Next row Patt to end.
Next row Work 2 tog, patt to end.

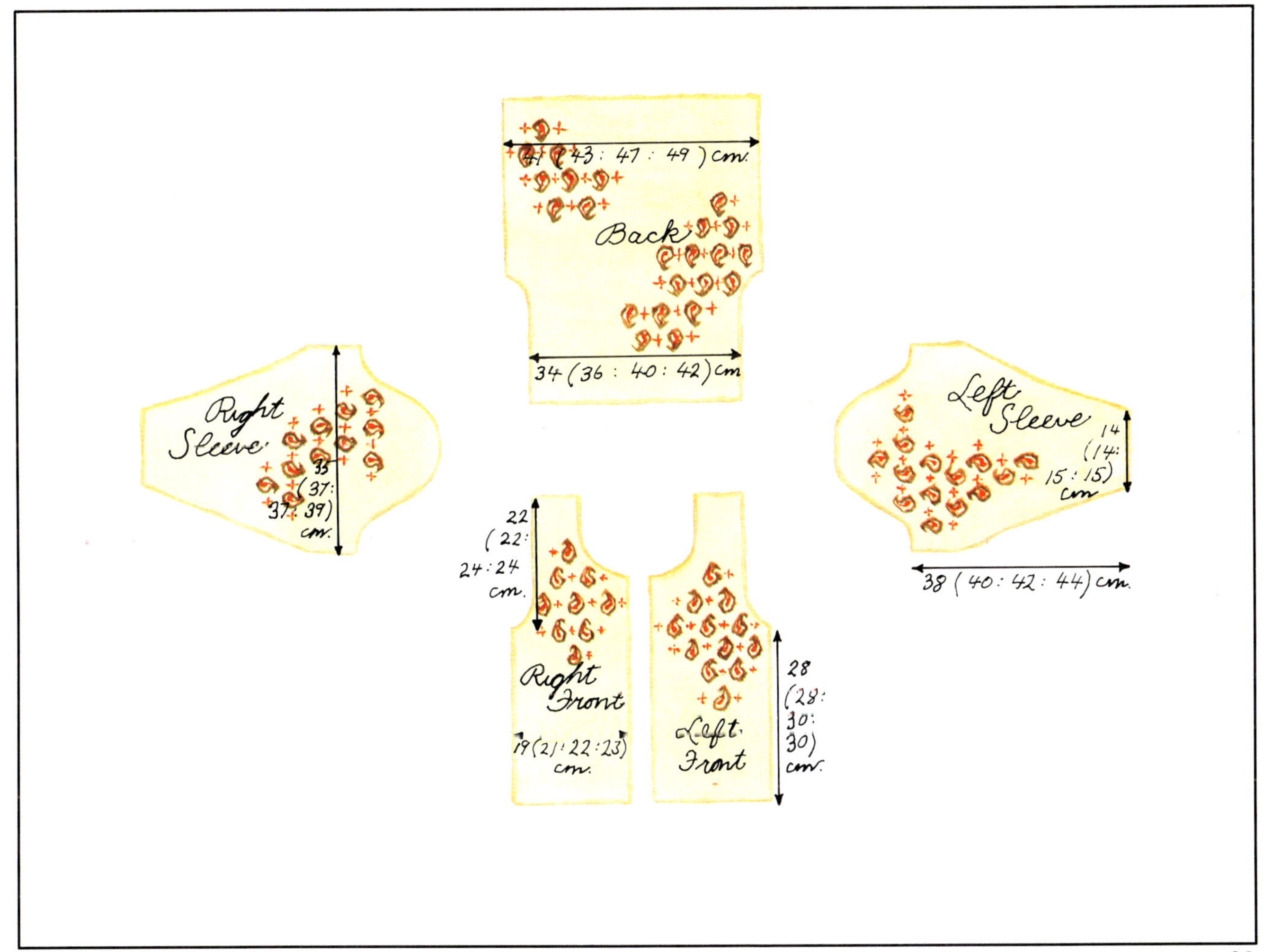

46[50:54:58] sts.
Cont without shaping until work measures 38[40:40]cm from cast-on edge, ending with a K row.

Shape neck
Next row Cast off 9 sts patt to end.
Next row Patt to end.
Next row Cast off 7[7:6:7] sts, patt to end.
Next row Patt to end.
Next row Cast off 6 sts, patt to end. 24[28:33:36] sts.
Cont without shaping until work matches back to shoulder shaping, ending at armhole edge.

Shape shoulder
Cast off rem sts.

Left front
Work as given for right front working patt from chart 3, reversing shaping.

Sleeves
Using 3¼mm needles and A, cast on 42[42:44:44] sts. Work 6 rows rib.
Change to st st and work in patt from chart 1. Inc 1 st at each end of every foll 4th row until there are 60[60:64:64] sts. Now inc 1 st at each end of every foll alt row until there are 102[108:108:112] sts.
Cont without shaping until work measures 38[40:42:44]cm from cast-on edge, ending with a P row.

Shape sleeve top
Cast off 4 sts at beg of next 2 rows and 2 sts at beg of foll 2 rows.
Dec 1 st at each end of next and every foll alt row until 54[66:54:62] sts rem, ending with a P row.
Cast off 2 sts at beg of next 8[14:8:12] rows, then 4 sts at beg of next 2 rows.
Cast off rem 30 sts.

To make up
Join shoulder seams.
Neckband
With RS of work facing, using 2¾mm needles and A, K up 53[53:55:55] sts up right side of neck, K up 50 across back neck, K up 53[53:55:55] sts down left side of neck. 156[156:160:160] sts.
Work 5 rows K1, P1 rib.
Cast off in rib.

Buttonhole band
With RS of work facing, using 2¾mm needles and A, K up 115[115:123:123] sts evenly along front and neckband edge.
1st row (WS) P1, *K1, P1, rep from * to end.
2nd row K1, *P1, K1, rep from * to end.
Rep the 1st row again.
Buttonhole row Rib 3, (yrn, work 2 tog, rib 7) 12[12:13:13] times, yrn, work 2 tog, rib to end.
Rib 4 more rows. Cast off in rib.

Buttonband
Work as given for buttonhole band omitting buttonholes.
Join side and sleeve seams.
Set in sleeves gathering sleeve top to form puff.
Sew on buttons.

Special technique — knitting up stitches from shaped and vertical edges

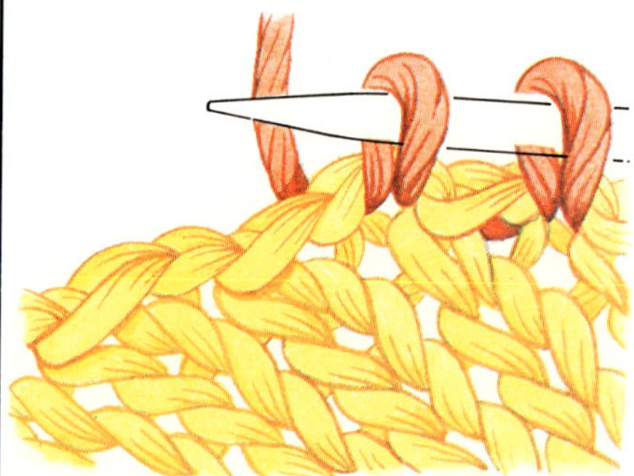

1 On a shaped edge, insert a needle from front to back through a cast-off stitch or the last stitch in a row. Take the yarn knitwise round the point of the needle and draw a loop through. On shaped edges one stitch is picked up for every two rows.

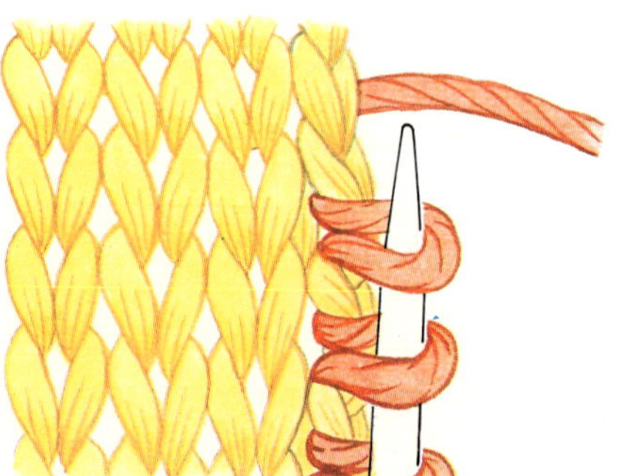

2 On vertical edges, insert a needle from front to back through the first stitch in a row. Take the yarn round the point of the needle knitwise and draw a loop through. Generally, on vertical edges, one stitch is picked up for every row.

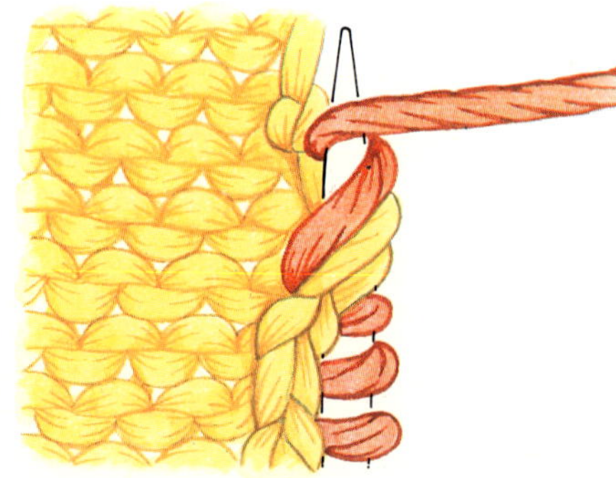

3 Similarly, stitches can be purled up along shaped or vertical edges. In this case work with the wrong side of the fabric facing.

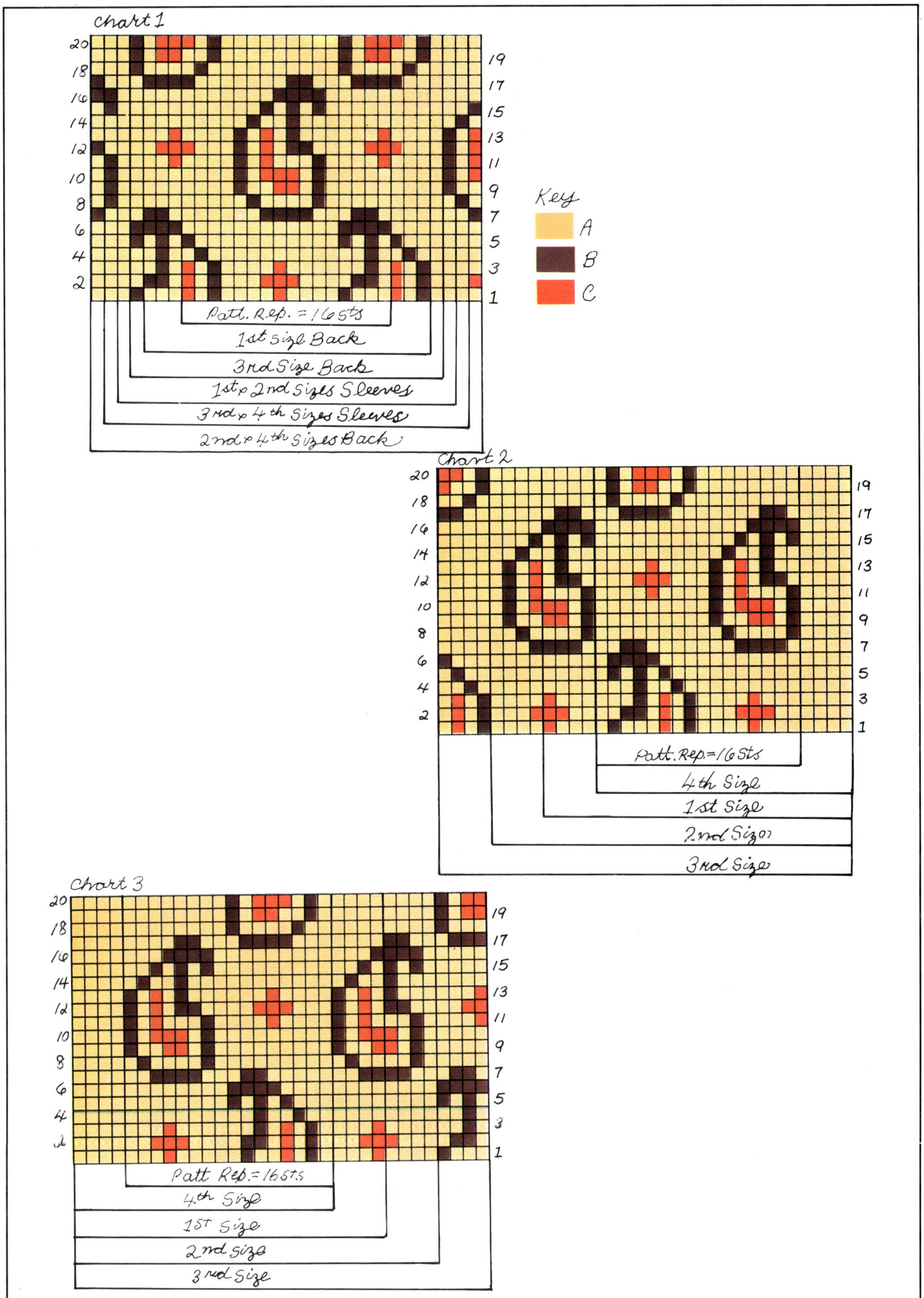

chart 1
Patt. Rep. = 16 sts
1st size Back
3rd Size Back
1st & 2nd Sizes Sleeves
3rd & 4th Sizes Sleeves
2nd & 4th Sizes Back
Key
A
B
C
Chart 2
Patt. Rep = 16 sts
4th Size
1st Size
2nd Size
3rd Size
Chart 3
Patt Rep.= 16 sts
4th Size
1st Size
2nd size
3rd size

Slipstitch Sweater

**The light crunchy textures of a three-colour slip-stitch pattern
and warm-autumnal colours made this shawl-collared sweater
an all-weather favourite for men or women.**

Sizes
To fit 96[101:106]cm chest
Length 63[64:65]cm
Sleeve seam 48[48:49]cm
Note Instructions for larger sizes are in square brackets []; where there is only one set of figures it applies to all sizes.

Tension
22 sts and 31 rows to 10cm over patt on 4mm needles

Materials
350 [400:450] g double knitting yarn in main colour (A)
175 [225:275] g in contrast colour (B)
125 [175:175] g in contrast colour (C)
1 pair each 3¼mm and 4mm knitting needles.

Back
**Using 3¼mm needles and A, cast on 104[112:116] sts.
Work in K2, P2 rib for 7cm.
Next row Rib 12[16:18], *work twice into next st, rib 7, rep from * to last 4[8:10] sts, K to end. 115[123:127] sts.
Change to 4mm needles, commence patt.
Sl all sl sts with yarn on WS of work.
1st row (RS) With A, K.
2nd row With A, P.
3rd row With B, K3, *sl 1, K3, rep from * to end.
4th row With B, P3, *sl 1, P3, rep from * to end.
5th row With C, K1, *sl 1, K3, rep from * ending last rep K1.
6th row With C, K1, *sl 1, K3, rep from * ending last rep K1.
7th and 8th rows As 3rd and 4th rows.
9th row As 5th row with A instead of C.
10th row With A, P1, *sl 1, P3, rep from * ending last rep P1.
11th-12th rows As 1st-2nd rows.
13th row With B, K1, *sl 1, K3, rep from * ending last rep K1.
14th row With B, P1, *sl 1, P3, rep from * ending last rep P1.
15th row With C, K3, *sl 1, K3, rep from * to end.
16th row With C, K3, *sl 1, K3, rep from * to end.

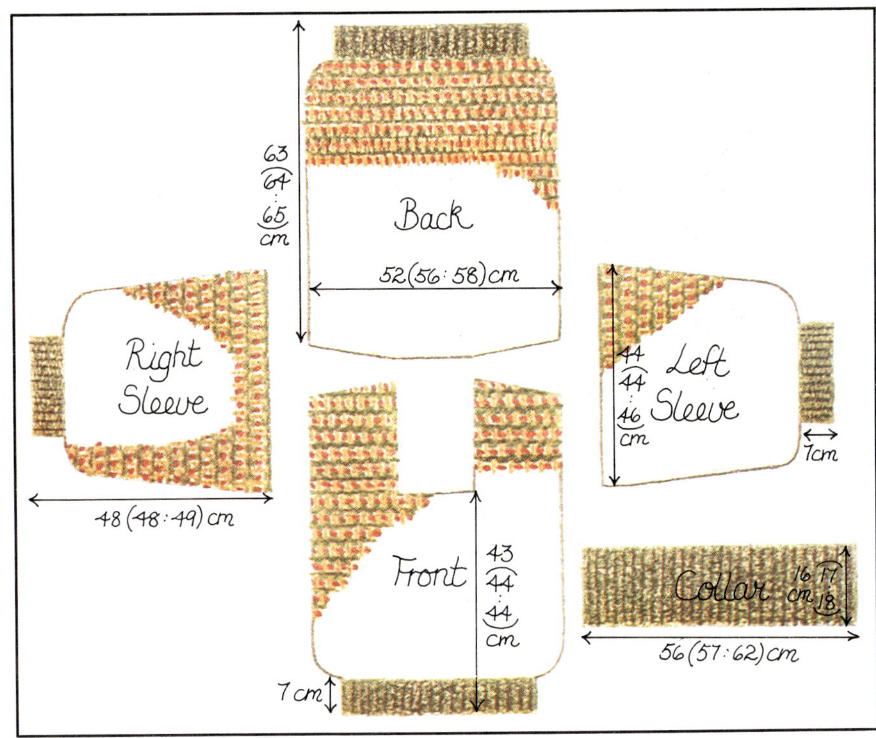

17th and 18th rows As 13th and 14th rows.
19th row As 15th row with A instead of C.
20th row With A, P3, *sl 1, P3, rep from * to end.
These 20 rows form the patt.**
Cont in patt until work measures 63[64:65]cm from cast-on edge, ending with a WS row.
Shape shoulders
Keeping patt correct, cast off 13[14:15] sts at beg of next 4 rows, then 14[15:14] sts at beg of foll 2 rows. Cast off rem 35[37:39] sts.

Front
Work as given for back from ** to **
Cont in patt until work measures 43[44:44]cm ending with a WS row.
Shape neck
Next row Patt 40[43:44], cast off 35[37:39], patt to end.
Work right side of neck first.
Cont without shaping until work matches back to shoulder shaping, ending at armhole edge.
Shape shoulder
Cast off 13[14:15] sts at beg of next and foll alt row. Work 1 row.

Cast off rem 14[15:14] sts.
With WS of work facing, return to sts for left side of neck. Join in yarn and complete to match first side, reversing shaping.

Sleeves
Using 3¼mm needles and A, cast on 56 sts. Work 7cm K2, P2 rib.
Next row Rib 5[5:1], *work twice into next st, rib 1, rep from * to last 5[5:1] sts, rib to end. 79[79:83] sts.
Change to 4mm needles.
Cont in patt as given for back, inc 1 st at each end of the next and every foll 12th row until there are 97[97:101] sts
Cont without shaping until work measures 48[48:49]cm from cast-on edge, ending with WS row. Cast off.

Collar
Using 3¼mm needles and A, cast on 172[176:192] sts. Work K2, P2 rib for 16[17:18]cm. Cast off in rib.

To make up
Join shoulder seams. Mark 22[22:23]cm down from shoulders. Set in sleeves. Join side and sleeve seams. Sew on collar.

Bow and Braces Sweater

This intriguing *trompe l'oeil* design is really easy to knit, but it's likely to attract some second glances from fascinated passers-by.

Sizes

To fit 86 [91:97]cm bust
Length 54 [55:56]cm
Sleeve seam 43 [43:45]cm
Note Instructions for the larger sizes are in square brackets []; where there is only one set of figures it applies to all sizes.

Tension

22 sts and 28 rows to 10cm over st st on 4mm needles

Materials

350 [350:400] g double knitting yarn in main colour (A)
50g in each of 3 contrast colours (B) (C) and (D)
1 pair 3¼mm and 4mm needles
3¼mm circular needle
6 buttons

Front

**Using 3¼mm needles and B, cast on 91 [97:103] sts.
1st row K1, *P1, K1, rep from *.
2nd row P1, *K1, P1, rep from *.
Rep the last 2 rows for 7cm, ending with a 1st row.
Next row Rib 4 [6:9], pick up loop between st just worked and next st, and work into back of it, — called M1 —, (rib 7, M1) 12 times, rib 3 [7:10]. 104 [110:116] sts.
Change to 4mm needles and beg with a K row work 2 rows st st.**
Cont to work in st st, reading patt from chart A as folls:
1st row K15 [18:21] B, K 1st row from chart A, K24B, K 1st row from chart A, K15 [18:21] B.
2nd row P15 [18:21] B, P 2nd row from chart A, P24B, P 2nd row from chart A, P15 [18:21] B.
These 2 rows establish the position of the brace thongs.
Cont until the 22 rows of chart A have been worked.
Next row K24 [27:30] A, 7D, 42A, 7D, 24 [27:30] A.
Next row P24 [27:30] A, 7D, 42A, 7D, 24 [27:30] A.
The last 2 rows establish the position of the braces.
Rep the last 2 rows 28 times more.
Shape armholes
Keeping patt correct as set, cast off 7 [7:8] sts at beg of next 2 rows. Dec 1 st at each end of the next and every foll alt row until 74 [78:82] sts rem.

Work 1 [1:3] rows straight.
Cont without shaping, keeping patt correct as set, commence patt from chart B as folls:
Next row Patt 26 [28:30] A, K 1st row from chart B, patt 26 [28:30] A.
Next row Patt 26 [28:30] A, P 2nd row from chart B, patt 26 [28:30] A.
These 2 rows establish the position of the bow tie. Cont as set until the 8 rows of chart B have been worked. Keeping the patt for braces correct work 4 rows straight.
Shape neck
Next row Patt 32 [33:34] sts, turn leaving rem sts on a spare needle, patt to end.
Complete left side of neck first.
Keeping patt correct, dec 1 st at neck edge on the next and every foll alt row until 22 [23:24] sts rem, ending at armhole edge.
Shape shoulder
Cast off 7 sts at the beg of next and foll alt row.

Patt 1 row. Cast off rem 8 [9:10] sts.
With RS of work facing return to sts on spare needle.
Sl centre 10 [12:14] sts on to a stitch holder, join in yarn to next st, patt to end. Patt 1 row.
Complete to match first side of neck reversing shapings.

Back

Work as given for front from ** to **. Cont to work in st st, reading patt from chart A as folls:
Next row K40 [43:46] B, K 1st row from chart A, K39 [42:45] B.
Next row P39 [42:45] B, P 2nd row from chart A, P40 [43:46] B.
The last 2 rows establish the position of the braces thong.
Cont until the 22 rows of chart A have been worked.
Next row K49 [52:55] A, 7D, 48 [51:54]A.
Next row P48 [51:54] A, 7D, 49 [52:55] A.

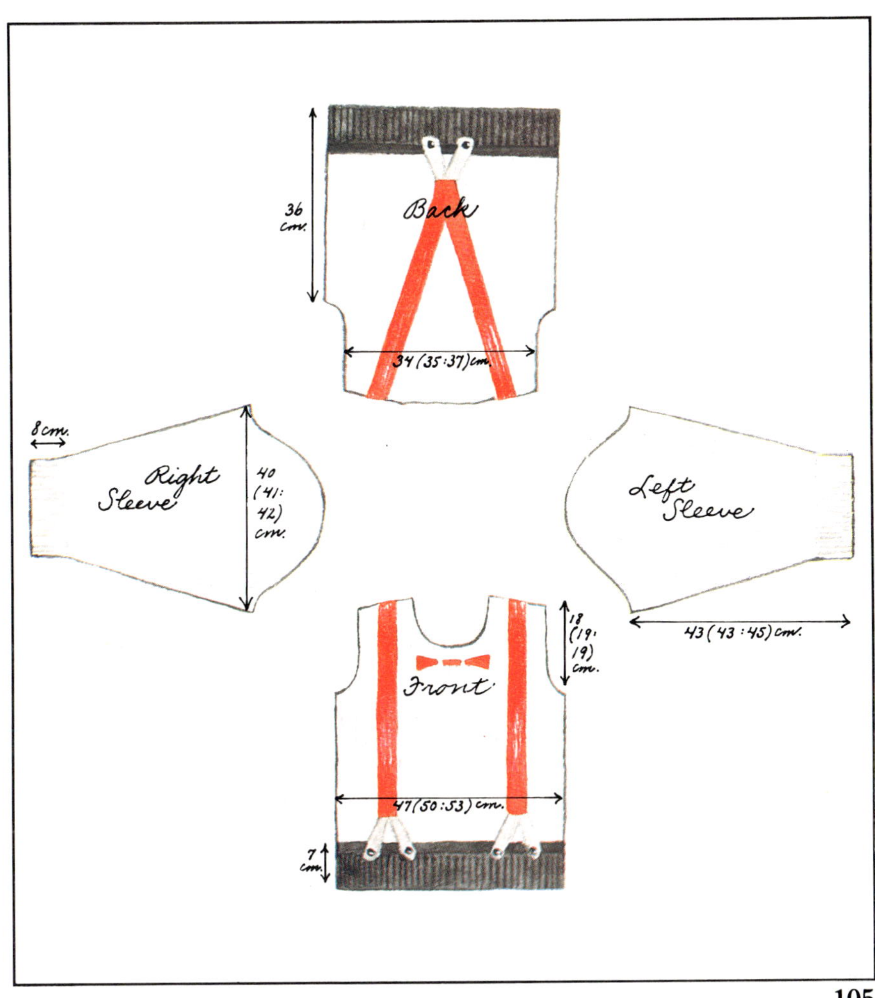

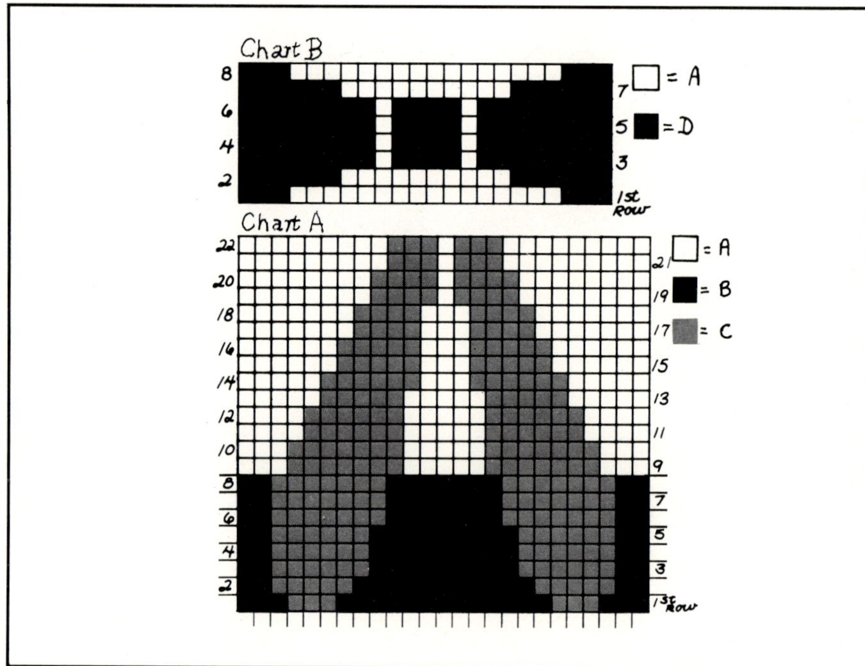

Rep the last 2 rows once more.
Next row K48 [51:54] A, 8D, 48 [51:54] A.
Next row P48 [51:54] A, 8D, 48 [51:54] A.
Rep the last 2 rows once more.
Next row K47 [50:53] A, 10D, 47 [50:53] A.
Next row P47 [50:53] A, 10D, 47 [50:53] A.
Rep the last 2 rows once more, then the first of them again.
Next row P46 [49:52] A, 12D, 46 [49:52] A.
Next row K46 [49:52] A, 12D, 46 [49:52] A.
Rep the last 2 rows once more.
Next row P45 [48:51] A, 14D, 45 [48:51] A.
Next row K45 [48:51] A, 14D, 45 [48:51] A.
Rep the last 2 rows once more.
Next row P44 [47:50] A, 7D, 2A, 7D, 44 [47:50] A.
Next row K44 [47:50] A, 7D, 2A, 7D, 44 [47:50] A.
Rep the last 2 rows once more.
Next row P43 [46:49] A, 7D, 4A, 7D, 43 [46:49] A.
Next row K43 [46:49] A, 7D, 4A, 7D, 43 [46:49] A.
Rep the last 2 rows once more.
Next row P42 [45:48] A, 7D, 6A, 7D, 42 [45:48] A.
Next row K42 [45:48] A, 7D, 6A, 7D, 42 [45:48] A.

Rep the last 2 rows once more, then the first of them again.
Next row K41 [44:47] A, 7D, 8A, 7D, 41 [44:47] A.
Next row P41 [44:47] A, 7D, 8A, 7D, 41 [44:47] A.
Rep the last 2 rows once more, then the first of them again.
Next row P40 [43:46] A, 7D, 10A, 7D, 40 [43:46] A.
Next row K40 [43:46] A, 7D, 10A, 7D, 40 [43:46] A.
Rep the last 2 rows once more.
Next row P39 [42:45] A, 7D, 12A, 7D, 39 [42:45] A.
Next row K39 [42:45] A, 7D, 12A, 7D, 39 [42:45] A.
Rep the last 2 rows once more, then the first of them again.
Next row K38 [41:44] A, 7D, 14A, 7D, 38 [41:44] A.
Next row P38 [41:44] A, 7D, 14A, 7D, 38 [41:44] A.
Rep the last 2 rows once more.
Next row K37 [40:43] A, 7D, 16A, 7D, 37 [40:43] A.
Next row P37 [40:43] A, 7D, 16A, 7D, 37 [40:43] A.
Rep the last 2 rows once more, then the first of them again.
Next row P36 [39:42] A, 7D, 18A, 7D, 36 [39:42] A.

Shape armholes
Next row Cast off 7 [7:8] sts, K29 [32:34] A, 7D, 18A, 7D, 36 [39:42] A.

Next row Cast off 7 [7:8] sts, P29 [32:34] A, 7D, 18A, 7D, 29 [32:34] A.
Keeping patt for braces correct by moving them to the armhole edges by one st on the 2nd then on every foll 5th and then 4th row as before, *at the same time*, dec 1 st at each end of the next and every foll alt row until 74 [78:82] sts rem.
Cont in patt without shaping until there are 9 [11:13] sts in A at armhole edge. Then cont as set until work measures same as front to shoulder shaping, ending with a P row.
Shape shoulders
Cast off 7 sts at beg of next 4 rows and 8 [9:10] sts at beg of foll 2 rows. Leave rem 30 [32:34] sts on a stitch holder.

Sleeves
Using 3¼mm needles and A, cast on 40 [42:44] sts and work in K1, P1 rib for 8cm.
Change to 4mm needles and cont in st st, inc 1 st at each end of the next and every foll 4th row until there are 88 [90:92] sts.
Cont without shaping until work measures 43 [43:45] cm from cast-on edge, ending with a P row.
Shape top
Cast off 7 [7:8] sts at beg of next 2 rows. Dec 1 st at each end of the next and every foll 3rd row until 38 sts rem. Cast off.

To make up
Join shoulder seams.
With RS of work facing, using 3¼mm circular needle and A, join in yarn to centre of sts on front stitch holder, K 5[6:7], K up 22 sts up right side of neck, K30 [32:34] sts on back neck, K up 22 sts down left side of neck, then K 5 [6:7] sts from front stitch holder. 84 [88:92] sts. Mark first st for beg of round.
Work in rounds of K1, P1 rib for 3cm, ending at the end of a round. Now work in rows for a further 5cm.
Cast off in rib. Join side and sleeve seams.
Set in sleeves, gathering fullness to form a puff top. Sew on buttons to brace thongs.
Lightly press corners of collar to form wings.

Patterned Two-piece

Put on the style in this super-sophisticated but unusual
two-piece combining a pocketed waistcoat and classic
cardigan in an interesting positive-negative colour scheme.

Sizes
To fit 81[86:91:97]cm bust
Waistcoat length 56[57:58:60]cm
Cardigan length 66[67:69:70]cm
Sleeve seam 43[43:44:44]cm

Note Instructions for larger sizes are in square brackets[]; where there is only one set of figures it applies to all sizes.

Tension
Waistcoat:
31 sts and 34 rows to 10cm over patt on 3¼mm needles
Cardigan:
19 sts and 24 rows to 10cm over patt on 4½mm needles

Materials
Waistcoat
225 [225:275:275] g four-ply yarn in main colour (A)
75 [75:100:100] g in contrast colour (B)
1 pair each 2¾mm and 3¼mm needles
6 buttons
Cardigan
600 [600:650:650] g Aran-weight yarn in main colour (C)
175 [175:225:225] g in contrast colour (D)
1 pair each 3¾mm and 4½mm needles
7 buttons

Waistcoat

Back
Using 2¾mm needles and A, cast on 103[109:115:123] sts.
Work in K1, P1 rib as foll:
1st row (RS) K1, *P1, K1, rep from * to end.
2nd row P1, *K1, P1, rep from * to end.
Rep the last 2 rows for 8cm ending with a 1st row.
Next row Rib 11[12:13:15], pick up loop between last st worked and next st and work into back of it — called M1 —, (rib 2, M1) 41[43:45:47] times, rib to end. 145[153:161:171] sts.
Change to 3¼mm needles and work in st st foll patt from Chart 1, working edge sts as shown and rep the 12 patt sts across the row.
Cont in patt until work measures 34[34:34:35]cm from cast-on edge, ending with a WS row.

Shape armholes
Keeping patt correct, cast off 7 sts at beg of next 2 rows.
Dec 1 st at each of the next 9[9:11:11] rows, then at each end of every foll alt row until 99[103:105:113] sts rem.
Cont without shaping until work measures 56[57:58:60]cm from cast-on edge, ending with a WS row.
Shape shoulders
Cast off 8[9:8:9] sts at beg of next 4 rows and 9[8:9:10] sts at beg of foll 2 rows.
Cast off rem 49[51:55:57] sts.

Pocket lining
Using 3¼mm needles and A, cast on 31 sts. Beg with a K row cont in st st until work measures 10cm from beg, ending with a P row. Leave these sts on as spare needle.

Left front
**Using 2¾mm needles and A, cast on 51[55:57:61] sts.
Work in K1, P1 rib as given for back for 8cm, ending with a 1st row.
Next row Rib 6[8:7:8], M1, (rib 2, M1) 20[20:22:23] times, rib to end. 72[76:80:85] sts.****
Change to 3¼mm needles and work in st st foll patt from Chart 2.
Cont in patt until work measures 18cm from cast-on edge, ending with a WS row.
Place pocket
Next row Patt 16[18:20:22], sl next 41 sts on to a stitch holder, patt across 31 sts of pocket lining at same time inc 10 sts evenly, patt to end.
Cont in patt until work matches back to underarm, ending with a WS row.
Shape armhole and neck
Next row Cast off 7 sts, patt to last 2 sts, K2 tog.
Next row Patt to end.
Dec 1 st at armhole edge on next 9[9:11:11] rows then on every foll alt row and *at the same time*, dec 1 st at neck edge on the next and every foll alt row until 36[36:35:38] sts rem.
Keeping armhole edge straight cont to dec at neck edge on every foll 3rd row until 25[26:25:28] sts rem.
Cont without shaping until work matches back to shoulder shaping ending with a WS row.

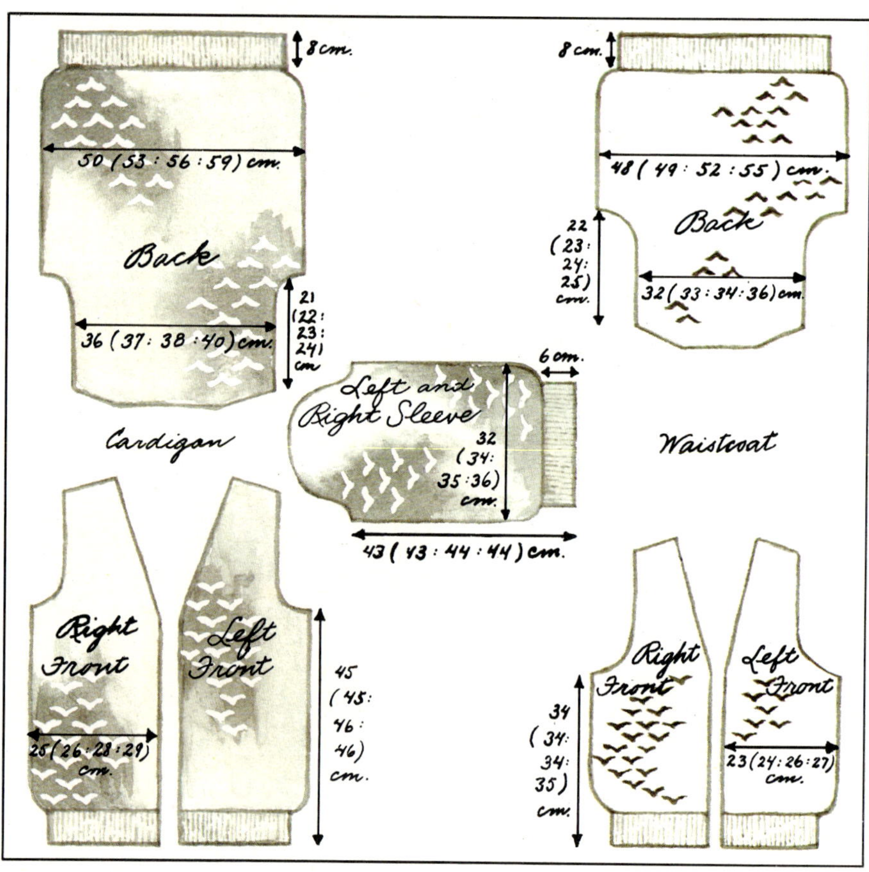

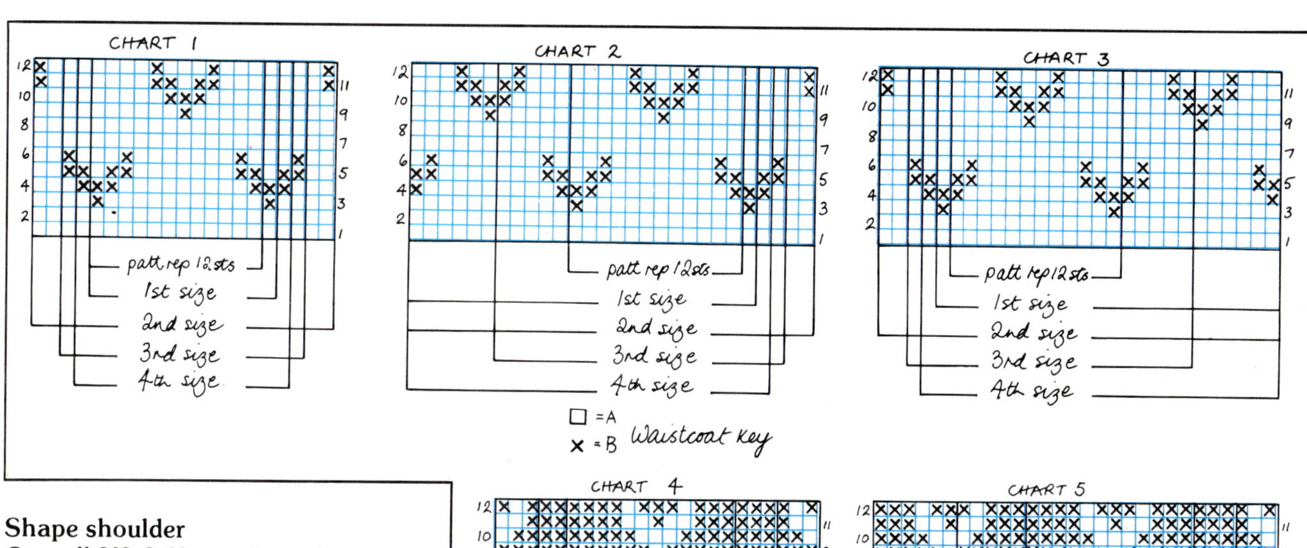

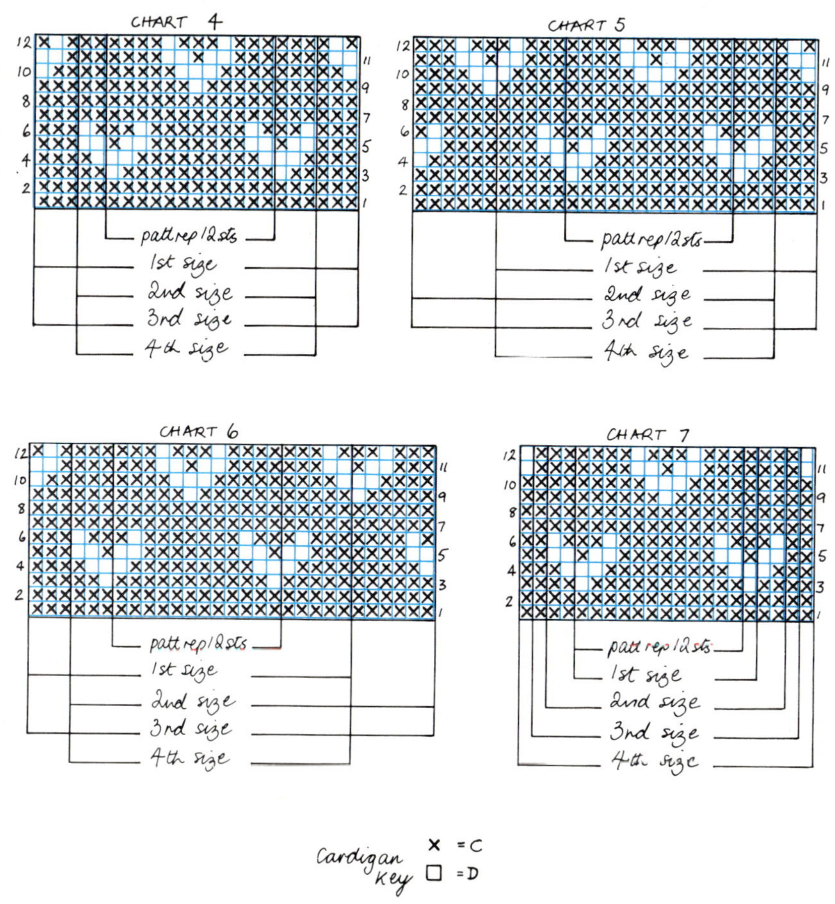

Shape shoulder

Cast off 8[9:8:9] sts at beg of next and foll alt row. Work 1 row. Cast off rem 9[8:9:10] sts.

Right front

Work as given for left front from ** to **.

Change to 3¼mm needles and work in st st foll patt from Chart 3.
Complete to match left front, omitting pocket and reversing shapings.

To make up

Do not press.
Join shoulder seams.

Pocket edging

With RS of work facing, using 2¾mm needles, join in A to 41 sts on stitch holder.
1st row K1, *P1, K1, rep from * to end.
2nd row P1, *K1, P1, rep from * to end.
Rep the last 2 rows 3 times more.
Cast off in rib.
Catch down pocket edging and pocket lining.

Buttonband

Using 2¾mm needles and A, cast on 11 sts.
1st row (RS) K2, *P1, K1, rep from * to last st, K1.
2nd row *K1, P1, rep from * to last st, K1.
Rep the last 2 rows until band, when slightly stretched, fits up left front edge to centre back neck.
Cast off in rib.

Buttonhole band

Sew on buttonband. Mark the position of six buttonholes, the first to come 2cm from lower edge, the last 2cm below front neck shaping, with the others evenly spaced between.
Using 2¾mm needles and A, cast on 11 sts.
Work as given for buttonband making buttonholes opposite markers as folls:
1st row (RS) Rib 5, cast off 2, rib 4.
2nd row Rib 4, cast on 2, rib 5.
Sew on buttonhole band, joining to buttonband at centre back neck.

Armbands

With RS of work facing, using 2¾mm needles and A, K up to 114[118:124:130] sts evenly around the armhole edge.
Work 10 rows K1, P1 rib. Cast off in rib.
Join side seams. Sew on button.

Cardigan

Back

Using 3¾mm needles and C, cast on 81[85:91:97] sts and work in K1, P1

rib as given for waistcoat back for 8cm, ending with a 1st row.
Next row Rib 8[5:8:4], M1, (rib 5[5:5:6], M1) 13[15:15:15] times, rib to end. 95[101:107:113] sts.
Change to 4½mm needles and work in st st foll patt from Chart 4. Cont in patt until work measures approx 45[45:46:46]cm from cast-on edge, ending with a WS row.

Shape armholes
Keeping patt correct, cast off 5 sts at beg of next 2 rows. Dec 1 st at each end of the next 3[3:5:5] rows, then on every foll alt row until 69 [71:73:77] sts rem.
Cont without shaping until work measures 66[67:69:70]cm from cast-on edge, ending with a WS row.

Shape shoulders
Cast of 6[6:6:7] sts at beg of next 4 rows and 7[7:7:6] sts at beg of foll 2 rows.
Cast off rem 31[33:35:37] sts.

Left front
***Using 3¾mm needles and C, cast on 39[41:45:47] sts and work in K1, P1 rib as given for waistcoat back for 8cm, ending with a 1st row.
Next row Rib 2[5:5:4], M1, (rib 5[4:5:5], M1) 7[8:7:8] times, rib to end, 47[50:53:56] sts. ***
Change to 4½mm needles and work in st st foll patt from Chart 5. Cont in patt until work matches back to underarm, ending with a WS row.

Shape armhole and neck
Next row Cast off 5 sts, patt to last 2 sts, K2 tog.
Next row Patt to end.
Dec 1 st at armhole edge on the next 3[3:5:5] rows then on every foll alt row *at the same time*, dec 1 st at neck edge on the next and every foll alt row until 19[19:19:20] sts rem.
Cont without shaping until work matches back to shoulder shaping, ending with a WS row.

Shape shoulder
Cast off 6[6:6:7] sts at beg of next and foll alt row.
Work 1 row.
Cast off rem 7[7:7:6] sts.

Right front
Work as given for left front from *** to ***.
Change to 4½mm needles and working in patt from Chart 6 complete to match left front reversing shapings.

Sleeves
Using 3¾mm needles and C, cast on 38[40:42:44] sts and work in K1, P1 rib for 6cm.
Next row Rib 8[8:9:10], M1, (rib 1, M1) 22[24:24:24] times, rib to end. 61[65:67:69] sts.
Change to 4½mm needles and work in st st foll patt from Chart 7. Cont in patt until work measures approx 43[43:44:44]cm from cast-on edge, ending with a 6th[6th:8th:8th] patt row.

Shape top
Keeping patt correct, cast off 5 sts at beg of next 2 rows.
1st size only
Dec 1 st at each end of the next and foll 4th row. Work 1 row. 47 sts.
All sizes
Dec 1 st at each end of the next and every foll alt row until 21 sts rem, ending with a WS row. Cast off.

To make up
Do not press.
Join shoulder, side and sleeve seams. Set in sleeves.
Buttonband
Using 3¾mm needles and C, cast on 9 sts. Work as given for buttonband of waistcoat.
Buttonhole band
Sew on buttonband. Mark the position of seven buttonholes, the first to come 2cm from lower edge, the last 2cm below front neck shaping, with the others evenly spaced between.
Using 3¾mm needles and C, cast on 9 sts.
Work as given for buttonband making buttonholes opposite markers as foll:
1st row (RS) Rib 4, cast off 2, rib 3.
2nd row Rib 3, cast on 2, rib 4.
Sew on buttonhole band, joining to buttonband at centre back neck.
Sew on buttons.

Special technique — working an armband

1 *The basic waistcoat has armbands which are knitted on to the main pattern pieces. Begin by joining the shoulder seams.*

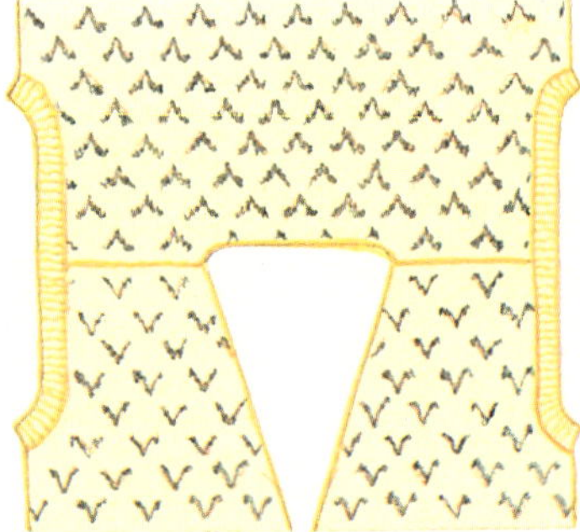

2 *With the right side of the work facing knit up the required number of stitches evenly round the armhole edge. Work in single rib to the required depth. Cast off in rib.*

3 *Finish by joining the side seams. Join the ribbed welt and armband with a flat seam. Join the stocking stitch parts with an invisible seam.*

Fireworks Sweater

Set a few sparks alight with this stunning design — a perfect example of the effectiveness of sharp, bright colours on a black background.

Size
To fit 82-94cm chest
Length 65cm
Sleeve seam 41cm

Tension
17 sts and 25 rows to 10cm over st st
on 5mm needles

Materials
450g Aran-weight yarn in main colour
(A)
50g each in 7 contrast colours
1 pair each 4mm and 5mm knitting
needles
Set of 4mm needles pointed at both
ends.

Back
*Using 4mm needles and A, cast on
71 sts. Work in K1, P1 rib as folls:
1st row K1, (P1, K1) to end.
2nd row P1, (K1, P1) to end.
Rep last 2 rows 9 times more.
Change to 5mm needles. Beg with a
K row cont in st st working from chart
inc 10 sts evenly across 1st row. 81 sts.
Cont until 98 rows have been worked in
st st, ending with a P row.
Shape raglan armholes
Dec 1 st at each end of next and
every foll alt row until 33 sts rem,
ending with a P row. Cast off.

Front
Work as given for back from * to *
Shape raglan armholes
Dec 1 st at each end of next and
every foll alt row until 77 sts rem,
ending with a P row.
Divide for neck
Next row K2 tog, patt 36, turn,
leaving rem sts on a spare needle.
Cont to dec at armhole edge as
before, *at the same time*, dec 1 st at
neck edge on the next, then every foll
4th and 2nd row until 1 st rem.
Fasten off.
With RS of work facing, sl centre st
on to a safety pin, join in yarn to next
st, patt to last 2 sts, K2 tog.
Complete to match first side of neck.

Sleeves
Using 4mm needles and A, cast on
35 sts. Work 15 rows K1, P1 rib.
Change to 5mm needles and st st
working patt from chart, inc 10 sts
evenly across 1st row. 45 sts. Inc 1 st
at each end of foll 9th and every foll

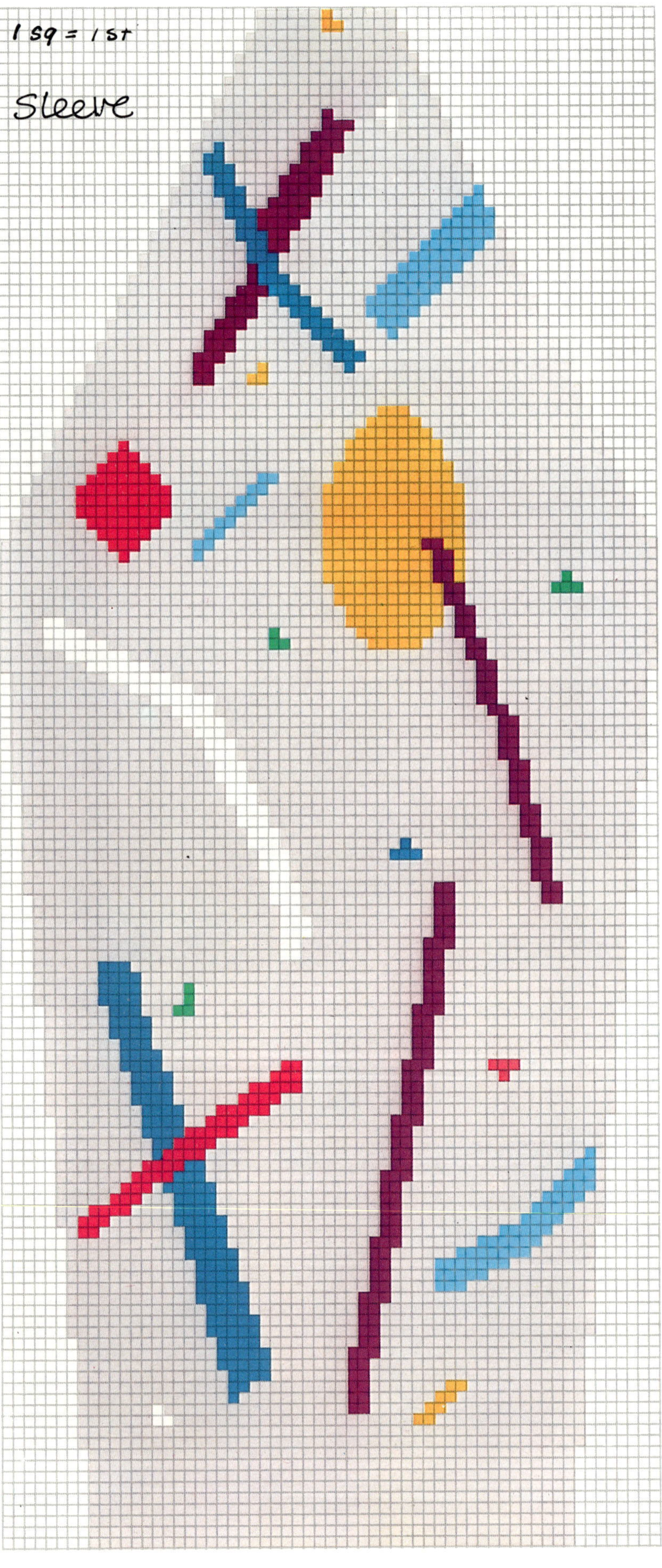

10th row until there are 61 sts. Cont until 91 rows have been worked in st st, ending with a K row.

Shape raglan top
Dec 1 st at each end of next and every foll alt row until 11 sts rem, ending with a P row. Cast off.

To make up
Press lightly on WS over a damp cloth. Join raglan seams neatly.

Neck border
With RS of work facing, using three of set of 4mm needles, K up 31 sts from back neck, 11 sts from sleeve top, 31 sts down left side of neck, K centre st, K up 31 sts up right side of neck and 11 sts from sleeve top. 116 sts. Using fourth needle work in rounds.
1st round Work in K1, P1 rib to within 1 st of centre st, sl 1, K2 tog, psso, rib to end. Rep 1st round for 3cm. Cast off in rib dec on this round as before.
Join side and sleeve seams.

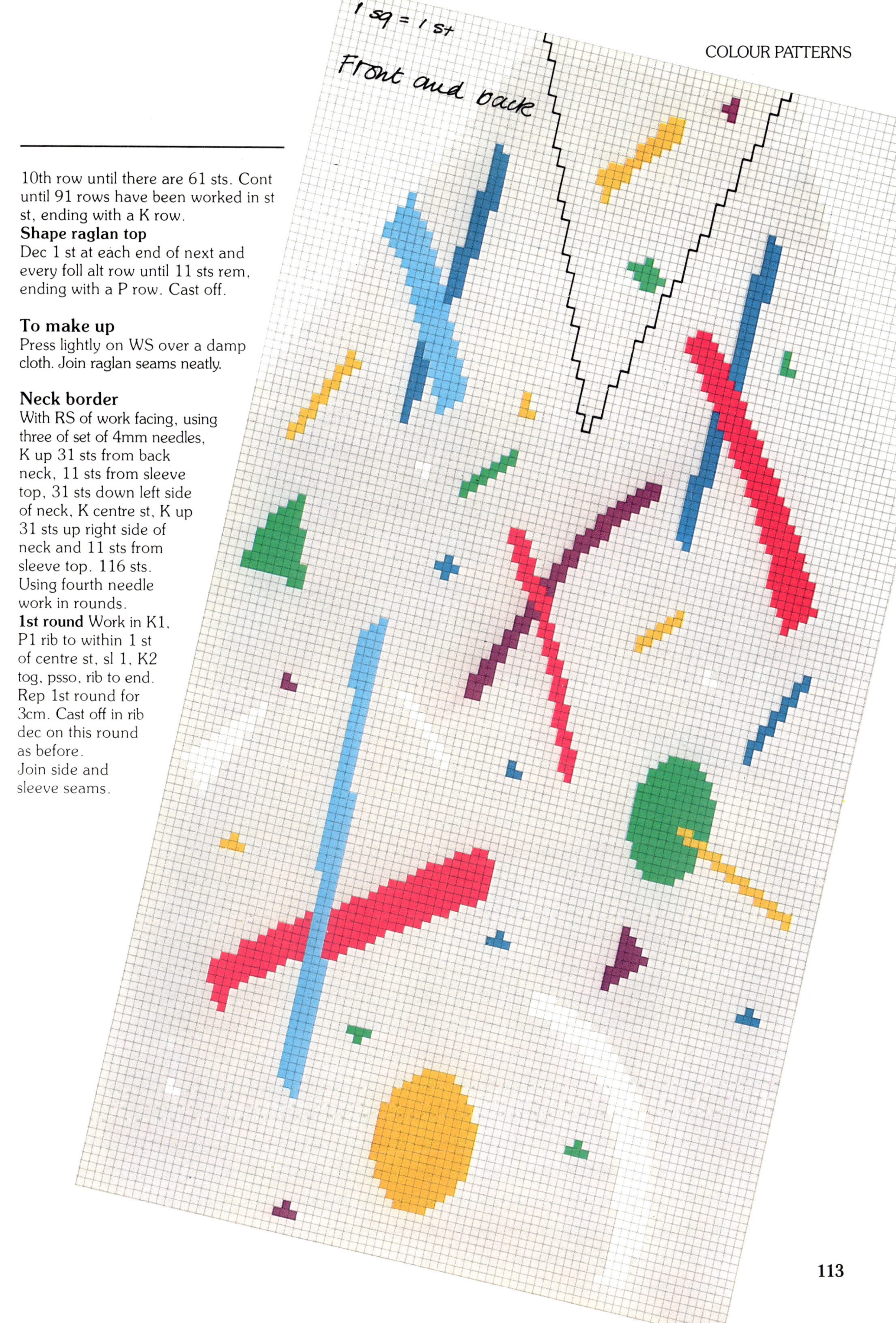

Harlequin Sweater and T-shirt

Join in the carnival spirit with this original, multicoloured
sweater, finished with flattering ruffles at the neck and waist.
The child's T-shirt is simply made from two rectangles.

Sweater
Sizes
To fit 76 [81:87] cm bust
Length 48 [52:56] cm
Sleeve seam 43cm
Note Instructions for the larger sizes
are in square brackets []; where there
is only one set of figures, it applies to
all sizes.

Tension
26 sts and 25 rows to 10cm over patt
on 4mm needles

Materials
200 [225:250] g four-ply yarn in main
colour (A)
150g each in two contrast colours (B)
and (C)
1 pair 4mm knitting needles
4mm circular needle

Back
**Using 4mm needles and B, cast on
202 [214:230] sts.
Next row K.
Change to C.
Next row P.
Next row K.
Change to A.
Beg with a P row work 18 rows st st.
Next row *P2 tog, rep from * to end.
101 [107:115] sts.
Using small separate balls of B and C,
commence patt from chart, twisting
yarns when changing colours to avoid
a hole. Read RS rows (odd-
numbered) from right to left and WS
rows (even-numbered) from left to
right.
Cont until work measures
29 [33:37] cm from cast-on edge,
ending with a P row.

Shape armholes
Keeping patt correct, cast off 6 sts at
beg of next 2 rows and 5 sts at beg of
foll 2 rows. Dec 1 st at each end of
next 1 [2:4] rows. 77 [81:85] sts. **
Cont without shaping until work
measures 48 [52:56] cm from cast-on
edge, ending with a WS row.

T-shirt chart (page 117)

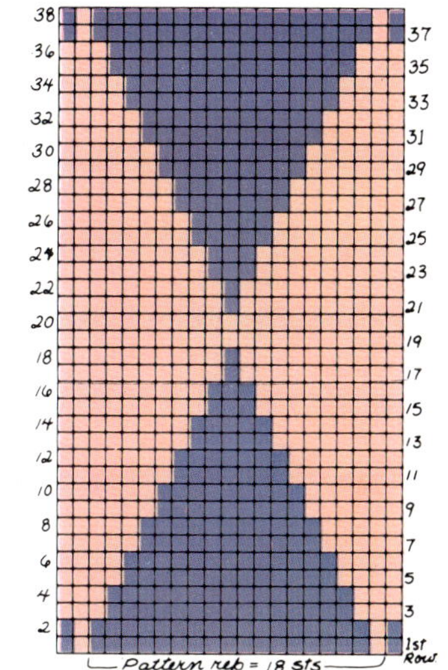

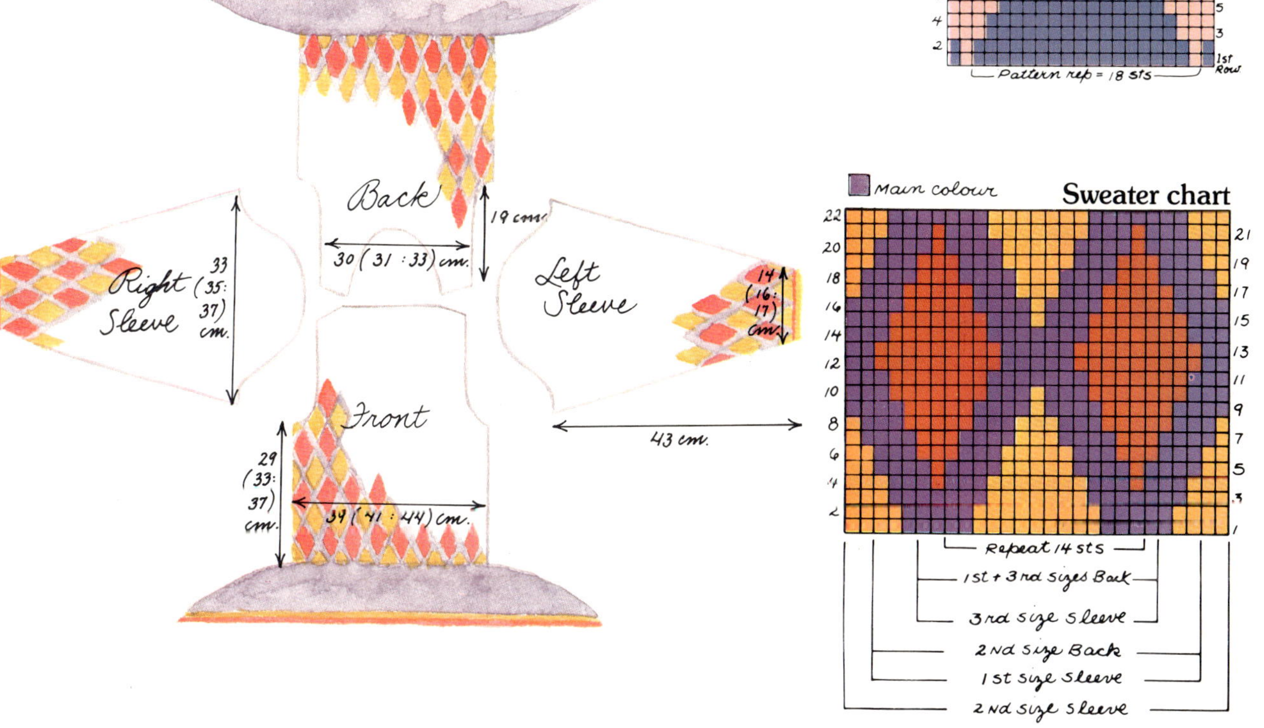

Shape shoulders
Cast off 8 sts at beg of next 2 rows and 15 [17:19] sts at beg of foll 2 rows. Cast off rem sts.

Front
Work as given for back from ** to **. Cont without shaping until work measures 41 [45:49] cm from cast-on edge, ending with a WS row.
Shape neck
Next row Patt 33 [35:37], cast off 11 sts, patt to end.
Complete right side of neck first.
Next row Patt to end.
***Next row** Cast off 5 sts, patt to end.
Next row Patt to end.
Next row Cast off 3 sts, patt to end.
Next row Patt to end.
Dec 1st at neck edge on next and foll alt row. 23 [25:27] sts.
Cont without further shaping until work matches back to shoulder shaping, ending at armhole edge.
Shape shoulder
Cast off 8 sts at beg of next row.
Work 1 row.
Cast off rem 15 [17:19] sts.
With WS of work facing return to sts for left side of neck.
Complete to match right side of neck, working from *** to end.

Sleeves
Using 4mm needles and A, cast on 37 [41:45] sts.
Beg with a K row work 3 rows in st st.
Change to C. Knit 2 rows.
Change to B.
Next row P.
Next row K.
Change to A.
Form hem
Next row *P next st and corresponding st of cast-on row tog, rep from * to end.
Using small separate balls of B and C commence patt from chart, *at the same time*, inc 1 st at each end of the 3rd and every foll 4th row until there are 87 [91:95] sts.
Cont without shaping until work measures 43cm from hem, ending with a P row.
Shape sleeve top
Keeping patt correct, cast off 3 sts at beg of next 2 rows and 2 sts at beg of foll 2 rows.
Dec 1 st at each end of foll 5th row.

Patt 2 rows.
Dec 1 st at beg of next 16 rows.
Cast off 2 sts at beg of foll 4 rows.
Dec 1 st at beg of foll 2 rows.
Cast off 2 sts at beg of foll 2 rows.
Dec 1 st at beg of next 6 rows.
Cast off.

To make up
Press pieces.
Join right shoulder seam.
Neck frill
With WS of work facing, using 4mm circular needle and A, K up 88 [100:112] sts around neck. Work in rows as foll.
Next row *P into front and back of next st, rep from * to end. 176 [200:224] sts.
Beg with a K row work 9 rows st st.
Next row *P into front and back of next st, rep from * to end. 352 [400:448] sts.
Change to C, beg with a K row and work 2 rows st st. Change to B.
Next row K.
Cast off P-wise.
Join left shoulder and collar.
Set in sleeves, gathering head to form puff. Join side and sleeve seams.

Special technique — knitted-in hem

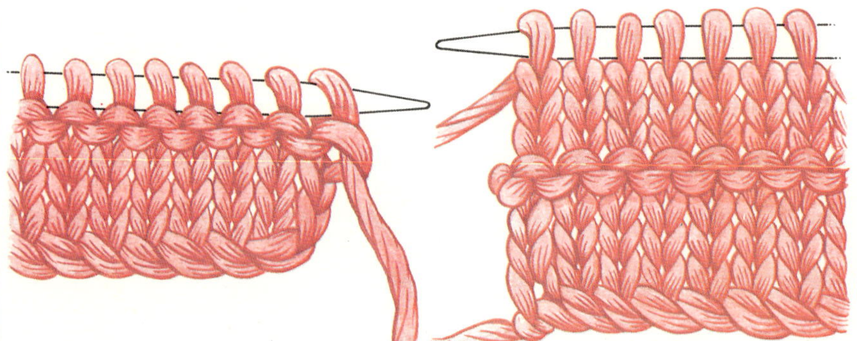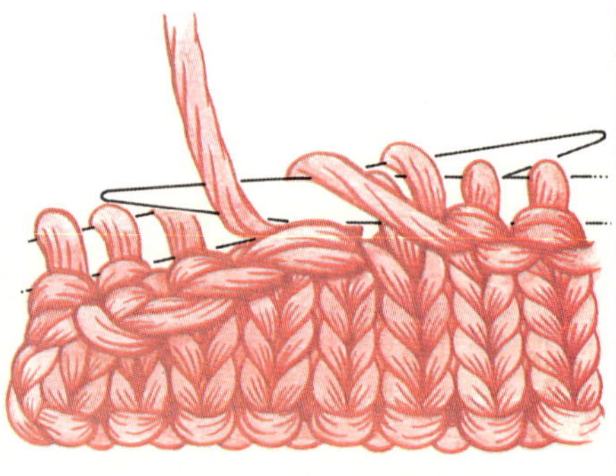

1 *The sleeves on the basic sweater have knitted-in hems. Work the underside of the hem in stocking stitch beginning and ending with a knit row. Knit the next row. This row forms the fold line of the hem.*

2 *Continue in stocking stitch for the same number of rows as for the underside beginning and ending with a knit row.*

3 *On the next row purl each stitch together with the corresponding stitch in the cast-on edge thus completing the hem.*

T-shirt
Size
To fit chest 65cm
Length 45cm

Tension
23 sts and 31 rows to 10cm over patt on 3¼mm needles.

Materials
125g four-ply yarn in each of 2 contrast colours (A) and (B)
1 pair each 2¾mm and 3¼mm needles

Back and front (alike)
Using 2¾mm needles and A, cast on 74 sts. Work in K1, P1 rib for 7cm, ending with a WS row. Inc 1 st at end of last row. 75 sts.
Change to 3¼mm needles. Join in B. Work 114 rows in diamond patt from chart on page 115, marking each end of 76th row for armholes.
Cont in A only, work 8 rows K1, P1 rib. Cast off in rib.

To make up
Sew shoulder seams together 20 sts in from each end.
Armbands Using 2¾mm needles and A, K up 80 sts between markers. Work in K1, P1 rib for 5 rows.
Cast off in rib. Sew side seams together.

'Round the World' Jacket

Warm and chunky with a colourful 'atlas' map design, this
stylish knitted jacket would make an ideal travelling
companion.

Sizes
To fit 86 [91:97] cm bust/chest
Length 61 [64:66] cm
Sleeve seam 45 [47:49] cm

Note Instructions for larger sizes are in square brackets []; where there is only one set of figures it applies to all sizes.

Tension
14 sts and 19 rows to 10cm over st st on 6mm needles

Materials
750 [750:800] g chunky yarn in main colour (A)
50g in each of 5 contrast colours (B), (C), (D), (E) and (F)
Five 2.5cm diameter buttons — 3 in A, 1 in B and 1 in E
1 pair each 5mm and 6mm needles.

Back
Using 5mm needles and A, cast on 76 [80:84] sts.
Work 14 rows in K1, P1 rib.
Change to 6mm needles and beg with a K row cont in st st working in patt from chart for the back section given overleaf, reading K rows from right to left and P rows from left to right.
Work 62 [66:70] rows.
Shape armholes
Cast off 6 sts at beg of next 2 rows.
Dec 1 st at beg of the next and every foll row until 56 sts rem.
Cont without shaping until 102 [106:110] rows have been worked from chart.
Shape shoulders
Cast off 16 sts at beg of next 2 rows.
Cast off rem 24 sts.

Left front
Using 5mm needles and A, cast on 41 [43:45] sts.
1st row P1, *K1, P1, rep from * to last 6 sts, K6.
2nd row K7, *P1, K1, rep from *.
Woman's version only
Rep 1st and 2nd rows 6 times more.
Man's version only
Rep 1st and 2nd rows once more.
1st buttonhole row P1, *K1, P1, rep from * to last 6 sts, K2, cast off 2 sts, K2.
2nd buttonhole row K2, cast on 2

sts, K3, *P1, K1, rep from * to end.
Rep 1st and 2nd rows 4 times more.
Both versions
Change to 6mm needles.
Next row Working from chart K to last 6 sts, K6.
Next row K6, working from chart P to end.
Cont in this way, keeping front edge sts in garter st, working patt and buttonholes for man's version as shown on chart.
Work a further 60 [64:68] rows.
Shape armhole
Cast off 6 sts at beg of next row.
Work 1 row. Dec 1 st at beg of next and every foll alt row until 31 sts rem.
Cont without shaping until 89 [93:97] rows have been worked from chart.
Shape neck
Cast off 11 sts at beg of next row.
Work 1 row.
Dec 1 st at beg of next and every foll alt row until 16 sts rem.
Cont without shaping until 102 [106:110] rows have been worked from chart.
Shape shoulder
Cast off rem sts.

Right front
Using 5mm needles and A, cast on 41 [43:45] sts.
1st row K6, *P1, K1, rep from * to last st, P1.
2nd row *K1, P1, rep from * to last 7 sts, K7.
Man's version only
Rep 1st and 2nd rows 6 times more.
Woman's version only
Rep 1st and 2nd rows once more.
1st buttonhole K2, cast off 2 sts, K2, *P1, K1, rep from * to last st, P1.
2nd buttonhole *K1, P1, rep from * to last 5 sts, K3, cast on 2 sts, K2.
Rep 1st and 2nd rows 4 times more.
Both versions
Change to 6mm needles.
Next row K6, working from chart, K to end.
Next row Working from chart, P to last 6 sts, K6.
Cont in this way, keeping front edge sts in garter st and working patt and buttonholes for woman's version as shown on chart.

Work a further 61 [65:69] rows.
Shape armhole
Cast off 6 sts at beg of next row.
Work 1 row.
Dec 1 st at beg of next and every foll alt row until 31 sts rem.
Cont without shaping until 88 [92:96] rows have been worked from chart.
Shape neck
Cast off 11 sts at beg of next row.
Work 1 row.
Dec 1 st at beg of next and every foll alt row until 16 sts rem.
Cont without shaping until 103 [107:111] rows have been worked from chart.
Shape shoulder
Cast off rem sts.

Sleeves
Using 5mm needles and A, cast on 38 sts. Work 14 rows K1, P1 rib.
Change to 6mm needles and beg with a K row work in st st and patt from chart, for left sleeve only.
Work 2 [6:10] rows. Inc 1 st at each end of the next and every foll 6th row until there are 56 sts. Cont without shaping until 70 [74:78] rows have been worked from chart.
Shape sleeve top
Cast off 6 sts at beg of next 2 rows.
Dec 1 st at beg of every foll row until 14 sts rem. Cast off.

Collar
Using 6mm needles and A, cast on 6 sts. Cont in garter st (every row K).
Work 2 rows.
Inc 1 st at the beg of the next and every foll alt row until there are 14 sts.
Cont without shaping until 60 rows have been worked from cast-on edge.
Dec 1 st at the beg of the next and every foll alt row until 6 sts rem.
Work 2 rows. Cast off.

To make up
Press lightly with a warm iron over a damp cloth.
Join, shoulder side and sleeve seams.
Set in sleeves.
Sew shaped edge of collar to neck edge.
Sew on buttons.

**Jacket
charts**

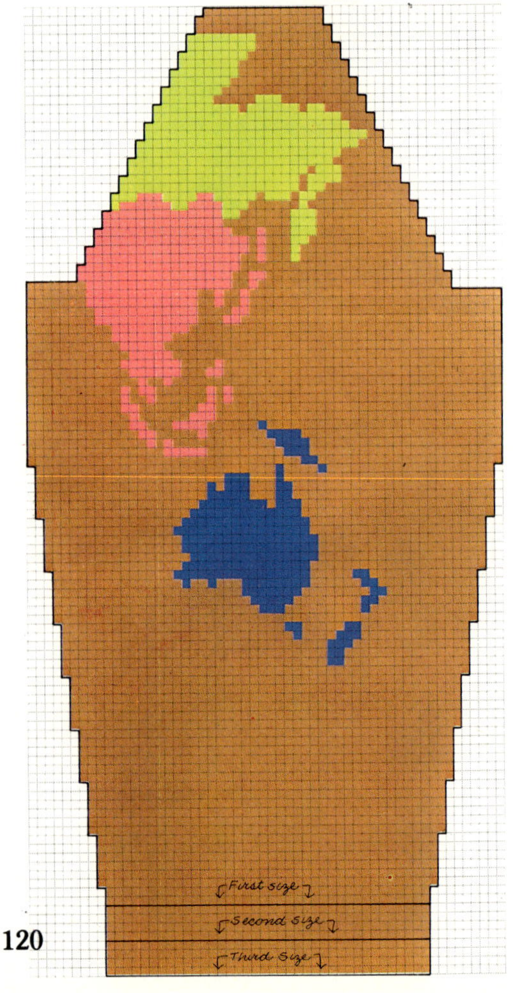

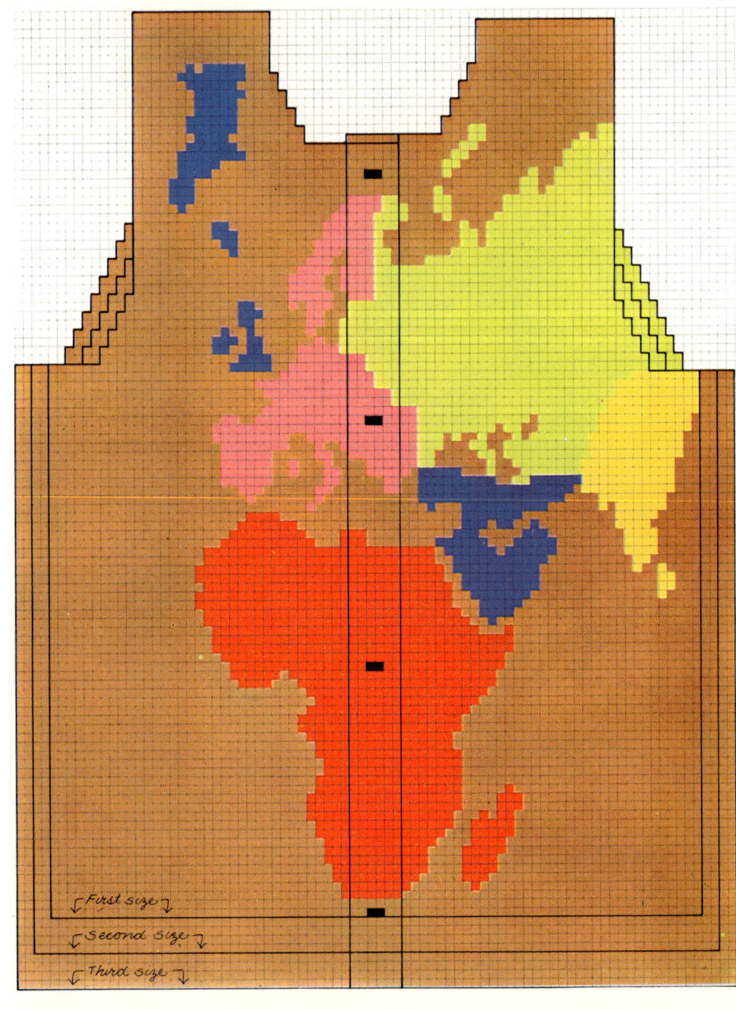

Summer Sweater

Even dull days will seem dazzling in this stunning sweater knitted in cool cotton. The stitch pattern may look intricate, but it's very easy to knit — only one colour is used in each row.

Sizes
To fit 81-86 [91-96]cm bust
Length 56[57]cm
Sleeve seam 11cm
Note Instructions for the larger size are in square brackets []; where there is only one figure it applies to both sizes.

Tension
22 sts and 36 rows to 10cm over patt on 4mm needles

Materials
400 [450] g double knitting yarn in main colour (A)
225 [275] g in contrast colour (B)
1 pair each 3¼mm and 4mm needles
3 buttons

Back
On all RS rows sl all the sl sts with yarn at back of work and on all WS rows sl all the sl sts with the yarn at front of work.
**Using 3¼mm needles and A, cast on 82[90] sts and work 8cm in K1, P1 rib.
Next row Rib 1, work twice into next st — called inc 1 —, *rib 3, inc 1, rep from * to end. 103[113] sts.
Change to 4mm needles.
Next row P.
Commence patt.
1st row (RS) With B, K7[12], *sl 2, K7, sl 2, K15, rep from * ending last rep K7[12].
2nd row With B, K7[12], *sl 2, P7, sl 2, K15, rep from * ending last rep K7[12].
3rd row With A, K2, sl 1, K1[K1, (sl 1, K1) 4 times], sl 1, K4, sl 2, K3, sl 2, K4, (sl 1, K1) 3 times, *(sl 1, K1) twice, sl 1, K4, sl 2, K3, sl 2, K4, (sl 1, K1) 3 times, rep from * ending last rep (sl 1, K1) twice, K1[(sl 1, K1) 5 times] instead of (sl 1, K1) 3 times.
4th row With A, K1, (K1, sl 1) twice, [(K1, sl 1) 5 times], P4, sl 2, K3, sl 2, P4, (sl 1, K1) 3 times, *(sl 1, K1) twice, sl 1, P4, sl 2, K3, sl 2, P4, (sl 1, K1) 3 times, rep from * ending last rep (sl 1, K1) twice, K1[(sl 1, K1) 5 times] instead of (sl 1, K1) 3 times.
5th row With B, K5[10], *sl 2, K4,

sl 1, K1, sl 1, K4, sl 2, K11, rep from * ending last rep K5[10].
6th row With B, K5[10], *sl 2, P4, sl 1, K1, sl 1, P4, sl 2, K11, rep from * ending last rep K5[10].
7th row With A, K2, sl 1[(K1, sl 1,) 4 times], K4, sl 2, K7, sl 2, K4, (sl 1, K1) twice, *sl 1, K1, sl 1, K4, sl 2, K7, sl 2, K4, (sl 1, K1) twice, rep from * ending last rep sl 1, K2[(sl 1, K1) 4 times] instead of (sl 1, K1) twice.
8th row With A, K2, sl 1[(K1, sl 1) 4 times], P4, sl 2, K7, sl 2, P4, (sl 1, K1) twice, *sl 1, K1, sl 1, P4, sl 2, K7, sl 2, P4, (sl 1, K1) twice, rep from * ending last rep sl 1, K2[(sl 1, K1) 4 times] instead of (sl 1, K1) twice.
9th row With B, K3[8], *sl 2, K4, (sl 1, K1) 3 times, sl 1, K4, sl 2, K7, rep from * ending last rep K3[8].
10th row With B, K3[8], *sl 2, P4, (sl 1, K1) 3 times, sl 1, P4, sl 2, K7, rep from * ending last rep K3[8].
11th row With A, K1[K3, sl 1, K1, sl 1], K4, sl 2, K11, sl 2, K4, sl 1, K1, *sl 1, K4, sl 2, K11, sl 2, K4, sl 1, K1, rep from * ending last rep K1[sl 1, K1, sl 1, K3] instead of sl 1, K1.
12th row With A, K1[K3, sl 1, K1, sl 1], P4, sl 2, K11, sl 2, P4, sl 1, K1, *sl 1, P4, sl 2, K11, sl 2, P4, sl 1, K1, rep from * ending last rep K1[sl 1, K1, sl 1, K3] instead of sl 1, K1.
13th row With B, K1, [K1, sl 2, K3], *sl 2, K4, (sl 1, K1) 5 times, sl 1, K4, sl 2, K3, rep from * ending last rep K1[K3, sl 2, K1] instead of K3.
14th row With B, K1[P1, sl 2, K3], *sl 2, P4, (sl 1, K1) 5 times, sl 1, P4, sl 2, K3, rep from * ending last rep K1[K3, sl 2, P1] instead of K3.
15th row With A, K3[8], *sl 2, K15, sl 2, K7, rep from * ending last rep K3[8].
16th row With A, P3[8], *sl 2, K15, sl 2, P7, rep from * ending last rep P3[8].
17th row With B, K1[K3, sl 1, K1, sl 1], K8, sl 2, K3, sl 2, K8, sl 1, K1, *sl 1, K8, sl 2, K3, sl 2, K8, sl 1, K1, rep from * ending last rep K1[sl 1, K1, sl 1, K3] instead of sl 1, K1.

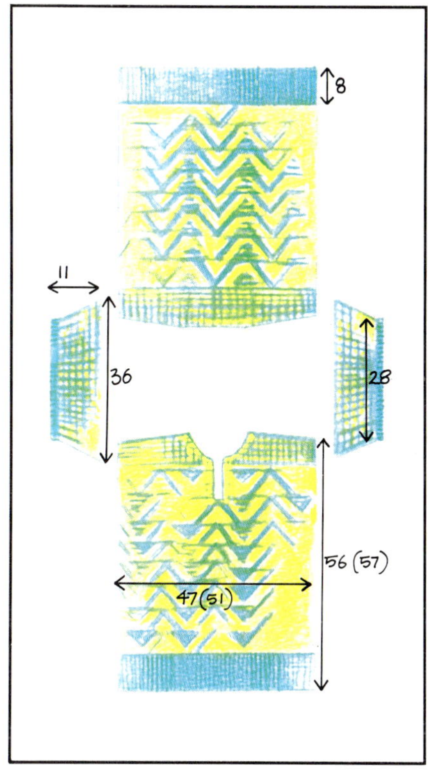

18th row With B, K1, [P3, sl 1, K1, sl 1], P8, sl 2, P3, sl 2, P8, sl 1, K1, *sl 1, P8, sl 2, P3, sl 2, P8, sl 1, K1, rep from * ending last rep K1[sl 1, K1, sl 1, P3] instead of sl 1, K1.
19th row With A, K1[K1, sl 2, K3], *sl 2, K8, sl 1, K1, sl 1, K8, sl 2, K3, rep from * ending last rep K1[K3, sl 2, K1] instead of K3.
20th row With A, P1[P1, sl 2, P3], *sl 2, P8, sl 1, K1, sl 1, P8, sl 2, P3, rep from * ending last rep P1[P3, sl 2, P1] instead of P3.
These 20 rows form the patt. **Rep these 20 rows 6 times more, then work 1st-18th rows again.
Commence yoke
1st-2nd rows With A, K.
3rd-4th rows With B, K1, *sl 1, K1, rep from * to end.
These 4 rows form the yoke patt.
Rep the last 4 rows 3[4] times more, then 1st-2nd rows again.
Shape shoulders
Keeping patt correct, cast off 9[10] sts at beg of next 8 rows. Leave the rem 31[33] sts on a stitch holder.

Front

Work as given for back from * * to
* *. Rep these 20 rows 5 times more,
then 1st-8th[1st-12th] rows again.

Divide for neck

Next row Patt 49[54] sts, cast off 5
sts, patt to end.
Complete right side of neck first.
Cont without shaping until the 20 patt
rows have been worked 7 times in all.

1st size only

Work 1st-16th rows again.

Shape neck

Next row (RS) Cast off 2 sts, patt to
end.
Dec 1 st at neck edge on next row.
Change to yoke patt as given on
back.
Rep the last 2 rows once.

2nd size only

Work 1st-18th rows again. Change to
yoke patt as given on back.

Shape neck

Next row (RS) Cast off 2 sts, patt to
end.
Dec 1 st at neck edge on next row.
Rep last 2 rows once.

Both sizes

Dec 1 st at neck edge on the 4[5] foll
alt rows, then on 2 foll 4th rows.

Shape shoulder

Dec 1 st at neck edge on next row.
Cast off 9[10] sts at beg of next and 2
foll alt rows. Work 1 row. Cast off
rem 9[10] sts. Return to sts for left
side of neck. With WS of work facing,
join in yarn and patt to end.
Complete to match first side of neck,
reversing shapings.

Sleeves

Using 3¼mm needles and A, cast on
52[56] sts. Work 8 rows K1, P1 rib.
Next row Rib 2[4], inc 1, *rib 2,
inc 1, rep from * to last 1[3] sts, rib to
end. 69[73] sts.
Change to 4mm needles.
1st-2nd rows With A, K.
3rd-4th rows With B, K1, *sl 1, K1,
rep from * to end.
The last 4 rows form the patt. Cont in
patt inc 1 st at each end of the next
and every foll 4th row until there are
83[87] sts. Cont without shaping.
Work 6 rows. Cast off.

To make up

Join shoulder seams.

Neck border

Using 3¼mm needles and A, with
RS of work facing, K up 24 sts from
right neck edge, K across 31[33] sts
on back neck, K up 24 sts down left
side of neck. 79[81] sts.
Next row P1, *K1, P1, rep from *.
Next row K1, *P1, K1, rep from *.
Rep the last 2 rows twice more. Cast
off in rib.

Right front border

Using 3¼mm needles and A, with
RS of work facing, K up 26 sts down
right neck border and front edge.
Work 3 rows K1, P1 rib.
1st buttonhole row Rib 4, *cast off
2 sts, rib 6, rep from * ending last rep
rib 4.
2nd buttonhole row Rib 4, *cast on
2 sts, rib 6, rep from * ending last rep
rib 4.
Rib 2 rows. Cast off in rib.

Left front border

Work to match right front border
omitting buttonholes.
Lap the right front border over left
and catch the row ends together
sewing to cast-off sts at centre front.
Place the centre of cast-off edge of
sleeve to shoulder seam and set in
sleeve. Join side and sleeve seams.
Sew on buttons.

Special technique — working a simple mosaic

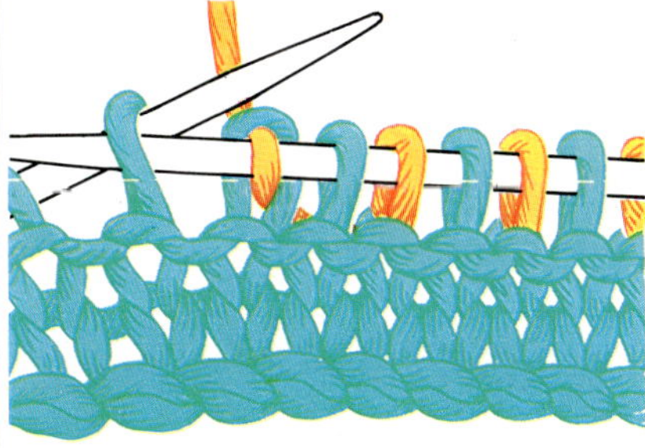

1 *This stitch is used on the sleeves and yoke of the sweater. With colour A knit the first two rows (odd-numbered rows are right-side rows). With colour B knit the third row slipping every alternate stitch purlwise with the yarn at the back of the work.*

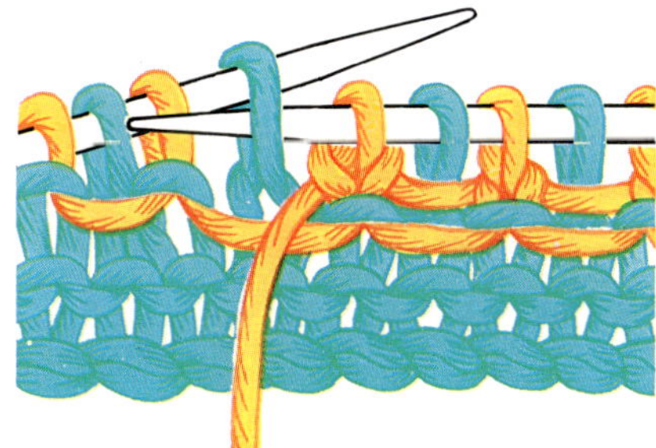

2 *With colour B knit the fourth row slipping purlwise the stitches that were slipped the previous row but this time with the yarn held at the front (that is, the wrong side) of the work.*

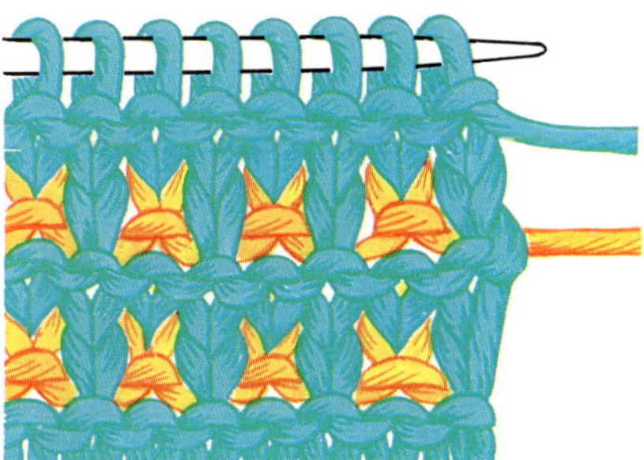

3 *Repeat these four rows to form the pattern. All mosaic stitches are based on the same principles: the yarn colour is changed every two rows, the slip-stitches are taken over two rows and are slipped with the yarn in front on wrong-side rows and at the back on right-side rows.*

Zigzag Jacket

Make yourself a genuine coat of many colours in a sizzling zigzag pattern. This one has an interesting double-breasted front and a cosy shawl collar.

Sizes

To fit 81-87[91-97]cm bust
Length 64[66]cm
Sleeve seam 43cm

Note Instructions for larger size are in square brackets []; where there is only one set of figures it applies to both sizes.

Tension

21 sts and 23 rows to 10cm over patt on 4mm needles

Materials

400 [450] g double knitting yarn in main colour (A)
175 [225] g in each of contrast colours (B) and (C)
100g in each of contrast colours (D) and (E)
1 pair each 3¾mm and 4mm knitting needles
4 buttons

Back

Using 3¾mm needles and A, cast on 104 [114] sts. Work 5 cm K1, P1 rib. Change to 4mm needles.
Beg with a K row cont in st st and patt from chart on page 126. Use small, separate balls of yarn for each colour area, twist yarns when changing colour to avoid a hole.
Work 90 rows.
Shape armholes
Cast off 4[5] sts at beg of next 2 rows.
Dec 1 st at each end of next and every foll alt row until 82[88] sts rem.
Cont without shaping until work measures 20[22]cm, ending with a WS row.
Shape shoulders
Cast off 9 sts at beg of next 4 rows and 7[10] sts at beg of foll 2 rows.
Cast off rem 32 sts.

Pocket lining (make 2)

Using 4mm needles and A, cast on 24 sts. Work in st st for 12cm, ending with a P row. Leave these sts on a spare needle.

Left front

Using 3¾mm needles and A, cast on 36[41] sts. Work 5cm K1, P1 rib.

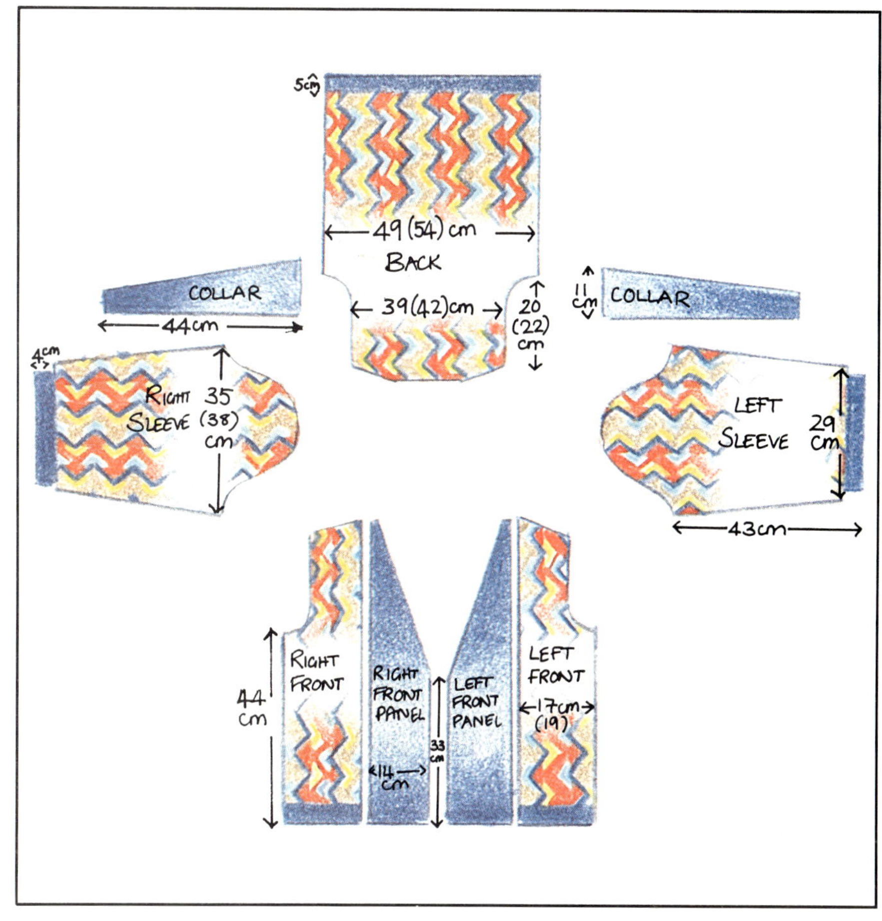

Change to 4mm needles.
Beg with a K row cont in patt from chart until work measures 17cm, ending with a WS row.
Place pocket
Next row Patt 6 sts, sl next 24 sts on to a st holder and patt across pocket lining sts on spare needle, patt to end.
Cont in patt until work matches back to armhole, ending with a P row.
Shape armhole
Cast off 4[5] sts at beg of next row.
Dec 1 st at armhole edge on foll alt rows until 25[28] sts rem.
Cont without further shaping until work matches back to shoulder shaping, ending at armhole edge.
Shape shoulder
Cast off 9 sts at beg of next and foll alt row.
Work 1 row. Cast off rem 7[10] sts.

Right front

Work as given for left front from ** to **

Change to 4mm needles.
Beg with a K row cont in st st and patt from chart until work measures 17cm, ending with a WS row.
Place pocket
Next row Patt 6[11] sts, sl next 24 sts on to a st holder, patt across pocket lining sts on spare needle, patt to end.
Cont in patt until work matches back to armhole, ending with a K row.
Shape armhole
Cast off 4[5] sts at beg of next row.
Dec 1 st at armhole edge on next and every foll alt row until 25[28] sts rem.
Complete to match left front.

Sleeves

Using 3¾mm needles and A, cast on 62 sts. Work 4cm K1, P1 rib.
Change to 4mm needles.
Beg with a K row cont in st st and patt from chart. Inc and work into patt 1 st at each end of the 11th and every foll 12th[9th] row until there are 74[80]

sts. Cont without shaping until work measures approx 43cm, ending with an 18th patt row.

Shape top
Cast off 4[5] sts at beg of next 2 rows. Dec 1 st at each end of next and every foll alt row until 50 sts rem, then at each end of every row until 18 sts rem. Cast off.

Right front panel
Using 3¾mm needles and A, cast on 36 sts.
Work 12cm K1, P1 rib.
1st buttonhole row Rib 7, cast off 2 sts, rib 18 including st used in casting off, cast off 2 sts, rib to end.
2nd buttonhole row Rib to end, casting on 2 sts over those cast off in previous row.
Cont in rib until work measures 22cm from cast-on edge.
Work 1st and 2nd buttonhole rows again.
Now cont in rib until work measures 33cm from cast-on edge, ending at front edge.

Shape front edge
Cast off 12 sts at beg of next row. Dec 1 st at front edge on 3 foll 4th[6th] rows, then on every foll 4th row until 2 sts rem.
Work 2 tog and fasten off.

Left front panel
Work to match right front panel, omitting buttonholes.

Collar (make 2 pieces)
Using 3¾mm needles and A, cast on 106[110] sts.
Work 14 rows K1, P1 rib.
Next row Rib to last 2 sts, turn.
Next row Sl 1, rib to end.
Next row Rib to last 4 sts, turn.
Next row Sl 1, rib to end.
Cont in this way until the row 'rib to last 10 sts, turn' has been worked.
Next row Sl 1, rib to end.
Next row Rib to last 20 sts, turn.

Next row Sl 1, rib to end.
Next row Rib to last 30 sts, turn.
Next row Sl 1, rib to end.
Next row Rib to last 40 sts, turn.
Next row Sl 1, rib to end.
Next row Rib to end across all sts on needle. Cast off.

To make up
Press with a warm iron over a damp cloth.
Pocket edgings
Using 3¾mm needles and A, K across 24 sts left on st holder. Work 2cm K1, P1 rib. Cast off in rib.
Sew down pocket linings on WS and edgings on RS.
Join shoulder, side and sleeve seams. Set in sleeves. Sew front panels to front edges. Join centre back neck seam of collar. Sew shaped edge of collar to neck edge, joining short ends to cast-off sts at front edge.
Sew on buttons and reinforce buttonholes.

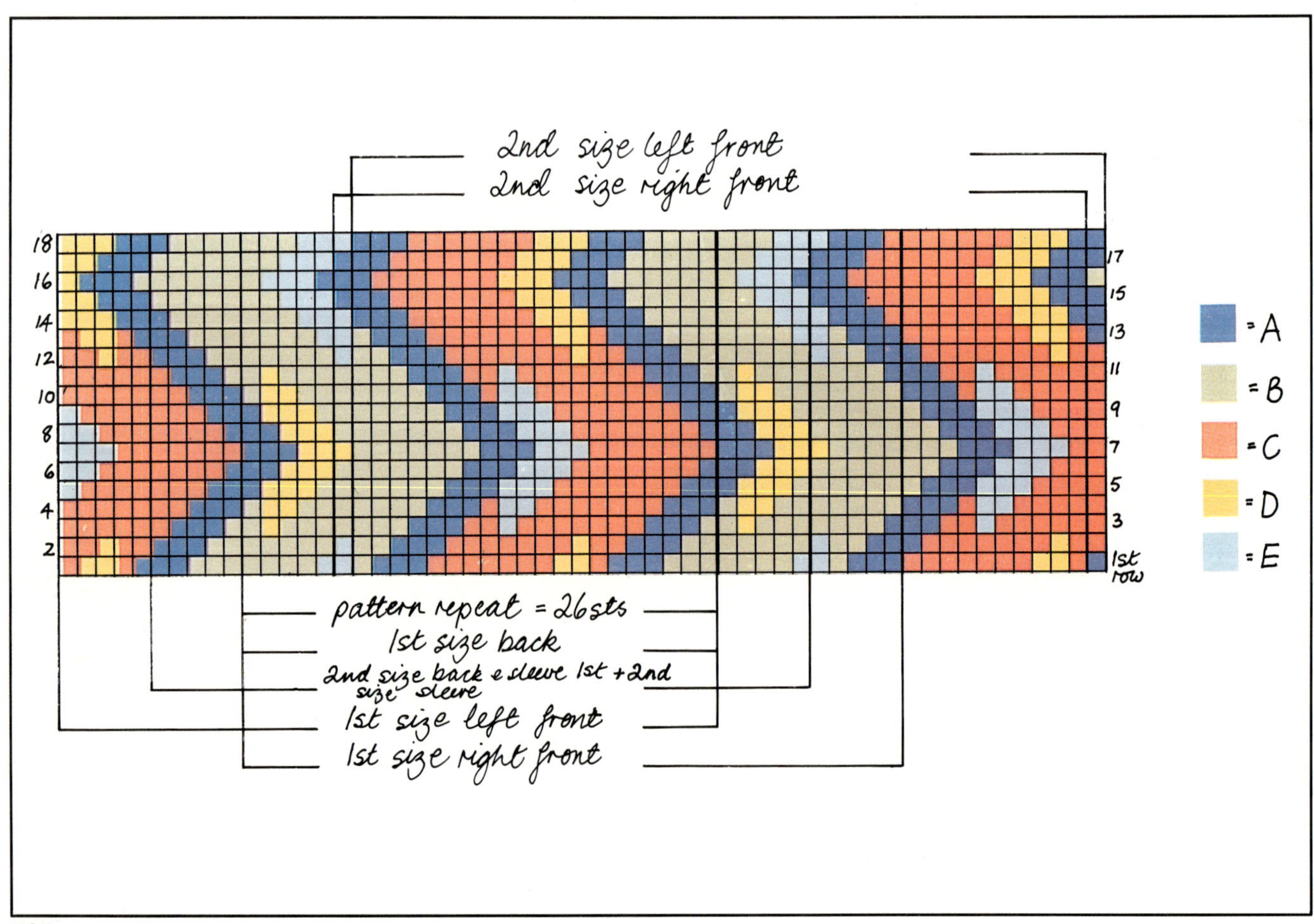

Folk Knitting

Knitting has a long history, going back, some say, as far as the ancient Egyptians. During that time several countries have developed their own particular knitting style —whether it be in the form of colour patterns, like Fair Isle and Scandinavian knitting, or a special kind of texture or stitch pattern, like those found in traditional Aran garments. In some cases (Guernsey knitting, for example) it is the actual shape of a garment and the yarn used for it that is distinctive; in others it is a special style of decoration—the brightly coloured wool embroidery on Tyrolean garments is an example of this last kind.

One of the most interesting features of folk knitting styles is that they are becoming more, rather than less, popular with the passage of time and there is a great demand for them to be absolutely authentic in every detail. All the patterns on the following pages are based on traditional patterns and use a wide range of stitches and motifs from all over the world, from Scotland to Peru.

Aran Sweater

The highly textured stitch patterns used in this classic sweater come from the Aran Islands, off the west coast of Ireland. The thick, crunchy fabric is specially designed to withstand the cruellest winter weather.

Size
To fit 81-86[91-96:101-106]cm bust / chest.
Length 61[67.5:70]cm.
Sleeve length 43[45.5:47]cm.
Note Instructions for larger sizes are in square brackets []; where there is only one set of figures it applies to all sizes.

Tension
22 sts and 28 rows to 10cm over Irish moss st on 4½mm needles.

Materials
825 [925:1025] g Aran-weight yarn
1 pair each 3¾mm and 4½mm knitting needles
1 cable needle

Irish moss stitch
Work over an even number of sts.
1st and 2nd rows (RS) *K1, P1; rep from * to end.

3rd and 4th rows *P1, K1; rep from * to end.
Rep these 4 rows.

Back
**Using 3¾mm needles, cast on 113 [123:131] sts. Work in K1, P1 rib for 5cm.
Change to 4½mm needles and work in patt as follows:
1st row K1, (P1, K1) 4 [6:8] times, P2, K4, *P2, C3B, K3, P5, Tw3B, K1, Tw3F, P5, C3B, K3, P2,* K1, (P1, K1) 8[9:9] times, rep from * to * once K4, P2, K1, (P1, K1) 4[6:8] times.
2nd row P1, (K1, P1) 4 [6:8] times, K2, P4, *K2, P6, K5, P2, K1, P1, K1, P2, K5, P6, K2,* P1, (K1, P1) 8 [9:9] times, rep from * to * once, P4, K2, P1, (K1, P1) 4 [6:8] times.
3rd row P1, (K1, P1) 4 [6:8] times, P2, C4B, *P2, K3, C3F, P4, Tw3B, K1,

P1, K1, Tw3F, P4, K3, C3F, P2,*P1, (K1, P1) 8[9:9] times, rep from * to * once, C4B, P3, (K1, P1) 4 [6:8] times.
4th row K1, (P1, K1) 4 [6:8] times, K2, P4, *K2, P6, K4, P2, (K1, P1) twice, K1, P2, K4, P6, K2, *K1, (P1, K1) 8 [9:9] times, rep from * to * once, P4, K3 (P1, K1) 4 [6:8] times.
5th row K1, (P1, K1) 4 [6:8] times, P2, K4, *P2, C3B, K3, P3, Tw3B, (K1, P1) twice, K1, Tw3F, P3, C3B, K3, P2, *K1, (P1, K1) 8 [9:9] times, rep from * to * once K4, P2, K1 (P1, K1) 4 [6:8] times.
6th row P1, (K1, P1) 4 [6:8] times, K2, P4, *K2, P6, K3, P2 (K1, P1) 3 times, K1, P2, K3, P6, K2, *P1, (K1, P1) 8 [9:9] times, rep from * to * once, P4, K2, P1, (K1, P1) 4 [6:8] times.
7th row P1, (K1, P1) 4 [6:8] times, P2, C4B, *P2, K3, C3F, P2, Tw3B, (K1, P1) 3 times, K1, Tw3F, P2, K3, C3F, P2, *P1, (K1, P1) 8 [9:9] times, rep

Aran abbreviations

CN — cable needle
C4F — **cable 4 front** (sl next 2 sts on to CN and leave at front of work, K2, then K2 from CN).
C4B — **cable 4 back** (sl next 2 sts on to CN and leave at back of work, K2, then K2 from CN).
C3F — **cable 3 front** (sl next st on to CN and leave at front of work, K2, then K1 from CN).
C3B — **cable 3 back** (sl next 2 sts on to CN and leave at back of work, K1, then K2 from CN).
Tw3F — **twist 3 front** (sl next 2 sts on to CN and leave at front of work, P1, then K2 from CN).
Tw3B — **twist 3 back** (sl next st on to CN and leave at back of work, K2, then P1 from CN).
Tw5B — **twist 5 back** (sl next 3 sts on to cable needle and leave at back of work, K2, then P1, K2 from CN).
Cr3B — **cross 3 back** (sl next st on to

CN and leave at back of work, K2, then K1 from CN).
Tw2B — **twist 2 back** (sl next st on to CN and leave at back of work, K1 tbl, then P1 from CN).
Tw2F — **twist 2 front** (sl next st on to CN and leave at front of work, P1, then K1 tbl from CN).
C2Ftbl — **cable 2 front through back of loop** (sl next st on to CN and leave at front of work, K1, tbl, then K1 tbl from CN).
C2Btbl — **cable 2 back through back of loop** (sl next st on to CN and hold at back of work, K1 tbl then K1 tbl from CN).
C2F P-wise — **cable 2 front purlwise** (sl next st on to CN and leave at front of work, P1, then P1 from CN).
C2Ftbl P-wise — **cable 2 front through back of loop purlwise** (sl next st on to CN and leave at front of work, P1 tbl, then P1 tbl from CN).

from * to * once, C4B, P3, (K1, P1) 4 [6:8] times.

8th row K1, (P1, K1) 4 [6:8] times, K2, P4, *K2, P6, K2, P2, (K1, P1) 4 times, K1, P2, K2, P6, K2, *K1, (P1, K1) 8 [9:9] times, rep from * to * once, P4, K3, (P1, K1) 4 [6:8] times.

9th row K1, (P1, K1) 4 [6:8] times, P2, K4, *P2, C3B, K3, P2, K3, (P1, K1) 4 times, K2, P2, C3B, K3, P2, *K1, (P1, K1) 8 [9:9] times, rep from * to * once, K4, P2, K1, (P1, K1) 4 [6:8] times.

10th row P1, (K1, P1) 4 [6:8] times, K2, P4, *K2, P6, K2, P3, (K1, P1) 4 times, P2, K2, P6, K2, *P1, (K1, P1) 8 [9:9] times, rep from * to * once, P4, K2, P1, (K1, P1) 4 [6:8] times.

11th row P1, (K1, P1) 4 [6:8] times, P2, C4B, *P2, K3, C3F, P2, Tw3F, (K1, P1) 3 times, K1, Tw3B, P2, K3, C3F, P2, *P1, (K1, P1) 8 [9:9] times, rep from * to * once, C4B, P3, (K1, P1) 4 [6:8] times.

12th row K1, (P1, K1) 4 [6:8] times, K2, P4, *K2, P6, K3, P3, (K1, P1) 3 times, P2, K3, P6, K2, *K1, (P1, K1) 8 [9:9] times, rep from * to * once, P4, K3, (P1, K1) 4 [6:8] times.

13th row K1, (P1, K1) 4 [6:8] times, P2, K4, *P2, C3B, K3, P3, Tw3F, (K1, P1) twice, K1, Tw3B, P3, C3B, K3, P2, *K1, (P1, K1) 8 [9:9] times, rep from * to * once, K4, P2, K1, (P1, K1) 4 [6:8] times.

14th row P1, (K1, P1) 4 [6:8] times, K2, P4, *K2, P6, K4, P3, (K1, P1) twice, P2, K4, P6, K2, *P1, (K1, P1) 8 [9:9] times, rep from * to * once, P4, K2, P1, (K1, P1) 4 [6:8] times.

15th row P1, (K1, P1) 4 [6:8] times, P2, C4B, *P2, K3, C3F, P4, Tw3F, K1, P1, K1, Tw3B, P4, K3, C3F, P2, *P1, (K1, P1) 8 [9:9] times, rep from * to * once, C4B, P3, (K1, P1) 4 [6:8] times.

16th row K1, (P1, K1) 4 [6:8] times, K2, P4, *K2, P6, K5, P3, K1, P3, K5, P6, K2, *K1, (P1, K1) 8 [9:9] times, rep from * to * once, P4, K3, (P1, K1) 4 [6:8] times.

17th row K1, (P1, K1) 4 [6:8] times, P2, K4, *P2, C3B, K3, P5, Tw3F, K1, Tw3B, P5, C3B, K3, P2, *K1, (P1, K1) 8 [9:9] times, rep from * to * once, K4, P2, K1, (P1, K1) 4 [6:8] times.

18th row P1, (K1, P1) 4 [6:8] times, K2, P4, *K2, P6, K6, P5, K6, P6, K2,

*P1, (K1, P1) 8 [9:9] times, rep from * to * once, P4, K2, P1, (K1, P1) 4 [6:8] times.

19th row P1, (K1, P1) 4 [6:8] times, P2, C4B, *P2, K3, C3F, P6, Tw5B, P6, K3, C3F, P2, *P1, (K1, P1) 8 [9:9] times, rep from * to * once, C4B, P3, (K1, P1) 4 [6:8] times.

20th row K1, (P1, K1) 4 [6:8] times, K2, P4, *K2, P6, K6, P2, K1, P2, K6, P6, K2, *K1, (P1, K1) 8 [9:9] times, rep from * to * once, P4, K2, K1, (P1, K1) 4 [6:8] times.

These 20 rows form patt. Cont in patt until work measures 39.5 [44.5:44.5]cm from beg, ending with a WS row.

Shape armholes
Keeping patt correct, cast off 6 [7:8] sts at beg of next 2 rows.
Dec 1 st at each end of next 5 rows.
Dec 1st at each end of foll 4 [2:3] alt rows (83[95:99])sts. **
Cont in patt without further shaping until work measures 20.5 [23:25.5]cm from beg of armhole shaping, ending with a WS row.

Shape shoulders
Keeping patt correct, cast off 7 sts at beg of next 6 rows. Cast off 4 [7:8] sts at beg of next 2 rows. Leave rem 33 [39:41] sts on a stitch holder.

Front

Work as given for back from ** to **
Cont in patt without further shaping until work measures 14.5 [17:19.5]cm from beg of armhole shaping, ending with a WS row.

Shape left front neck
Next row Patt 34 [37:38] sts, turn, leaving rem sts on a spare needle.
***Dec 1 st at neck edge on next and 8 foll alt rows. (25[28:29]) sts.

Shape left shoulder
Cast off 7 sts at beg of next and foll 2 alt rows.
Work 1 row.
Cast off rem 4 [7:8] sts. ***

Shape right front neck and shoulder
Return to sts on spare needle, sl next 15 [21:23] sts on a stitch holder. On rem 34 [37:38] sts patt to end of row. Complete to match left front and shoulder from *** to ***, reversing all shapings.

Sleeves (alike)

Using 3¾mm needles, cast on 43 [49:53] sts. Work in K1, P1 rib for 7.5cm, inc 1 st at each end of last row (45[51.55] sts).
Change to 4½mm needles and work in patt as follows:

1st row (P1, K1) 0 [1:2] times, K0[1:1], P2, K4, P2, C3B, K3, P5, Tw3B, K1, Tw3F, P5, C3B, K3, P2, K4, P2, K0 [1:1], (P1, K1) 0 [1:2] times.

2nd row (P1, K1) 0 [1:2] times, P0[1:1], K2, P4, K2, P6, K5, P2, K1, P1, K1, P2, K5, P6, K2, P4, K2, P0[1:1], (K1, P1) 0[1:2] times.

3rd row (P1, K1) 0 [1:2] times, P2 [3:3], C4B, P2, K3, C3F, P4, Tw3B, K1, P1, K1, Tw3F, P4, K3, C3F, P2, C4B, P2 [3:3], (K1, P1) 0 [1:2] times.

4th row (K1, P1) 0 [1:2] times, K2 [3:3], P4, K2, P6, K4, P2, (K1, P1) twice, K1, P2, K4, P6, K2, P4, K2 [3:3], (P1, K1) 0 [1:2] times.

5th row (K1, P1) 0 [1:2] times, K0 [1:1], P2, K4, P2, C3B, K3, P3, Tw3B, (K1, P1) twice, K1, Tw3F, P3, C3B, K3, P2, K4, P2, K0 [1:1], (P1, K1) 0 [1:2] times.

6th row (P1, K1) 0 [1:2] times, P0 [1:1], K2, P4, K2, P6, K3, P2, (K1, P1) 3 times, K1, P2, K3, P6, K2, P4, K2, P0 [1:1], (K1, P1) 0 [1:2] times.

7th row (P1, K1) 0 [1:2] times, P2 [3:3], C4B, P2, K3, C3F, P2, Tw3B, (K1, P1) 3 times, K1, Tw3F, P2, K3, C3F, P2, C4B, P2 [3:3], (K1, P1) 0 [1:2] times.

8th row (K1, P1) 0 [1:2] times, K2 [3:3], P4, K2, P6, K2, P2, (K1, P1) 4 times, K1, P2, K2, P6, K2, P4, K2 [3:3], (P1, K1) 0 [1:2] times.

9th row (K1, P1) 0 [1:2] times, K0 [1:1], P2, K4, P2, C3B, K3, P2, K3, (P1, K1) 4 times, K2, P2, C3B, K3, P2, K4, P2, K0 [1:1], (P1, K1) 0 [1:2] times.

10th row (P1, K1) 0 [1:2] times, P0 [1:1], K2, P4, K2, P6, K2, P3, (K1, P1) 4 times, P2, K2, P6, K2, P4, K2, P0 [1:1], (K1, P1) 0 [1:2] times.

11th row (P1, K1) 0 [1:2] times, P2 [3:3], C4B, P2, K3, C3F, P2, Tw3F, (K1, P1) 3 times, K1, Tw3B, P2, K3, C3F, P2, C4B, P2 [3:3], (K1, P1) 0 [1:2] times.

12th row (K1, P1) 0 [1:2] times, K2

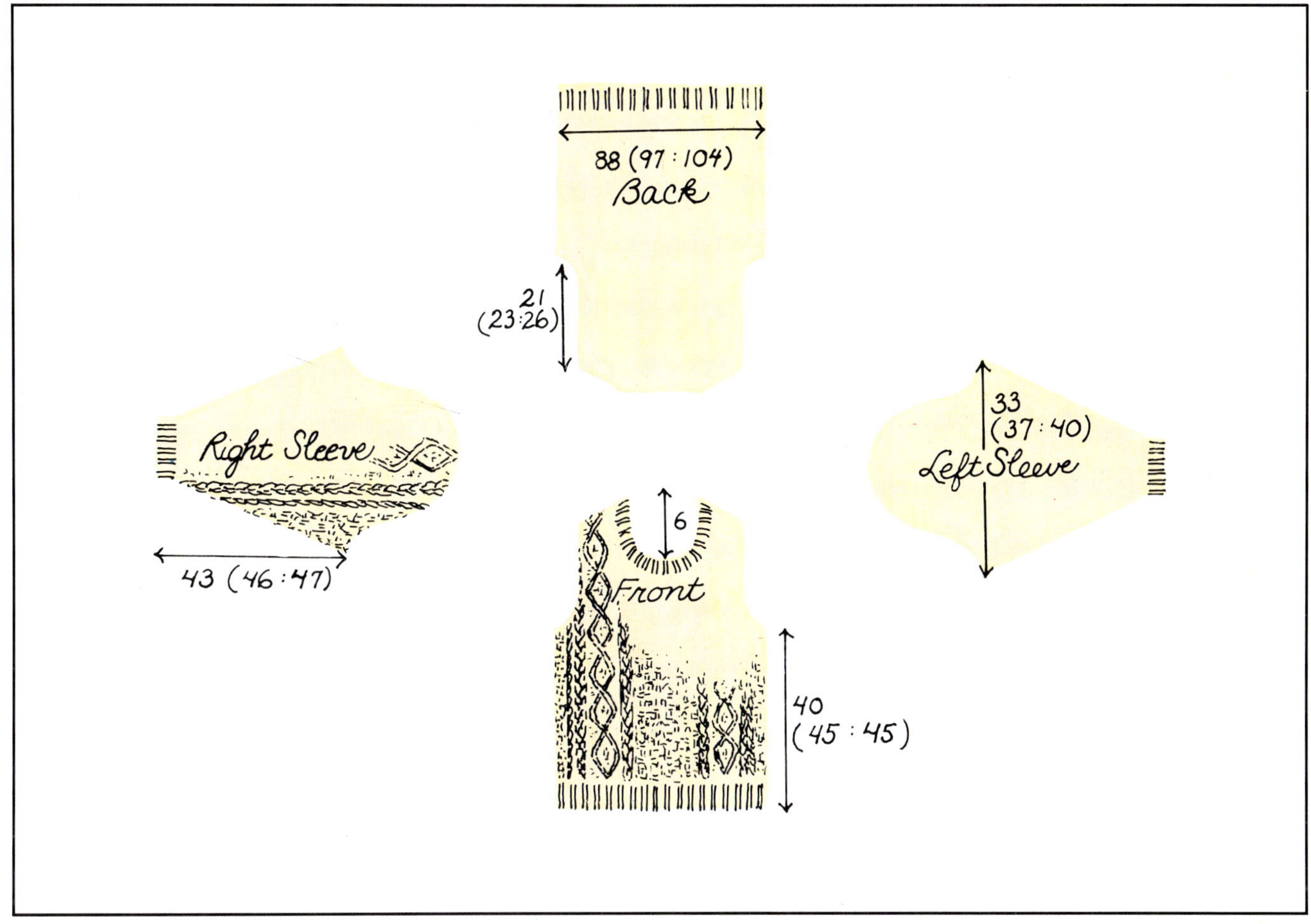

[3:3], P4, K2, P6, K3, P3, (K1, P1) 3 times, P2, K3, P6, K2, P4, K2 [3:3], (P1, K1) 0 [1:2] times.
13th row (K1, P1) 0 [1:2] times, K0 [1:1], P2, K4, P2, C3B, K3, P3, Tw3F, (K1, P1) twice, K1, Tw3B, P3, C3B, K3, P2, K4, P2, K0 [1:1], (P1, K1) 0 [1:2] times.
14th row (P1, K1) 0 [1:2] times, P0 [1:1], K2, P4, K2, P6, K4, P3, (K1, P1) twice, P2, K4, P6, K2, P4, K2, P0 [1:1], (K1, P1) 0 [1:2] times.
15th row (P1, K1) 0 [1:2] times, P2 [3:3], C4B, P2, K3, C3F, P4, Tw3F, K1, P1, K1, Tw3B, P4, K3, C3F, P2, C4B, P2 [3:3], (K1, P1) 0 [1:2] times.
16th row (K1, P1) 0 [1:2] times, K2 [3:3], P4, K2, P6, K5, P3, K1, P3, K5, P6, K2, P4, K2 [3:3], (P1, K1) 0 [1:2] times.
17th row (K1, P1) 0 [1:2] times, K0 [1:1], P2, K4, P2, C3B, K3, P5, Tw3F, K1, Tw3B, P5, C3B, K3, P2, K4, P2, K0 [1:1], (P1, K1) 0 [1:2] times.
18th row (P1, K1) 0 [1:2] times, P0

[1:1], K2, P4, K2, P6, K6, P5, K6, P6, K2, P4, K2, (K1, P1) 0 [1:2] times.
19th row (P1, K1) 0 [1:2] times, P2 [3:3], C4B, P2, K3, C3F, P6, Tw5B, P6, K3, C3F, P2, C4B, P2 [3:3], (K1, P1) 0 [1:2] times.
20th row (K1, P1) 0 [1:2] times, K2 [3:3], P4, K2, P6, K6, P2, K1, P2, K6, P6, K2, P4, K2 [3:3], (P1, K1) 0 [1:2] times.
These 20 rows form patt. Cont in patt for 4 rows.
Keeping patt correct and working the extra sts into the patt, inc 1 st at each end of next and every foll 4th row until there are 73 [79:79] sts on needle.
Keeping patt correct and working extra sts into patt, inc 1 st at each end of every foll 5th row until there are 77 [87:93] sts on needle.
Work straight until sleeve measures 43 [45.5:47]cm from cast-on edge.
Shape sleeve top
Keeping patt correct, cast off 6 [7:8] sts at beg of next 2 rows.

Dec 1 st at each end of next 5 rows.
Dec 1 st at each end of every foll alt row until 29 [33:33] sts rem.
Work 1 row.
Cast off 3 sts at beg of next 6 rows.
Cast off rem 11 [15:15] sts.

To make up
Press lightly on wrong side with a warm iron over a dry cloth. Join left shoulder seam.

Neckband
With RS facing, using 3¾mm needles, K up 33 [39:41] sts from back neck stitch holder, 26 sts from left side front neck, 15 [21:23] sts from centre front neck, 26 sts from right side front neck (100[112:116] sts).
Work in K1, P1, rib for 6.5cm.
Cast off in rib.
Join right shoulder seam. Fold neckband in half on to wrong side and slipstitch in position. Set in sleeves. Join side and sleeve seams.

Shetland Lace Shawl

This beautiful lace shawl, made in the traditional manner,
makes a fabulous fashion accessory but is soft enough for baby.

Size
Approx 150cm square after stretching

Tension
26 sts and 34 rows to 10cm over st st
on 4½mm needles

Materials
200g two-ply laceweight yarn
1 pair 4½mm knitting needles

To make
Cast on 3 sts.
Work centre
1st row (WS) Yrn, K3.
2nd row Yrn, K4.
3rd row Yrn, K5.
Cont in this way inc 1 st at beg of
every row until there are 12 sts. Place
a marker at beg of next row, to
denote the beg of RS rows.
Commence patt.
Next row (RS) Yrn, K3, K2 tog,
yfwd, K1, yfwd, K2 tog, K4.
Next row Yrn, K13.
Next row Yrn, K3, K2 tog, yfwd, K3,
yfwd, K2 tog, K4.
Next row Yrn, K15.
Next row Yrn, K6, yfwd, sl 1,
K2 tog, psso, yfwd, K7.
Next row Yrn, K to end.
Rep last row 6 times more so ending
with a WS row (marker is at beg of
next row). 24 sts.
Next row Yrn, *K3, K2 tog, yfwd,
K1, yfwd, K2 tog, K4, rep from * to
end.
Next row Yrn, K to end.
Next row Yrn, * K3, K2 tog, yfwd,
K3, yfwd, K2 tog, K2, rep from * to
last 2 sts, K2.
Next row Yrn, K to end.
Next row Yrn, * K6, yfwd, sl 1,
K2 tog, psso, yfwd, K3, rep from * to
last 4 sts, K4.
Next row Yrn, K to end.
Rep last row 6 times more. 36 sts.
Cont in this way, rep the last 12 rows
until there are 120 sts, ending with a
WS row.
Next row Yrn, *K3, K2 tog, yfwd,
K1, yfwd, K2 tog, K4, rep from * to
end.
Next row Yrn, K to end.
Next row Yrn, *K3, K2 tog, yfwd,
K3, yfwd, K2 tog, K2, rep from * to
last 2 sts, K2.

Next row Yrn, K3 tog, K to end.
Next row Yrn, K3 tog, K3, yfwd,
sl 1, K2 tog, psso, yfwd, K5, *K4,
yfwd, sl 1, K2 tog, psso, yfwd, K5,
rep from * to end.
Next row Yrn, K3 tog, K to end.
Rep the last row 6 times more. 114 sts.
Next row Yrn, K3 tog, *K4, K2 tog,
yfwd, K1, yfwd, K2 tog, K3, rep from
*to last 3 sts, K3.
Next row Yrn, K3 tog, K to end.
Next row Yrn, K3 tog, *K2, K2 tog,
yfwd, K3, yfwd, K2 tog, K3, rep from
* to last st, K1.
Next row Yrn, K3 tog, K to end.
Next row Yrn, K3 tog, K3, yfwd,
sl 1, K2 tog, psso, yfwd, K5, *K4,
yfwd, sl 1, K2 tog, psso, yfwd, K5,
rep from * to end.
Next row Yrn, K3 tog, K to end.
Rep last row 6 times more. 102 sts.
Cont in this way, rep the last 12 rows
until 6 sts rem.
Next row Yrn, K3 tog, K to end.
Rep last row twice more, 3 sts.
Next row K3 tog, fasten off, but do
not break yarn.

First side border
**With RS of work facing, K up 60
sts from first side of centre square as
foll:
K up 1, yfwd, (K up 2, yfwd) 29
times, K up 1. 90 sts.
Next row K. * *
Commence border patt.
1st row (RS) Yrn, K3, yfwd, sl 1, K2
tog, psso, yfwd, *K3, yfwd, K2 tog,
K2, yfwd, sl 1, K2 tog, psso, yfwd,
rep from * to last 4 sts, K4.
2nd and foll alt rows Yrn, K to end.
3rd row Yrn, K2, *K2 tog, yfwd, K3,
yfwd, K2 tog, K3, rep from * to end.
5th row Yrn, K2, *K2 tog, yfwd, K5,
yfwd, K2 tog, K1, rep from * to last 2
sts, K2.
7th row Yrn, K1, *yfwd, sl 1,
K2 tog, psso, yfwd, K3, yfwd, K2 tog,
K2, rep from * to last 5 sts, yfwd,
sl 1, K2 tog, psso, yfwd, K2.
9th row Yrn, *K2 tog, yfwd, K3,
yfwd, K2 tog, K3, rep from * to last 8
sts, K2 tog, yfwd, K3, yfwd, K2 tog,
K1.
11th row Yrn, *K2 tog, yfwd, K5,
yfwd, K2 tog, K1, rep from * to end.
13th row Yrn, K2 tog, yfwd, *K3,

yfwd, K2 tog, K2, yfwd, sl 1, K2 tog,
psso, yfwd, rep from * to last 10 sts,
K3, yfwd, K2 tog, K2, yfwd, K2 tog,
K1.
15th row Yrn, *K3, yfwd, K2 tog,
K3, K2 tog, yfwd, rep from * to last 4
sts, K4.
17th row Yrn, *K5, yfwd, K2 tog,
K1, K2 tog, yfwd, rep from * to last 6
sts, K6.
19th row Yrn, *K3, yfwd, K2 tog,
K2, yfwd, sl 1, K2 tog, psso, yfwd,
rep from * to last 8 sts, K3, yfwd,
K2 tog, K3.
21st row Yrn, K1, *yfwd, K2 tog,
K3, K2 tog, yfwd, K3, rep from * to
last 9 sts, yfwd, K2 tog, K3, K2 tog,
yfwd, K2.
23rd row Yrn, K3, *yfwd, K2 tog,
K1, K2 tog, yfwd, K5, rep from * to
last 9 sts, yfwd, K2 tog, K1, K2 tog,
yfwd, K4.
25th row Yrn, K1, *yfwd, K2 tog,
K2, yfwd, sl 1, K2 tog, psso, yfwd,
K3, rep from * to last 3 sts, yfwd,
K2 tog, K1.
27th row Yrn, K4, *K2 tog, yfwd,
K3, yfwd, K2 tog, K3, rep from * to last 2
sts, K2.
29th row Yrn, K1, *yfwd, K2 tog,
K1, K2 tog, yfwd, K5, rep from * to
last 7 sts, yfwd, K2 tog, K1, K2 tog,
yfwd, K2.
30th row As 2nd row.
31st-61st rows Rep 1st-30th rows
once, then 1st row again.
62nd row Yrn, K to end, turn and cast
on 16 sts for lace edging.

First side edging
Next row K15, K tog last st and 1st st
of border—called join 2 tog—turn.
Commence point.
1st row Sl 1, K1, yfwd, K2 tog, K8,
yfwd, K2 tog, yfwd, K2.
2nd row K14, yfwd, K2 tog, join 2
tog.
3rd row Sl 1, K1, yfwd, K2 tog, K2,
K2 tog, yfwd, K1, yfwd, K2 tog, K2,
yfwd, K2 tog, yfwd, K2.
4th row K15, yfwd, K2 tog, join 2
tog, turn.
5th row Sl 1, K1, yfwd, K2 tog, K1,
K2 tog, yfwd, K3, yfwd, K2 tog, K2,
yfwd, K2 tog, yfwd, K2.
6th row K16, yfwd, K2 tog, join 2 tog,
turn.

7th row Sl 1, K1, yfwd, K2 tog, K3, yfwd, sl 1, K2 tog, psso, yfwd, K5, yfwd, K2 tog, yfwd, K2.
8th row K17, yfwd, K2 tog, join 2 tog, turn.
9th row Sl 1, K1, yfwd, K2 tog, K12, yfwd, K2 tog, yfwd, K2.
10th row Cast off 5 sts loosely, K13 (including st used in casting off), yfwd, K2 tog, join 2 tog, turn.
These 10 rows form the first point.
Rep these 10 rows until all the border sts have been worked, ending with a WS row.
Sl these sts on to a stitch holder.

Second side border
Work as given for first side border from ** to **.
***Now cont in patt from 1st-61st rows as given for first side border, joining second border to first side on alt rows as foll:
2nd and foll alt rows Yrn, K to last st, K1 tog with corresponding row end of first border.
62nd row As 2nd row, then sl sts for edging from stitch holder on to end of needle.

Second side edging
Keeping patt correct, cont edging from first side.

Third side border and edging
Work as first side border from ** to **. Work as second side from *** to ***.

Fourth side border
Work as given for first side border from ** to **. Commence patt.
1st row (RS) Yrn, K3, yfwd, sl 1, K2 tog, psso, yfwd, *K3, yfwd, K2 tog, K2, yfwd, sl 1, K2 tog, psso, yfwd, rep from * to last 4 sts, K3, K1 tog with corresponding row end of first border.
2nd and foll alt rows Yrn, K to last st, K1 tog with corresponding row end of third border.
Cont in this way, working patt as given for first side of border joining at the end of every row until 61st row has been worked.
62nd row As 2nd row, then sl sts for edging from stitch holder on to end of needle.

Fourth side edging
Keeping patt correct, cont edging from third side. Graft rem 16 sts to cast-on sts of edging.

To make up
Roll shawl in a damp towel.
Fold a single bed sheet into a square 150cm × 150cm on a thickly carpeted floor or a folded blanket. Place the damp shawl on the sheet and pin out the work through the holes in the points of the edging in line with the edges of the square. Leave until completely dry.

Special technique — constructing the shawl

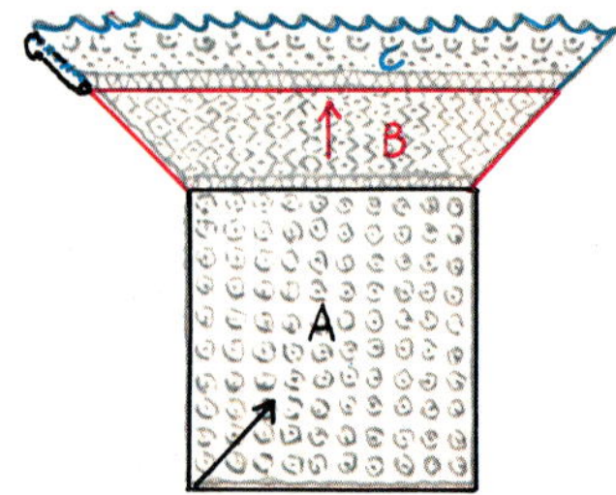
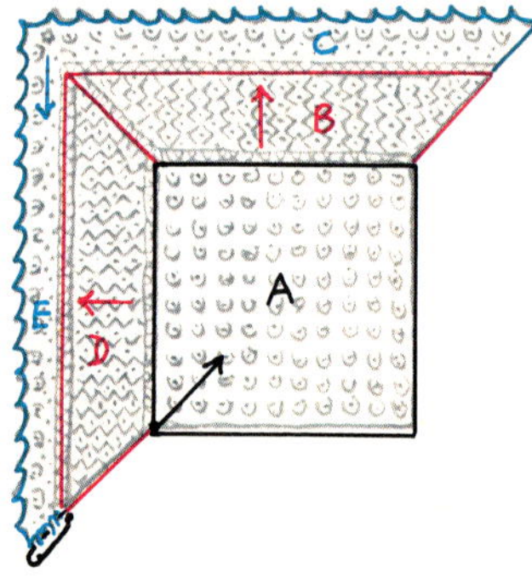
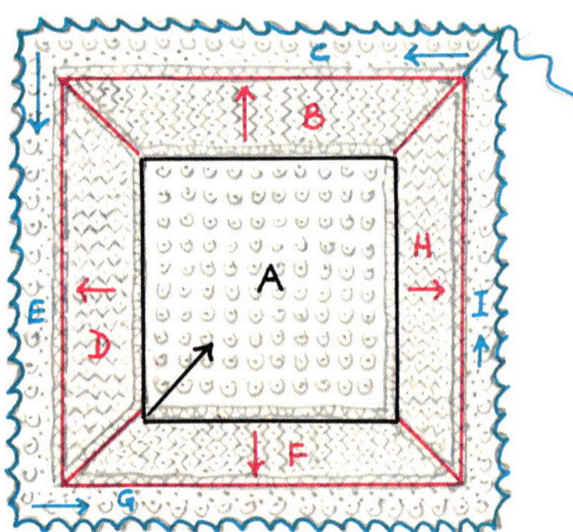

1 *Work the centre square (A) from corner to corner. Pick up stitches along one side and work the inner border (B). Cast on stitches for the edging (C) on to the last row of the border and work the edging, knitting into border stitches on every alternate row, thus joining the edging and border invisibly. When all the border stitches have been worked off leave the edging stitches on a stitch holder.*

2 *Now pick up stitches along the second side of the centre and work the inner border (D) as before, but this time knitting into the row ends of the first border (B) on every alternate row thus joining B and D invisibly. When the border is complete, slip the stitches from the stitch holder on to the end of the needle and work second side edging (E) as first side edging.*

3 *Work third side border (F) and edging (G) as given for the second side. Work the fourth side border (H) as before but knitting into the row ends from the first border on one side and the third border on the other side. Work the edging (I) as before, grafting the last row to the cast-on stitches. In this way the shawl is constructed entirely without seams or ugly joins.*

Shetland Lace Dress

This pretty little girl's dress has been knitted in stocking stitch with panels of eyelets and a Shetland lace edging. It is quite simple to work, and yet it is charmingly effective.

Size
To fit chest 60cm
Length 43cm

Tension
28 sts and 40 rows to 10cm over st st
on 2¾mm needles.

Materials
225g four-ply yarn (or No 5
cotton)
1 pair each 2¾mm and 4mm needles
4.5m narrow ribbon
3 small buttons

Back
**Using 2¾mm needles, cast on 155 sts.
1st row (RS) K.
2nd row P.
3rd-5th rows K.
6th row P.
7th row *K2 tog, yfwd, rep from * to
last st, K1.
8th-11th rows As 2nd-5th rows.
12th row P to last 2 sts, P2 tog.
154 sts.
13th row K1, *yrn, P2 tog, rep from
* to last st K1.
14th-22nd rows As 13th row.
23rd row K.
24th, 25th and 26th rows P.
27th row Inc 1, K to end. 155 sts.
28th row P2, * yrn, P2 tog, rep from *
to last st, P1.
29th-31st rows As 23rd-25th rows.
Beg with a P row, cont in st st until
work measures 23cm from cast-on
edge, ending with a P row. (This
length may be altered as required).
Next row K8, *K2 tog, rep from * to
last 9 sts, K9. 86 sts.
Next 3 rows P.
Next row K.
Next row P1, * yrn, P2 tog, rep from *
to last st, P1.

Next row K.
Next 2 rows P.**
Beg with a P row, cont in st st until
work measures 38cm from cast-on
edge, ending with a P row. Cast off,
marking centre 36 sts for back neck.

Front
Work as given for back from ** to
**. Beg with a P row, cont in st st
for 10cm, ending with a P row.
Shape neck
Next row K28, cast off next 30 sts,
K to end. Complete right side of neck
first. Cont in st st, dec 1 st at neck
edge on next 3 rows. 25 sts.
Cont without shaping until work
measures 38cm from cast-on edge,
ending with a P row. Cast off.
With WS of work facing rejoin yarn to
sts for left side of neck. Complete to
match first side.

Hem edging
Using 4mm needles cast on 7 sts and
work edging patt as foll:
1st row K.
2nd row P.
3rd row Sl 1 P-wise, K2, yfwd, K2
tog, yrn twice, K2 tog.
4th row Yrn, K2, P1, K2, yfwd, K2
tog, K1.
5th row Sl 1 P-wise, K2, yfwd, K2
tog, K4.
6th row K6, yfwd, K2 tog, K1.
7th row Sl 1 P-wise, K2, yfwd, K2
tog, yrn twice, K2 tog, yrn twice, K2
tog.
8th row (K2, P1) twice, K2, yfwd, K2
tog, K1.
9th row Sl 1 P-wise, K2, yfwd, K2
tog, K6.
10th row K8, yfwd, K2 tog, K1.
11th row Sl P-wise, K2, yfwd, K2
tog, (yrn twice, K2 tog) 3 times.

12th row (K2, P1) 3 times, K2, yfwd,
K2 tog, K1.
13th row Sl 1 P-wise, K2, yfwd, K2
tog, K9.
14th row Cast off 7 sts, K4 including
st used in casting off, yfwd, K2 tog,
K1.
The 3rd-14th rows form the pattern
repeat.
Rep the 3rd-14th rows until edging
measures approx 117cm, ending with a
14th patt row.
Cast off.

Armhole edgings
Using 4mm needles, cast on 7 sts
and work as for hem edging for
approx 22cm, ending with a 14th
patt row. Cast off.

To make up
Press all pieces as instructed on ball
band.
Join left shoulder seam.
With RS facing, using 2¾mm
needles, beg at right back neck
marker, K up 94 sts around neck
edge.
Next row Cast on 2 sts, cast off 3 sts,
*transfer st on RH needle to LH
needle, cast on 2 sts, cast off 3 sts,
rep from * to end.
Fasten off.
Join right shoulder for 2cm at
armhole edge.
Mark armholes 11cm down from
shoulder on back and front.
Join side seams leaving opening for
armholes.
Sew on sleeve and hem edgings.
Work button loops on right front
shoulder edge and sew on buttons.
Thread ribbon through eyelets,
bringing ends out at centre front waist
to tie.

Shetland Classics

You can put together a whole wardrobe of beautiful classics
from this cleverly constructed composite pattern. A back,
front and sleeves (long or short) makes a sweater; with
armbands instead of sleeves it's a slipover; with a front opening
it's a waistcoat.

Sizes

To fit 81[86:91:96]cm bust
Length 53[54:56:57]cm
Long sleeve seam 44cm
Short sleeve seam 15cm

Note Instructions for larger sizes are in square brackets []; where there is only one set of figures it applies to all sizes.

Tension

30 sts and 29 rows to 10cm over patt on 3¼mm needles

Materials

Waistcoat
150 [150:200:200] g four-ply yarn in main colour (A)
75g in contrast colour (B)
25g in each of 9 contrast colours (C, D, E, F, G, H, J, L,M)

Cardigan
250 [250:275:275] g in main colour (A)
50g in contrast colour (B)
25g in each of 9 contrast colours (C, D, E, F, G, H, J, L, M)

Short-sleeved sweater
275 [275:300:300] g in main colour (A)
50g in contrast colour (B)
25g in each of 9 contrast colours (C, D, E, F, G, H, J, L,M)
(add 75g in main colour for long-sleeved version)
1 pair each 2¾mm and 3¼mm needles
10[10:11:11] buttons (for waistcoat or cardigan)

Waistcoat

Back

**Using 2¾mm needles and A, cast on 113[121:129:135] sts. Work in K1, P1 rib as foll:

1st row (RS) K1, *P1, K1, rep from * to end.
2nd row P1, *K1, P1, rep from * to end.
Rep the last 2 rows for 7cm, ending with a 1st row.
Next row Rib 4[8:4:7], (work twice into next st — called inc 1 —, rib 6[6:7:7]) 15 times, inc 1, rib to end. 129[137:145:151] sts.
Change to 3¼mm needles and beg with a K row cont in st st working colour patt from chart on page 141. Read K rows from right to left and P rows from left to right. Cont in patt until work measures 33cm from cast-on edge, ending with a P row.

Shape armholes

Keeping patt correct, cast off 8[8:10:10] sts at beg of next 2 rows. Dec 1 st at each end of next and every foll alt row until 101[107:107:113] sts rem.
** Cont without shaping until work measures 20[21:23:24]cm from beg of armholes, ending with a K row.

Shape shoulders

Next row P86[91:91:96], turn.
Next row K71[75:75:79], turn.
Next row P55[58:58:61], turn.
Next row K39[41:41:43], turn.
Next row P39[41:41:43]. Leave these sts on a spare needle.

Pocket linings (make 2)

Using 3¼mm needles and A, cast on 25 sts. Beg with a K row cont in st st. Work 23 rows, inc 1 st at each end of last row. 27 sts. Leave these sts on a spare needle.

Left front

Using 2¾mm needles and A, cast on 67[71:75:77] sts. Work K1, P1 rib as for back for 7cm, ending with 1st row.
Next row Rib 11 and sl these sts on to a safety pin, rib 4[6:8:6], (inc 1, rib 5) 8[8:8:9] times, inc 1, rib to end. 65[69:73:76] sts.
Change to 3¼mm needles and beg with a K row cont in st st and patt from chart on page 141 thus: commence reading chart at S[T:U:V], work 1[5:9:2] sts at beg of row, then rep 32 patt sts twice.
Cont until work measures 13cm from cast-on edge, ending with a P row.

Place pocket

Next row Patt 19[21:23:24], with A, K1, (P1, K1) 13 times, patt to end.
Next row Patt 19[21:23:25], with A, P1, (K1, P1) 13 times, patt to end.
Rep the last 2 rows once more.
Next row Patt 19[21:23:24], with A, cast off in rib 27 sts, patt to end.
Next row Patt 19[21:23:25], patt across sts of one pocket lining, patt to end. Cont in patt until work measures same as back to underarm, ending at side edge.

Shape armhole

Cast off 8[8:10:10] sts at beg of next row. Dec 1 st at armhole edge on every foll alt row until 51[54:54:57] sts rem. Cont without shaping until work measures 14[15:17:18]cm from beg of armhole shaping, ending at front edge.

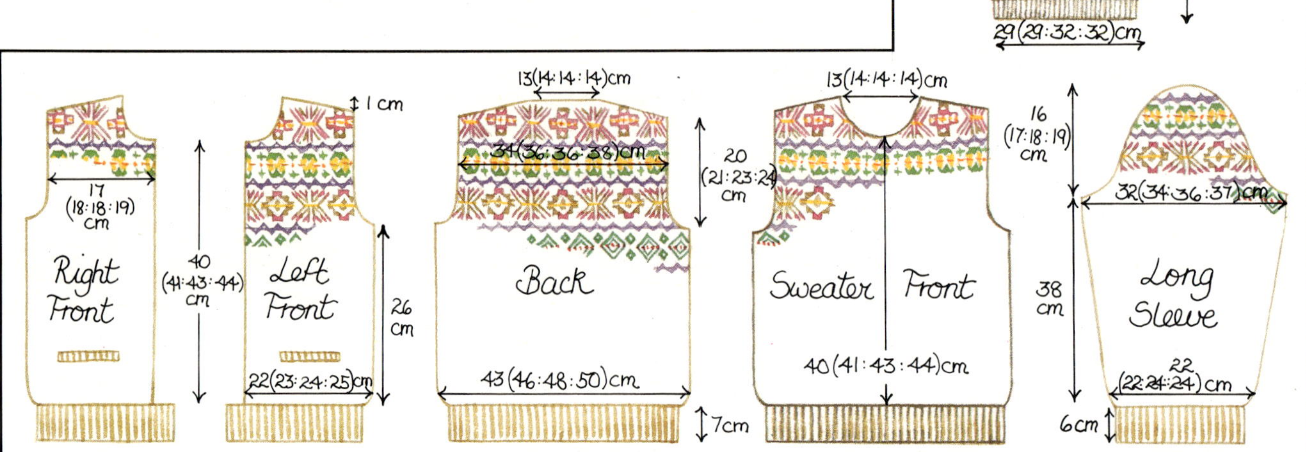

Shape neck

Next row Cast off 11 sts, patt to end.
Dec 1 st at neck edge on *every row*
until 31[33:33:35] sts rem.
Cont without shaping until work
matches back to shoulder shaping,
ending at neck edge.

Shape shoulder

Next row Patt 16 [17:17:18], turn.
Next row patt to end.
Leave these sts on a spare needle.

Right front

Using 2¾mm needles and A, cast on
67[71:75:77] sts.
Work in K1, P1 rib as given for back
for 1cm, ending with a 2nd row.
1st buttonhole row Rib 4, cast off 3
sts, rib to end.
2nd buttonhole row Rib to end,
casting on 3 sts over those cast off in
previous row.
Cont in rib until work measures 5cm
from base of previous buttonhole,
ending with a 2nd row. Work the 2
buttonhole rows again, then cont in
rib until work measures 7cm from
cast-on edge, ending with a 1st row.
Next row rib 3[5:7:5], (inc 1, rib 5)
8[8:8:9] times, inc 1, rib 4[6:8:6],
turn and leave rem 11 sts on a safety
pin. 65[69:73:76] sts.
Change to 3¼mm needles, beg with
a K row, cont in st st and patt from
chart on page 141 thus: commence
reading chart at S, work 1 st at beg of
row, rep 32 patt sts twice, then work
0 [4:8:11] sts, finishing at W [X:Y:Z].
Complete to match left front,
reversing placing of pocket on 4th size
and all shapings.

To make up

Graft shoulder seams.

Armbands

With RS of work facing, using 2¾mm
needles and A, K up
117[123:133:139] sts evenly around
armhole edge.
Beg with a 2nd row work in K1, P1
rib as given for back for 9 rows. Cast
off in rib.

Buttonband

With RS of work facing, using 2¾mm
needles and A, join in yarn to inner
edge of sts on safety pin on left front.
Work in K1, P1 rib as set until band is
long enough, when slightly stretched,
to fit up front edge to neck, ending
with a WS row. Break yarn, leave
these sts. Mark position of 9[9:10:10]
buttons, two on welt opposite

buttonholes already worked, one 4cm
above welt, one 4cm below neck
edge and others evenly spaced
between.

Buttonhole band

With WS or work facing, using
2¾mm needles and A, join in yarn to
inner edge of sts on safety pin. Cont
in rib as set making buttonholes
opposite markers until band measures
same as buttonband, ending with WS
row. Do not break yarn.

Neckband

With RS of work facing, using 2¾mm
needles and A, rib across sts of
buttonhole band, K up 26 sts up right
side of neck, K across 39[41:41:43]
sts on back neck, K up 26 sts down
right side neck, then rib across 11 sts
on buttonband. 113[115:115:117] sts.
Beg with 2nd row work 3 rows rib as
given for back. Work 2 buttonhole
rows again. Rib 4 more rows. Cast off
in rib. Join side seams. Catch down
pocket linings. Sew on front bands
and buttons.

Cardigan

**Back, pocket linings, left front
and right front**
Work as given for waistcoat.

Special technique — shaping with turning rows

1 *The shoulders of the basic
garments are shaped by working
turning rows. On the first row of
shoulder shaping purl the required
number of stitches then turn the work
so that the knit side is facing you,
leaving the remaining stitches on the
right-hand needle. Wrap yarn round
1st stitch on right-hand needle thus:
yarn forward, slip one from right-
hand needle, yarn back, slip stitch
back on right-hand needle.*

2 *Knit the required number of
stitches then turn the work so that
the purl side is facing you, leaving the
remaining stitches on the end of the
needle. Wrap yarn round 1st stitch on
right-hand needle thus: yarn back,
slip one from right-hand needle, yarn
forward, slip stitch back on right-hand
needle. Purl the required number of
stitches back to right shoulder then
turn again, wrapping yarn round 1st
stitch on right-hand needle as before.*

3 *Knit the required number of
stitches back. This point marks
the inner edge of the left shoulder.
Now turn, wrap yarn round first stitch
on right-hand needle as before and
purl the required number of stitches
back. This point marks the inner edge
of the right shoulder. Leave the
stitches on a spare needle. Working
turning rows in this way makes it
possible to graft the shoulders invisibly
in the making up.*

Key
A
B
C
D
E
F
G
H
J
K
L
Repeat: 32 patt sts.
1st size: Back, L & R front, long sleeves
2nd size: Long sleeve
3rd & 4th size: short sleeves
2nd size: Back
3rd & 4th size: long sleeves
3rd size: Back
4th size: Back
1st & 2nd size: Short sleeves

Long sleeves

Using 2¾mm needles and A, cast on 57[59:61:63] sts.
Work in K1, P1 rib as given for back for 6cm, ending with a 1st row.
Next row Rib 4[7:3:4], *inc 1, rib 6[8:4:5], rep from * to last 4[7:3:5] sts, inc 1, rib to end. 65[65:73:73] sts.
Change to 3¼mm needles and beg with a 129th row cont in st st and patt from chart, inc and work into patt 1 st at each end of 6th[9th:5th:5th] row and every foll 6th[5th:5th:5th] row until there are 97[101:107:111] sts. Cont without shaping until work measures approx 44cm from cast-on edge, ending with same patt row as back at underarm.

Shape top

Keeping patt correct, cast off 8[8:10:10] sts at beg of next 2 rows.
Dec 1 st at each end of next and every foll 4th row until 77[81:81:85] sts rem, then at each end of every foll alt row until 55[55:53:57] sts rem. Now dec 1 st at each end of every row until 25[25:27:27] sts rem. Cast off.

To make up

Graft shoulder seams. Join side and sleeve seams. Set in sleeves. Catch down pocket linings. Sew on frontbands and buttons.

Sweater

Back

Work as given for back of waistcoat.

Front

Work as given for back of waistcoat from ** to **.
Cont without shaping until work measures 14[15:17:18]cm from beg of armholes, ending with a P row.

Shape neck

Next row Patt 38[40:40:42] and turn, leaving rem sts on a spare needle.
Complete left side of neck first
Dec 1 st at neck edge on every row until 31[33:33:35] sts rem.
Cont without shaping until work matches back to shoulder shaping, ending at neck edge.

Shape shoulder

Next row Patt 16[17:17:18], turn.
Next row Patt to end.

Leave these sts on a spare needle. With RS of work facing return to sts for right side of neck. Sl centre 25[27:27:29] sts on to a spare needle, join in yarn to next st, patt to end.
Complete to match first side of neck.

Short sleeves

Using 2¾mm needles and A, cast on 79[81:89:91] sts. Work in K1, P1 rib as given for back for 3cm, ending with a 1st row.
Next row Rib 4[8:6:5], *inc 1, rib 9[12:10:15], rep from * to last 5[8:6:6] sts, inc 1, rib to end. 87[87:97:97] sts.
Change to 3¼mm needles and beg with a 41st row cont in patt from chart, inc and work into patt 1 st at each end of the 5th and every foll 4th row until there are 97[101:107:111] sts.
Cont without shaping until work measures approx 15cm from cast-on edge, ending with same patt row as back at under arm.

Shape top

Work as given for long sleeves on cardigan.

Shoulder pads (make 2)

Using 3¼mm needles and A, cast on 38 sts.
Work in K1, P1 rib, dec 1 st at each end of the 3rd and every foll alt row until 2 sts rem.
Work 2 tog and fasten off.

To make up
Neckband

Graft right shoulder seam.
With RS of work facing, using 2¾mm needles and A, K up 19 sts down left side of neck, K across 25[27:27:29] sts at centre front, K up 19 sts up right side of neck, K across 39[41:41:43] sts on back neck, inc 1 st at centre. 103[107:107:111] sts.
Beg with a 2nd row work in K1, P1 rib as given for back. Work 9 rows.
Cast off in rib.
Graft left shoulder seam and join neckband.
Join side and sleeve seams. Set in sleeves. Sew in shoulder pads.

Fair Isle Slipover

Knitted in marvellous muted earth colours, this neat
slipover looks good on men and women, and with clever
accessorizing the mood can be towny or countrified.

Sizes
To fit 81-86 [91-96] cm chest/bust
Length 60 [65] cm

Note Instructions for larger size are in square brackets [ ]; where there is one set of figures it applies to both sizes.

Tension
32 sts and 28 rows to 10cm over Fair Isle patt on 3¾mm needles

Materials
325g four-ply yarn in main colour (A)
25g in each of 5 contrast colours
1 pair each 3mm and 3¾mm knitting needles
3mm circular needle

Back
Using 3mm needles and A, cast on 144 [168] sts. Work in K1, P1 rib for 7 [8] cm, ending with a WS row. Change to 3¾mm needles and beg with a K row cont in st st working 45 rows in patt from chart on page 144. Read odd-numbered rows as K rows and even-numbered rows as P rows. Now repeat chart reading odd-numbered rows as P rows and even-numbered rows as K rows. These 90 rows form the patt. Work in patt until work measures 37 [39] cm from cast-on edge, ending with a WS row.

Shape armholes
Cast off 7 [8] sts at beg of next 2 rows. Dec 1 st at each end of the foll 9 [10] rows, then at each end of the 3 foll alt rows. 106 [126] sts. Cont without shaping until work measures 60 [66] cm from cast-on edge, ending with a WS row. Leave these sts on a spare needle.

Front
Work as given for back from * to *.
Shape armhole and neck
Next row Cast off 7 [8] sts, patt 63 [74], K2 tog, turn, leaving rem sts on a spare needle, patt to end. Complete left side of neck first.
Dec 1 st at armhole edge on the foll 9 rows and then on the 3 foll alt rows, *at the same time*, dec 1 st at neck edge on the next and every foll alt row until 24 [26] sts rem. Cont without shaping until work measures 60 [66] cm from cast-on edge, ending with a WS row. Leave these sts on a spare needle.
Return to sts for right side of neck. With RS of work facing, join in yarn to next st, K2 tog, patt to end.
Next row Cast off 7 [8] sts, patt to end. Complete as given for left side of neck from ** to **.

To make up
With RS of work facing, beg at armhole edge, graft 24 [26] sts from front shoulders to back.
Neck border
With RS of work facing, using 3mm circular needle and A, beg at centre

Special technique — grafting stocking stitch

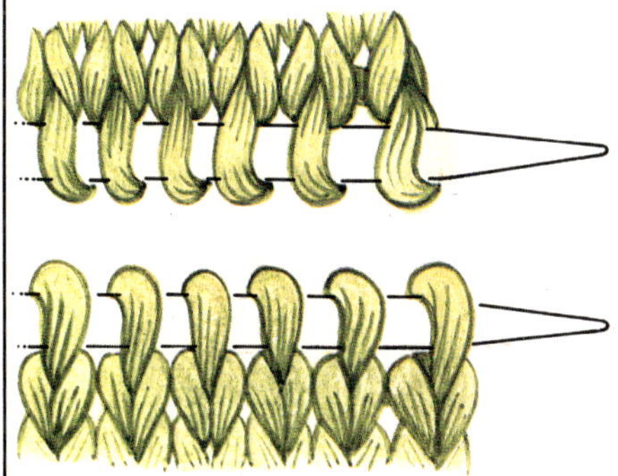

1 *This technique is used to join the shoulder seams of the basic slipover. Place the edges to be joined on a flat surface with the stitches facing each other. Thread a wool needle with a length of yarn at least four times the width of the edge.*

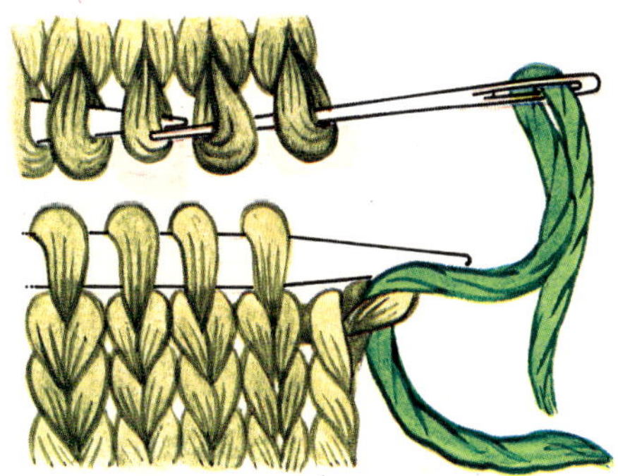

2 *Insert the needle through the first stitch on the lower edge from the back, then through the first stitch on the upper edge through the front then through the second stitch on the upper edge from the back withdrawing the knitting needle from each stitch as you work.*

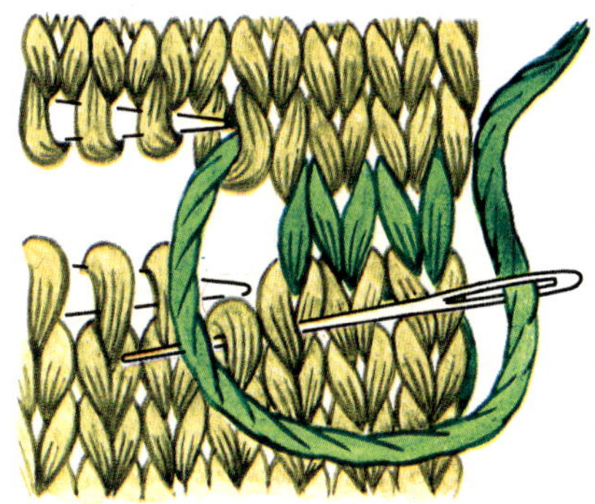

3 *Insert the needle through the first stitch on the lower edge from the front, then the second stitch on the lower edge from the back, then the second stitch on the upper edge from the front, then the third stitch on the upper edge from the back. Carry on across the row.*

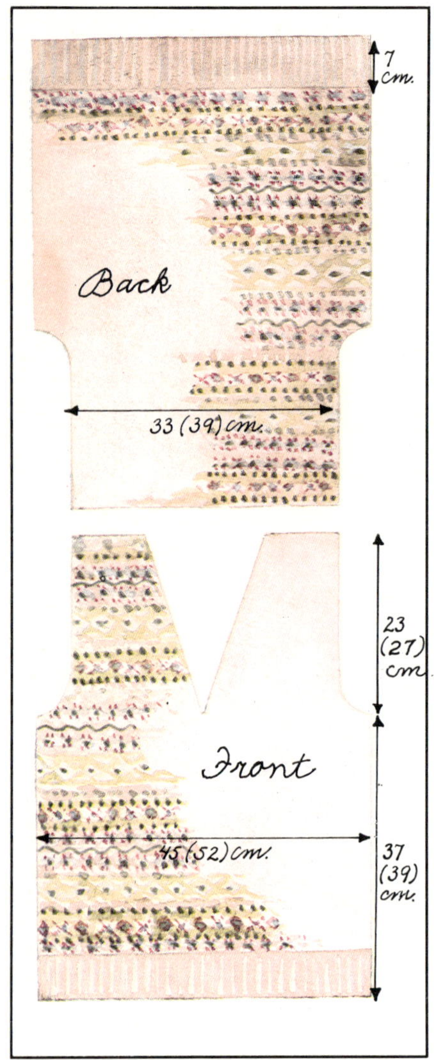

front, K up 60 [72] sts up right side of neck, K across the 58 [74] sts on back neck, K up 60 [72] sts down left side of neck. 178 [218] sts.

Work backwards and forwards.

1st row (WS) P2 tog, *K2, P2, rep from * to last 4 sts, K2, P2 tog.

2nd row P2 tog, P1, *K2, P2, rep from * to last 5 sts, K2, P1, P2 tog.

Cont in this way, keeping K2, P2 rib correct and dec 1 st at each end of every row. Work a further 11 [13] rows. Cast off in rib, dec on this row as before.

Arm borders

With RS facing, using 3mm needles and A, K up 120 [144] sts around armhole edge. Work 11 rows K2, P2 rib. Cast off in rib. Press with a warm iron over a damp cloth.

Join side seams and front neckband.

144

Chequered Accessories

Round off your wardrobe with this classic collection of
accessories — socks, gloves, scarf and beret — all knitted on
four needles in traditional patterns
from Sanquhar in Scotland.

Sizes

Gloves 19cm round hand above thumb
Fingerless gloves 19cm round hand above thumb
Beret to fit an average head
Ankle socks length of foot 22cm (adjustable)
Long socks length of foot 25cm (adjustable)
Length of leg to heel (top turned down) 48cm
Scarf length excluding fringe 153cm

Tension

28 sts and 28 rows to 10cm over patt on 3¾mm needles
32 sts and 40 rows to 10cm over st st on 2¾mm needles

Materials

Gloves
25g four-ply yarn in each of 2 colours (A) and (B)
Fingerless gloves
25g in each of 2 colours (C) and (D)
Beret
50g in main colour (A)
25g in contrast colour (B)
Ankle socks
50g in main colour (A)
25g in contrast colour (B)
Long socks
125g in main colour (C)
25g in contrast colour (D)
Scarf
300g in main colour (C)
150g in contrast colour (D)
1 set each 2¾mm, 3¼mm and 3¾mm knitting needles pointed at both ends

Gloves

Right glove

***Using 2¾mm needles and A, cast on 44 sts and divide on to 3 needles. (Mark next st as first st of round). Using 4th needle work in rounds of K1, P1 rib for 6cm.
Next round Rib 2, pick up loop between last st and next st on ĽH needle and work into the back of it — called M1, (rib 6, M1) 7 times. 52 sts. Change to 3¾mm needles and cont in st st, commence patt from chart 1

as foll (read every round from right to left):
1st round K1A, *K1B, K1A, rep from * to last 27 sts, patt 1st round from chart 1.
2nd round K1B, *K1A, K1B, rep from * to last 27 sts, patt 2nd round from chart 1.
These 2 rows establish the patt for the palm with the back of hand worked from chart.
Keeping chart correct, work a further 13 rounds.**

Place thumb
Next round K1, sl next 11 sts on to a safety pin, cast on 11 sts, patt to end. Work 11 rounds.
1st finger
Change to 3¼mm needles and A.
Next round K8, sl next 37 sts on to a length of yarn, cast on 2 sts, K7. 17 sts.***
K 30 rounds.
Shape top
Next round K1, *K2 tog, rep from * to end.
K one round.
Break off yarn and thread it through rem sts, draw up tightly and fasten off.
2nd finger
Join in yarn to next st of round.
Next round K6, cast on 2 sts, K last 7 sts of round, K up 2 sts from base of 1st finger. 17 sts.
K 36 rounds.
Complete as given for 1st finger.
*****3rd finger**
Join in yarn to next st of round.
Next round K6, cast on 2 sts, K last 6 sts of round, K up 2 sts from base of 2nd finger. 16 sts.*****
K 30 rounds.

Shape top
Next round *K2 tog, rep from * to end.
K one round.
Thread yarn through rem sts, draw up and fasten off.
4th finger
Join in yarn to rem sts.
Next round K12, K up 2 sts from base of 3rd finger. 14 sts.
K 26 rounds.
Complete as given for 3rd finger.
Thumb
With RS of work facing, using 3¼mm needles and A, K 11 sts from safety pin, then K up 11 sts from cast-on sts. 22 sts.
K 26 rounds.
Complete as 3rd finger.

Left glove

Work as given for right glove from *** to **.
Place thumb
Next round Patt 13, sl next 11 sts on to a safety pin, cast on 11 sts, patt to end.
Work 11 rounds.
1st finger
Change to 3¼mm needles and A.
Next round K17, sl these sts on to a length of yarn, K15, cast on 2 sts, leave rem sts on a length of yarn.
Complete as given for 1st finger of right glove.
2nd finger
Next round Sl last 6 sts from first length of yarn on to needle, join in A, K up 2 sts from base of 1st finger, K7 sts from second length of yarn, cast on 2 sts. 17 sts.
Complete as given for 2nd finger of right glove.
3rd finger
Next round Sl last 6 sts from first length of yarn on to needle, join in A, K up 2 sts from base of 2nd finger, K 6 sts from second length of yarn, cast on 2 sts. 16 sts.
Complete as given for 3rd finger of right glove.
4th finger
Next round Sl last 5 sts on first length of yarn on to needle, join in A, K up 2 sts from base of 3rd finger, K 7 sts rem on second length of yarn. 14 sts.
Complete as 4th finger of right glove.
Thumb
Work as given for right glove.

Fingerless gloves
Right fingerless glove
Work as given for right glove from
*** to ***, working from chart 2.
Next round K7, K2 tog, K8. 16 sts.
K 4 rounds. Work 3 rounds K1, P1
rib. Cast off loosely in rib.
2nd finger
Join in yarn to next st of round.
Next round K6, cast on 2 sts, K last 7
sts of round, K up 2 sts from base of
1st finger. 17 sts.
Next round K15, K2 tog, 16 sts.
Complete as 1st finger.
3rd finger
Work as 3rd finger of right glove from
**** to ****.
K 4 rounds. Complete as 1st finger.
4th finger
Join in yarn to rem sts.
Next round K12, K up 2 sts from
base of 3rd finger. 14 sts.
K 3 rounds. Complete as 1st finger.
Thumb
Using 3¼mm needles and A, with
RS of work facing K 11 sts from
safety pin, then K up 11 sts from cast-on
sts. 22 sts.
Complete as 1st finger.

Left fingerless glove
Work as given for left glove working
from chart 2, completing fingers as
given for right fingerless glove.

Beret
Using 2¾mm needles and A, cast on
126 sts and divide on to three
needles. (Mark next st as first of
round).
Work 11 rounds K1, P1 rib.
Next round * (K2, M1) 27 times, (K1,
M1) 9 times, rep from * once more.
198 sts.
Change to 3¾mm needles and
commence patt from chart 1.
Work 27 rounds.
Shape crown
Cont in A only.
Next round * K2 tog, K2, rep from *
to last 2 sts, K2 tog, 148 sts.
Next round K.
Next round (K12, sl. 1, K2 tog, psso) 9
times, K13. 130 sts.
Next round Sl first st on to end of last
needle, K to end.
Next round (K10, sl 1, K2 tog, psso)
10 times, 110 sts.
Next round (K8, sl 1, K2 tog, psso)

10 times, 90 sts.
Cont to dec in this way until the round
'(sl 1, K2 tog, psso) 10 times'
has been worked. 10 sts.
Next round K.
Next round (K2 tog) to end. 5 sts.
Thread yarn through the rem sts,
draw up and fasten off.

Ankle socks
Using 2¾mm needles and A, cast on
72 sts and divide on to 3 needles.
(Mark next st as first of round). Work
4 rounds K1, P1 rib.
Change to 3¾mm needles and
commence patt from chart 1.
Work 18 rounds.
Change to 2¾mm needles and
cont in A only.
Next round (K3, K2 tog) 4 times,
(K2, K2 tog) 8 times, (K3, K2 tog)
4 times. 56 sts.
Work in K1, P1 rib for 5cm.
Turn work inside out, so reversing
fabric.
K12 rounds.
Divide for heel
Next round K13, sl last 14 sts of

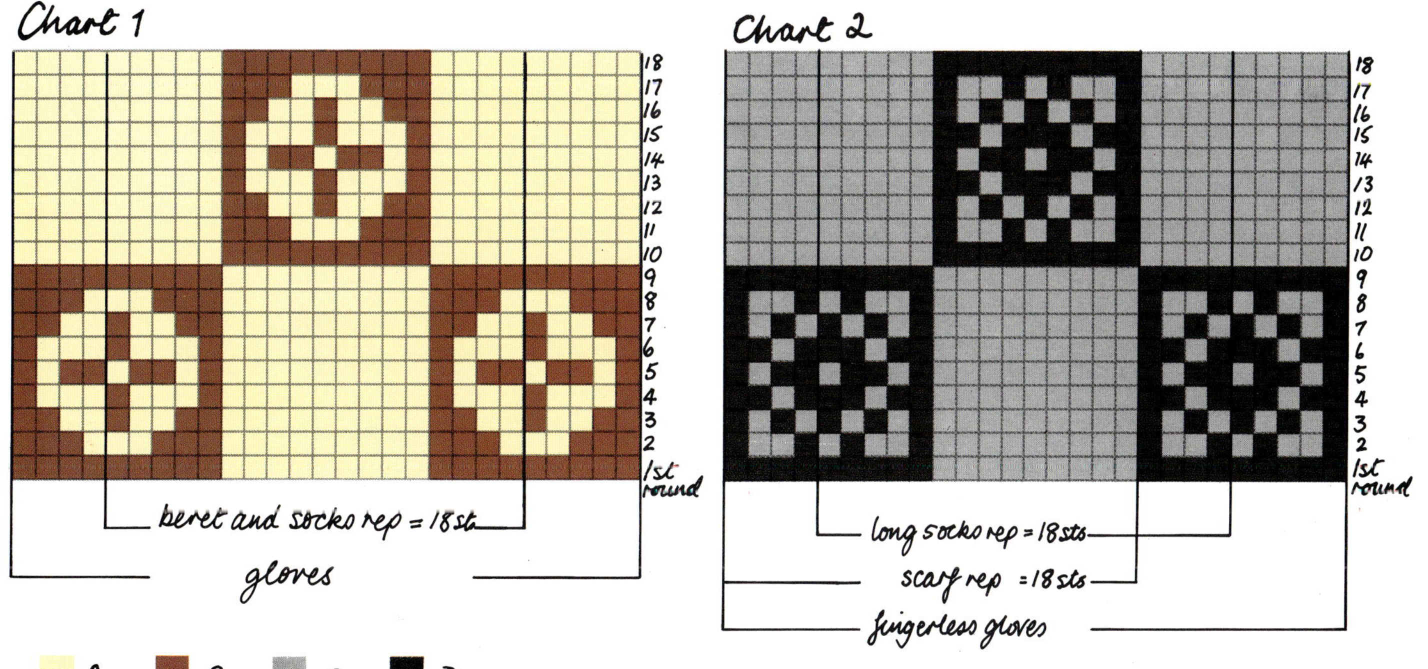

round to other end of same needle.
27 sts.
Divide rem sts on to 2 needles and
leave for instep.
Cont on 27 sts for heel in rows as foll:
1st row (WS) Sl 1, P to end.
2nd row Sl 1, K to end.
Rep these 2 rows 15 times more,
then the 1st row again.
Turn heel
1st row K19, K2 tog tbl, turn.
2nd row P12, P2 tog, turn.
3rd row K12, K2 tog tbl, turn.
Rep 2nd and 3rd rows 5 times more,
then the 2nd row again.
Next row K7 to complete heel (6 sts
rem on LH needle).
Sl all instep sts on to one needle.
With spare needle, K6 sts rem for
heel, K up 16 sts along side of heel,
with 2nd needle K29 instep sts, with
3rd needle K up 16 sts along side of
heel, K7 heel sts. 74 sts.
Shape instep in rounds as foll:
1st round K.
2nd round 1st needle—K to last 3
sts, K2 tog, K1, 2nd needle—K to
end, 3rd needle—K1, K2 tog tbl, K
to end.
Rep these 2 rounds until 56 sts rem.
Cont without shaping. Work 48
rounds.
(Length of foot may be adjusted here
if necessary.)
Next round 1st needle—K to end,
2nd needle—K1, K2 tog tbl, K to
last 3 sts, K2 tog, K1, 3rd needle—
K to end.
Shape toe
1st round 1st needle—K to last 3
sts, K2 tog, K1, 2nd needle—K1,
K2 tog tbl, K to last 3 sts, K2 tog, K1,
3rd needle—K1, K2 tog tbl, K to
end.
2nd round K.
Rep last 2 rounds until 30 sts rem.
K sts from 1st needle on to end of 3rd
needle. Graft or cast off sts tog from 2
needles.

Long socks
Using 2¾mm needles and C, cast on
72 sts and divide on to 3 needles.
(Mark next st as first of round). Work
4 rounds K1, P1 rib.
Change to 3¾mm needles and
commence patt from chart 2.
Work 18 rounds.

148

Change to 2¾mm needles and cont
in A only.
Next round K.
Next round (K 6, M1) 12 times.
84 sts.
Work in K1, P1 rib for 6cm.
Turn work inside out so reversing
fabric.
K40 rounds.
Shape leg
1st round K2 tog, K to last 3 sts. K2
tog tbl, K1.
K5 rounds.
Rep the last 6 rounds until 60 sts rem.
Cont without shaping until work
measures 35cm from reversing of
fabric.
Divide for heel
Next round K14, sl last 15 sts of
round to other end of same needle.
29 sts.
Divide rem sts on to 2 needles and
leave for instep.
Cont on 29 sts for heel in rows as foll:
1st row (WS) Sl 1 P-wise, P to end.
2nd row Sl 1 K-wise, * K1, ybk, sl 1
P-wise, rep from * to last 2 sts, K2.

Rep these 2 rows 16 times more,
then the 1st row again.
Turn heel
1st row K17, sl 1, K1, psso, turn.
2nd row P6, P2 tog, turn.
3rd row K7, Sl 1, K1, psso, turn.
4th row P8, P2 tog, turn.
Cont in this way until all sts are
worked on to one needle ending with
a P row. 17 sts.
Next row K9 to complete heel (8 sts
rem on LH needle).
Sl all instep sts on to one needle.
With spare needle, K8 sts rem for heel,
K up 18 sts along side of heel,
with 2nd needle K31 instep sts, with
3rd needle K up 18 sts along side of
heel, K9 heel sts. 84 sts.
Shape instep in rounds as foll:
1st round K.
2nd round 1st needle—K to last 3
sts, K2 tog, K1, 2nd needle—K, 3rd
needle—K1, K2 tog tbl, K to end.
Rep these 2 rounds until 58 sts rem.
Cont without shaping. Work 56
rounds. (Length may be adjusted
here.) S1 first st of 2nd needle on to
end of 1st needle and last st of 2nd
needle on to 3rd needle.
Shape toe
1st round 1st needle—K to last 3
sts, K2 tog, K1, 2nd needle—K1,
K2 tog tbl, K to last 3 sts, K2 tog, K1,
3rd needle—K1, K2 tog tbl, K to
end.
2nd round K.
Rep these 2 rounds until 26 sts rem,
ending with a 2nd round.
K sts from 1st needle on to end of 3rd
needle. Graft or cast off sts tog from 2
needles.

Scarf
Using 3¾mm needles and C, cast on
144 sts and divide on to 3 needles.
(Mark next st as first of round).
K one round.
Cont in st st, commence patt from
chart 2 until work measures approx
153cm from cast-on edge ending with
a 9th patt row.
Cast off.

To make up
Press scarf flat and join ends.
Cut rem yarn into 36cm lengths.
Using 3 strands of C and 3 strands of
D tog make a fringe along the short
ends of scarf.

Guernsey Family Sweaters

This happy family of sweaters shows three traditional
Guernsey styles—including the plain workday garment and
the more decorative versions for Sundays and celebrations.

Sizes
Man's sweater
To fit 96 [101:106] cm chest
Length 66 [67:69] cm
Sleeve seam 46 [47:48] cm
Woman's sweater
To fit 81 [86:91] cm bust
Length 61 [62:63] cm
Sleeve seam 42cm
Child's sweater
To fit 66 [71:76] cm chest
Length 48 [52:56] cm
Sleeve seam 30 [34:38] cm

Note Instructions for larger sizes are in square brackets []; where there is only one set of figures it applies to all sizes.

Tension
27 sts and 36 rows to 10cm over st st ˙on 3mm needles.

Materials
Man's sweater
650 [750:850] g Guernsey five-ply yarn
Woman's sweater
550 [650:750] five-ply Guernsey yarn
Child's sweater
450 [450:550] g five-ply Guernsey yarn
1 pair 3mm needles
One 3mm circular needle or a set of 4 long double-pointed 3mm needles

Man's sweater
Back and front (one piece)
**Using pair 3mm needles, cast on 132 [140:148] sts for front.
Next row Sl 1, *K1 tbl, rep from * to end.
Rep the last row 24 times more. Break yarn and leave these sts on spare needle.**
Rep from ** to ** for back.
Using 3mm circular needle, join back and front by slipping both sets of sts on to needle, marking first st of back as first st of round. 264 [280:296] sts. Work in rounds.
Work 6 rounds K2, P2 rib.
Next round (Pick up the loop between last st knitted and next st and knit into the back of it — called M1 —, K132 [140:148]) twice. 266 [282:298] sts.
Next round (P1, K132 [140:148]) twice.
Rep last round until work measures 43 [43:44] cm from cast-on edge.
Shape underarm gussets
1st round (M1, K1, M1, K132 [140:148]) twice.
2nd and every alt round K.
3rd round (M1, K3, M1, K132 [140:148]) twice.
5th round (M1, K5, M1, K132 [140:148]) twice.
Cont to inc in this way until the round (M1, K17, M1, K132 [140:148])

twice has been worked.
Next round (Sl 19 sts on to a stitch holder, K132 [140:148]) twice. Leave the 132 [140:148] sts of back on a spare needle and cont in rows on sts for front.
Next row (WS) P5, K5, P112 [120:128], K5, P5.
Next row K.
Rep the last 2 rows until front measures 66 [67:69]cm, ending with a WS row. Leave these sts on a spare needle.
With WS of work facing, join in yarn to sts for back. Complete as given for front.
Shape shoulders
With WS of work tog, using a 3mm needle, beg at left armhole edge, join shoulder as folls.
(K1 st from front and 1 st from back tog to make 1 st) 38 [41:44] times, turn and cast off these sts. Fasten off. Join in yarn to right shoulder and complete to match left shoulder, leaving centre 56 [58:60] sts for neck opening.
Shape neck gussets
With RS of work facing, using 3mm needles, K up 1 st from neck edge of left shoulder, K1 from front, turn.
Next row Sl 1 P-wise, P1, P1 from back, turn.
Next row Sl 1 K-wise, K2, K1 from front, turn.

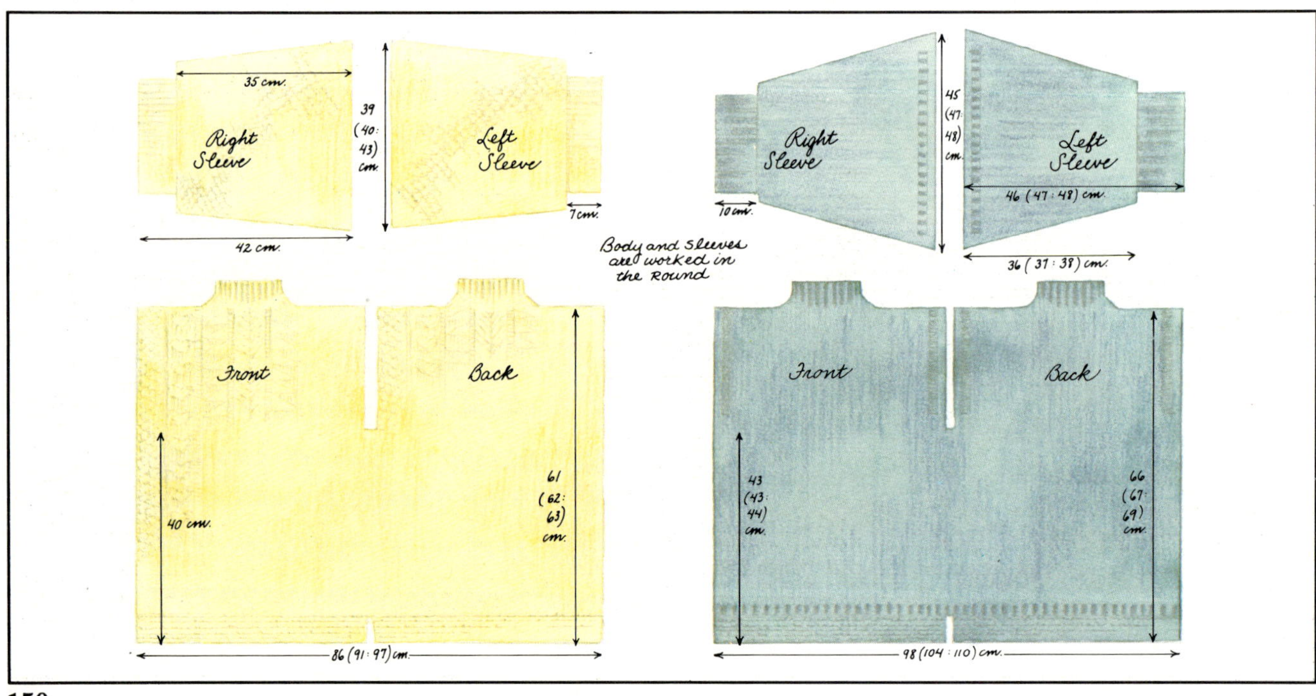

Cont in this way until there are 15 sts. Break yarn and leave these sts. Work right neck gusset in the same way.

Neckband

Using 3mm circular needle, with RS of work facing, K across back neck sts, inc 1 st at each end, K left neck gusset sts, K across sts on front, K right neck gusset sts. 116 [120:124] sts.

Mark first gusset st as first st of round. Work 12 [14:16] rounds K2, P2 rib. Cast off in rib.

Sleeves

Using 3mm circular needle, with RS of work facing, beg at underarm, K19 sts from gusset, K up 104 [108:112] sts round armhole edge. 123 [127:131] sts. Mark first gusset st as first st of round.

1st round K2 tog, K15, K2 tog tbl, P1, work in K2, P2 rib to last st, P1,

2nd and 3rd rounds K17, P1, rib to last st, P1.

4th round K2 tog, K13, K2 tog tbl, P1, rib to last st, P1.

5th and 6th rounds K15, P1, rib to last st, P1.

7th round K2 tog, K11, K2 tog tbl, P1, K to last st, P1.

8th and 9th rounds K13, P1, K to last st, P1.

Cont as set, dec 1 st at each side of gusset until 105 [109:113] sts rem.

Next round P1, K104 [108:112].

Next round P1, K2 tog tbl, K to last 2 sts, K2 tog.

Next round P1, K to end. Rep the last round 4 times more. Rep the last 6 rounds until 71 [73:75] sts rem.

Cont without shaping until sleeve measures 36 [37:38] cm (sleeve may be lengthened here).

Next round P1, K4 [3:3], K2 tog, (K8 [6:9], K2 tog) 6 [8:6] times), K to end. 64 [64:68] sts.

Work in rounds of K2, P2, rib for 10cm. Cast off in rib.

To make up

Press lightly on WS omitting ribbing and garter st.

Woman's sweater

Back and front (one piece)

**Using pair 3mm needles, cast on 117 [125:133] sts for front.

Next row Sl 1, *K1 tbl, rep from * to end.

Rep the last row 24 times more. Break yarn and leave these sts on a spare needle.**

Rep from ** to ** for back.

Using 3mm circular needle, join back and front by slipping both sets of sts on to needle, marking first st of back as first st of round.

Commence patt

When working from chart, read each row from right to left.

1st round P1, K2, (P2, K2) 2 [3:4] times, work 1st row from chart, K2 (P2, K2) 5 [7:9] times, work 1st row from chart, K2, (P2, K2) 2 [3:4] times, P1.

2nd round As 1st round, working 2nd row from chart.

3rd round K1, P2, (K2, P2) 2 [3:4] times, work 3rd row from chart, P2, (K2, P2) 5 [7:9] times, work 3rd row from chart, P2 (K2, P2) 2 [3:4]. times, K1.

4th round As 3rd round, reading 4th row from chart.

These 4 rounds establish the edge st patt and place the centre patt panel. Keeping edge sts and patt panel from chart correct cont until work measures 40cm from cast-on edge.

Shape underarm gussets

1st round (Pick up loop between last st knitted and next st and knit into the back of it — called M1 —, patt 117 [125:133]) twice.

2nd round (K1, patt 117 [125:133]) twice.

3rd round (M1, K1, M1, patt 117 [125:133]) twice.

4th round (K3, patt 117 [125:133]) twice.

5th round (M1, K3, M1, patt 117 [125:133]) twice.

6th round (K5, patt 117 [125:133]) twice.

Cont to inc in this way until the round (M1, K15, M1, patt 117 [125:133]) twice has been worked.

Next round (Sl 17 sts on to a stitch holder, patt 117 [125:133]) twice. Leave the 117 [125:133] sts of back on a spare needle and cont in rows

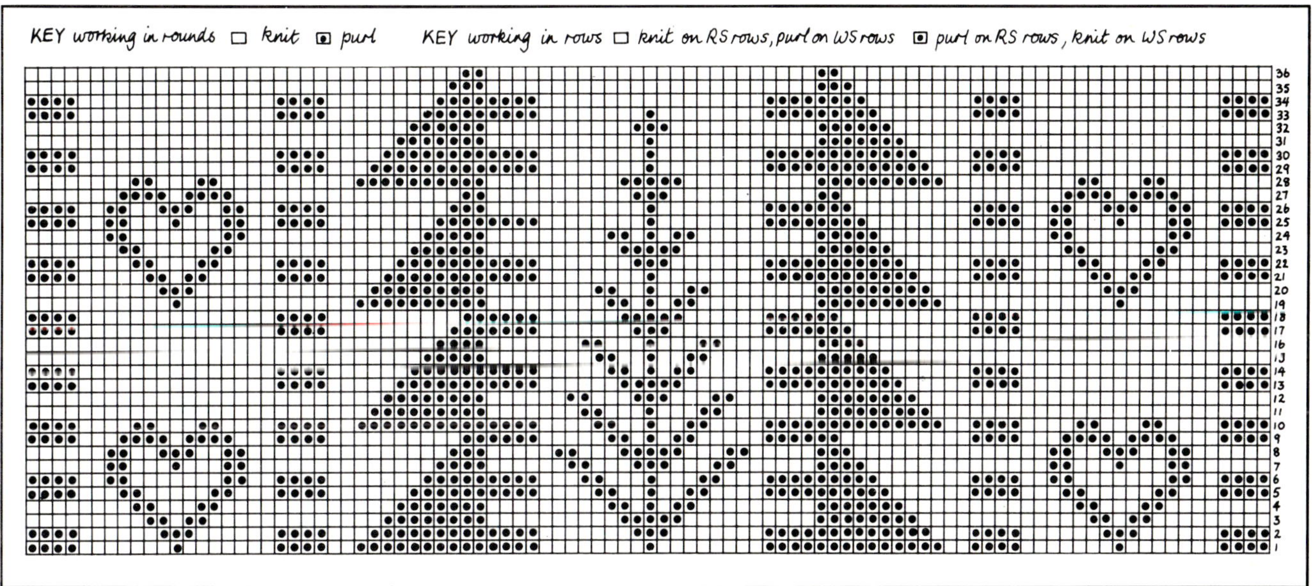

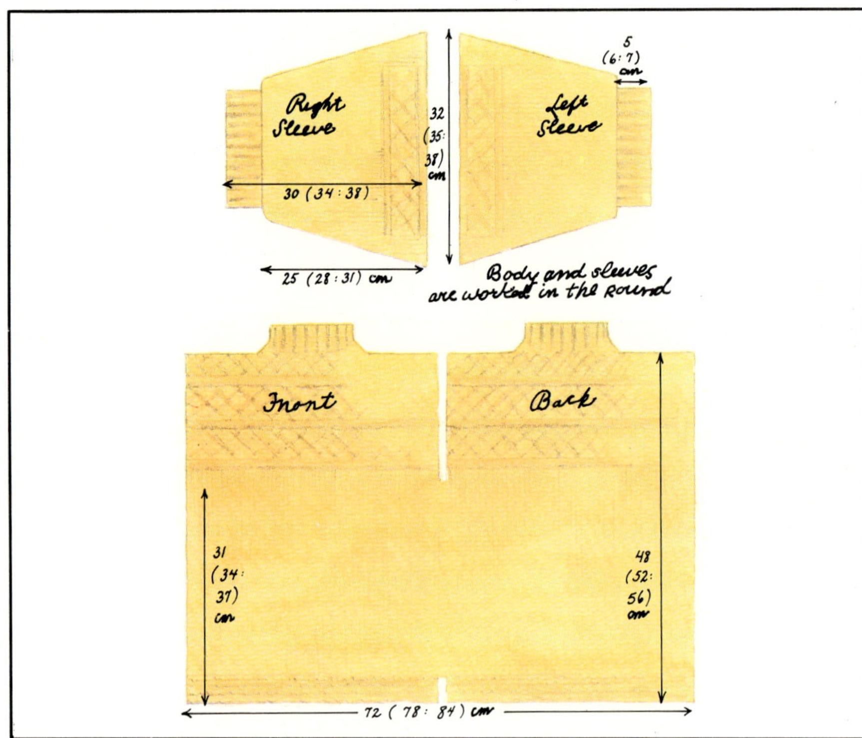

and patt on sts for front until work measures 61 [62:63]cm, ending with a WS row.

With WS of work facing, join in yarn to sts for back. Complete as given for front.

Shape shoulders

With WS of work tog, using a 3mm needle, beg at left armhole edge, join shoulders as foll.

(K1 st from front and 1 st from back tog to make 1 st) 34 [37:40] times, turn and cast off these sts. Fasten off. Join in yarn to right shoulder and complete to match left shoulder, leaving centre 49 [51:55] sts for neck opening.

Shape neck gussets

With RS of work facing, using 3mm needles, K1 st from neck edge of left shoulder, K1 from front, turn.

Next row Sl 1 P-wise, P1, P1 from back, turn.

Next row Sl 1 K-wise, K1 from front, turn.

Cont in this way until there are 13 sts. Break yarn and leave these sts. Work right neck gusset in the same way.

Neckband

Using 3mm circular needle, with RS of work facing, K across right neck gusset, K back neck sts, K across left neck gusset sts and front. 100 [104:108] sts. Mark next st as first st of round. Work 12 rounds K2, P2 rib. Cast off in rib.

Sleeves

Using 3mm circular needle, with RS of work facing, beg at underam, K17 sts from gusset, K up 92 [96:104] sts round armhole edge. 109 [113:121] sts. Mark first gusset st as first st of round.

1st round K2 tog, K13, K2 tog tbl, P1, K2, *P2, K2, rep from * to last st, P1.

2nd round K15, P1, K2, *P2, K2, rep from * to last st, P1.

3rd round K2 tog, K11, K2 tog tbl, K1, P2, *K2, P2, rep from * to last st, K1.

4th round K14, P2, *K2, P2, rep from * to last st, K1.

Cont in this way, dec 1 st at each side of gusset until 93 [97:105] sts rem.

Next round K2 tog, patt to end. Patt 3 [3:5] rounds.

Next round Patt 1, work 2 tog, patt to last 3 sts, work 2 tog tbl, patt 1. Patt 7 [7:5] rounds.

Rep the last 8 [8:6] rounds until 64 [68:70] sts rem.

Cont without shaping until sleeve measures 35cm (sleeve may be lengthened here).

Next round K3 [5:3], K2 tog, (K6 [6:5], K2 tog) 7 [7:9] times, K to end. 56 [60:60] sts.

Work in rounds of K2, P2 rib for 7cm. Cast off in rib.

To make up

Press lightly on WS omitting ribbing and garter stitch.

Child's sweater

Back and front (one piece)

**Using pair of 3mm needles, cast on 97 [105:113] sts for front.

Next row Sl 1, *K1 tbl, rep from * to end.

Rep the last row 20 times more. Break yarn and leave these sts on a spare needle. **

Rep from ** to ** for back.

Using 3mm circular needle, join back and front by slipping both sets of sts on to needle, marking first st of back as first st of round. Work in rounds.

Next round (Pick up the loop between last st knitted and next st and knit into the back of it — called M1 —, K97 [105:113]) twice. 196 [212:228] sts.

Next round (P1, K97 [105:113]) twice.

Rep the last round until work measures 31 [34:37] cm from cast-on edge.

Shape underarm gussets

1st round (M1, K1, M1, K97 [105:113]) twice.

2nd and every alt row K.

3rd round (M1, K3, M1, K97 [105:113]) twice.

5th round (M1, K5, M1, K97 [105:113]) twice.

Cont to inc in this way until the round '(M1, K13, M1, K97 [105:113]) twice' has been worked.

Next round (Sl 15 sts on to a stitch holder, K97 [105:113]) twice.

Leave the 97 [105:113] sts of back on a spare needle and cont in rows on sts for front.

Next row (WS) P.

Now work in patt.

1st, 3rd and 4th rows P.

2nd row K.

5th row (RS) P1, *K7, P1, rep from * to end.

6th row P1, *K1, P5, K1, P1, rep from * to end.

7th row K2, *P1, K3, rep from * ending last rep K2.

8th row P3, *K1, P1, K1, P5, rep from * ending last rep P3.
9th row K4, *P1, K7, rep from * ending last rep K4.
10th row As 8th row.
11th row As 7th row.
12th row As 6th row.
13th row As 5th row.
14th-21st rows As 6th-13th rows.
22nd row P.
These 22 rows form the patt.
Cont in patt until front measures 48 [52:56] cm, ending with a WS row. Leave these sts on a spare needle. With WS of work facing, join yarn to back sts. Complete as given for front.
Shape shoulders
With WS of work tog, using a 3mm needle, beg at left armhole edge, join shoulders as folls, (K1 st from front and 1 st from back tog to make 1 st) 27 [30:33] times, turn and cast off these sts. Fasten off. Join in yarn to right shoulder; complete to match left, leaving 43 [45:47] sts for neck opening.
Shape neck gussets
With RS facing, using 3mm needles, K up 1 st from neck edge of left shoulder seam, K1 from front, turn.
Next row Sl 1 P-wise, P1, P1 from back, turn.
Next row Sl K-wise, K2, K1 from front, turn.
Cont in this way until there are 11 sts. Break yarn and leave these sts. Work right neck gusset in the same way.

Neckband

Using 3mm circular needle, with RS of work facing, K across back neck sts, K left neck gusset sts, K across sts on front, K right neck gusset sts. 88 [92:96] sts. Mark first st as first st of round. Work 10 [10:12] rounds, K2, P2 rib. Cast off in rib.

Sleeves

Using 3mm circular needle, with RS of work facing, beg at underarm, K15 sts from gusset, K up 73 [81:89] sts round armhole edge. 88 [96:104] sts. Mark first gusset st as first st of round.
1st round K2 tog, K11, K2 tog tbl, P to end.
2nd round K13, P to end.
3rd round K2 tog, K9, K2 tog tbl, P to end.
4th round K to end.
5th round K2 tog, K7, K2 tog tbl, P1, *K7, P1, rep from * to end.
6th round K10, *P1, K5, P1, K1, rep from * to end.
7th round K2 tog, K5, K2 tog tbl, K2, *P1, K3, rep from * ending last rep K2.
8th round K10, *P1, K1, P1, K5, rep from * ending last rep K3.
9th round K2 tog, K3, K2 tog tbl, K4, *P1, K7, rep from * ending last rep K4.
10th round K8, *P1, K1, P1, K5, rep from * ending last rep K3.
11th round K2 tog, K1, K2 tog tbl, K2, *P1, K3, rep from * ending last rep K2.
12th round K4, *P1, K5, K1, rep from * to end.
13th round K3 tog, P1, *K7, P1, rep from * to end.
14th round P1, K1, *P1, K5, P1, K1, rep from * to end.
15th round P1, K2, *P1, K3, rep from * ending last rep K2.
16th round P1, K3, *P1, K1, P1, K5, rep from * ending last rep K3.
17th round P1, K4, *P1, K7, rep from * ending last rep K4.
18th round As 16th round.
19th round As 15th round.
20th round As 14th round.
21st round P2, * K7, P1 rep from *.
22nd round P1, K2 tog tbl, K to last 2 sts, K2 tog. 72 [80:88] sts.
Next round P.
Rep the last round twice more.
Next round P1, K to end.
Rep the last round 6 times more.
Next round P1, K2 tog tbl, K to last 2 sts, K2 tog.
Rep the last 6 rounds until 52 [56:60] sts rem. Cont. without shaping until sleeve measures 25 [28:31]cm.
Next round K3 [2:4], K2 tog, (K5 [6:6], K2 tog) 6 times, K3 [2:4], K2 tog, 44 [48:52] sts. Work in rounds of K2, P2 rib for 5 [6:7]cm. Cast off.

To make up
Press lightly on WS.

Special technique—shaping underarm gussets

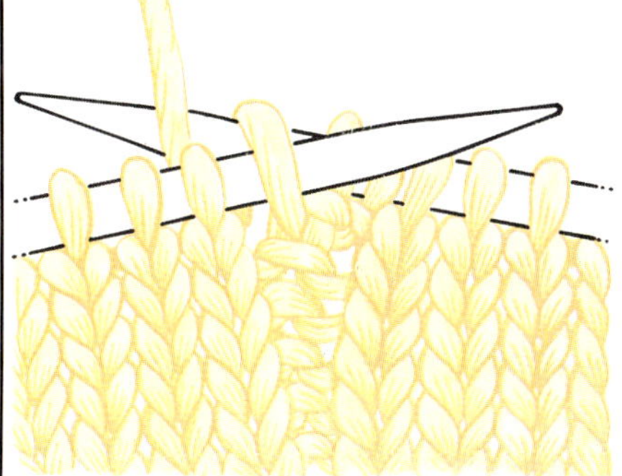

1 *Work in rounds to armhole position. On next round begin working right underarm gusset. Make one, knit one, make one. Work across back stitches then begin left underarm gusset in the same way, then work across stitches for front.*

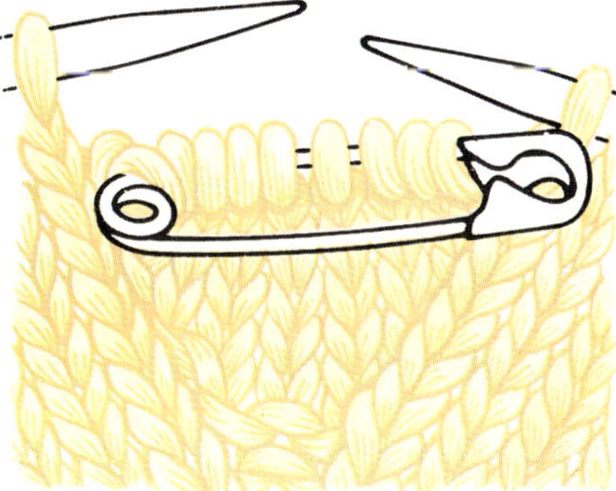

2 *Continue shaping gussets by increasing one stitch on each side on every alternate row until gusset is required width. Slip gusset stitches on to stitch holder and work back and front yokes separately on two needles.*

3 *When back and front yokes are completed pick up stitches for sleeves and, working in rounds, continue shaping gussets by decreasing one stitch on each side on every alternate row until one gusset stitch remains.*

Hebridean Guernsey

This version of the Guernsey fisherman's sweater comes
from the Hebridean islands off the west coast of Scotland.
It features lace panels and motifs as well as the more
usual cables and textures.

Sizes
To fit 71-76 [81-86:91-96]cm chest or bust
Length 63[65:67]cm
Sleeve seam 43[45:47]cm

Note Instructions for larger sizes are in square brackets []; where there is only one set of figures it applies to all sizes.

Tension
30 sts and 40 rows to 10cm over st st on 3¼mm needles

Materials
450 [500:550] g four ply yarn
1 pair 3¼mm needles
Set of four 2¾mm and 3¼mm double-pointed needles
Cable needle

Panel patt A (worked over 6[10:16] sts)
1st row (WS) K.
2nd row P.
3rd row K1, P to last st, K1.
4th row P1, (yfwd, K2 tog) 2[4:7] times, P1.
5th row As 3rd.
6th row P1, K to last st, P1.
These 6 rows form panel patt A.

Panel patt B (worked over 8 sts)
1st row (WS) K1, P1, K1, P4, K1.
2nd row P1, K4, P3.
3rd and 4th rows Rep 1st and 2nd rows.
5th row As 1st row.
6th row P1, sl next 2 sts on to a cable needle and hold at front of work, K2, then K2 sts from cable needle — called C4F —, P3.
These 6 rows form panel patt B.

Panel patt C (worked over 17 sts)
1st row (WS) P.
2nd row K5, P7, K5.
3rd row P4, K2, P1, K3, P1, K2, P4.
4th row K3, P2, K2, P3, K2, P2, K3.
5th row P2, K2, P3, K3, P3, K2, P2.
6th row K1, P2, K4, P3, K4, P2, K1.
7th row P1, (K3, P3) twice, K3, P1.
8th row As 6th row.
9th row P2, K1, P4, K3, P4, K1, P2.
10th row K7, P3, K7.
11th and 13th rows P8, K1, P8.
12th and 14th rows K8, P1, K8.
15th and 17th rows P3, (K1, P1) twice, K3, (P1, K1) twice, P3.
16th row K4, (P1, K1) 5 times, K3.

18th and 19th rows As 12th and 11th rows.
20th row As 10th row.
21st row P7, K1, P1, K1, P7.
22nd row As 20th row.
23rd row P.
24th row K.
25th and 26th rows (K1 tbl) 17 times.
These 26 rows form panel patt C.

Panel patt D (worked over 8 sts)
1st row (WS) K1, P4, K1, P1, K1.
2nd row P3, K4, P1.
3rd and 4th rows As 1st and 2nd rows.
5th row As 1st row.
6th row P3, sl next 2 sts onto cable needle and hold at back of work, K2, then K2 from cable needle — called C4B —, P1.
These 6 rows form panel patt D.

Panel patt E (worked over 11 sts)
1st and 3rd rows (WS) P.
2nd row K1, yfwd, K3, sl 1, K2 tog, psso, K3, yfwd, K1.
4th row P1, K1, yfwd, K2, sl 1, K2 tog, psso, K2, yfwd, K1, P1.
5th and 7th rows K1, P9, K1.
6th row P1, K2, yfwd, K1, sl 1, K2 tog, psso, K1, yfwd, K2, P1.
8th row P1, K3, yfwd, sl 1, K2 tog, psso, yfwd, K3, P1.
These 8 rows form panel patt E.

Panel patt F (worked over 17 sts)
1st row (WS) P.
2nd row K8, P1, K8.
3rd row P7, K3, P7.
4th row K6, P5, K6.
5th row P5, K2, P1, K1, P1, K2, P5.
6th row K4, P2, K2, P1, K2, P2, K4.
7th row P3, K2, P3, K1, P3, K2, P3.
8th row K2, P2, K3, P3, K3, P2, K2.
9th row P1, K2, P3, K5, P3, K2, P1.
10th row K5, P2, K1, P1, K1, P2, K5.
11th row P4, K2, P2, K1, P2, K2, P4.
12th row K3, P2, K3, P1, K3, P2, K3.
13th row P2, K2, P3, K3, P3, K2, P2.
14th-17th rows Rep 4th-7th rows.
18th row K7, P3, K7.
19th row P6, K5, P6.
20th and 21st rows As 10th and 11th rows.

22nd and 23rd rows As 2nd and 3rd rows.
24th row K.
25th and 26th rows (K1 tbl) 17 times.
These 26 rows form panel patt F.

Panel patt G (worked over 17 sts)
1st and every foll alt row (WS) P.
2nd row K6, K2 tog, yfwd, K1, yfwd, sl 1, K1, psso, K6.
4th row K5, K2 tog, yfwd, K3, yfwd, sl 1, K1, psso, K5.
6th row K4, K2 tog, yfwd, K5, yfwd, sl 1, K1, psso, K4.
8th row K3, (K2 tog, yfwd, K1) twice, yfwd, sl 1, K1, psso, K1, yfwd, sl 1, K1, psso, K3.
10th row K2, K2 tog, yfwd, K1, K2 tog, yfwd, K3, yfwd, sl 1, K1, psso, K1, yfwd, sl 1, K1, psso, K2.
12th row K1, K2 tog, yfwd, K1, K2 tog, yfwd, K5, yfwd, sl 1, K1, psso, K1, yfwd, sl 1, K1, psso, K1.
14th row K3, (yfwd, sl 1, K1, psso, K1) twice, K2 tog, yfwd, K1, K2 tog, yfwd, K3.
16th row K4, yfwd, sl 1, K1, psso, K1, yfwd, sl 1, K2 tog, psso, yfwd, K1, K2 tog, yfwd, K4.
18th row K5, yfwd, sl 1, K1, psso, K3, K2 tog, yfwd, K5.
20th row K6, yfwd, sl 1, K1, psso, K1, K2 tog, yfwd, K6.
22nd row K7, yfwd, sl 1, K2 tog, psso, yfwd, K7.
24th row K.
25th and 26th rows (K1 tbl) 17 times.
These 26 rows form panel patt G.

Back and Front (worked in one piece)
Using set of four 2¾mm needles, cast on 240[264:288] sts. Divide on to three needles, join into a round. Mark first st to denote beg of round.
Work in rounds of K1, P1 rib for 7[8:9]cm.
Next round (Rib 10[11:12], pick up loop between st just worked and next st on LH needle and work into the back of it — called M1 —) 24 times. 264[288:312] sts.
Change to 3¼mm needles and commence patt.
1st round *Marking next st for side seam, (P2, K4, P1, K4, P1) 11[12:13] times*, rep from * to * again.

2nd round *K1, P1, K5, P1, K3, P1, rep from * to end.

3rd round *P2, K6, P1, K2, P1, rep from * to end.

4th round *K1, P1, K7, P1, K1, P1, rep from * to end.

5th round *P2, K9, P1, rep from * to end.

6th round * (K1, P1) twice, K7, P1, rep from * to end.

7th round *P2, K2, P1, K6, P1, rep from * to end.

8th round *K1, P1, K3, P1, K5, P1, rep from * to end.

These 8 rounds form the patt.

Cont in patt until work measures 41[42:43]cm from cast-on edge. Leave first 132[144:156] sts on a spare needle for front, sl rem sts on to a needle and work in rows as foll for back.

****Next row** (WS) *K1 tbl, rep from * to last st, leave rem st on a safety pin for side seam.

Next row K tbl to end, inc[dec:dec] 1 st at each end of row. 133[141:153] sts.

Place panel patts as foll:

Next row (WS) Work 1st row of panels A, D, C, B, E, D, F, B, E, D, C, B and A.

Next row Work 2nd row of panels A, B, C, D, E, B, F, D, E, B, C, D and A.

Cont in this way until 26 rows of panel patts C and F have been completed *at the same time,* marking each end of 15th row to denote sleeves.

Now cont as set, placing panel patt G instead of C and C instead of F. Work 26 rows.

Now cont as set, placing panel patt F instead of G and G instead of C. Work 26 rows.

Next row (WS) K tbl to end.

Rep last row until work measures 18[19:20]cm from sleeve markers, ending with a RS row.

Shape shoulders

Next 2 rows K tbl to last 5[6:6] sts, turn.

Next 2 rows K tbl to last 10[12:12] sts, turn.

Next 2 rows K tbl to last 15[18:18] sts, turn.

Next 2 rows K tbl to last 20[24:24] sts, turn.

Next 2 rows K tbl to last 25[30:30] sts, turn.

Next 2 rows K tbl to last 30[36:36] sts, turn.

Next 2 rows K tbl to last 35[42:42] sts, turn.

Next 2 rows K tbl to last 44[46:50] sts, turn.

Leave these sts on a spare needle. With WS of work facing, rejoin yarn to sts for front.

Cont as given for back from * * until work measures 15[15:16] cm from sleeve markers, ending with a WS row.

Shape neck

Next row Patt 51[52:57], K2 tog and turn, leaving rem sts on a spare needle. Complete left side of neck first.

Dec 1 st at neck edge on *every row* until 44[46:50] sts rem.

Cont without shaping until work matches back to shoulder shaping, ending with a RS row.

Shape shoulder

Next row K tbl to last 5[6:6] sts, turn.

Next and foll alt rows K tbl to end.

Next row K tbl to last 10[12:12] sts, turn.

Next row K tbl to last 15[18:18] sts, turn.

Next row K tbl to last 20[24:24] sts, turn.

Next row K tbl to last 25[30:30] sts, turn.

Next row K tbl to last 30[36:36] sts, turn.

Next row K tbl to last 35[42:42] sts, turn.

Next row K tbl to end.

Leave these sts on a spare needle. With RS of work facing, return to sts for right side of neck, sl centre 27[33:35] sts on to a stitch holder, join in yarn to rem 53[54:59] sts, K2 tog tbl, patt to end.

Complete to match first side of neck, reversing shapings.

Gussets

With RS of work facing, using pair 3¼mm needles, K seam st from safety pin.

New row Inc 1, P1, inc 1.

Next row K3.

Cont in this way, working in st st, inc 1 st at each end of next and every foll alt row until there are 17 sts.

Leave these sts on a safety pin.

Sleeves

Graft shoulder seams.

With RS of work facing, using set of 3¼mm needles, commencing at underarm, K17 sts from gusset, K up 49[54:59] sts from sleeve marker to shoulder, K up 1 st at shoulder seam, K up 49[54:59] sts down to sleeve marker. 116[126:136] sts.

Mark first gusset st as first of round and cont as foll, noting that WS rows of panel patts will now be worked as RS rows, therefore, read K for P and P for K on these rows.

Next round K2 tog, K13, K2 tog tbl, K31[36:41], P1, K1, work 1st row of panel patts D, G and B, K1, P1, K to end.

Next round K46[51:56], P2, work 2nd row of panel patts D, G and B, P2, K to end.

Next round K2 tog, K11, K2 tog tbl, K31[36:41], P1, K1, work 3rd row of panel patt D, G and B, K1, P1, K to end.

Next round K44[49:54], P2, work 4th row of panel patts, D, G and B, P2, K to end.

Cont in this way, keeping panel patts correct, dec 1 st at each side of underarm gusset on next and foll alt row until 100[110:120] sts rem. (1 st rem in gusset.)

Next round P1, patt to end.

Rep the last round 1[5:3] times more.

Next round P1, K2 tog tbl, patt to last 2 sts, K2 tog.

Dec 2 sts in this way on every foll 5th[4th:4th] round until 52[52:58] sts rem.

Cont as set without shaping until sleeve measures 37[39:40]cm.

Change to set of 2¾mm needles and work in rounds of K1, P1 rib for 6[6:7]cm.

Cast off in rib.

Neckband

With RS of work facing, using set of 2¾mm needles, beg at left shoulder, K up 19[20:21] sts down left side of neck, K across 27[33:35] sts at centre front, K up 19[20:21] sts up right side of neck and K across 45[49:53] sts on back neck. 110[122:130] sts.

Mark next st as beg of round.

Work 14 rounds K1, P1 rib.

Cast off in rib.

To make up

Sew underarm gussets neatly in place with a flat seam.

Special technique — grafting garter stitch

1 The shoulders of the sweater are grafted rather than seamed together. Place the back and front sections with the loops facing each other as shown. Thread a needle with matching yarn or use a long end from one of the sections. Bring the needle through from back to front of first loop on lower edge, then from back to front of first loop on upper edge.

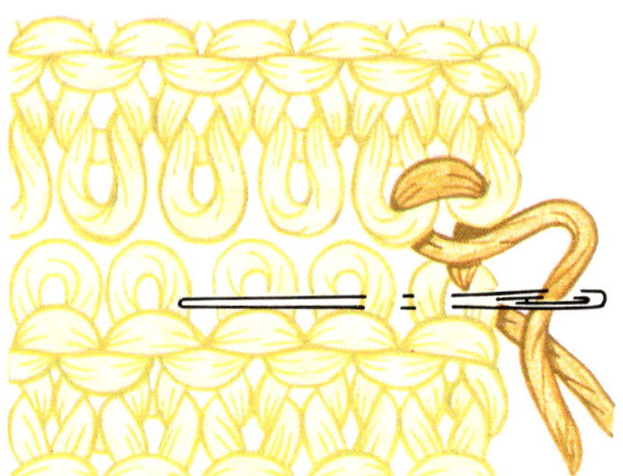

2 Pull the yarn through. Now take the needle from front to back of the second loop on the upper section. Pull the yarn through. Take the needle from front to back of the first loop on the lower section and bring it out from back to front of the next stitch along on the lower section.

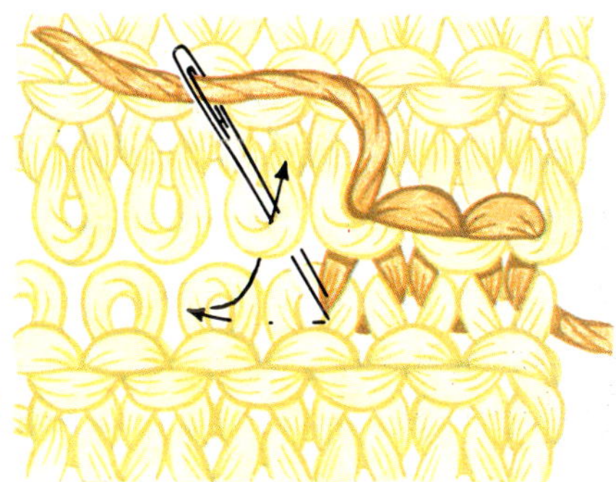

3 Pull the yarn through. Continue in this way until all the stitches are grafted together. This produces a much neater join than a seam and is especially suitable for joining across the shoulders.

Peruvian-patterned Garments

Look elegantly ethnic in this key-patterned alpaca
waistcoat or knit an Inca bird into a sweater for a child. The
poncho on page 163 is decorated with another version
of the key pattern.

Sizes
Waistcoat
To fit 81 [87:91:97]cm bust
Length 53 [53:56:56]cm
Sweater
To fit 64 [71:79]cm chest
Length 46 [51:56]cm
Sleeve seam 33 [36:38]cm

Note Instructions for larger sizes are in square brackets []; where there is only one set of figures it applies to all sizes.

Tension
Waistcoat
30 sts and 32 rows to 10cm over patt on 3¼mm needles

Sweater
25 sts and 26 rows to 10cm over patt on 3¾mm needles

Materials
Waistcoat
175g four-ply yarn in main colour (A)
100g in each of 2 contrast colours (B) and (C)
1 pair each 2mm, 3mm and 3¼mm knitting needles
6 buttons
Sweater
125 [150:150] g double knitting yarn in main colour (A)
100g in each of 2 contrast colours (B) and (C)
1 pair each 3mm and 3¾mm knitting needles
Set of four 3mm needles pointed at both ends.

Waistcoat
Back
Using 2mm needles and A, cast on 90 [98:106:114] sts.
Work in K1, P1 rib for 6cm, ending with a RS row.
Next row Rib 13 [1:4:8]; *pick up loop between last st worked and next st and work into back of it — called M1 —, rib 2 [3:3:3], rep from * to last 13 [1:6:10] sts, rib to end. 122 [130:138:146] sts.
Change to 3¼mm needles and commence patt from chart on page 160, reading K rows from right to left and P rows from left to right.
1st row K1, *K 1st row from chart, rep from * to last st, K1.
2nd row K1, * P 2nd row from chart,

rep from * to last st, K1.
Cont in this way, keeping patt from chart correct until 80 [80:90:90] rows have been worked from chart.
Shape armholes
Keeping patt correct, cast off 8 sts at beg of next 2 rows.
Next row K1, sl 1, K1, psso, patt to last 3 sts, K2 tog, K1.
Next row K1, patt to last st, K1.
Rep the last 2 rows 7 times more. 90 [98:106:114] sts.
Cont in patt until 70 rows have been worked from the beg of armhole shaping, ending with a 30th [30th: 10th:10th] patt row.
Change to 3mm needles, B and cont in st st.
Work 2 rows.
Shape shoulders
Cast off 7 [8:8:9] sts at beg of next 4 rows, 7 [8:9:9] sts at beg of foll 2 rows and 7 [7:9:10] sts at beg of next 2 rows. Cast off rem 34 [36:38:40] sts.
Pocket linings (make 2)
Using 3mm needles and B, cast on 40 sts. Work 40 rows in st st. Leave these sts on a spare needle.

Left front
**Using 2mm needles and A, cast on 50 [50:58:58] sts.
Work in K1, P1 rib for 6cm, ending with a RS row.
Next row Rib 1 [1:4:4], *M1, rib 3, rep from * to last 1 [1:6:6] sts, rib to end. 66 [66:74:74] sts.
Change to 3¼mm needles and work in patt as given for back until 40 rows have been worked from chart.
Place pocket
Next row (RS) Patt 13 [13:17:17] sts, sl next 40 sts on to a st holder, patt 13 [13:17:17].
Next row Patt 13 [13:17:17] sts, patt across 40 sts of pocket lining, patt 13 [13:17:17] sts.
Cont in patt until 80 [80:90:90] rows have been worked from chart.**
Shape armhole and neck
Next row Cast off 8 sts, patt to end.
Next row Patt to end.
Next row K1, sl 1, K1, psso, patt to last 3 sts, K2 tog, K1.
Next row Patt to end.
Next row K1, sl 1, K1, psso, patt to end.
Next row K1, P2 tog, patt to end.

Next row K1, sl 1, K1, psso, patt to end.
Next row Patt to end.
Rep the last 6 rows again, then the first 4 of them again. 44 [44:52:52] sts.
Keeping armhole edge straight, cont to dec at neck edge as before on every foll 3rd [3rd:2nd:3rd] row until 28 [31:34:37] sts rem.
Cont without shaping until 70 rows have been worked from beg of armhole shaping, ending with a 30th [30th:10th:10th] patt row.
Change to 3mm needles, B and cont in st st.

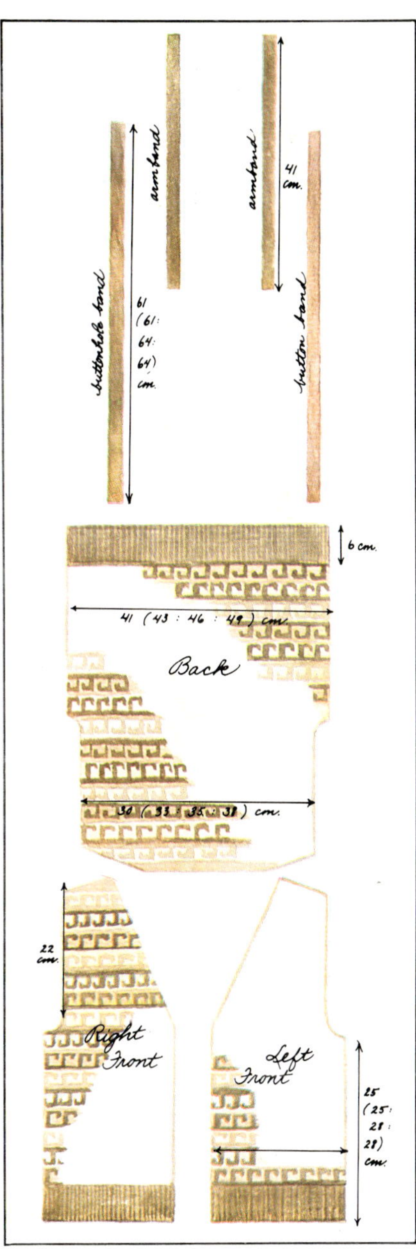

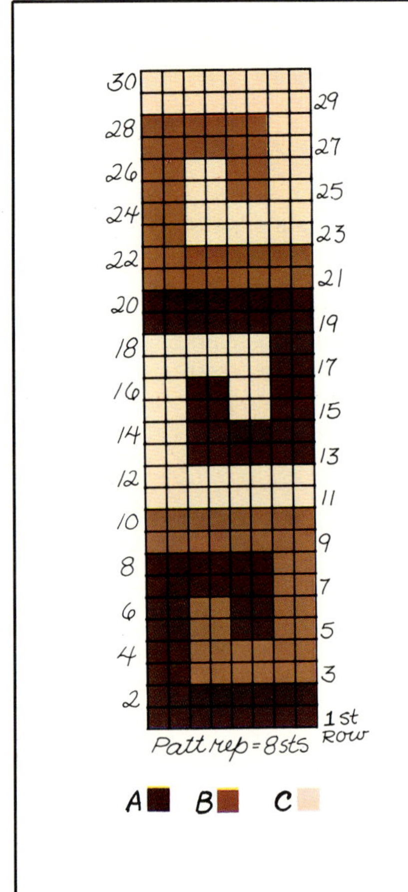

Work 2 rows.

Shape shoulder
Cast off 7 [8:8:9] sts at beg of next and foll alt row. Work 1 row. Cast off 7 [8:9:9] sts at beg of next row. Work 1 row. Cast off rem 7 [7:9:10] sts.

Right front
Work as given for left front from ** to **.
Patt 1 row.
Shape neck and armhole
Next row Cast off 8 sts, patt to end.
Next row K1, sl 1, K1, psso, patt to last 3 sts, K2 tog, K1.
Next row Patt to end.
Next row Patt to last 3 sts, K2 tog, K1.
Next row Patt to last 3 sts, P2 tog, K1.
Next row Patt to last 3 sts, K2 tog, K1.
Next row Patt to end.
Rep the last 6 rows again, then the first 4 of them again. 44 [44:52:52] sts.
Complete to match left front, working 1 extra row before shaping shoulder.

160

Pocket edgings
With RS of work facing, using 2mm needles and A, K across 40 sts on st holder. Work in K1, P1 rib for 3cm, ending with a WS row. Cast off in rib.

Armbands (make 2)
Using 2mm needles and A, cast on 11 sts.
1st row K1, *P1, K1, rep from * to end.
2nd row K1, *K1, P1, rep from * tc last 2 sts, K2.
Rep the last 2 rows until work measures 41cm from cast-on edge, ending with a 2nd row. Cast off in rib.

Button band
Work as given for armbands until band measures 61 [61:64:64]cm, ending with a 2nd row. Cast off in rib.

To make up
Press as instructed on ball band. Join shoulder seams.
Sew button band to left front edge, ending at centre back neck.
Mark the position of 6 buttonholes as folls, one at 2cm from lower edge, one at 7cm from lower edge, one slightly below beg of neck shaping and 3 more evenly spaced between.
Buttonhole band
Work buttonhole band as given for button band, making buttonholes opposite markers as folls,
1st buttonhole row (RS) K1, (P1, K1) twice, K2 tog, yfwd, (P1, K1) twice.
2nd buttonhole row K1, *K1, P1, rep from * to last 2 sts, K2.
Cont in rib until band measures 61 [61:64:64]cm, ending with a 2nd row. Cast off in rib.
Join side seams. Sew armbands to armhole edge. Sew buttonhole band to right front, ending at centre back neck, join to button band. Sew pocket linings to WS and pocket edgings to RS. Sew on buttons.

Sweater
Back
**Using 3mm needles and A, cast on 82 [90:102] sts.
1st row *K2, P2, rep from * to last 2 sts, K2.
2nd row K1, P1, *K2, P2, rep from *

to last 4 sts, K2, P1, K1.
Rep the last 2 rows for 6cm, ending with a 2nd row.
Change to 3¾mm needles and B.
Next row K, inc 1 st at each end on 2nd size only. 82 [92:102] sts.
Next row P.
Cont in st st, working from chart on page 162 until 58 [66:74] rows have been worked from chart.
Shape armholes
Keeping chart correct, cast off 6 sts at beg of next 2 rows.
Next row K1, sl 1, K1, psso, work to last 3 sts, K2 tog, K1.
Next row Work to end.
Rep the last 2 rows 3 times more. 62 [72:82] sts.
Cont to work from chart until 76 [88:100] rows have been worked. Change to B. **
Work 30 rows st st, ending with a P row.
Shape shoulders
Cast off 5 [7:8] sts at beg of next 4 rows and 6 [6:8] sts at beg of foll 2 rows. Leave rem 30 [32:34] sts on a spare needle.

Front
Work as given for back from ** to **. Work 14 [12:10] rows st st, ending with a P row.
Shape neck
Next row Work 22 [26:30] sts and turn, leaving rem sts on a spare needle.
Work left side of neck first.
Next row P1, P2 tog, work to end.
Next row Work to last 3 sts, K2 tog, K1.
Rep the last 2 rows twice more. 16 [20:24] sts.
Cont without shaping. Work 9 [11:13] rows, ending with a P row.
Shape shoulder
Cast off 5 [7:8] sts at beg of next and foll alt row. Work 1 row. Cast off rem 6 [6:8] sts.
With RS of work facing, return to sts on spare needle, sl centre 18 [20:22] sts on to a st holder, join in B and work to end.
Next row Work to last 3 sts, P2 tog tbl, P1.
Next row K1, sl 1, K1, psso, work to end.
Rep the last 2 rows twice more. 16 [20:24] sts.
Complete to match left side of neck.

Sleeves

Using 3mm needles and A, cast on
42 [42:46] sts.
Work in rib as given for back for 6cm,
ending with a 2nd row.
Change to 3¾mm needles and B.
Next row * K twice into every st, rep
from * to last 2 [2:0] sts, K2 [2:0].
82 [82:92] sts.
Commence patt.
1st row K1B, *4B, 2C, 4B, rep from
* to last st, K1B.
2nd row P1B, *3B, 4C, 3B, rep from
* to last st, P1B.
3rd row K1B, *2B, 6C, 2B, rep from
* to last st, K1B.
4th row P1B, *1B, 8C, 1B, rep from
* to last st, P1B.
5th-8th rows Work 4 rows st st in C.
9th-12th rows Work 4 rows st st in
A.
13th row K1B, *1B, 8A, 1B, rep
from * to last st, K1B.
14th row P1B, *2B, 6A, 2B, rep
from * to last st, P1B.
15th row K1B, *3B, 4A, 3B, rep
from * to last st, K1B.
16th row P1B, *4B, 2A, 4B, rep
from * to last st, P1B.
17th-20th rows Work 4 rows st st in
B.
21st-24th rows Work 4 rows st st in
C.
25th row K1C, *4C, 2A, 4C, rep

Special technique — holding yarn in left hand

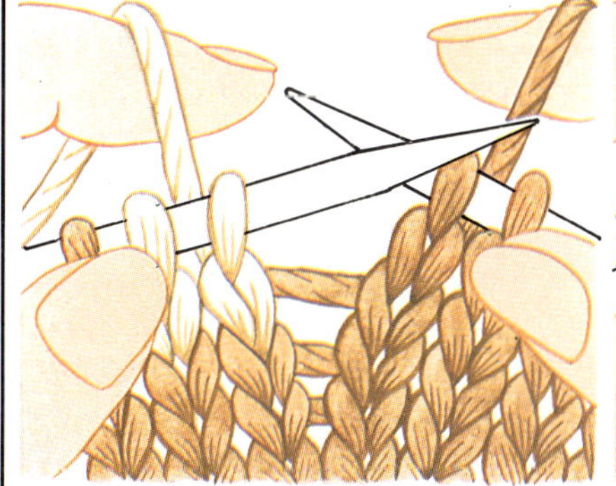

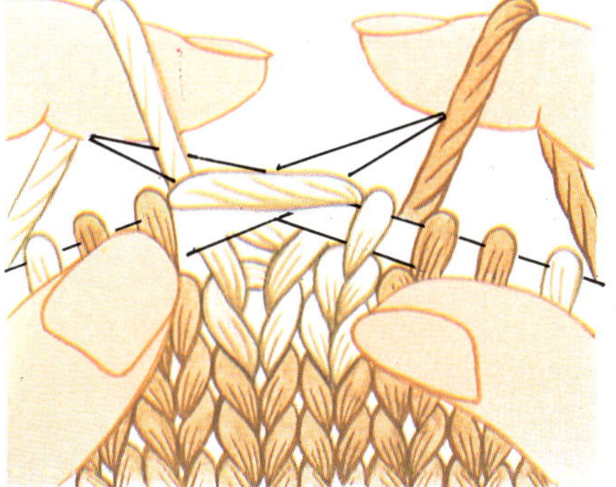

1 When working with two different
colours in a row, it is often easier to
hold one colour in the right hand and knit
it as usual, and the second colour in the
left hand and use it to knit as follows.

2 To work knit stitches, use the
forefinger of the left hand to hold the
yarn in position. Insert the right-hand
needle knitwise into the first stitch on the
left-hand needle. Take the needle behind
the yarn and pull a loop through the stitch
as usual.

3 To work purl stitches, hold the yarn in
position with the left forefinger. Insert
the right-hand needle purlwise into the
first stitch on the left-hand needle. Move
the needle round the yarn making a loop.
Take the loop through the stitch as usual.

from * to last st, K1C.
26th row P1C, *3C, 4A, 3C, rep from * to last st, P1C.
27th row K1C, *2C, 6A, 2C, rep from * to last st, K1C.
28th row P1C, *1C, 8A, 1C, rep from * to last st, P1C.
29th-32nd rows Work 4 rows st st in A.
33rd-36th rows Work 4 rows st st in B.
These 36 rows form the patt. Cont in patt until work measures 33 [36:38]cm from cast-on edge, ending with a P row.

162

Shape sleeve top
Keeping patt correct, cast off 6 sts at beg of next 2 rows.
Next row K1, sl 1, K1, psso, work to last 3 sts, K2 tog, K1.
Next row Work to end.
Rep the last 2 rows until 58 [48:62] sts rem, ending with a WS row.
Next row K1, sl 1, K1, psso, work to last 3 sts, K2 tog, K1.
Next row P1, P2 tog, work to last 3 sts, P2 tog tbl, P1.
Rep the last 2 rows until 30 [32:34] sts rem, ending with a WS row.
Cast off.

To make up
Do not press. Join shoulder seams.
Neckband
With RS of work facing, using set of four 3mm needles and A, K up 30 [32:34] sts from back neck, K up 16 [18:20] sts down left side of neck, K across 18 [20:22] sts at centre front, K up 16 [18:20] sts up right side of neck. 80 [88:96] sts.
Work in rounds of K2, P2 rib for 5cm. Cast off very loosely.
Join side and sleeve seams. Set in sleeves. Fold neckband in half on to WS and catch down.

Poncho

Size
To fit 7-8 years
Length 63cm
Width 96cm at widest point

Tension

15 sts and 20 rows to 10cm over st st
on 5½mm needles

Materials

750g chunky yarn in main colour (A)
200g in contrast colour (B)
1 pair each 4½mm and 5½mm needles,
1.25 mm crochet hook

Back and front (alike)

Using 5½mm needles and A, cast on
2 sts.
Beg with a K row, work 2 rows in st
st. Cont in st st inc 1 st at each end of
every row until there are 86 sts.
Now inc 1 st at each end of next and
every foll alt row until there are 144
sts, ending with a P row.
Join in B and work 1st-20th rows in key
patt from chart.
Cont in A. Beg with a K row, cont in
st st until work measures 62cm,
ending with a P row.
Shape shoulders Cast off 51 sts at
beg of next 2 rows. 22 sts.
Neck Change to 4½mm needles and
work in K1, P1 rib for 3cm, ending
with a WS row. Join in A and K to
end. Cast off loosely in rib.

To make up

Join shoulder and neckband seams.
Using 1.25mm crochet hook and A,
work 1 row dc all round edge of
poncho. Mark down 15cm from
shoulder and catch together
at armholes. Fringe edges.

Tyrolean Cardigan

A profusion of flowers blooms on the brilliantly patterned
cardigan. It has a traditional peplum, pompon ties and
detachable collar, and there is also a matching hat and mittens.

Sizes
To fit 81[86:91:96]cm bust
Length 55[56:57:57]cm
Sleeve seam 43[46:46:47]cm

Note Instructions for larger sizes are in
square brackets []; where there is only
one set of figures it applies to all
four sizes.

Tension
29 sts and 31 rows to 10cm over patt
on 4mm needles

22 sts and 31 rows to 10cm over st st
on 4mm needles

Materials
Cardigan
850 [900:950:1000] g double knitting
yarn
Collar
100g double knitting yarn
Beanie
100g double knitting yarn
Mittens
100g double knitting yarn
4 skeins tapestry wool in red
3 skeins in blue
2 skeins each in yellow and green
1 pair each 3¼mm and 4mm knitting
needles
9 buttons
Shoulder pads (optional)

Back
Using 4mm needles, cast on
152 [156:160:164] sts.
K 4 rows.
Work peplum
Commence patt.
1st row (RS) P1[3:5:7], *K the 3rd st
on LH needle, then K the 1st and
2nd st — called TW3 —, K1, P2, sl
next 3 sts on to cable needle and hold
at back of work, K3, then K3 from
cable needle — called C6B, K3, sl
next 3 sts on to cable needle and hold
at front of work, K3, then K3 from
cable needle — called C6F, P2, K1,
TW3 ***, K1, P5, K tbl 2nd st on LH
needle then K 1st st — called TW2B
—, K1, (K1, P1, K1, P1, K1) all into
next st, turn, P5, turn, K5, sl 4th, 3rd,
2nd and 1st st over 5th — called MB
—, K1, K 2nd st on LH needle, then
K 1st st — called TW2F —, P5, K1
, rep from * to * once, P4, rep

from * to ** once, rep from * to ***
again, P1[3:5:7].
2nd row K1[3:5:7], *P3, K3, P6 tbl,
P3, P6 tbl, K3, P3 ***, K6, P7, K6
, rep from * to * once, K4, rep
from * to ** once, rep from * to ***
again, K1[3:5:7].
3rd row P1[3:5:7], *K4, P2, K6 tbl,
K3, K6 tbl, P2, K4 ***, K1, P4,
TW2B, K5, TW2F, P4, K1 **, rep
from * to *** once, P4, rep from *
to ** once, rep from * to *** again,
P1[3:5:7].
4th row K1[3:5:7], *P3, K3, P6 tbl,
P3, P6 tbl, K3, P3 ***, K5, P9, K5
, rep from * to * once, K4, rep
from * to ** once, rep from * to ***
again, K1[3:5:7].
5th row P1[3:5:7], *TW3, K1, P2,
K6 tbl, K1, MB, K1, K6 tbl, P2, K1,
TW3 ***, K1, P3, TW2B, K1, MB,
K3, MB, K1, TW2F, P3, K1 **, rep
from * to *** once, P4, rep from *
to ** once, rep from * to *** again,
P1[3:5:7].
6th row K1[3:5:7], *P3, K3, P6 tbl,
P3, P6 tbl, K3, P3 ***, K4, P11, K4,
, rep from * to * once, K4, rep
from * to *** once, rep from * to
*** again, K1[3:5:7].
7th row P1[3:5:7], *K4, P2, K6 tbl,
K3, K6 tbl, P2, K4 ***, K1, P2,
TW2B, K9, TW2F, P2, K1 **, rep
from * to *** once, P4, rep from * to
** once, rep from * to *** again,
P1[3:5:7].
8th row K1[3:5:7], *P3, K3, P6 tbl,
P3, P6 tbl, K3, P3 ***, K3, P13, K3
, rep from * to * once, K4, rep
from * to ** once, rep from * to ***
again, K1[3:5:7].
9th row P1[3:5:7], *TW3, K1, P2,
K6 tbl, K1, MB, K1, K6 tbl, P2, K1,
TW3 ***, K1, P1, TW2B, K1, MB,
K7, MB, K1, TW2F, P1, K1 **, rep
from * to *** once, P4, rep from *
to ** once, rep from * to *** again,
P1[3:5:7].
10th row K1[3:5:7], *P3, K3, P6 tbl,
P3, P6 tbl, K3, P3 ***, K2, P15, K2
, rep from * to * once, K4, rep
from * to ** once, rep from * to ***
again, K1[3:5:7].
11th row P1[3:5:7], *K4, P2, K6 tbl,
K3, K6 tbl, P2, K4 ***, K1, TW2B,
K13, TW2F, K1 **, rep from * to
*** once, P4, rep from * to ** once,
rep from * to *** again, P1[3:5:7].
12th row K1[3:5:7], *P3, K3, P6 tbl,

P3, P6 tbl, K3, P3 ***, K1, P17, K1
, rep from * to * once, K4, rep
from * to ** once, rep from * to ***
again, K1[3:5:7].
13th row P1[3:5:7], *TW3, K1, P2,
K6 tbl, K1, MB, K1, K6 tbl, P2, K1,
TW3***, TW2B, K1, MB, K11, MB,
K1, TW2F **, rep from * to ***
once, P4, rep from * to ** once, rep
from * to *** again, P1[3:5:7].
14th row As 12th row.
15th row P1[3:5:7], *K4, P2, K6 tbl,
K3, K6 tbl, P2, K4 ***, TW2F, K15,
TW2B **, rep from * to *** once,
P4, rep from * to ** once, rep from
* to *** again, P1[3:5:7].
16th row As 12th row.
17th row P1[3:5:7], *TW3, K1, P2,
K6 tbl, K1, MB, K1, K6 tbl, P2, K1,
TW3 ***, K1, P5, TW2B, K1, MB,
K1, TW2F, P5, K1 **, rep from * to
*** once, P4, rep from * to ** once,
rep from * to *** again, P1[3:5:7].
18th row As 2nd row.
19th row P1[3:5:7], *K4, P2, K6 tbl,
K3, K6 tbl, P2, K4 ***, K1, P4,
TW2B, K5, TW2F, P4, K1 **, rep
from * to *** once, P4, rep from *
to ** once, rep from * to *** again,
P1[3:5:7].
20th row As 4th row.
21st row P1[3:5:7], *TW3, K1, P2,
C6F, K3, C6B, P2, K1, TW3 ***,
K1, P3, TW2B, K1, MB, K3, MB,
K1, TW2F, P3, K1 **, rep from * to
*** once, P4, rep from * to ** once,
rep from * to *** again, P1[3:5:7].
22nd row As 6th row.
23rd row P1[3:5:7], *K4, P2, K6 tbl,
K3, K6 tbl, P2, K4 ***, K1, P2,
TW2B, K9, TW2F, P2, K1 **, rep
from * to *** once, P4, rep from *
to ** once, rep from * to *** again,
P1[3:5:7].
24th row As 8th row.
25th row P1[3:5:7], *K4, P2, K6 tbl,
K3, K6 tbl, P2, K4 ***, K1, P1,
TW2B, K1, MB, K7, MB, K1, TW2F,
P1, K1 **, rep from * to *** once,
P4, rep from * to ** once, rep from
* to *** again, P1[3:5:7].
26th row As 10th row.
27th row P1[3:5:7], *K4, P2, K6 tbl,
K3, K6 tbl, P2, K4 ***, K1, TW2B,
K13, TW2F, K1 **, rep from * to
*** once, P4, rep from * to ** once,
rep from * to *** again, P1[3:5:7].
28th row As 12th row.
29th row P1[3:5:7], *K4, P2, K6 tbl,

K3, K6 tbl, P2, K4 ***, TW2B, K1, MB, K1, MB, K1, TW2F **, rep from * to *** once, P4, rep from * to ** once, rep from * to *** once, P1[3:5:7].
30th row As 12th row.
31st row P1[3:5:7], *K4, P2, K6 tbl, K3, K6 tbl, P2, K4 ***, TW2F, K15, TW2B **, rep from * to *** once, P4, rep from * to ** once, rep from * to *** again, P1[3:5:7].
32nd row As 12th row.
These 32 rows form the patt.
Next row K1[3:5:7], *K2 tog, K1, rep from * to last 1[3:5:7] sts, K to end. 102[106:110:114] sts.
Change to 3¼mm needles and work 3 rows K1, P1 rib.
Next row (make eyelets) Rib 4[2:4:2], *yrn, rib 2 tog, rib 2, rep from * to last 2[0:2:0] sts, rib to end. Work 2 rows in rib.
Next row Rib 38[27:16:5], *work twice into next st, — called inc 1, — rib 12, rep from * 1[3:5:7] times more, rib to end. 104[110:116:122] sts.

Change to 4mm needles, and recommence patt as foll, working from corresponding rows of peplum.
1st row P1[4:7:10], TW3, work from *** to ** of peplum, then work from * to ***, P4, rep from * to ***, then from *** to ** again, TW3, P1[4:7:10].
2nd row K1[4:7:10], P3, work from *** to ** of peplum, then from * to ***, K4, rep from * to ***, then *** to ** again, P3, K1[4:7:10].
3rd row P1[4:7:10], *K3, work from *** to ** of peplum, then from * to **, P4, rep from * to ***, then from *** to ** again, K3, P1[4:7:10].
4th row As 2nd row.
5th row P1[4:7:10], TW3, work from *** to ** of peplum, then from * to ***, P4, rep from * to ***, then *** to ** again, TW3, P1[4:7:10].
Cont working patt sections in this order, *at the same time,* inc and work in to reverse st st 1 st at each end of the next and every foll 6th row until there are 124[130:136:142] sts.
Cont without shaping.

Work 10 rows.
Shape armholes
Keeping patt correct, cast off 4 sts at beg of next 2 rows and 3 sts at beg of for 2 rows.
Dec 1 st at each end of next 3[5:6:8] rows.
104[106:110:112] sts.
Cont without shaping until work measures 20[21:22:22]cm from beg of armholes, ending with a WS row.
Shape shoulders
Cast off 30[30:32:32] sts at beg of next 2 rows.
Leave rem 44 [46:46:48] sts on a spare needle.

Left front
Using 4mm needles, cast on 76[78:80:82] sts.
K 4 rows.
Commence patt as foll, working from corresponding rows of back peplum.
1st row P1[3:5:7], work as for back from * to ** once, then from * to *** once, P1, K1.
2nd row K2, work as for back from *

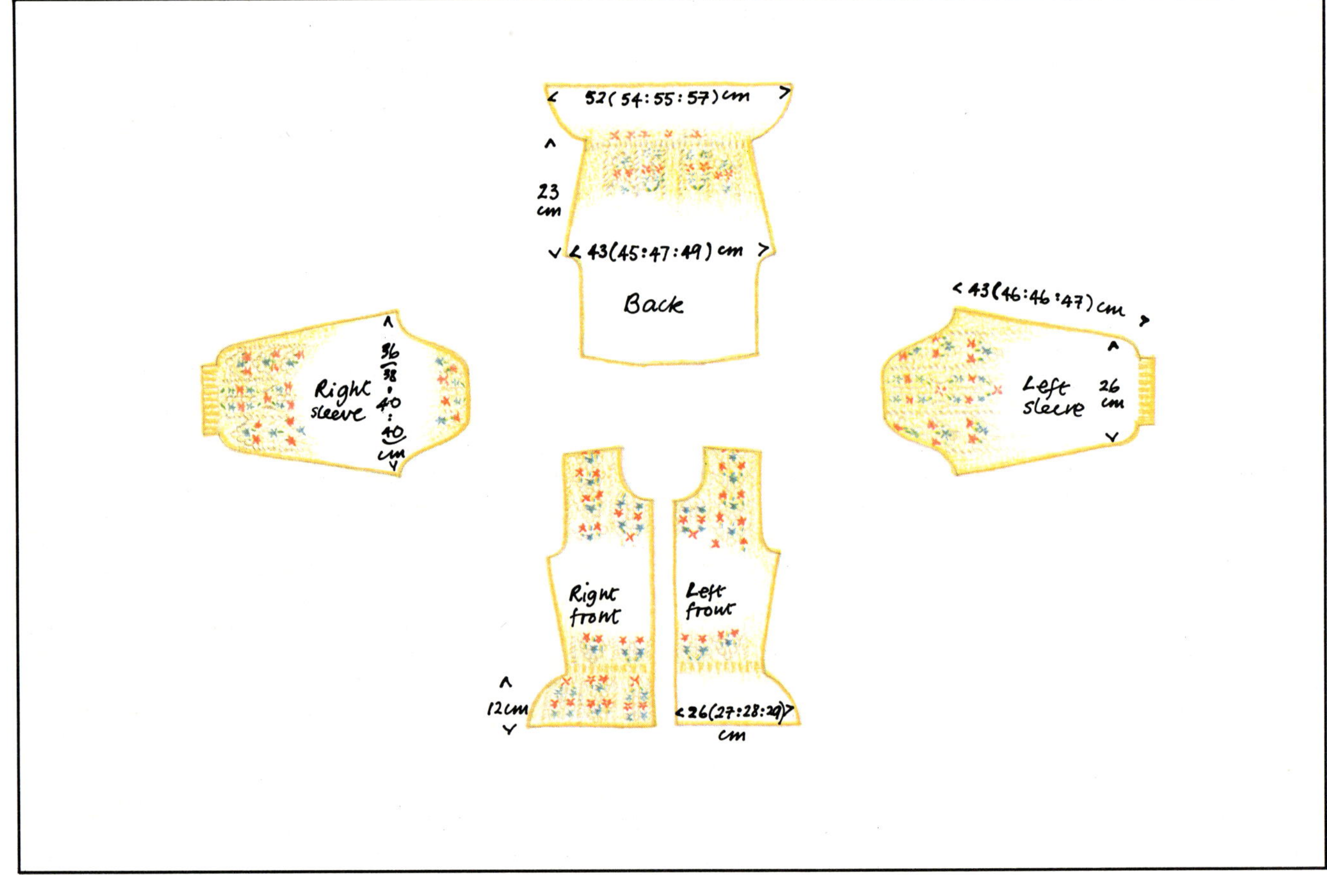

to **, then from * to *** once,
K1[3:5:7].
3rd row P1[3:5:7], work as for back
from * to ** once, then from * to
*** once, P1, K1.
4th row K2, work as for back from *
to ** once, then from * to *** once,
K1[3:5:7].
Cont working in this way, work a
further 28 rows.
Next row K1[3:5:7], *K2 tog, K1,
rep from * to end. 51[53:55:57] sts.
Change to 3¼mm needles.
Work in K1, P1 rib as foll:
Next row K1, *P1, K1, rep from * to
end.
Next row P1, *K1, P1, rep from * to
end.
Cont in rib as set. Work 1 more row.

Next row (make eyelets) Rib
4[2:4:2], *yrn, work 2 tog, rib 2, rep
from * ending last rep rib 1.
Work 3[2:2:2] rows in rib.
2nd, 3rd and 4th sizes only
Next row Rib [26:21:15], *inc 1, rib
12, rep from * [0:1:2] times more, rib
to end. [54:57:60] sts.
All sizes
Change to 4mm needles and
recommence patt as foll working from
corresponding rows of back peplum:
1st row P1[4:7:10], TW3, work as
for back from *** to ** once, then
from * to *** once, K1.
2nd row K1, work as for back from *
to **, P3, K1[4:7:10].
3rd row P1[4:7:10], K3, work as for

back from *** to **, then from * to
***, K1.
4th row K1, work as for back from *
to **, P3, K1[4:7:10].
5th row P1[4:7:10], TW3, work as
for back from *** to **, then from *
to ***, K1.
Cont working in this way, *at the same
time*, inc and work into reverse st st 1
st at side edge on the next and every
foll 6th row until there are
61[64:67:70] sts.
Cont without shaping.
Work 10 rows.
Shape armholes
Keeping patt correct, cast off 4 sts at
beg of next row and 3 sts at beg of foll
alt row.
Dec 1 st at armhole edge on
foll 3[5:6:8] rows. 51[52:54:55] sts.
Cont without shaping until work
measures 12[13:13:13]cm from beg
of armhole, ending at front edge.
Shape neck
Cast off 8 sts at beg of next row and 4
sts at beg of foll alt row. Dec 1 st at
neck edge on every row until
30[30:32:32] sts rem.
Cont without shaping until work
matches back to shoulder shaping,
ending at armhole edge.
Shape shoulder
Cast off rem sts.

Right front
Using 4mm needles, cast on
76[78:80:82] sts. K 4 rows.
Commence patt as foll working from
corresponding rows of back peplum.
1st row K1, P1, work as for back
from * to ** once, then from * to
*** once, P1[3:5:7].
2nd row K1[3:5:7], work as for back
from * to ** once, then from * to
*** once, K2.
3rd row K1, P1, work as for back
from * to ** once, then from * to
*** once, P1[3:5:7].
4th row K1[3:5:7], work as for back
from * to ** once, then from * to
*** once, K2.
Cont in this way, work a further 28
rows.
Next row *K1, K2 tog, rep from * to
last 1[3:5:7] sts, K to end.
51[53:55:57] sts.
Change to 3¼mm needles. Work 3
rows K1, P1 rib as given for left front.
Next row (make eyelets) Rib 1, work

2 tog, yrn, *rib 2, work 2 tog, yrn,
rep from * to last 4[2:4:2] sts, rib to
end.
Work 3[2:2:2] rows in rib.
2nd, 3rd and 4th sizes only
Next row Rib [26:21:15], * inc 1, rib
12, rep from * [0:1:2] times more, rib
to end. [54:57:60] sts.
All sizes
Change to 4mm needles and
recommence patt as foll:
1st row K1, work as for back from *
to ** once, TW3, P1[3:5:7].
2nd row K1[3:5:7], P3, work as for
back from *** to ** once, then from * to
***, K1.

Complete to match left front,
reversing all shaping.

Sleeves
Using 3¼mm needles, cast on
52[54:56:58] sts.
Work in K1, P1 rib for 3[4:4:5]cm.
Next row Rib 5[8:11:14], * inc 1, rib
1, rep from * to last 5[8:11:14] sts,
rib to end. 73 sts.
Change to 4mm needles. Commence
patt, working corresponding rows
from back peplum as foll:
1st row K1, TW3, work as for back
from *** to ** once, then from * to
**, TW3, K1.
2nd row P4, work as for back from
*** to ** once, then from * to **,
P4.
3rd row K4, work as for back from
*** to ** once, then from * to **,
K4.

4th row P4, work as for back from *** to ** once, then from * to **, P4.

5th row K1, TW3, work as for back from *** to ** once, then from * to **, TW3, K1.

Cont working in this way, *at the same time,* inc and work into reverse st st 1 st at each end of the next and every foll 6th row until there are 103[109:113:113] sts.

Work 34[22:10:10] rows.

Shape top

Cast off 4 sts at beg of next 2 rows and 3 sts at beg of foll 2 rows. Dec 1 st at each end of next and every foll alt row until 45 sts rem. Cast off.

Button band

Using 3¼mm needles, cast on 6 sts. Work in K1, P1 rib until band, when slightly stretched, fits from beg of rib to neck edge of left front, ending at inner edge. Leave sts on a safety pin. Sew band in place. Mark 8 button positions on band, the first 3cm from neck edge, the last 1cm from cast-on edge with the others evenly spaced between.

Buttonhole band

Using 3¼mm needles, cast on 6 sts. Work in K1, P1 rib for 1cm.

1st buttonhole row Rib 3, cast off 1, rib to end.

2nd buttonhole row Rib 2, cast on 1, rib to end.

Cont in rib making buttonholes opposite markers, until band fits up right front edge, ending at outer edge. Do not break yarn. Sew band in place.

To make up

Join shoulder seams.

Neckband

Using 3¼mm needles, rib across sts of buttonhole band, K up 34[36:38:38] sts up right side of neck, K21[22:22:23], K2 tog, K21[22:22:23] across sts on back neck, K up 34[36:38:38] sts down left side of neck, rib across buttonband. 123[129:133:135] sts.

Beg with a 2nd row work 3 rows K1, P1 rib as given for left front.

Work the 2 buttonhole rows again. Rib 2 more rows. Cast off in rib.

Work embroidery using 2 strands of

168

yarn. (See Special Technique.) Join side and sleeve seams. Set in sleeves easing fullness at top. Sew on buttons and shoulder pads. Make a twisted cord and thread through waist eyelets. Make two small pompons and sew to ends of cord.

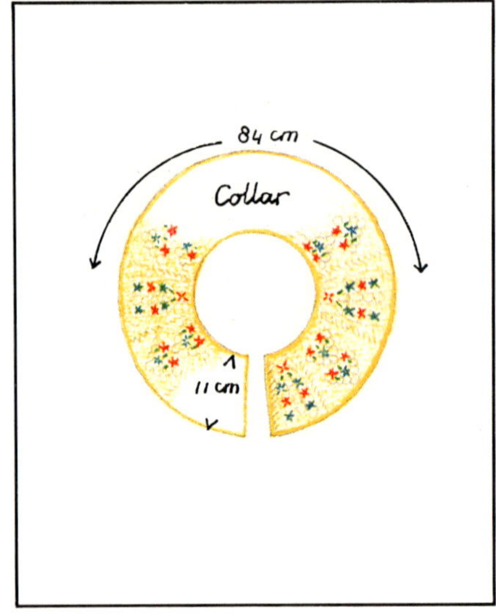

Detachable collar

Using 4mm needles, cast on 244 sts. K 4 rows.

Commence patt, working from corresponding rows of back peplum.

1st row K1, work as for back from * to ** twice, then from * to *** once, P4, rep from * to ** twice, then from * to *** again, K1.

2nd row K1, work as for back from * to ** twice, then from * to *** once, K4, rep from * to ** twice, then from * to *** again, K1.

Cont in this way. Work a further 30 rows.

Next row (K2 tog) to end.

Next row (K2 tog) to end. 61 sts.

Make edging

1st row K.

2nd row K1, *yfwd, K2 tog, rep from * to end.

3rd row *K1, (K1, P1) all into yfwd of previous row, rep from * to last st, K1.

4th row Cast off 1, *insert LH needle into st below yfwd of 2nd row, draw through a loop and sl previous st over, cast off 3, rep from * to end.

Make a twisted cord and thread through at neck edge.

Beanie

Using 4mm needles, cast on 131 sts. Beg with a K row cont in st st for 6cm, ending with a P row.

Commence patt.

1st row K.

2nd and every foll alt row P.

3rd row * K12, MB, rep from * to last st, K1.

4th row P.

Rep these 4 rows 4 times more.

Commence shaping.

1st row *K2 tog, K11, rep from * to last st, K1.

2nd and every foll alt row P.

3rd row *K2 tog, K9, MB, rep from * to last st, K1.

Keeping patt correct, cont to dec in this way on every alt row until 11 sts rem.

Next row K2 tog, K to last st, K1. Break off yarn, thread through rem sts, draw up and fasten off securely.

To make up

Embroider flowers in 'wedges' between rows of bobbles.

Join seam. Roll brim on to RS and catch in place. Make a twisted cord, tie in a neat bow, sew to crown. Make two small pompons and sew to each end of cord.

Right mitten

**Using 3¼mm needles, cast on 40 sts.

Work 9 rows K1, P1 rib.

Next row Rib 3, * work twice into next st — called inc 1 —, rib 6, rep from * to last 2 sts, rib 2. 45 sts.**

Commence patt and thumb gusset.

1st row *K1, P2, TW3, P2, sl next 2 sts on to cable needle and hold at back of work, then K2 from cable needle — called C4B, sl next 2 sts on to cable needle and hold at front of work, K2, then K2 from cable needle — called C4F —, P2, TW3, P2, K1, P1, * K2, P1, K17.

2nd and every foll alt row K1, P to last 24 sts, P1, K2, P3, K2, P8, K2, P3, K3.

3rd row *K1, P2, K3, P2, K8, P2, K3, P2, K1, P1, * work into front, back and front of next st, K1, P1, K17.

5th row K1, P2, TW3, P2, K8, P2, TW3, P2, K1, P1, K4, P1, K17.

7th row K1, P2, K3, P2, C4F, C4B,

P2, K3, P2, K1, P1, (inc 1, K1) twice, P1, K17.
8th row As 2nd row.
These 8 rows establish the cable patt.
Next row As 1st row from * to *, K6, P1, K to end.
Next and every foll alt row As 2nd row.
Next row As 3rd row from * to *, inc 1, K3, inc 1, K1, P1, K to end.
Cont in this way inc 1 st at each side of gusset on every foll 4th row until there are 55 sts.
Work 5 rows without shaping.
Divide for thumb
Next row Patt 37, turn leaving palm sts on spare needle.
Next row K1, P11, cast on 4 sts, turn.
Next row K16.
Next row K1, P to last st, K1.
Rep last 2 rows 8 times more.
Shape top
1st row (K2 tog) to end.
2nd row K1, P to last st, K1.

Break off yarn, thread through rem sts, draw up and fasten off securely.
With RS of work facing, rejoin yarn to palm sts, K to end. 43 sts.
Dec 1 st at each end of next and every foll alt row until 7 sts rem.
Cast off.

Left mitten
Work as given for right mitten from ** to **.
Commence patt and thumb gusset.
1st row K17, P1, K2, P1, K1, P2, TW3, P2, C4B, C4F, P2, TW3, P2, K1.
2nd and every foll alt row K3, P3, K2, P8, K2, P3, K2, P3, K2, P to last st, K1.
3rd row K17, P1, work into front, back and front of next st, K1, P1, patt to last st, K1.
Cont in this way, inc 1 st at each side of gusset on every foll 4th row until there are 55 sts.
Work 5 rows without shaping.

Divide for thumb
Next row K30, cast on 4 sts, turn leaving back of hand sts on spare needle.
Next row K1, P14, K1, turn.
Complete as thumb of right mitten.
With RS of work facing, rejoin yarn to sts for back of hand, patt to end.
Keeping patt correct, complete as given for right mitten reversing shaping.

Mitten edging
Using 3¼mm needles and RS of work facing, K up 39 sts along rib edge.
K 1 row.
Work edging as given for detachable collar.

To make up
Embroider mitten backs (see Special Technique.)
Join thumb and side seam.

Special technique — Tyrolean embroidery

1 *Tyrolean embroidery stitches are simple ones like detached chain stitch and French knots. Work floral motifs to follow the lines of the stitch pattern. On the chevron panel work one flower in the point of each 'V' and one above it on each side in a different colour.*

2 *On the cable and bobble panel work three flowers and two leaves on each side of the bobbles, and one flower between each pattern repeat, alternating the contrast colours as shown.*

3 *The medallion cable running along the centre of the mitten backs makes a perfect 'frame' for a string of lazy-daisy motifs in alternating contrast colours.*

American Indian Sweater

The brilliant geometric patterns of the American Indians
have been used on this long, lean sweater. It looks
marvellous with trousers, or with boots
and a mid-calf skirt.

Sizes
To fit 81[86:91:96]cm bust
Length 66cm
Sleeve seam 46cm
Note Instructions for larger sizes are in square brackets []; where there is only one set of figures it applies to all sizes.

Tension
22 sts and 26 rows to 10cm over patt on 4mm needles

Materials
275 [275:325:325] g double knitting yarn in main colour (A)
150 [150:200:200] g in each of two contrast colours (B) and (C)
100 [100:150:150] g in each of two contrast colours (D) and (E)
1 pair each 3¼mm and 4mm knitting needles
Set of four 3¼mm needles pointed at both ends

Back
**Using 3¼mm needles and A, cast on 97[103:109:115] sts. Work in K1, P1 rib as foll:
1st row K1, *P1, K1, rep from * to end.
2nd row P1, *K1, P1, rep from * to end.
Rep the last 2 rows for 5cm, ending with a 2nd row.
Change to 4mm needles and beg with a K row cont in st st working patt as foll:
Work 1st-22nd rows from chart 1.

Work 23rd-41st rows from chart 2.
Work 42nd-90th rows from chart 3.
Work 91st-106th rows from chart 4.**
Work 107th-143rd rows from chart 5.
Work 144th-160th rows from chart 6.
See pages 172-174 for charts.
Shape shoulders
Next row Cast off 28[31:34:37] sts, K41 and slip these sts on to a holder, cast off rem 28[31:34:37] sts.

Front
Work as given for back from ** to **.
Work 107th-142nd rows colour patt from chart 5.
Shape neck
Cont working from chart 5 and chart 6, keeping patt correct.
Next row K40[43:46:49] sts, and turn, leaving rem sts on a spare needle.
Complete left side of neck first.
Cast off 3 sts at beg of next row and 2 sts at beg of foll 3 alt rows. Now dec 1 st at beg of foll 3 alt rows. 28[31:34:37] sts.
Cont without shaping to match back until 160th row has been worked from chart 6.
Shape shoulder
Cast off these sts.
With RS of work facing return to sts on spare needle, sl centre 17 sts on to a holder, join in yarn to next st, K to end.
Work 1 row.
Complete to match first side of neck, reversing shaping.

Sleeves
Using 3¼mm needles and A, cast on 45[49:53:57] sts.
Work in K1, P1 rib as given for back for 7cm, ending with a 1st row. Inc 12 sts evenly across last row. 57[61:65:69] sts.
Change to 4mm needles and beg with a P row cont in st st and patt as foll, *at the same time*, inc 1 st at each end of 7th and every foll 6th row.
Work 42nd-90th rows from chart 3. 73[77:81:85] sts.
Work 91st-106th rows from chart 4. 77[81:85:89] sts.
Work 107th-143rd rows from chart 5. 89[93:97:101] sts.
Cast off loosely.

To make up
Join shoulder seams.
Neckband
Using three of set of four 3¼mm needles, with RS of work facing and A, K across 41 sts on back neck, K up 20 sts down left side of neck, K across 17 sts at centre front and K up 20 sts up right side of neck. 98 sts.
Using fourth needle work in rounds.
Work in K1, P1 rib for 7cm. Cast off loosely in rib.
Press with a warm iron over a damp cloth omitting rib.
Place centre of cast-off edge of sleeve to shoulder seam, set in sleeves. Join side and sleeve seams. Fold neckband in half on to WS and slip-stitch down.

Special technique — introducing new yarn

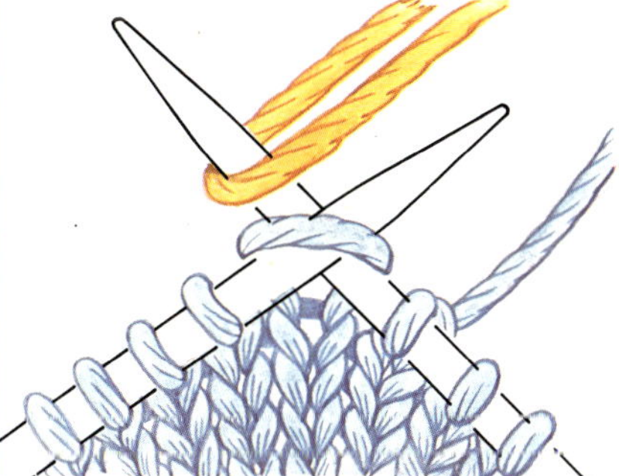

1 *Insert right-hand needle into stitch on left-hand needle. Wind new yarn around right-hand needle and pull through the stitch, thus knitting one stitch with new yarn. Leave old yarn at back of work.*

2 *Knit next stitch in the same way but this time wind both strands of new yarn over right-hand needle and knit. This secures the end of the new yarn, as shown.*

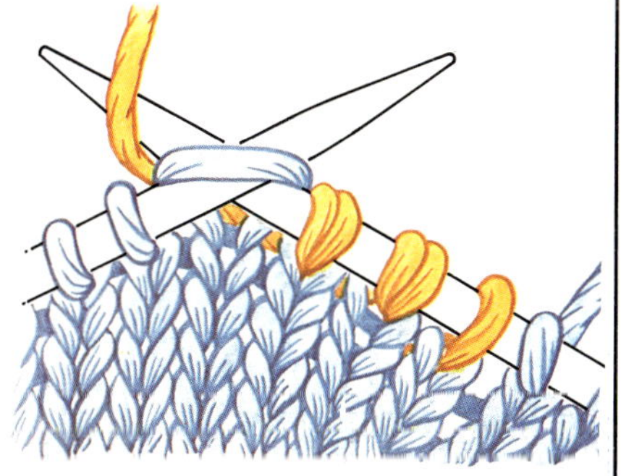

3 *Repeat as for second stitch and thereafter leave the end at the back of the work and knit with one strand only.*

Reading the charts

Work in stocking stitch reading K rows (odd-numbered) from right to left and P rows (even-numbered) from left to right.

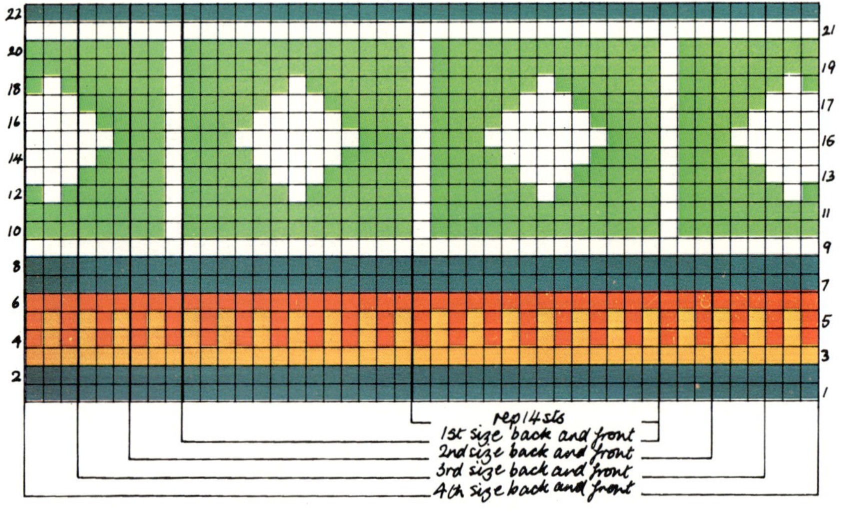

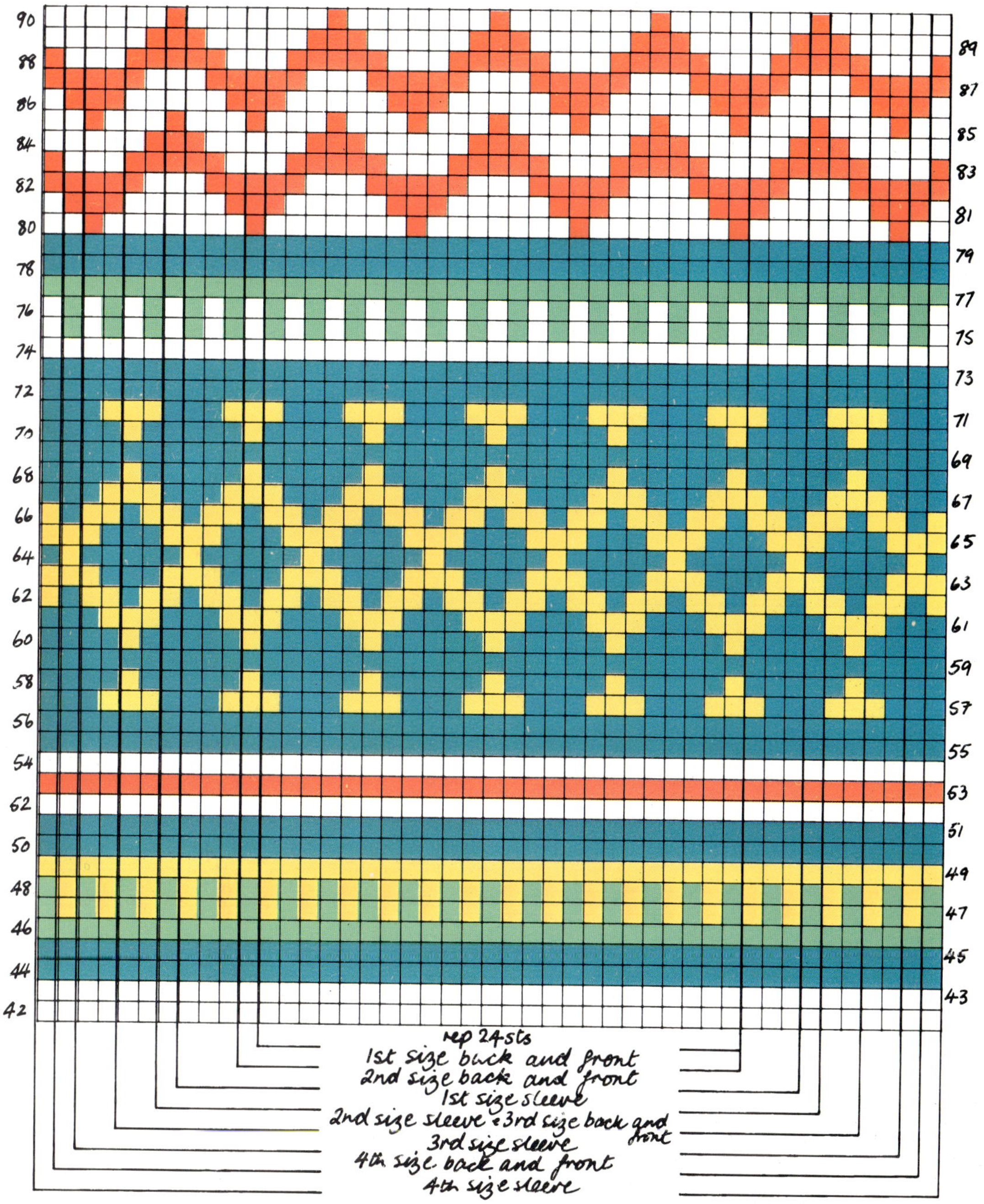

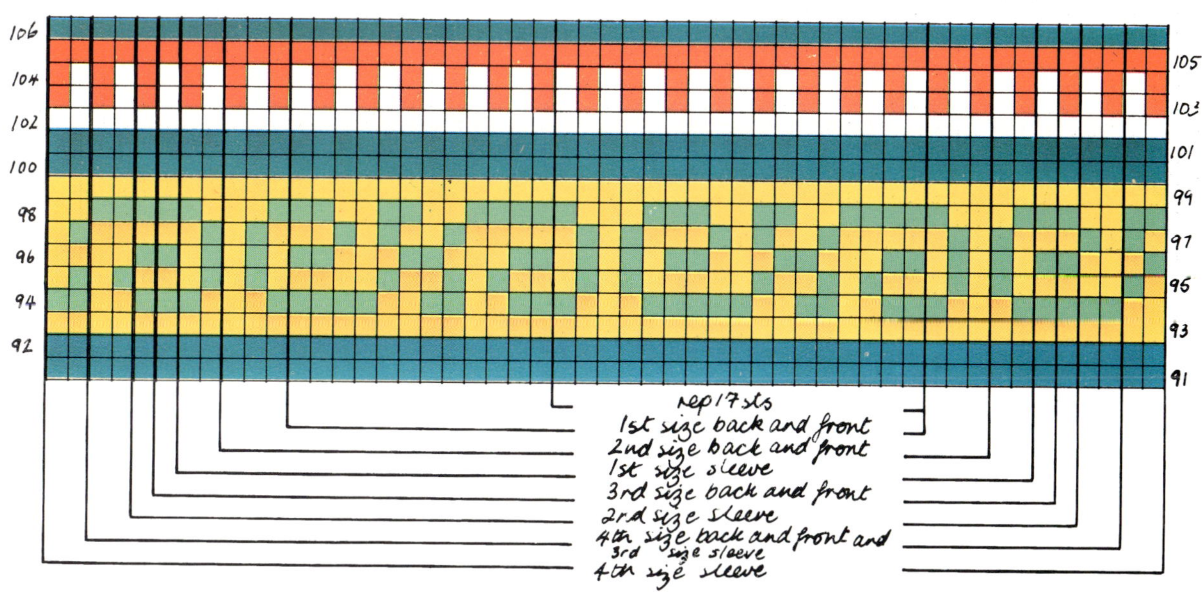

90
88
86
84
82
80
78
76
74
72
70
68
66
64
62
60
58
56
54
62
50
48
46
44
42
89
87
85
83
81
79
77
75
73
71
69
67
65
63
61
59
57
55
63
51
49
47
45
43
rep 24 sts
1st size back and front
2nd size back and front
1st size sleeve
2nd size sleeve + 3rd size back and front
3rd size sleeve
4th size back and front
4th size sleeve

106
104
102
100
98
96
94
92
105
103
101
99
97
95
93
91
rep 17 sts
1st size back and front
2nd size back and front
1st size sleeve
3rd size back and front
2nd size sleeve
4th size back and front and 3rd size sleeve
4th size sleeve

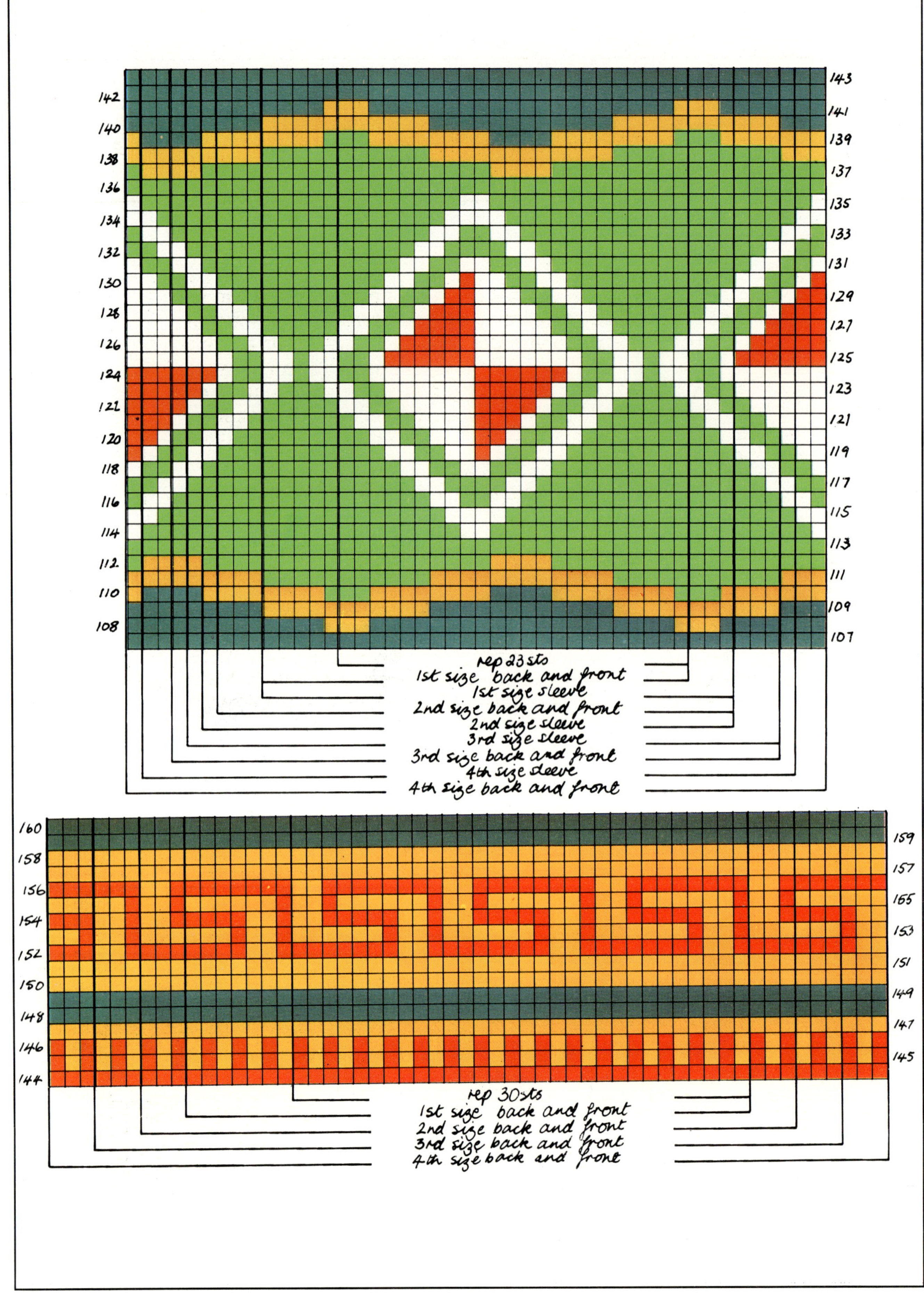
rep 23 sts
1st size back and front
1st size sleeve
2nd size back and front
2nd size sleeve
3rd size sleeve
3rd size back and front
4th size sleeve
4th size back and front
rep 30 sts
1st size back and front
2nd size back and front
3rd size back and front
4th size back and front

Finishing Touches

There are many kinds of decorative finishes which can be added to knitted garments. They can be used to add interest to an otherwise plain sweater or dress or to create an entirely original texture or fabric. Pompons and tassels can be made up in matching or contrasting yarns and simply sewn on wherever you like. Use them to trim collars and necklines; add them to cords for ties; tassel an entire edge to make a thick, sweeping fringe.

Beads and sequins can either be sewn on after the garment is finished or knitted in as you go along (they have to be threaded on to the yarn before knitting it). Special techniques for knitting in beads are shown on page 29.

Knitting, like any other fabric , can be embroidered. You can use many of the usual embroidery stitches—chain stitch, cross stitch, satin stitch, smocking, stem stitch and so on. There is also a stitch, Swiss darning (page 28), which is specially intended for knitted fabrics. With this you can create colour patterns and motifs which look as if they have been knitted in.

Tasselled Sweater

Huge fluffy tassels add a light-hearted touch to a soft cosy
sweater with an unusual pointed collar patterned in a
rich combination of contrast colours.

Sizes
To fit 81[86:91:96]cm bust
Length 62[62:63:63]cm
Sleeve seam 46cm

Note Instructions for the larger sizes
are given in square brackets []; where
there is only one set of figures it
applies to all sizes.

Tension
15 sts and 19 rows to 10cm over st st
on 5½mm needles

Materials
550 [550:600:600] g mohair in main
colour (A)
100g in contrast colour (B)
50g in each of two contrast colours (C)
and (D)
1 pair each 4½mm and 5½mm
knitting needles
Set of four 4½mm needles pointed at
both ends

Back
**Using 4½mm needles and A, cast
on 62[66:70:74] sts.
1st row *K2, P2, rep from * to last 2
sts, K2.
2nd row *P2, K2, rep from * to last 2
sts, P2.
Rep the last 2 rows until work
measures 13cm from cast-on edge,
ending with a 2nd row.
Change to 5½mm needles.
Next row (K2, work into front and
back of next st — called inc 1)
2[3:4:5] times, K to last 6[9:12:15]
sts, (inc 1, K2) 2[3:4:5] times.
66[72:78:84] sts.**
Beg with a P row cont in st st until
work measures 62[62:63:63]cm from
cast-on edge, ending with a P row.
Cast off, marking centre 20 sts for
back neck.

Front
Work as given for back from ** to **.
Beg with a P row cont in st st until
work measures 55[55:56:56]cm from
cast-on edge, ending with a P row.
Shape neck
Next row K25[28:31:34], cast off 16
sts, K to end.
Complete right side of neck first.
Dec 1 st at neck edge on next 2 rows.
23[26:29:32] sts.
Cont without shaping until work
measures 62[62:63:63]cm from cast-

on edge, ending with a P row.
Cast off. With WS of work facing,
return to sts for left side of neck.
Rejoin yarn at neck edge and
complete to match first side.

Sleeves
Using 4½mm needles and A, cast on
30 sts. Work in rib as given for back
for 6cm ending with a 2nd row.
Change to 5½mm needles.
Beg with a K row cont in st st. Inc 1 st
at each end of every foll 4th row until
there are 64 sts.
Cont without further shaping until
work measures 46cm from cast-on
edge, ending with a P row. Cast off.

Back collar
Using 5½mm needles and B, cast on
2 sts.
Commence working from chart on
page 178 as foll:
1st row (RS) K.

2nd-5th rows K, inc 1 st at each end
of every row.
6th row With B, inc into first st, K3,
P2A, K3B, inc into last st.
7th row With B, inc into first st, K3,
K4A, K3B, inc into last st.
8th row With B, inc into first st, K3,
P6A, K3B, inc into last st.
Keeping chart correct, cont in this
way inc 1 st at each end of every row
until there are 80 sts.
Cont without shaping until 71 rows of
chart have been worked, ending with
a RS row.
Cast off.

Front collar
Work as given for back collar until 57
rows of chart have been worked,
ending with a RS row.
Shape neck
Next row Patt 32, turn leaving rem
sts on a spare needle.
Complete right side of neck first.

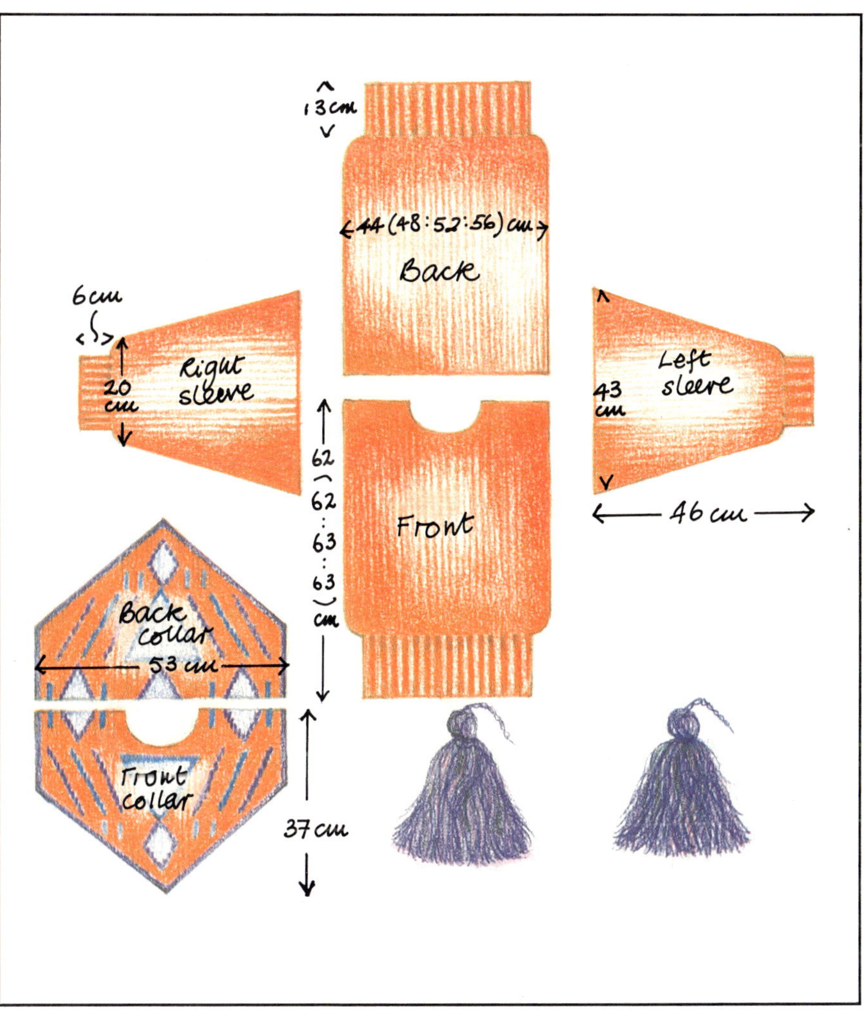

Keeping chart correct, dec 1 st at neck edge on next 2 rows.

Cont without shaping until 71 rows of chart have been worked, ending with a RS row. Cast off.

With WS of work facing, rejoin yarn to neck edge, cast off 16 sts, patt to end.

Complete to match first side of neck.

To make up
Join shoulder seams.
Neckband
With RS of work facing, using set of four 4½mm needles and A, K up 14 sts down left side of neck, 16 sts from front neck, 14 sts up right side of neck and 20 sts from back neck. 64 sts.

Work in rounds of K2, P2 rib for 3cm. Cast off in rib.

Sew front and back pieces of collar together at shoulders, matching pattern carefully. Neatly sew to neck edge below neckband.

Placing centre of cast-off edge of sleeve to shoulder seam, set in sleeves.

Join side and sleeve seams.

Using B, make two large tassels approximately 20cm long and attach to collar points at front and back with a corded tie (see Special Technique).

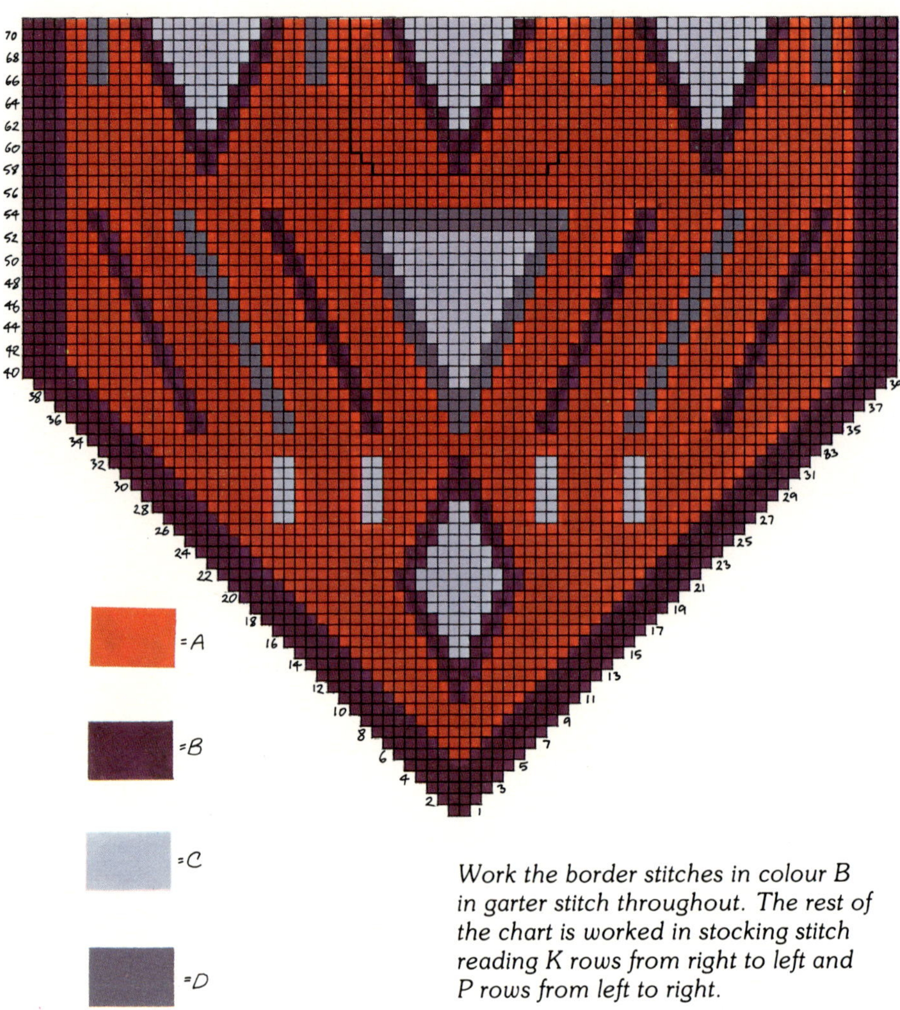

Work the border stitches in colour B in garter stitch throughout. The rest of the chart is worked in stocking stitch reading K rows from right to left and P rows from left to right.

Special technique — making a corded tie

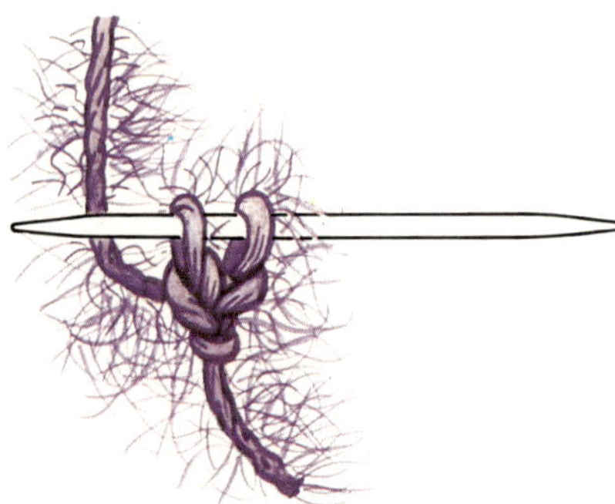

1 *The tassels are attached to the collar of the basic sweater by corded ties. Using double-pointed needles cast on two stitches on to one of the needles (three stitches can be cast on for a thicker tie). Knit these two stitches as usual.*

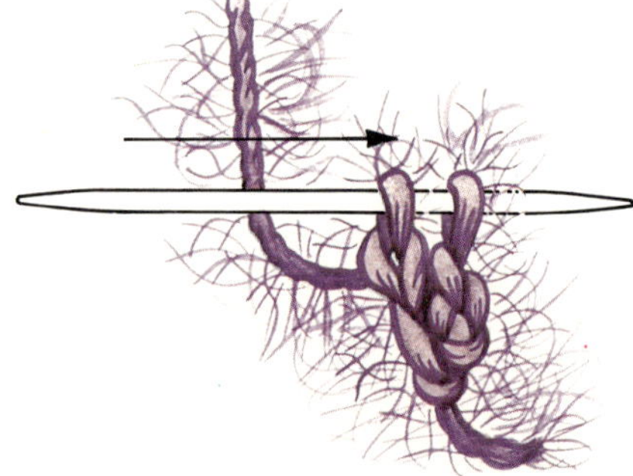

2 *Do not turn the work. Push the two stitches up to the working end of the needle and knit the two stitches again pulling the working yarn firmly round to the first stitch.*

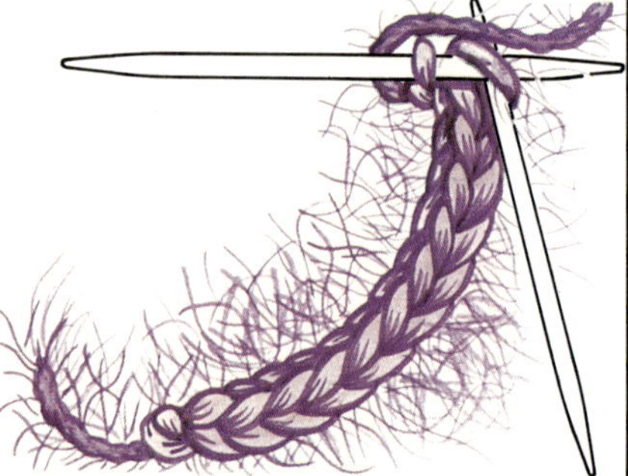

3 *Do not turn the work. Push the two stitches up to the working end again and knit the stitches as before. Carry on in this way until the cord is the required length. Knit the two stitches together and fasten off.*

Rose-patterned Sweater

The square collar on this flattering simple sweater makes a perfect 'canvas' for Swiss darning, whether traditional like these soft pink cabbage roses or more abstract and modern.

Sizes
To fit 86[91:96]cm bust
Length 56[57:57]cm
Sleeve seam 43cm

Note Instructions for larger sizes are in square brackets []; where there is only one set of figures it applies to all sizes.

Tension
24 sts and 30 rows to 10cm over st st on 4mm needles

Materials
650 [650:700] g double knitting yarn
1 pair each 3¼mm and 4mm knitting needles
3¼mm circular needle
1 skein tapestry wool in each of light, medium and dark tones of a 'rose' colour.
1 skein in green

Back
**Using 3¼mm needles, cast on 96[102:108] sts. Work 21 rows K1, P1 rib.
Next row Rib 5[8:11], *work into front and back of next st — called inc 1 —, rib 5, rep from * to last 7[10:13] sts, inc 1, rib to end. 111[117:123] sts. Change to 4mm needles. Beg with a K row cont in st st until work measures 36cm from cast-on edge, ending with a P row.
Shape armholes
Cast off 3 sts at beg of next 6 rows. Dec 1 st at each end of every foll row until 79[81:85] sts rem.**
Cont without shaping until work measures 20[21:21]cm from beg of

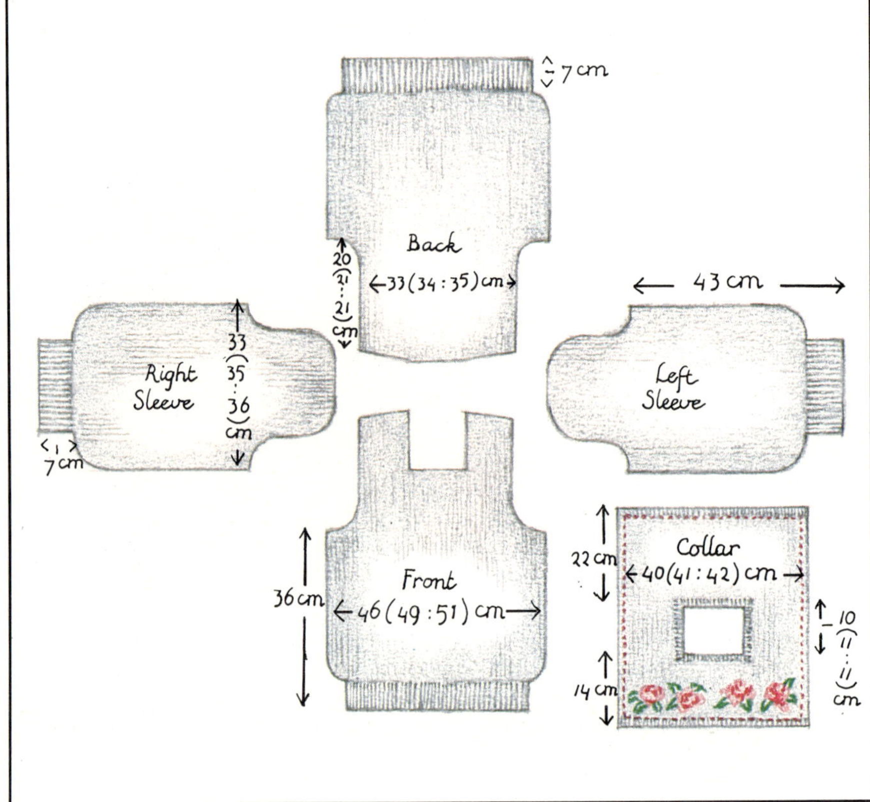

armholes, ending with a P row.
Shape shoulders
Cast off 10[10:11] sts at beg of next 2 rows and 11 sts at beg of foll 2 rows. Cast off rem 37[39:41] sts.

Front
Work as given for back from ** to **. Cont without shaping until work measures 10cm from beg of armhole shaping, ending with a P row.
Shape neck
Next row K21[21:22] sts, leave these

on a spare needle, cast off next 37[39:41] sts, K to end.
Complete right side of neck first. Cont without shaping until work matches back to shoulder shaping, ending at armhole edge.
Shape shoulder.
Cast off 10[10:11] sts at beg of next row. Work 1 row. Cast off rem 11 sts. With WS of work facing return to sts on spare needle. Join in yarn to neck edge. Complete to match first side, reversing shaping.

Sleeves
Using 3¼mm needles, cast on 48[52:56] sts.
Work 21 rows K1, P1 rib.
Next row Rib 9[11:13], (inc 1) 31 times, rib to end. 79[83:87] sts.
Change to 4mm needles. Beg with a K row cont in st st until work measures 43cm from cast-on edge, ending with a P row.
Shape top
Cast off 3 sts at beg of next 6 rows.
Dec 1 st at each end of the next and every foll alt row until 53[55:57] sts rem.
Cont without shaping until work measures 54[55:55]cm from cast-on edge, ending with a P row.
Dec 1 st at each end of every row until 19[21:23] sts rem.
Cast off 3 sts at beg of next 4 rows.
Cast off rem sts.

Collar
Using 4mm needles, cast on 97[99:101] sts. Cont in rib as foll:
1st row (RS) K1, *P1, K1, rep from * to end.
2nd row P1, *K1, P1, rep from * to end.
Rep the last 2 rows twice more.
Next row (K1, P1) twice, K to last 4 sts, (P1, K1) twice.
Next row (P1, K1) twice, P to last 4 sts, (K1, P1) twice.
Rep the last 2 rows until work measures 14cm from cast-on edge, ending with a WS row.
Shape neck
Next row (K1, P1) twice, K26, leave these sts on a spare needle, cast off next 37[39:41] sts, work to end.
Complete right side of neck first.
Cont without shaping until work measures 24[25:25]cm from cast-on edge, ending with a WS row. Break yarn and leave these sts.
With WS of work facing return to sts on spare needle. Join in yarn to next st, work to end.
Cont until work matches first side of neck, ending with a P row.
Next row Work 30 sts, cast on 37[39:41] sts, then work across sts for other side of neck. 97[99:101] sts.
Cont on sts as set for a further 22cm, ending with a WS row.
Rep 1st-2nd rib rows 3 times. Cast off in rib.

To make up
Join shoulder seams.
With RS of front and back facing WS of collar, place collar in position, matching neck edges.

Front neck edge
Using 3¼mm needles, beg at left front corner of neck, working through two thicknesses of garment and collar, K up 37[39:41] sts.
Rep 1st-2nd rib rows as given for collar 4 times, *at the same time*, dec 1 st at each end of every row. Cast off in rib.

Back neck edge
Using 3¼mm circular needle, beg at right front corner of neck, K up 30[33:33] sts up right side of neck, 37[39:41] sts across back neck, 30[33:33] sts down left side of neck. 97[105:107] sts. Work in rows.
Complete as given for front neck edge. Join corners of edging. Join side and sleeve seams.
Set in sleeves.

Swiss darning
Using two strands embroidery wool Swiss-darn roses on to collar following chart. Place pattern by matching centre stitch of collar to centre stitch on chart and working bottom row on chart on first knit row of collar. Continue working border dots every fifth stitch up the sides of the collar and across lower back edge. Press darning under a damp cloth.

Special technique — making up a square collar

1 *Join shoulder seams. Place the collar in position on the sweater with the wrong side of the collar facing the right sides of the back and front. Match the neck edge of the collar to the neckline of the sweater.*

2 *Pick up the required number of stitches along the front neck edge through the cast-off edges of the collar neck edge and the sweater neckline for each stitch. Work in single rib as instructed decreasing one stitch at each end of every row. Cast off in rib.*

3 *Pick up the required number of stitches along sides and back neck edge working through both layers as before. Work in single rib for the required depth, decreasing one stitch at each end of every row. Join the lower front corners of the rib.*

Beaded Cardigan

This beautifully shaped cardigan with frilled peplum has
glass beads knitted into a simple textured pattern.
Alternatively, the beads could be sewn on after the knitting
is completed.

Sizes
To fit 86 [91:97]cm bust
Length 54 [55:56]cm
Sleeve seam 43cm

Note Instructions for larger sizes are in square brackets []; where there is only one set of figures it applies to all sizes.

Tension
28 sts and 28 rows to 10cm over bead patt on 4mm needles

Materials
700 [750:800] g double knitting yarn
1 pair each 3¼mm and 4mm needles
9 buttons
Approx 1000 beads

Back
Before commencing work, thread approx 120 beads on to each of 8 balls of yarn.
Using 4mm needles, and yarn without beads, cast on 243 [253:263] sts.
Commence peplum
****Knit 2 rows.**
Next row (RS) P3, *K7, P3, rep from * to end.
Next row K3, *P7, K3, rep from *. Rep the last 2 rows for 7cm, ending with a WS row.
Next row P3, *sl 1, K1, psso, K3, K2 tog, P3, rep from * to end.
Next row K3, *P5, K3, rep from *.
Next row P3, *sl 1, K1, psso, K1, K2 tog, P3, rep from * to end.
Next row K3, *P3, K3, rep from *.
Next row P3, *sl 1, K2 tog, psso, P3, rep from * to end.
Next row K3, *P1, K3, rep from * to end. 99 [99:107] sts.
Change to 3¼mm needles.
*****Next row** *P1, K1, rep from * to last st, P1.
Next row *K1, P1, rep from * to last st, K1.
Next row *P1, K1, rep from * to last st, P1.
Next row K1, *P1, K1, P2 tog, yrn, rep from * to last 2 sts, P1, K1.**
1st and 3rd sizes only
Work a further 2[0] rows in rib.
2nd size only
Next row Rib 19, (inc into next st, rib 19) 3 times, inc into next st, rib to end. 103 sts.
All sizes
Now work 0 [1:2] rows in rib, inc 1 st

at each end of every row. 99 [105:111] sts. Change to 4mm needles and yarn with beads. Commence bead patt.
1st row (RS) K1, *K4, P2, rep from * to last 2 sts, K2.
2nd row K1, P1, *K2, P4, rep from * to last st, K1.
3rd-5th rows Rep 1st-2nd rows once, then 1st row again.
6th row K1, P1, *K2, P1, ybk, push bead up close to RS of work, sl 2, yfwd, — called place bead, P1, rep from * to last st, K1.
7th row K1, *insert RH needle between 4th (K st) and 5th (P st) on LH needle, draw through a loop and sl on to LH needle, K it tog with next st on LH needle, P2, K3, rep from * to last 2 sts, K2.
8th row K1, *P4, K2, rep from * to last 2 sts, P1, K1.
9th row K2, *P2, K4, rep from * to last st, K1.
10th-13th rows Rep 8th-9th rows twice.
14th row K1, *P1, place bead, P1, K2, rep from * to last 2 sts, P1, K1.
15th row K2, *P2, insert RH needle between 4th (K st) and 5th (P st) on LH needle, draw through a loop, sl it on to LH needle, K it tog with next st on LH needle, P2, K3, rep from * ending last rep K2.
16th row As 2nd row.
These 16 rows form the patt.

Cont in patt, inc 1 st at each end of the next and every foll 3rd row until there are 123 [129:137] sts, working extra sts in patt.
Cont without shaping until work measures 23cm from beg of bead patt, ending with a WS row.
Shape armholes
Keeping patt correct, cast off 4 sts at beg of next 4 rows. Dec 1 st at each end of next 4 [7:8] rows.
Dec 1 st at each end of every foll alt row until 91 [93:97] sts rem.
Cont without shaping until work measures 20 [21:22] cm from beg of armhole shaping, end with a WS row.
Shape shoulders
Cast off 13 sts at beg of next 2 rows, then 13 [13:14] sts at beg of foll 2 rows. Leave rem 39 [41:43] sts on a spare needle.

Left front
Using 4mm needles and yarn without beads, cast on 123[133:143] sts.
Work as given for back from ** to **.
Work 2 [1:0] rows in rib.
Now work 0 [1:2] rows in rib, inc 1 st at each end of every row. 51 [57:63] sts.
Change to 4mm needles and yarn with beads.
Commence bead patt as given for back. Inc and work into patt 1 st at side edge on the 17th and every foll 3rd row until there are 63 [69:75] sts.
Cont without shaping until work

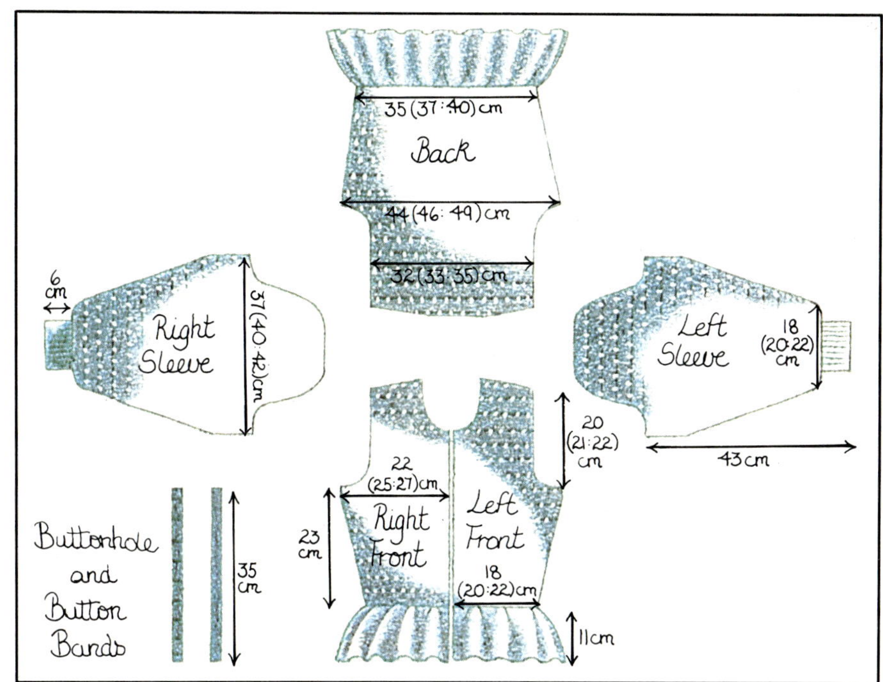

matches back to underarm, ending at side edge.

Shape armhole
Keeping patt correct, cast off 4 [5:5] sts at beg of next row and 4 [4:5] sts at beg of foll alt row. Dec 1 st at armhole edge on foll 4 [7:9] rows and then 1 st on every foll alt row until 47 [49:52] sts rem.
Cont without shaping until work measures 12cm from beg of armhole shaping, ending at front edge.

Shape neck
Keeping patt correct, cast off 8 sts at beg of next row, then dec 1 st at neck edge on every row until 26 [26:27] sts rem. Cont without shaping until work matches back to shoulder shaping, ending at armhole edge.

Shape shoulder
Cast off 13 sts at beg of next row.
Work 1 row.
Cast off rem 13 [13:14] sts.

Right front
Work as given for left front reversing shapings.

Sleeves
Using 3¼mm needles and yarn without beads, cast on 48 [54:60] sts. Work in K1, P1 rib for 6cm.
Next row Rib 9 [12:15], (work twice into next st, rib 13) twice, work twice into next st, rib to end. 51 [57:63] sts.
Change to 4mm needles and yarn with beads.

Commence bead patt as given for back, inc 1 st at each end of every foll 3rd row until there are 105 [111:117] sts. Cont without shaping until work measures 43cm from cast-on edge, ending with a same patt row as back at underarm.

Shape top
Keeping patt correct, cast off 4 [5:5] sts at beg of next 2 rows and 4 [4:5] sts at beg of foll 2 rows. Now dec 1 st at each end of every row until 59 [61:63] sts rem, then at each end of every alt row until 33 sts rem.
Cast off 3 sts at beg of next 6 rows.
Cast off rem 15 sts.

Shoulder pads (make 2)
Using 3¼mm needles and yarn without beads, cast on 38 sts. Work in K1, P1 rib for 26 rows. Cast off in rib.

To make up
Join shoulder seams.
Neck edging
Using 3¼mm needles, with RS of work facing, K up 30 [33:36] sts up right front neck edge, K across 39 [41:43] sts on back neck, K up 30 [33:36] sts down left front neck edge. 99 [107:115] sts. Now work in rib as given for back from * * * to * *.
Work a further 3 rows in rib.
Work frill
1st row (RS), P3, *K1, P3, rep from *
2nd row K3, * (P1, K1, P1) all into next st, K3, rep from * to end.

3rd row P3, *K3, P3, rep from *.
4th row K3, * (P1, K1) all into next st, P1, (K1, P1) all into next st, K3, rep from * to end.
5th row P3, *K5, P3, rep from *.
6th row K3, *(P1, K1) all into next st, P3, (K1, P1) all into next st, K3, rep from * to end.
7th row P3, *K7, P3, rep from *.
8th row K3, *P7, K3, rep from *.
9th row As 7th.
Keeping patt correct, cast off.
Buttonband
Using 3¼mm needles cast on 8 sts. Work in K1, P1 rib until band is long enough, when slightly stretched, to fit left front edge from top of peplum to neck edge. Cast off in rib.
Mark the positions of 9 buttons, the first to come 2cm above base of band, the last 2cm below the neck edge, with the other 7 evenly spaced between them.
Buttonhole band
Work to match buttonband making button holes opposite markers as foll:
1st row (RS) Rib 3, cast off 2, rib 3.
2nd row Rib to end, casting on over cast-off sts of previous row.
Join side and sleeve seams. Set in sleeves. Fold shoulder pads in half diagonally and oversew edges. Sew in position. Sew on bands and buttons. Using 4 lengths of yarn 300cm long, make a twisted cord for waist tie, and using 200cm long lengths make a neck tie. Thread through eyelet holes, bringing ends out to tie.

Special technique — placing the beads

1 In this pattern beads are placed on wrong-side rows. Thread beads on to yarn before starting to knit. Work in pattern to bead position. Take yarn to back of work, push bead up close to work, slip two stitches, bring yarn forward. Work to next bead.

2 On the next row, work to the bead, insert the right-hand needle between the 4th and 5th stitches on the left-hand needle from front to back. Take the working yarn under and over the needle and draw a loop through to the front of the work.

3 Take the loop under the bead and place it on the left-hand needle. Knit the loop together with the next stitch on the left-hand needle. Work in pattern to the next bead position.

Sequinned Dress

Make a dramatic entrance to any party in a flouncy
sequined sizzler of a dress that's a lot easier to make than
it looks. The sequins are knitted in as the work
progresses and the frills are made separately and sewn on.
The skimpy bodice is fastened with narrow straps
criss-crossing the back.

Size
To fit 87-92cm bust
Length at side seam 65cm

Tension
28 sts and 36 rows to 10cm over st st
on 3¼mm needles

Materials
600g four-ply yarn
1 pair 3¼mm knitting needles
approx 8,000 sequins 10mm in
diameter

Special note The sequins must be
threaded on to the yarn before
beginning to knit. Thread
sequins concave side down.

Front
**Using 3¼mm needles, cast on 184
sts. Beg with a K row cont in st st until
work measures 21cm from cast-on
edge, ending with a P row.
Next row (K2 tog) to end. 92 sts.
Beg with a P row work 3 rows st st.
Commence sequin patt.
1st row K2, *place sequin as foll:
yfwd, move a sequin up close to RS
of work, P1, — called place sequin
—, K1, rep from * to end.
2nd-4th rows Beg with a P row work
3 rows st st.
5th row K3, *place sequin, K1, rep
from * to last st, K1.
6th-8th rows As 2nd-4th rows.
These 8 rows form the patt.
Cont in patt. Work 2 rows.
Keeping patt correct, commence hip
shaping.
Next row K1, K2 tog, K26, K3 tog,
K28, K3 tog, K26, K2 tog, K1. 86 sts.
Patt 7 rows.
Next row K1, K2 tog, K24, K3 tog,
K26, K3 tog, K24, K2 tog, K1. 80 sts.
Patt 7 rows.
Next row K1, K2 tog, K22, K3 tog,
K24, K3 tog, K22, K2 tog, K1. 74
sts.**
Patt 39 rows.
Commence bodice shaping.
Next row K1, pick up loop between
last st worked and next st on LH
needle and K it tbl — called M1 —,
K25, M1, K1, M1, K20, M1, K1, M1
K25, M1, K1. 80 sts.
Patt 7 rows.
Next row K1, M1, K27, M1, K1, M1,
K22, M1, K1, M1, K27, M1, K1. 86
sts.

Patt 7 rows.
Next row K1, M1, K29, M1, K1, M1,
K24, M1, K1, M1, K29, M1, K1. 92
sts.
Patt 39 rows.
Next row K28, (M1, K1) 5 times,
K26, (M1, K1)5 times, K28. 102 sts.
Patt 3 rows. Begin neck shaping.
Next row K2 tog, K to last 2 sts,
K2 tog.
Next row P2 tog, P47, cast off 2 sts,
P to last 2 sts, P2 tog.
Complete left side of neck first.
Keeping patt correct, dec 1 st at each
end of every foll alt row until 28 sts
rem. Now dec 1 st at each end of
every foll 4th row until 16 sts rem,
ending with a P row.
Next row (K2 tog) to end. 8 sts.
Next row (P2 tog) to end. 4 sts.

Next row (K1, place sequin) twice.
Next row (P2 tog) twice.
Next row K.
Cast off. With RS of work facing,
return to sts for right side of neck.
Complete to match first side.

Back
Work as given for front from ** to
**. Patt 18 rows.
Shape back waist
Next row P22, cast off 30 sts, P to
end.
Complete right side of waist first.
Keeping patt correct, dec 1 st at inner
edge on every foll 4th row until 3 sts
rem. Cast off. With RS of work
facing, return to sts for left side of
waist. Join in yarn to next st and
complete to match first side.

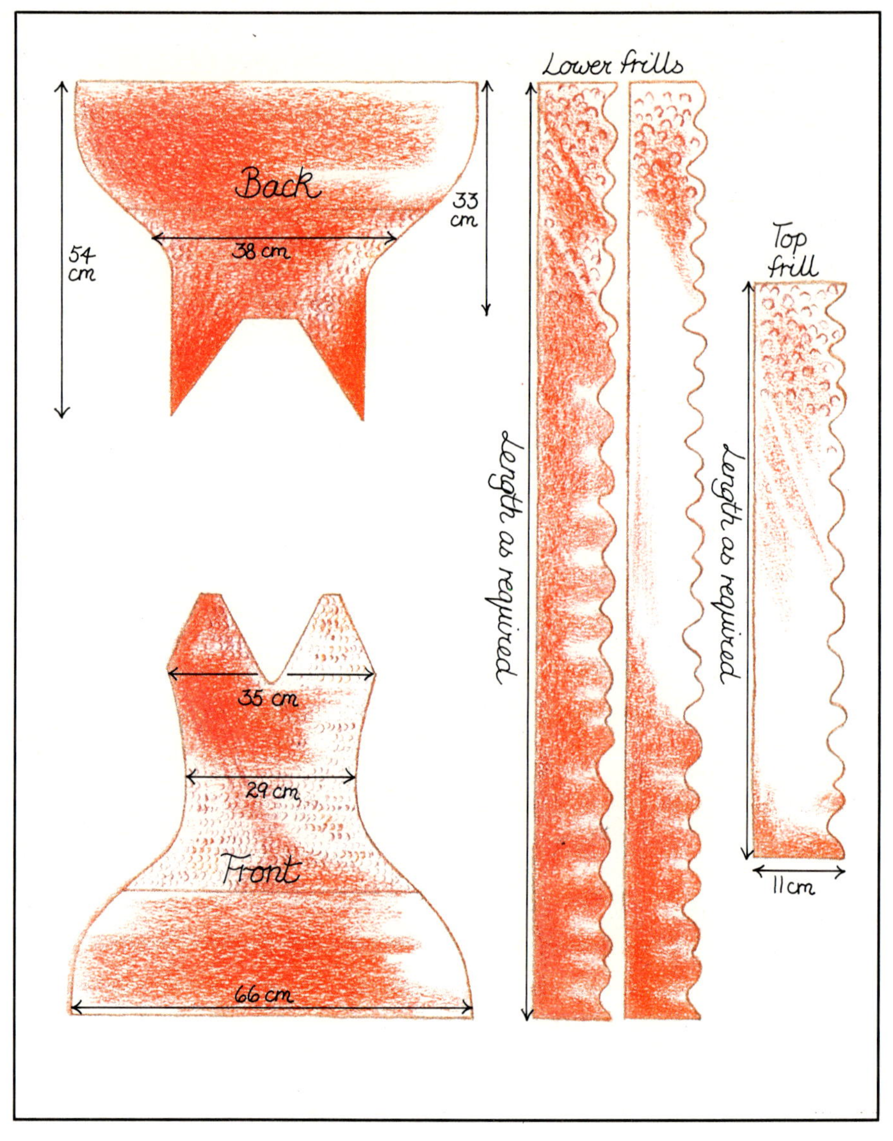

Top frill
Using 3¼mm needles, cast on 30 sts.
Next row K.
Next row P24, K6.
Rep the last 2 rows once more.
Commence sequin patt.
1st row K2, *place sequin, K2, rep
from * to last 3 sts, K3.
**2nd, 4th, 6th, 8th, 10th and 12th
rows** P24, K6.
3rd, 7th and 11th rows K.
5th row K3, *place sequin, K2, rep
from * to last 2 sts, K2.
9th row K1, *place sequin, K2, rep
from * to last 2 sts, place sequin K1.
13th row K2, turn.
14th and foll alt rows K to end.
15th row K2, place sequin, turn.
17th row K4, turn.
19th row K3, place sequin, K1, turn.
21st row K6, turn.
23rd row K1, (place sequin, K2)
twice, turn.
24th and foll alt rows P to last 6 sts,
K6.
25th row K8, turn.
27th row (K2, place sequin) 3 times,
turn.
29th row K10, turn.
31st row K3, (place sequin, K2)
twice, place sequin, K1, turn.
33rd row K12, turn.
35th row K1, (place sequin, K2) 4
times, turn.
37th row K14, turn.
39th row (K2, place sequin) 5 times,

turn.
41st row K16, turn.
43rd row K3, (place sequin, K2) 4
times, place sequin, K1, turn.
45th row K18, turn.
47th row K1, (place sequin, K2) 6
times, turn.
49th row K20, turn.
51st row (K2, place sequin) 7 times,
turn.
53rd row K22, turn.
55th row K3, (place sequin, K2) 6
times, place sequin, K1, turn.
57th row K24, turn.
59th row K1, (place sequin, K2) 8
times, turn.
61st row As 57th row.
63rd row As 55th row.
65th row As 53rd row.
67th row As 51st row.
69th row As 49th row.
71st row As 47th row.
73rd row As 45th row.
75th row As 43rd row.
77th row As 41st row.
79th row As 39th row.
81st row As 37th row.
83rd row As 35th row.
85th row As 33rd row.
87th row As 31st row.
89th row As 29th row.
91st row As 27th row.
93rd row As 25th row.
95th row As 23rd row.
97th row As 21st row.
98th and foll alt rows K to end.

99th row As 19th row.
101st row As 17th row.
103rd row As 15th row.
105th row As 13th row.
106th row K to end.
107th-118th rows Rep 1st-12th rows
inclusive once.
These 118 rows form the patt. Cont
in patt until straight edge fits hipline at
beg of sequin patt.
Cast off.

Lower frills (make 2)
Work as given for top frill until straight
edge fits lower edge of skirt, ending
with a WS row.
Cast off.

Ties (make 2)
Using 3¼mm needles, cast on 4 sts.
Beg with a K row, cont in st st until
work measures 118cm from beg,
ending with a P row.
Cast off.

To make up
Join side seams.
Sew top frill to top of skirt at
beginning of sequin pattern, one
lower frill to hem edge and the
second lower frill between them.
Sew ties to top of bodice. Make a
button loop on each inner back edge.
Take ties over shoulders, cross over on
the back, thread through loops and tie
in a bow.

Special technique — placing sequins

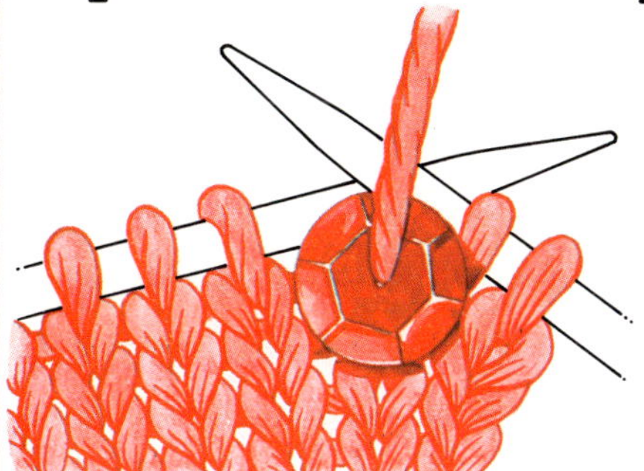

1 *The sequins on the dress are placed on right-side rows on the 1st and 5th pattern rows as follows: On the 1st row knit the first two stitches. Bring the yarn forward from the back to the front of the work. Push a sequin up close to the right side of the work.*

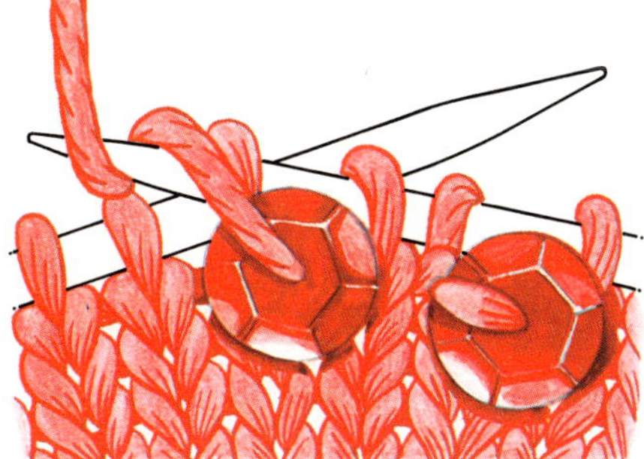

2 *Purl the next stitch. The first sequin is now in position. Knit the next stitch then place the second sequin in the same way. Continue placing the sequins after every alternate stitch.*

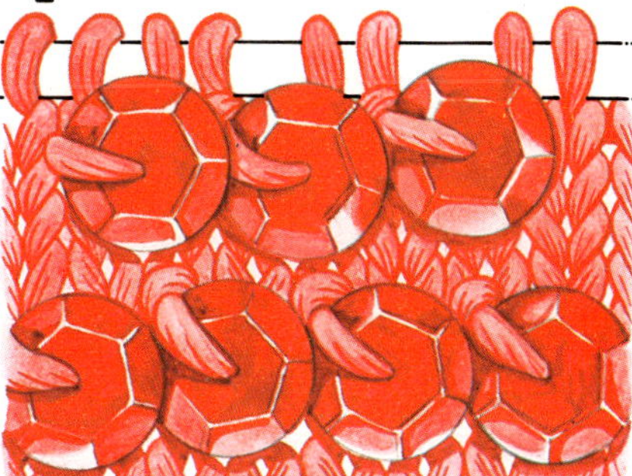

3 *On the 5th row the sequins are placed after the third stitch in the row, and then after every alternate stitch, thus staggering them between the sequins on the 1st row.*

Smocked Sweater

A prettily pointed frill and a beaded smocked front panel
give this beautifully shaped sweater
a romantic medieval look.

Sizes
To fit 87[91:97]cm bust
Length including frill 54[55:57]cm
Sleeve seam including frill 46cm

Note Instructions for the larger sizes are in square brackets []; where there is only one set of figures it applies to all sizes.

Tension
24 sts and 30 rows to 10cm measured over main rib patt on 4mm needles

Materials
650 [700:750] g double knitting yarn
1 pair 3¼mm and 4mm needles
1 4mm circular needle
approx 110 small beads

Front
Using 4mm needles, cast on 3 sts.
Commence shaping.
1st row K3.
2nd row (RS) Cast on 4 sts and work across sts as foll: P2, K1, P4.
3rd row Cast on 4 sts and work as foll: K2, P1, K5, P1, K2.
4th row Cast on 5 sts and work as foll: P1, K1, (P5, K1) twice, P2.
5th row Cast on 5 sts and work as foll: K1, P1, (K5, P1) 3 times, K1.
6th row Cast on 5 sts and work as foll: K1, (P5, K1) 4 times, P1.
7th row Cast on 5 sts and work as foll: P1, (K5, P1) 5 times.
Cont in this way, casting on 5[6:6] sts at beg of next 4[8:6] rows, working extra sts into patt. Then cast on 6[7:7] sts at beg of foll 6[8:8] rows.
1st and 3rd sizes only
Cast on 7[8] sts at beg of next 6[4] rows.
All sizes
Cont in patt as set on these 129[135:141] sts until work measures 29[29:30]cm measured at side edge, ending with a WS row.
Shape armholes and divide for neck
Next row Cast off 4[5:6] sts, patt 58[60:62] including st used in casting off, K2 tog and turn, leaving rem sts on a spare needle.
Complete left side of neck first.
Work 1 row.
**Dec 1 st at armhole edge on next 3[5:5] rows, then on *every foll alt row*, *at the same time*, dec 1 st at neck edge on next and every alt row

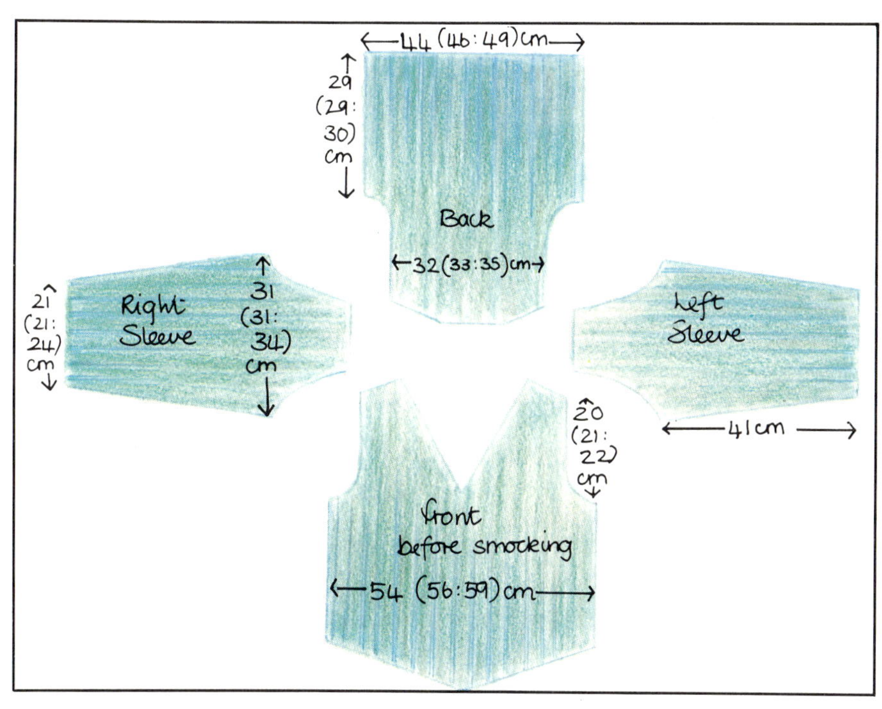

until 40[41:43] sts rem.
Keeping armhole edge straight cont to dec at neck edge only as before until 20[20:21] sts rem, ending with a RS row.
Cont without shaping. Work 3 rows.
Shape shoulder
Cast off 7 sts at beg of next and foll alt row.
Work 1 row.
Cast off rem 6[6:7] sts**
With RS of work facing, return to sts on spare needle. Sl centre st on to a safety pin, join in yarn to rem sts, K2 tog, patt to end.
Next row Cast off 4[5:6], patt to end.
Complete to match first side of neck, work from ** to **, reversing shapings, and working 4 rows before shoulder shaping.

Front lower edge frill
With RS of work facing, using 4mm circular needle, K up 129[135:141] sts around lower edge. Work in rows.
1st row (WS) K1[4:1], *P1, K5, rep from * to last 2[5:2] sts, P1, K1[4:1].
2nd row P1[4:1], pick up loop between last st and next st on LH needle and work into the back of it — called M1 —, *K1, M1, P5, M1, rep from * to last 2[5:2] sts, K1, M1, P1[4:1].
3rd row K1[4:1], *P3, K5, rep from * to last 4[7:4] sts, P3, K1[4:1].
4th row P1[4:1], M1, *K3, M1, P5, M1, rep from * to last 4[7:4] sts, K3, M1, P1[4:1].
5th row K1[4:1], *P5, K5, rep from * to last 6[9:6] sts, P5, K1[4:1].
6th row P1[4:1], M1, *K5, M1, P5, M1, rep from * to last 6[9:6] sts, K5, M1, P1[4:1].
7th row K1[4:1], *P7, K5, rep from * to last 8[11:8] sts, P7, K1[4:1].
8th row P1[4:1], M1, *K7, M1, P5, M1, rep from * to last 8[11:8] sts, K7, M1, P1[4:1].
9th row K1[4:1], *P9, K5, rep from * to last 10[13:10] sts, P9, K1[4:1].
10th row P1[4:1], M1, *K9, M1, P5, M1, rep from * to last 10[13:10] sts, K9, M1, P1[4:1].
11th row K1[4:1], *P11, K5, rep from * to last 12[15:12] sts, P11, K1[4:1].
12th row P1[4:1], *K11, P5, rep from * to last 12[15:12] sts, K11, P1[4:1].
Rep last 2 rows until frill measures 5cm from beg, ending with a WS row.
Cast off in rib as set.

Back
Using 4mm needles, cast on 105[111:117] sts.
Commence patt.
1st row (RS) P1[4:1], *K1, P5, rep from * to last 2 [5:2] sts, K1, P1 [4:1].
2nd row K1 [4:1], *P1, K5, rep from * to last 2[5:2] sts, P1, K1[4:1].

These 2 rows form the rib patt. Cont in patt until work measures same as front to underarm at side seam, ending with a WS row.

Shape armholes
Keeping patt correct, cast off 4 [5:6] sts at beg of next 2 rows.
Dec 1 st at each end of next 3[5:5] rows, then on every foll alt row until 77[79:83] sts rem.
Cont without shaping until work matches front to shoulder shaping, ending at armhole edge.

Shape shoulders
Cast off 7 sts at beg of next 4 rows, then 6[6:7] sts at beg of foll 2 rows. Leave rem 37[39:41] sts on a spare needle.

Back lower edge frill
With RS of work facing, using 4mm circular needle, K up 105[111:117] sts around lower edge.
Work as given for front lower edge frill.

Sleeves
Using 3¼mm needles, cast on 51[51:57] sts.
1st row K1, *P1, K1, rep from * to end of row.
2nd row P1, *K1, P1, rep from * to end.
Rep the last 2 rows for 2cm, ending with a 2nd row.
Change to 4mm needles and commence patt as given for back. Inc and work into patt 1 st at each end of the 5th and every foll 8th row until there are 75[75:81] sts.
Cont without shaping until work measures 41cm from cast-on edge, ending with a WS row.

Shape top
Cast off 4[5:6] sts at beg of next 2 rows. Dec 1 st at each end of next and every foll 4th row until 51[45:49] sts rem, then at each end of every foll alt row until 37 sts rem, ending with a WS row.
Next row K2 tog, K2, * (K2 tog) twice, K2, rep from * to last 3 sts, K2 tog, K1. 25 sts.
Cast off.

Sleeve frills
With RS of work facing, using 4mm needles, K up 51[51:57] sts along lower edge of sleeve.
Work as given for front lower edge frill.

To make up
Work smocking over central panel of 55 sts. (See Special Technique.) Join right shoulder.

Neck frill
With WS of work facing, using 4mm needles, K across 37[39:41] sts on back, K up 49[54:60] sts down right side of neck, K centre st, K up 50[55:59] sts up left side of neck. 137[149:161] sts.
1st row (WS) K2[2:5], *P1, K5, rep from * to last 3[3:6] sts, P1, K2[2:5].
2nd row P2[2:5], M1, *K1, M1, P5, M1, rep from * to last 3[3:6] sts, K1, M1, P2[2:5].
3rd row K2[2:5], *P3, K5, rep from * to last 5[5:8] sts, P3, K2[2:5].
4th row P2[2:5], M1, *K3, M1, P5, M1, rep from * to last 5[5:8] sts, K3, P2[2:5].
5th row K2[2:5], *P5, K5, rep from * to last 7[7:10] sts, P5, K2[2:5].
6th row P2[2:5], M1, *K5, M1, P5, M1, rep from * to last 7[7:10] sts, K5, M1, P2[2:5].
7th row K2[2:5], *P7, K5, rep from * to last 9[9:12] sts, P7, K2[2:5].
8th row P2[2:5], M1, *K7, M1, P5, M1, rep from * to last 9[9:12] sts, K7, M1, P2 [2:5].
9th row K2[2:5], *P9, K5, rep from * to last 11[11:14] sts, P9, K2[2:5].
10th row P2[2:5], M1, *K9, M1, P5, M1, rep from * to last 11[11:14] sts, K9, M1, K2[2:5].
11th row K2[2:5], *P11, K5, rep from * to last 13[13:16] sts, P11, K2[2:5].
12th row P2[2:5], *K11, P5, rep from * to last 13[13:16] sts, K11, P2[2:5].
Rep last 2 rows until frill measures 5cm, ending WS. Cast off in rib as set. Join left shoulder, neck frill, side and sleeve seams. Set in sleeves.

Special technique — working the smocking

1 The smocking is worked over the centre ten knit ribs on front of sweater. Begin with centre two ribs. Thread needle with matching yarn. Secure yarn at back of work. Bring needle through to front on left of pair. Take it through to back on right, then to front again. Thread bead on to yarn, push it up to work, drawing ribs together.

2 Leaving four rows between, draw together the pairs of ribs on either side of the first pair as shown, placing a bead on each one as before.

3 Leaving four rows between, draw together the middle pair of ribs and two pairs on either side of the middle pair. Carry on in this way smocking alternate pairs of ribs to produce a honeycomb effect, working regularly from right to left on each smocking row.